HEROES

OF A

DIFFERENT STRIPE

HOW ONE TOWN RESPONDED
TO THE WAR IN IRAQ

BY

OLGA BONFIGLIO

GLOBAL VISIONS
2005

Bonfiglio, Olga M., 1950–
    Heroes of a different stripe : How one town responded to
the war in Iraq. / by Olga Bonfiglio. – Kalamazoo, Mich. :
Global Visions, 2005.
    xxxviii, 531 p. ; 22 cm. Includes index
    1. Peace movements—Michigan—Kalamazoo County
2. Iraq War, 2003—Public opinion—Kalamazoo County
3. KNOW (Organization)   4. Women in Black (Organization)
I. Title   II. Kalamazoo Interfaith Coalition for Peace and
Justice.   III. Project for the New American Century
JZ5584.U65 B66   327.17567 B66

ISBN -0-9773641-0-0

Printed by Fidlar Doubleday, Inc.
Kalamazoo, Michigan

TABLE OF CONTENTS

Heroes of a Different Stripe

PREFACE

While most books on the war in Iraq today focus on the words and experiences of soldiers, generals, politicians and pundits, this book chronicles how ordinary citizens responded to this crisis from January 2003 to June 2004 in Kalamazoo, a medium-sized city in southwestern Michigan.

I began researching this book by attending the national peace march on January 18, 2003, in Washington, D.C., and then by going to the events and weekly peace vigils of the organized group called the Kalamazoo Nonviolent Opponents to War (KNOW). I also attended six of the seven Bush rallies held in March–April 2003. Throughout this time, I surveyed peace activists and Bush supporters, interviewed their leaders, monitored the responses their demonstrations aroused from street traffic and followed newspaper stories from our local paper, the *Kalamazoo Gazette*. Several key points describe the mood in Kalamazoo during this critical time.

First, Kalamazooans were incredibly divided over the war with each side lacking any understanding of the other's positions because people simply didn't talk, socialize or debate with those they disagreed with about the war in Iraq. The *Kalamazoo Gazette* printed wire service news from Washington and Iraq and provided several stories on the local peace activists and a couple stories about the Bush supporters. Various columnists offered their opinions on the war *before* it started, but the paper largely shied away from analytical pieces on its consequences or implications. As the war commenced, it covered stories about soldiers, their families and the dead.

Second, Kalamazooans were idealistic and passionate about the war regardless of how informed they were about it. People had an opinion and freely shared it, but the peace activists did so through their own reading, study and attention to the independent media, while the Bush supporters generally relied on the mainstream media and the president's word as their sources of information.

Third, many Kalamazooans' view of the war and America's role in the world was influenced by their religious beliefs. The Bush supporters saw the president as a moral man who was right to use the swords of vengeance against the 9/11 perpetrators. In this way he could bring justice into the world and rid it of terrorists. Some more radical right-wing people viewed this war as a prelude to Jesus' Second Coming as described in the New Testament book of Revelation. Some of the peace activists, on the other hand, regarded Jesus' Sermon on the Mount and Isaiah's prophecy of "beating swords into plowshares and spears into pruning hooks" as their model for creating a more just and peaceful world.

Fourth, the local political parties in Kalamazoo, which had been very quiet since the 2000 election, remained silent on the war during the 18 months covered in this book. The rallies and vigils that took place by both the peace and Bush groups were organized by individuals. Flyers, websites and signs were made and distributed by individuals. Spokespersons who took on a particular project were individuals. The peace activists did coalesce into the Kalamazoo Nonviolent Opponents to War (KNOW), but the group remained an informal organization with no set leadership or membership and no alignment with the Kalamazoo County Democratic Party.

Fifth, Kalamazooans from both sides expressed a desire for the same things: security, a good life and a future for their children.

Sixth, many Kalamazooans were consumed by fear. The Bush supporters feared terrorists and approved of the president's move to eliminate them by military force. The peace activists feared that military force would augment terrorism and encourage the spread of war throughout the world. The Bush supporters liked the president's strong arm in confronting this crisis; he appealed to their conceptions of leadership. The peace activists were repulsed by Bush machismo and found it difficult to tolerate his arrogance, his unwillingness to work with our allies or the United Nations and his administration's attack on Americans' civil liberties in the name of national security. Their advocacy for peace and justice, whether inspired by religion or humanism, sought to end all war—forever.

Originally I had planned to present an account of these two major factions within my town and how they responded to a war with Iraq, but the Bush rallies ended in April 2003 and those who supported the president no longer assembled publicly as a group. Part III and Appendices G and I, however, provide material I did manage to gather about them during that short period of time. As the peace activists continued their activities beyond the start of the war, this book evolved into a story about them and how they advocated for peace as a minority voice in the midst of all the dramatic national and international events that occurred before and during the war.

· I pursued this story for several reasons. First, the national media had systematically dismissed and distorted the activists' message with images of jobless anti-war "hippies" chaining themselves to buildings, being hauled off to jail or creating traffic jams in the city streets. They consistently gave low-ball numbers for the national marches that took place in cities all over the country and barely covered the huge marches that took place throughout the world. Although authorities no longer "count" the demonstrators, it was obvious to me that the numbers of people present at these events were largely underreported since I witnessed the massiveness of the January 2003 peace march in Washington and the August 2004 pre-GOP Convention in New York City. I wanted to provide a more comprehensive picture of how the peace activists thought about the war, why they were dedicated to the cause of peace and why they continue to demonstrate even today. I do this by describing their activities in the run-up to war (Part I), the beginning of the war (Part II), the occupation (Part IV) and during first six months of 2004 leading up to the U.S. handover of Iraq to Iraqis (Part VII) on June 30, 2004. Profiles of their leaders are presented in Part VI, preceded in Part V by national and internationally-known peace activists who came to the Kalamazoo area.

There were other reasons why I wrote this book. Critiques about a war with Iraq were largely blocked or buried deep in the newspapers. Rumors or impressions, like the link between 9/11 and Saddam Hussein, were not corrected and instead were allowed to fester. News from abroad that challenged the United States' actions and policies wasn't coming in. Unfortunately, in this environment, the media were not giving American citizens a complete picture of why we were going after Iraq or why most of the world protested our plans to do so. It is for this reason that I have also provided many footnotes to the text and news summaries of events in an attempt to fill in the gaps of the news that went unreported or for readers who may have forgotten them. These summaries also provide a context for the activists' responses during this very intense time.

In truth, I did not intend to write this book. At first, it served as a means of re-channeling my frustration at the media. As I wrote the book, it quickly became a coping mechanism that allowed me to deal with my growing fears about the war for those who might be drawn into it, for the families who might sacrifice their children for it and for the retaliatory consequences that might result in the homeland and around the world. Some days I literally fell into a panic about a reinstatement of the draft because I knew too many people who would be of age and forced to serve in the war. So my writing became an outlet while I waited for the war to end, which like most Americans, I believed would be as short as the 100-hour Persian Gulf War was in 1991.

However, as I interacted with the demonstrators, I became intrigued by what they said and did. My pen, paper and listening ear became vehicles for them to express their concerns, fears, tensions and hopes and I felt privileged that they trusted me enough to share so much of themselves. I soon realized that what I collected from the Kalamazoo peace activists might reflect the sentiments of millions of other Americans who made a stand for peace. Then my purpose changed once more and the book became a spiritual endeavor to understand what it takes to be a peacemaker and how one sustains that ambition, especially in the face of public ridicule and loathing.

Like many people, I considered peace a passive activity or, at least an absence of war. After spending months of observing and talking with the Kalamazoo peace activists, I learned that peacemaking is really an action-oriented endeavor that takes much time, ingenuity, determination, discipline, restraint and sacrifice. To adopt a vision of peace and to enact it in one's daily life requires a faith-filled belief that one *can* make a difference in the world—or as Gandhi reportedly put it: "Be the change you wish to see." Such peaceful, nonviolent aspirations are radical departures from the assumptions about war and violence where forcefulness changes or isolates people.

What I also discovered in writing this book is that while all people are capable of being peacemakers, they will find it difficult to pursue this noble cause in isolation. They must be part of a group, a community or some public entity that constantly challenges its members to be true to the virtues of peacemaking. So peacemaking is also a community-building process that attempts to work for justice and equality among all people in the world by starting with its own members. This is heroic work and surely a 21st century skill we need to learn for the survival of our dear earth! I believe that the collective leadership of the people involved in the Kalamazoo peace movement—and in peace movements all over the world— provide a witness to peacemaking as well as the hope that a world without war IS possible. For this reason, I call the peace activists—heroes of a different stripe.

A Note on Pseudonyms

The aim of this book is to record the unheard voices of grassroots Americans. However, I am conscious that time may have shed a different light on some people's comments and that some of the things they said in the first year-and-a-half of war may make them uncomfortable now. My intent in recording their remarks is not to violate their privacy or to hold them up to public ridicule. Sometimes people specifically requested that I not share their names or, in the case of the Bush supporters, I chose not to identify them because I didn't know them. I don't use children's real names. For purposes of keeping the flow of the narrative, I use pseudonyms. If a person's job or position may be jeopardized through his/her comments, I use a pseudonym or change certain details in the descriptions to impede identification. However, in keeping with journalistic standards, public officials are identified. In this way, it is my hope that I have treated all the interviewees respectfully, especially since they graciously gave me their time, thoughts and feelings about this important issue.

Whenever I approached people for an interview, I explained that I was writing a book and wanted to know their thoughts about the war. If the person consented, I recorded what was said with pen and paper, and not with any electronic devices. Because I'm a good note-taker, I felt confident that I could present a reliable account of what people said and the way they said it.

Sometimes I overheard pertinent conversations or remarks at the demonstrations. Since they occurred in public assembly on a public street or in a public park, I didn't feel I violated anyone's privacy by recording what s/he said. As I constantly showed up at vigils, rallies and events, people came to recognize me and know that I was taking notes for the book. Sometimes they approached me and I gladly recorded their comments.

Acknowledgements

To the peace activists and Bush supporters of Kalamazoo for consenting to my interviews and surveys and for the valuable insights they shared that comprise the bulk of this book.

To John Titus, Raelyn Joyce and Gary Dorrien for allowing me to reprint their speeches.

To Jim Rodbard, attorney and president of the local branch to Michigan's ACLU affiliate, for reviewing the section on the USA PATRIOT Act.

To Shadia Kanaan for reviewing the section on Father Chacour.

To Beth Johnson who read the manuscript, helped me improve the narrative and encouraged me in the publishing process.

To Diane Worden and Holley Lantz for editing, indexing and formatting of the book as well as for guiding me through the printing process and all the necessary paperwork for this exciting new venture.

To Mark E. Miller for the photographs of the peace activists and their signs on the front and back covers and to John A. Lacko for my portrait photo.

To Marti Faketty, Beth Johnson, Deb Killarney and Barbara Owings, members of my writers group, who saw me through this project and encouraged me every month to complete it.

To Lucy the Cat, R.I.P., who sat with me at the computer during those long nights of writing. To Tucker the Cat who picked up the slack after Lucy's death and made the room calm enough for me to finish the book.

And, of course, to my husband, Kurt, for all his loving support in this endeavor.

INTRODUCTION

I was unaware of the burgeoning peace movement until I drove through downtown Kalamazoo one Sunday afternoon in October 2002. I saw Ron Kramer among those holding a sign: "No war in Iraq." I rolled down my window and said to him rather flippantly: "Here we go again."

President Bush had been talking about war with Iraq all summer and I couldn't believe that we would actually go after Saddam in retaliation for September 11. After all, there was no connection between 9/11 and Saddam Hussein. Fifteen of the 19 hijackers were Saudis. Who would be crazy enough to start a war in the volatile Middle East anyway? Such a prospect could bring on World War III, as I had been told long ago in my high school history classes. Besides, we invaded Afghanistan the previous October to "hunt down" Osama bin Laden. Why did we want to "take out" Iraq?

Ron nodded back at me and shrugged his shoulders as if to read my mind. His engaging smile under his bushy mustache assured me that this early protest would indeed avert a war. At least, that was what I wanted to believe. And if war protesters were appearing in Kalamazoo, surely they were appearing in many other American cities as well. Too many people would remember Vietnam, I reasoned, and they wouldn't allow another fiasco like that to get out of control before it started. Surely they wouldn't! That's how out of touch I was with the national mood at this time.

As I left Ron, I honked my horn in support of peace and a cheer arose from the crowd as it usually does when a driver wants to show agreement with the demonstrators. I recognized many of the people there that day, even though my encounter was rather brief—and I would meet many others as the months went on.

The Kalamazoo Peace Movement Re-Emerges

On Sunday, September 1, 2002, Tom Small asked his wife, Nancy, what she wanted to do for her birthday. "I'd like to stand in front of the Federal Building with a sign saying 'No war in Iraq,'" she said.

Tom thought that to be a good idea so he called his friend, Patrick Jones, and the three of them arranged to meet at noon in front of the Federal Building in downtown Kalamazoo and hold signs protesting a war against Iraq. The threesome continued their demonstrations each week and other people found out about their "Sunday peace vigil." The group grew to 10, 15, and 20 and consisted of many people who had stood for peace for many, many years, including those who demonstrated against the Vietnam War. Later that fall, as many as 200 to 250 people joined the group that included students and professors from Kalamazoo College and Western Michigan University, Quakers, pacifists, members of the clergy and laity, Muslims, Veterans for Peace, local activists and senior citizens.

As the administration's talk about war with Iraq continued, Ron Kramer began holding luncheon meetings with about 20 local peace activists in the basement of the Wesley Foundation, a campus ministry center at Western Michigan University. Ron wanted to gather a group to voice opposition to a war with Iraq.

"I was amazed at how many people came," said Ron as he contrasted this war's response to the invasion of Afghanistan. He and others had opposed that war, too, but "weren't real organized" to do anything more than put an ad in the *Kalamazoo Gazette*. Even at that time Ron recognized that the president wanted to invade Iraq—yet another act of violence in the United States' response to 9/11.

Meanwhile, the WMU Progressive Student Alliance planned a teach-in for the first anniversary of 9/11. Members asked Ron to be a part of a panel to discuss why a war with Iraq would be considered illegal and immoral. They chose him because he had co-authored a 1998 book entitled *Crimes of the American Nuclear State*. It discussed how U.S. foreign policy was shaped around the threat of nuclear hostility and how acts relating to the manufacture, deployment and testing of nuclear weapons violated international and federal regulatory law.

Later that night Ron attended a 9/11 memorial service at the Friends Meeting House and learned about the Sunday peace vigils that Tom and Nancy had started and that the Quakers joined them in the effort to avert war with Iraq. The Quakers had already been holding Tuesday afternoon demonstrations at the Federal Building to protest against U.N. sanctions on Iraq as part of the "Voices in the Wilderness" national campaign (http://vitw.org/) that called for an end to economic sanctions and military bombings against the Iraqi people. Jean and Joe Gump were among those who had been demonstrating with the Quakers since 1998.

"Since the Gumps had gathered no more than half a dozen people, they were glad to have us all join them," Tom Small told me as he reflected on the origins of the Sunday peace vigils. However, as these groups came together they realized they needed some structure, so Tom assumed the leadership of this new alliance and held weekly strategy and organizational meetings. One of the first things the group discussed was its name.

"Joe Gump came up with KNOW—Kalamazoo Non-Violent Opposition to War," said Tom. He had gotten the idea by tracking the activities of other peace organizations over the Internet. The group also decided to focus itself on a war with Iraq.

"We were careful not to dwell on opposition of *all* war and violence, like domestic violence or nuclear weapons," said Nancy Small. "We wanted to focus on anyone who was against a war on Iraq."

"But we were pretty clear right from the beginning that war with Iraq would happen anyway," conceded Tom. Consequently, KNOW's mission became an educational one because of the mainstream media's reluctance to inform the American people about war plans against Iraq. It instead began "diluting" information about Bush policies and activities. In Kalamazoo, KNOW was pledged to fill that gap (*see* Appendix A).

In the fall many college students in Kalamazoo also formed or re-activated their student peace groups. The WMU-KNOW recruited and sent many students to the peace marches in Washington and New York prior to the war. Members of the Non-Violent Student Association at Kalamazoo College, founded in the 1990s by Jerry Berrigan, son of Vietnam peace activists Phil Berrigan and Liz McAlister, wanted to focus their activities on advocating peace with Iraq. Thirty-five students went to the Washington peace march in January and the other peace marches held in spring 2003.

"The students were just invaluable," said Nancy, who admitted that while the middle-aged leaders sometimes saw them as "a little pushy," the students' enthusiasm, positive attitude, and commitment really drove KNOW. For example,

Noah Dillard organized the bus trips to Washington (October, January, March) and New York (February). In the summer Noah and Stephanie Higdon started a Monday night film and discussion series on peace and justice issues at the downtown Kalamazoo Public Library.[1] In the months prior to the war, these young people recruited other students who stayed up all night to paint huge banners for peace. They hung up the banners on various overpasses in the city and on the I-94 freeway so that drivers would see them on their way to work in the morning. Although no one was arrested, the police asked the students to take down the signs. Then Kevin Fuchs came up with the idea for the blue and white yard signs that read: "Another Family for Peace." He ordered and distributed the yard signs and also arranged to make buttons and bumper stickers.

"The young members would have liked more action," said Tom. "We older activists were more cautious, like when they wanted to order yard signs in 1,000-piece lots instead of 500-piece lots, which the group finally agreed to do. The young people did most of the fundraising, too."

"We talked at length about how to phrase what the signs should say," said Nancy. Finally, the group came up with "Another Family for Peace" with "peace" emphasized in large white letters on a light blue background. KNOW's name and website (www.kzoo4peace.com) were written on the bottom of the sign. In November 2002 the light blue and white yard

---

[1] This film series, eventually called "Be-in-the-KNOW Films" (www.beintheknowfilms.org) was continued on Tuesday nights by Wade and Sandy Adams, Elke Schoffers, Tony and Joan Badalamenti, Shadia Kanaan, and Jacob Libby at WMU's Sangren Hall. It ran throughout the spring and summer of 2004 on a bi-monthly basis and then two and three times a week during the last eight weeks before the November 2004 election. The group continues to show films at local coffee shops and brew pubs.

signs suddenly appeared on 3,000 front lawns all over Kalamazoo.

"People at national and regional peace meetings saw the Kalamazoo buttons and heard about the yard signs," said Tom, "and the city became known as a peace activist town that sent delegates to demonstrations and meetings." The yard signs especially caught on as several other communities imitated the KNOW signs, notably Lafayette, Indiana; Lansing; Ann Arbor; and a community in Pennsylvania.

Overview of the Book

In January 2003 when the number of Americans protesting the war began to mount, several hundred people also began to demonstrate regularly at "peace vigils" held every Sunday at noon in front of the Federal Building on Michigan Avenue, the main drag of downtown Kalamazoo. They eventually organized themselves into a group called the Kalamazoo Non-violent Opponents to War (KNOW). When the second national peace march was held in Washington, D.C., on January 18, KNOW sent 224 people on four buses to participate in a 36-hour round-trip mission.

As the prospect for war intensified, more peace activists showed up for scheduled events. On Sunday, February 25 nearly 600 people came to Stetson Chapel at Kalamazoo College to hear Professor Gary Dorrien, an Episcopalian priest and religion scholar, discuss how the Bush administration had adopted the neoconservatives' plans for "perpetual war" as its post-9/11 foreign policy.[2] This policy became known as the Bush Doctrine, but it was the product of a neoconservative think tank called the Project for the New American Century.

---

[2] From this and several other lectures, Dorrien eventually published the book entitled *Imperial Designs: Neoconservatism and the New Pax Americana* (Routledge, 2004). (*See* Appendix E.)

On the evening of Thursday, March 20, twenty-four hours after the war had started, KNOW held a silent candlelight vigil at the Federal Building. Seven hundred people lined both sides of the street for an hour on that cold, misty night. They came to express their sorrow and distress at the administration's decision to go to war. The event was low key and there were a few policemen posted just in case trouble erupted, which it didn't. The next night the Kalamazoo InterFaith Coalition held a prayer service at the First Presbyterian Church. Representatives from the town's major religions were there to reinforce their faith's belief in peace. The service was very moving and a feeling of solidarity pervaded the sanctuary. It was small comfort for the disastrous turn of events, but a community-oriented comfort nonetheless. People needed to be together that night just as they needed to be together after 9/11, the presumed provocation of this war. During the early months of the war until May 1st when, according to President Bush, "major combat operations in Iraq [had] ended," [3] 400 to 500 people continued to stand for peace at the Sunday vigils.

The KNOW demonstrators weren't the only demonstrators in town, however. In February 2003 a lone man stood in front of the Federal Building waving to traffic and holding a picture of Saddam with a target drawn around him. Sometimes two to four other people joined this demonstrator. Then on March 15 a pro-Bush contingent began to hold regular rallies on Saturday mornings in front of the Federal Building. They were there every Saturday until April 26 when it looked as though the war were drawing to a close. At their peak they attracted 160 people. However, Bush supporters never gathered as a group again until a year later when the president came to Kalamazoo for a campaign rally at the 4,500-seat Wings Stadium. They were joined by 200

---

[3] www.cnn.com/2003/WORLD/meast/05/01/sprj.irq.main/

demonstrators outside the stadium and 100 more peace activists who made a stand five miles away on a hill overlooking the I-94 freeway and in view of the presidential motorcade's approach to the stadium. On the other side of the freeway a small group of Bush supporters countered with their greeting signs for the president.

KNOW continued to draw 40 to 60 people to its Sunday vigils each week for the rest of 2003 and into the next year. In April 2004 after news of the Abu Ghraib prisoner abuses surfaced, attendance climbed to 100 people. Attendance at the Sunday peace vigils, which had waned during the winter, began to pick up again from 40 people each week to 60 and 80 people, a number sustained until the November 2004 election. Some people went to the vigils *every week,* which in one faithful activist's opinion "was the only place to be at noon on Sunday." The Tuesday vigils consistently drew about a dozen demonstrators and about 20 miles west of Kalamazoo, a small group of activists stood for an hour on Saturdays at noon in Paw Paw.

Indeed, the peace vigils in front of the Federal Building became the place for Kalamazooans to express their opposition to the war and their anger at the Bush administration. The vigils also became a place of refuge, mutual support and friendship, especially when a majority of Americans backed Bush on the war. However, the honking horns of approval from passing cars increased steadily as more and more citizens lost faith in Bush and his war effort. With each passing season I wondered how long the peace activists would continue their vigils. At press time for this book, they are still out there—and they intend to stay because they see themselves as a vital and contributing force for peace in the world.

The Setting and Scene

The Federal Building is a stately, art deco, yellow sandstone building at the corner of Michigan Avenue and Park Street erected in 1938 during the Franklin D. Roosevelt administration. It currently houses the 6th Circuit Court. Near the building's cornerstone on the southeast side is a free-standing bronze plaque of the Bill of Rights. It is at this end of the building that the peace activists and the Bush supporters hold their demonstrations.

As the county seat, Kalamazoo serves as the center for political, economic and social activity in southwestern Michigan. People come downtown usually in their cars and they typically exceed the 30-mile-per-hour speed limit on Michigan Avenue, the one-way, seven-lane trunk-line that runs east and perpendicular to the northbound one-way, five-lane business loop traffic of Park Street. Only a traffic light at the intersection slows down this mad rush of cars to give the demonstrators some "face time" as well as a split-second opportunity for the drivers to interact with them. So the demonstrators from both sides did what they could to attract the attention of passing motorists—and the media.

For their vigils the peace activists mostly made their own signs with messages against the war and President Bush. The biggest impact of their message, however, was in the city's neighborhoods. KNOW printed 3,000 light blue yard signs with white letters that read: "Another family for peace" and sold them for $5. The signs first appeared on people's lawns in November 2002 and many of them lasted through late fall 2003. In spring 2004 more signs were printed and distributed to replace the old signs, but not nearly as many of them stood on people's lawns as in the previous year. The peace activists were highly organized and aggressive in distributing their yard signs to homeowners and in replacing missing or destroyed signs. They also produced and sold bumper stickers, buttons, calendars and books that they distributed at the vigils and through a few downtown stores.

At the Bush rallies demonstrators also held hand-made signs but there was a preponderant number of red-white-blue mass-produced yard signs that read: "We support President Bush and our troops." The signs left out any attribution to a distributor and homeowners did not seem as willing to post these signs in their yards as did those who supported peace. Before these signs appeared, one local businessman printed and distributed his own sign, which read: "Another family that supports the USA." He put his name and website on the bottom of the sign and it appeared to double as a Bush endorsement and an advertisement for his company. This sign wasn't widely distributed but the *Gazette* did publish a story about it in March 2003, one of two stories that appeared about the Bush supporters during this time. In July 2003, a new mass-produced sign appeared: "Pray for peace. Pray for our troops." No group name was identified as the source of these signs either, although they were available through the Kalamazoo County Republicans and a few Republican business owners in town. Rumor had it that the Clear Channel was behind these signs.

Bush supporters used a plethora of American flags in their rallies and a couple of them vigorously waved Marine Corps flags. The peace activists, identified with the liberal wing of politics, only began using a few American flags during their vigils after the war started when their patriotism was questioned.

During both the peace vigils and the Bush rallies, drivers and their passengers mostly looked curiously at the demonstrators. If they approved of their message, they honked their horns. If they disapproved, they either ignored the demonstrators or made nasty remarks or obscene hand gestures. However, only the peace demonstrators received jeers or "drive-by-shoutings" from passing cars, and these expressions usually came from white men, mostly young to middle-aged and a few elderly. Disapproving drivers also revved up their car engines as they passed the demonstrators. Women drivers did not yell out of their cars or gesture; they usually looked straight ahead if they were in disagreement. On only a few occasions did drivers stop to discuss the war with demonstrators of either side.

Political Climate in Kalamazoo

Michigan, with a population of over 10 million people and 17 electoral votes, is typically a Republican state, except for the Detroit area which is Democratic due to the large labor union population that resides there. However, in the 2000 and 2004 presidential elections, Michigan turned out to be a "blue" state. Kalamazoo County, together with Muskegon and Lake Counties, were the only counties in the western part of the state that went for Kerry.[4] Of course, the local Democratic Party worked hard for Kerry with an unprecedented group of over 1,000 volunteers. A local chapter of MoveOn.org helped to organize voter registration campaigns and door-to-door support of Kerry as did the National Coalition on Black Civic Participation,[5] which specifically targeted minorities through their UNITY '04 Voter Empowerment campaign.

---

[4] Election results in 2004 (www.usatoday.com/news/politics elections/vote2004/countymap.htm). In the 2000 presidential election, Manistee, Wexford and neighboring Calhoun Counties voted for Democrat Al Gore (www.usatoday.com/news/politicselections/vote2004/countymap2000.htm).

[5] The UNITY 04 campaign (www.UNITY04.net) registered 17,000 voters across the state and worked in Detroit, Kalamazoo and Benton Harbor implementing GOTV efforts including a voter registration effort in Kalamazoo County.

Southwest Michigan is not only Republican territory, but it is the national headquarters of the Christian Reformed Church, which fosters a tradition of conservatism, decency, industriousness, stability, decorum and a more provincial view of the world. As the area's population has become more ethnically, racially and religiously diverse, local politics have been influenced and grown more vociferous, especially in the wake of the Roe v. Wade ruling in 1973. Because of the area's strong Republican and conservative religious traditions, candidates win elections on the abortion issue alone, usually during the primaries.[6] In general elections Democrats have made strides but have been unable to overcome the abortion issue or to persuade moderate pro-choice Republicans to vote for them. Democratic voters also shy away from selecting all the candidates on "bed sheet" ballots that include a host of county and township commission seats. Conservative Republicans, however, are highly organized and schooled in voting all the way down the ballot, and they consequently win in the general elections.

---

[6] According to Democratic sources, the conservative right-wing churches in Kalamazoo have created an effective political machine that sanctions candidates and advocates issues from the pulpit. Candidates are screened and selected based on their zealous opposition to one issue and one issue alone: abortion. Pro-life advocates are said to have a plan extending 10 to 12 years out where members of their "farm club" serve on local commissions and boards for experience and then advance to county and state-level positions as opportunities arise. Since Michigan has term limits, vacancies for state representative seats arise after three two-year terms and for state senate seats after two four-year terms. The pro-life base of operations is the Alternatives of Kalamazoo (formerly the Crisis Pregnancy Center), a $1.8 million building positioned right across the street from the Planned Parenthood building. Leaders gather there for meetings and planning sessions.

In 1964 Democrats began to gain a foothold in the city of
Kalamazoo when Democrat Paul H. Todd, won the U.S.
congressional seat, albeit for one term. President Lyndon B.
Johnson had huge coattails in a Democratic sweep across the
nation and the sympathy vote for the assassinated President
John F. Kennedy in 1963 also helped. Another Democrat,
Howard Wolpe, recaptured this congressional seat in 1978 and
held it until 1993 when he chose not to run for re-election. As
a former WMU political science professor, he had slowly
gained a Democratic and moderate Republican constituency by
previously serving on the Kalamazoo City Commission and
then by winning a state representative seat in 1976.

Kalamazoo County has three state representative seats
and, since Wolpe's win, a Democrat has occupied the one that
encompasses the city. The state senate seat, which includes the
entire county, has been consistently Republican, although
Democrats have aggressively gone after it for the past three
elections (1994, 1998, 2002) winning between 45 and 48
percent of the vote. During the late 1990s the Kalamazoo
Democrats made a concerted effort to transform the county in
their direction through a program of candidate recruitment,
fundraising and campaigning. Democratic candidates for
president, governor and the U.S. Senate had won in
Kalamazoo County since the 1980s, and party leaders believed
they could win some county, township and state representative
races.

In the 2000 election the nine-person County Commission
achieved a majority of Democrats for the first time in history
while the county drain commissioner post went to a Democrat
for the first time in 70 years. The 2001 redistricting process
diluted Democratic hopes for a continued majority, however,
especially when the Commission increased from a nine-
member board to a 17-member board, courtesy of the
Republican majority on the five-member committee charged

with redistricting.[7] The Republicans then held power in the county's townships and county boards and controlled every branch of government in Michigan (and, of course, in Washington). Kalamazoo Democrats quietly licked their wounds after this sound beating—until the 2002 election when they went after the state senate seat, but lost again. Their only consolation was that then-Attorney General Jennifer Granholm became governor. Republicans surrounded the state's first woman governor in both legislative houses, the attorney general, the secretary of state, and the non-partisan Michigan Supreme Court.[8]

Socio-Economic Climate of Kalamazoo

Over the past 100 years or so, the influence of many new people and institutions has contributed to Kalamazoo's more progressive social climate, which has provided for a greater tolerance of racial, ethnic and religious diversity as well as an exuberant appreciation of and support for the arts. This climate was led by an ever-growing higher education community,[9] the Roman Catholic Church,[10] and various left-

---

[7] This committee consisted of the county prosecutor, treasurer, clerk (who were all Republicans) and the county chairs of the Democratic and Republican Parties.

[8] In the 2000 election Debbie Stabenow did capture the U.S. Senate seat from Spencer Abraham, who later became Bush's pick for Secretary of the Department of Energy. Michigan currently has two Democratic senators: Carl Levin and Debbie Stabenow.

[9] Kalamazoo hosts a major research university; a prestigious small, private liberal arts college; an excellent community college, and a small, private, for-profit university.

[10] Although the Church established the first Christian mission in 1690 in St. Joseph on the shores of Lake Michigan, it continues to be a

leaning protestant churches. The biggest influence, however, came from the international array of scientists and corporate managers who worked at The Upjohn Company, the once-prominent pharmaceutical firm.

"The Company" was run by the powerful Upjohn family that in the 19th century had merged by marriage with the equally powerful Gilmore family, whose wealth was rooted in retail department stores and expanded to broadcasting, car dealerships and real estate. Non-profit and charitable organizations became quite dependent on these families who also ran the area's banks and contributed to a steadfast and bountiful support of the arts. In the early 1980s Kalamazoo was said to be one of the richest and most financially secure cities east of the Mississippi River.

All of that changed in the 1990s. The Gilmore's stores began to close and The Upjohn Company went through a series of mergers until it was eventually sold in 2002 to Pfizer & Company. A series of job cuts ensued over the next few years and the city lost many people to re-location. The paper industry, which had also contributed to Kalamazoo's diverse business base, also began to wither away. During 1998–2000 five plants closed. The third-generation offspring of the wealthy families had been leaving town since the 1970s. These changes accumulated and dealt the community a serious decrease in the city's tax base and a downswing in contributions to non-profit services and organizations. The members of one extremely wealthy family did remain in town, however, the Strykers—and they were Democrats, although generally quiet ones. This family has given much to Kalamazoo of late and its presence is still not yet fully recognized or accepted by the populace—or the remaining old guard.

---

minority presence of about 14 percent of the population in southwest Michigan.

The Demonstrators

I didn't take a formal profile of the demonstrators but I can describe the kind of people who participated in the demonstrations. The KNOW peace activists were mainly middle-aged to elderly professionals. A few of the men wore beards. Many people were long-time political, peace and/or environmental advocates. Among them were Vietnam veterans and a few World War II and Korean vets; some were members of a group called Veterans for Peace. People from various religions showed up regularly, including members of clergy, Roman Catholic nuns and priests, Muslims and Jews and pacifists like the Quakers or Church of the Brethren. No organized recruitment effort prompted people to attend the vigils. Standing for peace was their main motivation whether it was religious or not.

KNOW activists also formed several spin-off groups. The Women in Black emerged shortly after the war began. This local group was part of an international movement of women who dressed in black and silently mourned the victims of war and violence. Another women's group formed after several participated in the nationally-organized CodePink demonstration held in Washington in March just before the war began. Kalamazoo CodePink subsequently sponsored a couple events and brought Peace Momma, a 12-foot *papier-mâché* puppet with moveable arms to various events.

The Kalamazoo County Democratic Party was not officially involved in the peace demonstrations, although many participants at the vigils were known Democrats or Green Party members. A couple of elected Democrats attended a few vigils.

Bush supporters were mostly middle-aged people and senior citizens. I was unable to determine their social status. Many of the men wore beards. These demonstrators comprised three major groups: Bush supporters, family members of Marines and soldiers and veterans of Vietnam or the post-Vietnam era. A couple of the demonstrators were Republican office holders or party members but group leaders always insisted that their rallies were *not* sponsored by the local Republicans. In fact, they said that they didn't know most of the people who "just showed up."

That both major political parties were not officially involved in the rallies or vigils is noteworthy, but not a complete surprise. After my short stint in local politics during the late 1990s, I became convinced that the parties were broken and unresponsive to the populace. So if anything, the war in Iraq drew out citizens to take the streets and express their grassroots approval or disapproval. Unfortunately, public assembly, a First Amendment right—as important as it is to the political process—does not allow much room for reasoned debate. It's an emotional outlet in which sides are taken, much like teams at a sporting match. When a high-pitched competitive attitude mixes with politics, the discussion sometimes descends to an unhealthy level and people don't listen to one another; they shout at each other and fight to win at all costs. No one learns another's position because no dialogue occurs. Although Kalamazoo lacked any public confrontation, it became evident to me that the two sides did not talk to each other and did not know each other's opinions, motivations or values. (This book attempts to fill that gap as well.)

The racial make-up of the demonstrators from both sides was almost exclusively white. Many individuals from the Muslim community participated in the early KNOW activities but dropped out once the war commenced; most people felt vulnerable taking a stand for peace in public. College students joined in the KNOW vigils and went to the national peace marches. Their attendance faded, however, as the school year drew to a close in April 2003 and never picked up again.

WMU created a student KNOW group and Kalamazoo College already had the Non-Violent Student Association and they held their own activities on campus, although they received minor attention from the media. I was unaware of any Bush-supporting college groups other than the already-established College Republicans at both WMU and Kalamazoo College. My focus for the book remained on the Kalamazoo community activities.

Several articles on the peace activists had filled the pages of the *Kalamazoo Gazette* in the run-up to the war and the Bush supporters received just two front-page articles about their rallies during the seven weeks they were there. TV cameras and radio recorders also appeared from time to time. After May 1, 2003, however, the media only covered special occasions like the peace activists' September 11 candlelight vigil and their Sunday, December 14 vigil, the day Saddam Hussein was captured.

A major student story did emerge in May 2004 when President Bush visited Kalamazoo. Several members of Kalamazoo College Republicans who worked the event spotted a small group of Kalamazoo College Democrats and then reported them to security. The "K" Dems were regarded as Bush opponents and were not welcome at this "private rally"[11] even though they had procured tickets through proper channels. This story received attention in *The Nation* (May 5, "Capital Gains" the online blog by David Corn) and *The Progressive* (May 13, "McCarthyism Watch"). The *Kalamazoo Gazette* covered the story on May 10. (Kalamazoo culture typically avoids sharing bad or embarrassing news. People also shun negative political campaigns.)

---

[11] A mid-August 2004 Reuters article reported that holding "private rallies" was a regular practice for Bush-Cheney appearances.

It is especially interesting to note that individuals joined the peace vigils or the Bush rallies on their own volition. This indicates to me the importance people place on their ability to demonstrate in a *public* way. The right of public assembly allows individuals to express themselves in a group. It creates a feeling of solidarity among its participants and assures them that they are not alone in their beliefs for their cause. It also provides citizens with a check-and-balance mechanism to alert political officials of "the people's will." Nevertheless, the peace activists' voices throughout the country went largely unheard as the White House refused to listen or respond to them. Consequently, the demonstrators' only recourse was to appeal to the local populace and remain a presence for peace. The following is a chronological and a reflective account of my interactions with the peace movement in Kalamazoo beginning with my attendance at the January 18, 2003, peace march held in Washington, D.C.

Heroes of a Different Stripe

I.

RUN~UP
TO
WAR

MARCH–APRIL 2003

Heroes of a Different Stripe

36 HOURS: NATIONAL PEACE MARCH IN WASHINGTON, D.C.

Saturday, January 18, 2003

I take a shower at the last possible moment since it will be a while before I have another. The long, hot blasts of water calm me and I mentally store them in anticipation of the long, cold journey ahead. After drying myself with a thick terrycloth towel, I spread lotion all over my body in a kind ritualistic anointing for the mission ahead of me: to write a chronicle about the peace movement in Kalamazoo. This must be what it is like for soldiers as they mentally prepare themselves for battle. This must be what American soldiers and Marines are doing now as they converge on the Middle East and ready themselves for war with Saddam Hussein in Iraq.

My mind shifts to imagining Dad being drafted into World War II. He was only 18, so young to leave home and place his life in danger. How did he do it? How did so many young men like him leave home? And how did families let go of their sons? How do governments send their young men to war— over and over and over again? Now we are at it once more. There must be a better way to settle disputes. The millions of people in the emerging worldwide peace movement are going to try.

Growing up in the 1950s and 60s has prepared me to be apprehensive about the world. It was the Cold War and I learned to fear a Soviet takeover and the possibility of nuclear holocaust. Even today I shutter at the words of that period: communism, Soviet Union, Khrushchev, Cuba and Castro. To make matters worse, the arms race of the 1970s and 80s somehow encouraged, rather than prevented nuclear proliferation as the Nuclear Club of Nations increased its membership and only furthered the likelihood of the "eve of destruction," as the 1965 Barry McGuire hit song lamented.

Now, in this new century and new millennium, the fear of the impending war in Iraq—with the prospect of chemical and biological warfare not to mention the rush for valuable oil resources—has gripped me and I feel a need to do something. My news sense also tells me that the national peace march in January will be a tipping point event. I'm a freelance writer and I wanted to write about the march, so I called my editor at the *Gazette* to pitch the story. A few weeks went by without an answer but as the numbers of Kalamazooans planning to attend the march rose to 224, the editors decide that the story is worth doing (it is a national event with a local angle) but they will send their own seasoned reporter and photographer instead of me, still a rookie writer. However, since the *Gazette* reporter plans to fly back to Kalamazoo to write his story, he asked me to gather quotes from participants on the bus ride home.

I feel a keen sense of mission about this trip. I've never attended a peace march before and I wasn't involved in the protest demonstrations of the Vietnam era, but I promised myself that if the prospect of war ever came up again I wouldn't be a bystander. Now I am a war correspondent on the home front.

7:00 PM — Arrival

After feasting on a dinner of broiled salmon with rosemary, a buttery baked potato, broccoli with olive oil and carrot salad with raisins, my husband, Kurt, takes me to the gathering site, St. Thomas More Student Parish. The buses haven't yet arrived but people are slowly converging on the church. As I gather my things to leave the car, Kurt leans over to kiss me good-bye. "I'm very proud of you," he says. That makes me feel validated; he doesn't think I'm crazy or wasting my time and he doesn't try to discourage me as Dad would have with concerns about my safety—or my patriotism.

I make my way down to the church basement of St. Thomas Moore Student Parish where Sister Sue has laid out a table full of snacks and soft drinks for those who will make the 14-hour bus ride to Washington, D.C. and their family and friends who are here to see them off. Kalamazoo is sending four of the 12 busloads from Michigan that will join the expected 500,000 marchers who will come from Maine to Texas and Florida and as far west as Missouri.

People from all ages and persuasions are at St. Tom's tonight: high school students and college students, a few children with their parents, Vietnam veterans, business people, professionals, craftsmen, religious people from a variety of faiths. And although they differ in age, background, and experience, they all come with one purpose: to dissuade President Bush from going ahead with his plan for a pre-emptive, unilateral war with Iraq. Then there is another important element to this march, too. It is part of a 24-hour worldwide call for peace with marches held in cities all over the world starting in Australia and Japan and ending in California. Such a vociferous demand for peace has never occurred before in the world's history—and the war hasn't even started. Clearly, this coordinated effort is made possible by the Internet.

8:00 PM — Prayer Service and Rally

Friends and family gather with the peace marchers in the church for a short prayer service and send-off rally. There must be 300 people here tonight and the energy of the room is one of conviction and solidarity of purpose. These people think that they *can* avert this war! (Little did the country know, then, how stubborn Bush would be once he made up his mind. But neither did the country know how persistent the peace activists would be to stand against this war.)

People are dressed in their heavy coats, hats, boots and gloves. They carry placards for the march and backpacks of food, water and amusements for the long journey. My backpack is filled with a supply of Cheerios, pasta, a couple turkey sandwiches, water, an inflatable travel pillow, Chapstick, Kleenex, heavy socks, notebook, and big yellow scarf. (It turns out that I had enough of everything to sustain me over the next 36 hours and through the 20-degree cold except warm gloves. A Michigander should have known better.)

Some of the marchers here tonight attended the peace march in D.C. last October. At that time the prospect of war was less apparent, but with the New Year the administration's drumbeats toward war have grown louder and more intense.

The service is simple and prayerful with a couple songs and a couple prayers. A perfect beginning for this mission. Next came the speeches from KNOW leaders.

"Maybe we didn't fight hard enough the last time," says Don Cooney referring to the Vietnam War protests of 35 years ago when people gathered at St. Tom's and filled several buses to march on Washington. Don is a WMU professor of social work and a long-time social justice advocate for the poor and for peace. The former priest is also a four-term city commissioner. "Maybe our voices against war weren't loud enough. This time, if we don't stop this war from starting, we may fall into World War III." This shuddering thought stirs me as I nervously consider the gravity of Don's words and remember the warnings of my high school history teachers that conflict in the Middle East could lead to the worst kind of war.

Rick Stahlhut, a medical doctor and activist gives the marchers tips on what to do in case the police use fire hoses on the demonstrators. The thought of being hosed down further sobers the excitement of this occasion. In the 1960s police used fire hoses to break up crowds of Vietnam War protesters and civil rights advocates. I now realize that we are just as vulnerable in this march. "Because water freezes, it can harm you," says Rick. "On the other hand, drink enough water to avoid dehydration during this trip."

"The purpose of the march is to call for peace," says Tom Small. "To have the effect of a peace movement, you must move and act peacefully. If you get arrested or hassled by the police, don't put up a resistance. Be peaceful always."

8:30 PM — Leave Kalamazoo for D.C.

We leave the church with hope-filled enthusiasm and energy to find four huge buses lined up on the street outside the church. After marchers pile their parade signs into the bus storage bins, they climb on board, find their seats and hoist their backpacks into the overhead racks. The din of the crowd and the roar of the buses' engines fill the street until everyone is settled and ready to go. It is an otherwise quiet and clear, crisp winter night, the best Michigan has to offer at this time of year.

The buses lumber through the city streets until they reach the eastbound I-94 freeway and then sail swiftly through the night with only headlights and exit streetlights breaking up the darkness of the countryside. That's one thing I've always appreciated about Kalamazoo, the countryside is never that far away. And we're going to see a lot of countryside on this trip tonight!

Our first stop is a rest stop center near Battle Creek where we pick up a few more people and head southeast on I-69 to Ohio. As I watch the two buses in front of ours go around the long curve of the freeway, I am moved at the thought of being a part of this historic moment. Hundreds of thousands of people are driving at this very moment to Washington or San Francisco (the other site of the international peace march) to stand for peace. These people represent a growing grassroots movement that has yet to be acknowledged by the Bush administration or the media or either political party, for that matter. Their action signifies a renewed movement toward democracy where the people speak for themselves rather than through a filtered intermediary like a union, a party, a politician, or a corporation. Part of this group's mission this weekend is to be seen and heard—and only the big numbers of the crowd will accomplish this.

Dayton and Columbus Crossroads on I-75

The lighted signs on the freeway have a romantic quality to them as we travel in the pitch-black night. Mile by mile as we move closer to Washington it feels as though we are gathering energy. It also feels like a pilgrimage, only it is not to honor a sacred event of the past but to persuade the leadership from committing the country to a disaster in Iraq in the near future—and for a long time to come. During this stretch of the journey I search the bus for people to interview about their reasons for going to the march and find a family of three.

"We are the strongest nation in the world. Why can't we use our strength for world peace?" asks Colleen Harmon (pseudonym), 45. "So much money for war. Why not work with the U.N. and find a way to negotiate? Why must we go to war?"

"I kept watching the news and reading, and things kept getting worse. Enough is enough. I had to do something," says Michael Harmon (pseudonym), who was 10 during the Vietnam War, his own son's age. Michael works for an aerospace company that makes fighter jets, the same planes that will bomb Baghdad if this war occurs. "I find it ironic," he says, "that I'm helping to build these jets. I do believe there's a need for defense but I'm not quite sure the president in charge is doing the job he should. I have to tell myself that it's still necessary to have an armed defense but that it's still hard to justify that. Then again, we've got to eat. I hope that a thousand years from now the borders of countries will be looked at as antiquity. All these resources we have are put into arms. If they could be redirected, how much better life could be for everyone."

"I want to convince George W. Bush that war isn't the right way to solve problems," says son, Brian. Brian goes to school in Kalamazoo where students learn conflict resolution skills through what they call a peace rug. The peace rug works like this. When children have a dispute with each other, they go off to a designated corner of the room and sit or kneel on a rug facing each other. They take turns speaking and listening and control their talk by agreeing that the person holding a pen, flower, block, or some object, is the speaker while the other child is the listener. The objective of the discussion is to find a workable solution to their conflict. Teachers, aides, and other adults avoid imposing solutions on the children, however, they teach more aggressive children to temper themselves and encourage shy children to speak up on their own behalf. Brian believes that the president should use a peace rug with Saddam Hussein in the same way students in his class do.

11:15 PM –Midnight — First Stop near Toledo, Ohio

Everyone is glad to stop and stretch—and we get 45 minutes to do it. Some of us find an ice cream machine that uses a tube to suck up the bar of your choice from a box and then drops it down the dispenser. Very clever and it amuses us, especially after riding a cramped bus for so long. But spirits remain high and people are generally joyful about this trip.

One woman passes out red plastic peace-symbol necklaces and people put them on right away. I take one, too, and put it on. The last time I saw these symbols was during the Vietnam War, which, I must admit I missed. That seems incomprehensible to me now but it shows how it is possible to live in this country and be oblivious to what's going on in it and in the world. Now we are poised to engage in a new war. We are also engaged in a new kind of peace movement, one that protests the war before it begins.

At this scheduled stop we have a bus driver change but are delayed another 20 minutes until our new driver arrives. This glitch is not the worst thing to happen since we will arrive in D.C. way before the 11 a.m. rally begins followed by the 1 p.m. march. We will be outdoors until 5 p.m. and have no place to go to warm ourselves. So this delay is OK—and it's a prolonged opportunity to stretch our legs.

Aaron, our new driver, finally arrives and after he introduces himself with a chatty banter and obvious confidence, we give him a cheer, which he readily appreciates. As we merge onto the freeway and slip into cruise control, he turns off the inside overhead lights of the bus. Time to get some sleep. We move our seats to the backward position and settle down for a night's sleep—if we can.

We are driving under the light of a full moon and there are no clouds, so I can see a lot even in the dark night. The moon has a halo around it and except for the surging engines of our bus and the quiet talk of a few passengers, all is peaceful and calm. I ponder the question Steve Senesi posed while we ate our ice cream during the Toledo break: Was Jesus a lion or a lamb? It's a trick question and people tried to puzzle it out as Steve chuckled at their struggle. Before we boarded the bus he realized he had teased us long enough and gave us the answer: Jesus was both because he could adapt himself to the situation.

Sometime in the Middle of the Night — Pennsylvania Border

I can't sleep and am uncomfortable, but I remind myself about American soldiers who are camped out in the desert and how miserable it must be for them. If war is averted, they can come home. If not, who knows how long they will stay there.

It's snowing but not enough to impede our travel. The wetness of the white stuff just adds the slap of the windshield wipers to the sounds of the night. It's a pleasing sound that complements the low and continuous drone of the bus's motor.

Our four buses are pretty much the only vehicles on the road tonight. They stay close together. Good thing, too, because Bus #2 develops a problem. The cold and ice have made the door leak. We stop on the side of the freeway as the drivers converge to fix the door. After 15 minutes they solve the problem and we continue on to Washington.

6:15–7:10 AM — Breezewood, Pennsylvania

Breezewood is an astounding rendition of tourist neon in the middle of nowhere. It's ugly, overdone, and a place I wouldn't want to live. However, tonight, after 11 hours on the road, it's a welcome stop. We park at The Post, where we see many other buses going to the Washington today. As we enter the building, hundreds of sleepy-eyed people stand in long lines waiting for the restroom, the cafeteria or one of the many snack machines. A man on the public address system intermittently calls out the names of places for bus re-loading. While I wait in the restroom line, I ask people in the crowd where they are from and how many buses they have sent: St. Louis (3 buses), Wisconsin (17 buses), Minneapolis (4 buses with 10 statewide). We also meet up with two buses from Traverse City, Michigan.

People of all ages have converged here and they are generally joyful and cooperative with each other despite the early hour and the long rides they've endured. Some people buy a "home-cooked" meal of turkey, mashed potatoes and gravy, corn, pie and hot coffee. A few members from our bus decide to avoid the long lines and instead walk to a nearby bakery, but they miss the incredible energy and excitement pulsating throughout this place. Once again, it's that sensation of determination of purpose in stopping a move toward war.

There are so many buses coming and going that the fumes are sneaking into the building and making it a little unpleasant. However, no one complains because the more buses going to Washington, the better. The more people who show up for this march, the more effectively the message of dissent can get through to President Bush.

As the long restroom line snakes around this congested mass of tables and chairs and hundreds of bodies in motion, I bump into a couple people I know from Detroit: Maggie and Deborah. Maggie is 80 years old and a member of the Detroit Raging Grannies, one of the local chapters that has emerged across the U.S. to protest a war with Iraq.[12] To see these older

---

[12] Originally started in February 1987, a group of eight women from Victoria, BC, Canada, worried about nuclear-powered vessels carrying nuclear weapons in Canadian waters and decided to protest by singing song parodies. They continued their activist agenda with other political and economic issues (http://nsvow.chebucto.org/grannies.htm). As their idea grew in Canada, the first American

women here makes a strong statement to me about their commitment to peace. Some of the grannies will participate in the march in wheelchairs!

We leave "Breezewood madness" at 7:10 a.m. and head east on I-70 with only 127 miles to go before we reach Washington. We are driving on a cold and crisp morning still under a shining full moon. Spirits and expectations continue to run high despite the long ride.

Traveling in eastern Pennsylvania has made me feel like a time traveler. We are in one of the original 13 colonies where our nation began as patriots fought off the ruling British "red coats." Seeing the turn-off signs to Gettysburg reminds me of another important era in our history when our country divided into "blue" states and "gray" states. How many lives were lost and overturned in that war? Then my thoughts return to today as I contemplate how we have become a nation divided once

---

group started in Seattle in 1996. As their website (www.raginggrannies.com) states:

"In the tradition of wise women elders, the mission of the Seattle Raging Grannies is to promote global peace, justice, and social and economic equality by raising public awareness through the medium of song and humor.

"Our goal is to challenge our audiences to work to bring about the social changes that are required in order to end economic oppression, particularly of women and children, and to end racial inequality, environmental destruction, human rights violations, and arms proliferation.

"We are enraged about the poor conditions that people are forced to endure in their lives, and about the condition of the earth that will be left to our precious grandchildren. We sing out to gain respect for all persons and encourage everyone to grow above their prejudices. We rage against 'corporate greed' and sign for 'one world' in which JUSTICE is evident everywhere and PEACE reigns."

again over this war with Iraq, just as we did 30 years ago over another war in another faraway place. What are we willing to lose this time and do we really know the price?

A lot of people I meet on the buses think war is outmoded because our advanced technology and sophisticated weapons have the capacity to exterminate large civilian populations. "Atrocitologists" estimate that during the 20th century between 130–175 million lives were lost in war[13] alone—and that does not include civilian deaths or politically-motivated slaughter. Surely we can do better in the 21st century and stop this death and destruction! Isn't this what this march in Washington is all about?

Approaching Washington, D.C.

With about 35 miles to go we are greeted by a brilliant morning sun, a snow-covered countryside and clear roads. The weather has been amazingly cooperative during this trip. Tobi Hanna-Davies, one of the bus trip organizers, leads the group in song and a spiritual reading. The reading requires our response, which is: "We are one." The few people still sleeping are gradually roused by this morning liturgy, especially as we sing "We Shall Overcome." Tobi struggles to lead the singing and asks for a "great singer" to emerge. Only Aaron, our bus driver, volunteers because he knows all the words. Our repertoire includes "This Land Is My Land," "Blowing in the Wind" and "This Little Light of Mine." Aaron then gives our bus a name: Aaron and His Choir. His occasional banter with the riders makes the journey pleasant. He is a rare gift!

Singing these songs makes it feel like the 1960s all over again. The only difference is that many of us who remember these songs are now middle-aged—and there's a whole generation behind us. My thoughts about a war surface again

---

[13] http://users.erols.com/mwhite28/warstat8.htm#Total

as I wonder whether we can spare this next generation its ugly costs. As we turn on I-66 to Washington we sing "Let There Be Peace on Earth." Then it's "America the Beautiful." I get a lump in my throat as we pass familiar scenes of D.C. and sing "Michael Row the Boat Ashore" and *"Dona nobis pacem."* A light rail train glides by as we sing "Kum-Bay-Ya." The singing loosens up some people who add harmony and beauty to the music. I'm so glad we are singing! We just don't do that often enough. Soldiers during the Civil War used to sing for amusement only they did it so much that officers had to quiet them at night to protect them from the enemy detecting them. Singing brings a group together. It promotes bonding and relieves the tension of everyday life for just a little while.

Now the Lincoln Memorial is in sight. This monument always thrills me because Lincoln was one of my favorites. His courage and faithfulness to the nation during its greatest crisis is a model for us. As we turn down Constitution Boulevard, we pass the buildings that make the nightly news: Federal Reserve, Washington Monument, Commerce Department, E.P.A., Justice Department, and the Archives where the Constitution, Bill of Rights and Declaration of Independence are kept. The buildings are so stately and they represent such great ideals. They are a reminder of what America stands for and I feel such great pride in that!

Finally, our bus comes to a stop right on the edge of the Great Mall. As we find a place to unload, Tobi once again reminds us that this rally is a peace rally and that we need to remember to be peaceful—no matter what happens. The leaders of this trip have been consistently apprehensive of the potential for violence with the huge crowd and they continue to keep us focused on our purpose.

About 10 AM on The Mall

We get off the bus and are told where our meeting point is for the return trip home. The speeches begin at 11 a.m. and the march at 1 p.m. There is a lot of time to kill—and we will all be outside in the cold, 20-degree weather for the next six hours or so. I look around to find people I know and can only find George, my seatmate for the past 14 hours. He looks lost and doesn't have anybody with him. I invite him to spend the time with me and then we talk about what we can do while we wait for the march to begin. Because he's a Navy Vietnam War veteran I ask him if he'd like to go to the memorial. He's never visited it, so we head for it. George and I no sooner start walking down the mall than a toenail starts scraping against my toe. My heavy socks, which I brought for warmth, are now scrunching the toes in my narrow boot. It's going to be a long day.

George and I reach the Vietnam War Memorial and I feel an ache in the pit of my stomach start. He has said nothing as we approach the black gouge in the earth and I try to be silent. We walk a few yards into the memorial and look at the names engraved on the shiny, black wall. It is obvious the memorial has touched him deeply. He becomes more silent. What a rare privilege it is to be with a veteran who is here for the first time. And yet how disconcerting it is. I'm not sure how to be with him, so I just stay quiet. We continue walking about a quarter of the way along the wall's walkway and George stops. He has a "peace on earth" sign with him and we take photos of each other holding the sign at the memorial. Then he wants to turn back, so we do. As we leave, a solitary security guard suddenly appears near the entrance to the memorial. He tells us signs are prohibited at the site and I feel awful that we violated this rule even though we didn't know about it.

"Peace on earth," the guard says as he reads our sign out loud. "What an idea." As George rolls up the sign and puts it under his arm, the guard sees us fumbling to capture his meaning. "You don't think I'm for war, do you?" he snaps. The guard probably sees hundreds of people each day while he's on duty here at the memorial. As the prospect of a new war looms, it's ironic that he has to pull duty at the stark, black wall in the earth with the 58,000 names etched on it.

George and I walk on to the huge white temple that houses the Lincoln Memorial, climb the steps, and gaze at the giant sculpture of Lincoln. It's difficult to look at this memorial and not imagine the wounds of our nation during the 1860s and how this man tried to hold the states all together, even those that seceded. Now 142 years later, we're a divided nation once again and without a leader trying to unify us.

We walk a short distance to the Korean War Memorial, which I've never seen before. Photos of it haven't appealed to me but being here makes a difference, especially today. The memorial's triangular shape and position on the mall, opposite the Vietnam and Lincoln Memorials, call to mind the sacrifices of war—which the young men of the nation must always bear. The faces of the figures are grim. Their hunched stance caused by the weight of their equipment and the wear of war contradicts their otherwise youthful strength and optimism in the future. The Korean War Memorial moves me deeply, but once again it makes me wonder: Why must we kill off our young for these "just" causes? Who decides this? Do we have an alternative way of settling our conflicts?

12:30 PM — Rally

George and I return to the crowd gathered on the other side of the mall. The Capitol Building stands in the background like a symbolic theatrical backdrop to today's event. In that building the decision was made last fall to give the president the power to pursue this war if it were necessary. In that building Democrats and Republicans afraid to look unpatriotic in light of 9/11 committed yet another generation of young men—and women—to war.

Today's speeches blast the president and declare 9/11 not to be an appropriate factor for war with Iraq. Of course, these speeches appeal to the crowd with wild applause. Speakers call the administration a bunch of warmongers and declare Bush a "selected" rather than an elected president. To the people gathered here today, the 2000 election remains a factor against war more strongly than retribution for 9/11. Former Attorney General Ramsey Clark under President Lyndon B. Johnson cites a long list of Bush's "high crimes and misdemeanors" that threatens the Bill of Rights, civil liberties and international law. He pleads with the crowd not to be bystanders and even calls for Bush's impeachment. (I can't believe my ears. Impeachment. Is the nation going to go through this again?)

Al Sharpton speaks about Martin Luther King's legacy of world peace and the fight against segregation. (This peace march is held in conjunction with the observation of MLK Day.) He points out that the White House is willing to wage war against Iraq, where no WMDs have been found, but not against North Korea, which has nuclear weapons as everyone knows. He says that plenty of money will be spent for "weapons of mass distraction" but not for health care or the elderly in America.

"We are beginning the extraordinary process of renewing our country here today," says Ron Kovic, Vietnam veteran and subject of the film, "Born on the Fourth of July." "When you don't give up, when you're willing to endure, there is always rebirth and redemption. We are shouting out today, 'No blood for oil!'"

"No blood for oil! No blood for oil" shouts back the crowd several times.

Speakers pound on the president over the Florida election debacle, the Enron scandal, legislation that leaves homeless veterans of past wars empty-handed, and the passing of the $1.3 trillion stimulus package (Tax Cut I) that has turned out to be a huge advantage to the wealthy 1 percent of our country. One woman says the work we do today in this march is "noble and good." One man urges Muslim men not to feel ashamed for the sins of a few bad Muslims. Other speakers call for the elimination of weapons of mass destruction not just in Iraq, but from the entire planet—including in the United States.

Actress Jessica Lange says that the protesters of this "possible war" must not be silenced. "I address this assembly as a mother, and American woman, a legacy to the next generation. This administration keeps us mesmerized with the USA PATRIOT Act and eviscerates our civil rights. How far are they willing to go to silence dissent? We are demonized, reviled and made to look foolish."

Jessie Jackson challenges college students to march for peace on their campuses—and to fight racism, sexism, ethnicism, too. "Don't let them discredit you," he warns.

Congressman John Conyers of Michigan says that the administration has miscalculated the people's will.

The emcee of the rally calculates that 200,000 people have already arrived by 12:30 p.m. and that people are still coming. The crowd cheers. Actually, there's no way of knowing how many people attend these things, especially since the media low-balls the count while organizers high-ball it. Despite the turnout of this demonstration, however, the president is not in Washington to see it; he is spending the weekend at Camp David, even though he's undoubtedly aware of the peace march. I can't say I blame him for wanting to be out of town. I wonder how he sustains all this negative energy not only from Americans but from people all over the world. Curiously, as the next 18 months drag on, he seems almost buoyed by the protests and dissentions.

As George and I make our way to the march's starting position, the Raging Grannies take their place in the parade with their banners. Most of the older women walk but a few ride in wheelchairs. I see Maggie again and she is beaming in her black wool hat and heavy red coat and scarf. People know why they are here. They feel purposeful and hopeful that they can avert a war. There are posters everywhere and many giant puppets with messages of peace or anti-war sentiments. Here is a sample of the posters:

> Billions for bombs, pennies for people.
> How will war prevent terrorism?
> What would W do if N. Korea had oil?
> Regime Change – Impeach Bush
> Bomb Texas they have oil, too.
> Drop Bush, not bombs.
> $200 billion for health care.
> Who would Jesus bomb?
> Say no to American imperialism.
> Money for jobs not war.
> Bush's foreign policy is a bomb.
> Big cars, big war, big mistake. No war for oil.
> We must fight poverty, ignorance, disease. No
>   war.
> War for oil is wrong.
> No blood for oil.
> United States of Arrogance
> Smart bombs, misguided leaders.
> Money for jobs, not war.
> Take back the flag.

Peace is patriotic.

I will not teach my child to kill your child.

Don't make me ashamed of my country, my
home.

We need jobs, education, health care, not war.

Using technology to make enemies.

The walk is slow and the parade covers the entire width of
the street. Occasionally protesters chant this war's anthem:
"No, no, we won't go, won't fight for Texaco." It is
reminiscent of the Vietnam protest chant, "Hell no, we won't
go." In key spots, probably due to the nature of the buildings,
police are stationed in heavy numbers. In one building young
men in white shirts and ties hang out the window, yelling and
waving American flags. They deride the marchers, but even
these critics are a rare sight on this day. There are no incidents
as we pass these counter-protesters—and I don't hear of
anything significant afterward.

Food vendors line the commercial district as we walk
through and the smells of the hot dogs and tacos coming from
their steamy food containers are tempting. We pass many
coffee shops and restaurants. A little warmth would go well
right now on this cold day, but I stick with the march, almost
as if it were a discipline for the cause of peace. As the march
continues, people's different paces allow them to encounter
different people and swap stories about their local peace
activities. For example, Maine has a huge peace movement
where people are even holding vigils on bridges and overpasses
every Sunday from 1–3 p.m. The state sent 14 buses to
Washington.

4:30 PM — End of the March

It has taken us quite a while to reach our destination, the Navy Yard, two or three miles on the parade route from the Capitol. As we pass the building, marchers jeer at it. Demonstration organizers chose to pass by this building because it contains U.S. weapons of mass destruction. Many questions emerge as I gaze on it: If WMDs are so dangerous and if Saddam shouldn't have them, why do we have them? What kind of people develop such weapons, finance them, activate them? What kind of people want to use them? Why are governments so hell-bent on using WMD—or at least threatening to use them? Who wants to destroy the world?

5 PM

I am quite tired by now and am anxious to sit down on a warm bus, but we have another half mile to go before we reach our meeting site. The organizers have done a good job of positioning the buses on various streets so that marchers can board them and reduce congestion as much as possible. While the plan is great, the timing is off for us because police blocked the streets due to a disturbance. We have to wait an extra hour for our bus. People mill around and share their impressions of the march. Many engage each other in small talk as if to take their minds off the long wait. All in all people are pretty patient despite the cold air and their tired feet. When the buses finally arrive, we are all especially jubilant—and grateful.

6 PM

As we drive through Washington, many people eat the food they have brought with them. Many people take naps. We have a long ride ahead of us, but for now, being in a warm bus with a soft seat is all that matters. After I finish the penne pasta I brought, I interview various people on the bus to get their impressions of the march. Here are the comments I collected:

> *There is a tremendous groundswell against a pre-emptive, unilateral strike. So many people were here in Washington for the first time at a protest. That's very impressive to me. I was deeply moved by many of the speakers. What moved me the most was Ramsey Clark, former Attorney General, who cited the Constitution of the United States calling for the impeachment of George Bush and giving a long list of grounds for impeachment. I felt tremendous hope today being part of a collective action with a half million people. It was real democracy today.*

Tobi Hanna-Davies
(former city commissioner)

> *Since it was my first time, it seemed overwhelming and inspiring. I kept looking at the Capitol Building against the blue sky and realized what an historic place I was standing in. I was surprised that I didn't see an overwhelming police presence. I thought the people that came from all over were so supportive and so committed to peace. All ages, families. And the creative signs and costumes. How creative people are in their expression of protest. I would go again.*

Sara Wick
(librarian)

> *I was eternally grateful that this time I was not crying to myself about the war. In 1991 I wrote anti-war poetry I never published and was amazed I could pull it all out and it had the same meaning and names as today—Bush, Cheney. I didn't sit on the sidelines today. No matter what happens, I stood up and now I can live with myself. And it beats crying. I attended the D.C. rally as my next step following the Sunday vigils [in Kalamazoo.] It was*

more of a spiritual thing for me rather than complaining about Bush. I felt called to be there.

Bobbe Taber
(addictions counselor)

I was most impressed by the kids who had a real enthusiasm, not a circus, a real concern about problems of this world. They're politically savvy. They see what's happening in front of them: deviousness, lying, mendacity of this administration: a president, vice president, and five cabinet members from the oil industry is a reason to go to Iraq? This administration is part of a world conspiracy that involves efforts to control the rest of the world to control oil. Oil doesn't last forever. We should be looking for alternatives to fossil fuels.

Dick Becker
(retired social worker)

It's my first time in a peace march and I'm impressed by the crowd and its size, how orderly and friendly it is. I think everyone got the feeling they were conveying to the powers that be that they didn't want war and war is bad. It seems like everyone was sincere....I've never been on a march. I'm here to try and stop a war and to convince them that there are other means to killing children and other people. We're in the 21st century....There's always a need for the military as a deterrent, but we need to figure out another way to settle disputes....People I know are not thinking about [a war] and they feel it's out of their control. If enough people show up to the rally, I think it will have a big enough effect.

George Theodoru
(Vietnam veteran and business manager)

I'm against war in general. If someone asked me if I'd go, I could not kill anyone. I'm protesting the loss of civil liberties, the apparent disregard of the voice of the American people. War is irrational. If they instituted a draft they wouldn't have enough support. I am afraid of the draft—it's not a super threat. I'm just not willing to die for this cause.

Ted Hufstader
(college student)

The more I heard the speakers and read the signs, the more I saw the cause was so right. To see that all this Bush propaganda doesn't get to everyone and that there is such a large contingent that sees through it. I did feel liberated to be immersed in it.

Michael Harmon
(engineer)

I was surprised at how many people were there. I thought some of the signs were pretty interesting. I would do this again. It was important. We were trying to make world peace. World peace means there is no fighting or war.

Brian Harmon
(son)

I was thrilled that I got to share this experience with Brian and Michael. I was overwhelmingly surprised that so many people feel the way we do and are striving for the same causes.

Colleen Harmon
(wife and mother)

6:15 PM — Ann Arbor Area

After being awake most of the night I finally get some rest because I learned how to sleep on a bus: like a duck.

7:05 PM — Battle Creek Area

It's sleeting and a trucker wants to pass our bus. First, he calls our driver to tell him he's coming. He doesn't want to spray the bus's front windows. Our driver and the trucker exchange travel information and simple road talk. The trucker says he's headed for I-69 near Battle Creek. As he prepares to turn off I-94, the two men wish each other a safe drive and a good morning. The simple conventions and courtesies of the road. It's peaceful and it feels as though all's right with the world just now on this slightly wet and very quiet morning.

7:45 AM — Home Again

We return to St. Tom's this morning 36 hours after we began this journey. Sister Sue greets us at the bottom of the church sidewalk with her big smile and tender hand shakes and congratulations. It is good to see her, especially as her presence acknowledges our effort. She conveys the kind of support people need when they stick their necks out to try to do something. And standing for peace IS doing something! So many people will not do anything during this critical period and instead prefer to live a life of denial, paralysis and cowardice.

LOCAL GROUP ATTENDS
CODEPINK PEACE MARCH IN WASHINGTON

Saturday, March 8, 2003

Lisa Dallacqua found the spirit of Saturday's CodePink peace march in Washington, D.C. different from the January peace march. Probably because the possibility of war was more imminent and probably because it was a women's march.

"It was amazing that we made our statement without any violence. And that is a statement about war itself: that you can change things without violence," said Lisa, 19, a first year Kalamazoo College student. "It was another form of diplomacy."

Lisa and 50 others from the Kalamazoo area joined approximately 10,000 women from across the country in the Saturday march. Organized by a national group called CodePink (www.codepink4peace.org), the women's protest demonstration over a possible war with Iraq included the formation of a human ring for peace around the White House.

The Kalamazoo group met for a Friday night send-off ceremony at St. Thomas Moore Student Parish before boarding a bus for their 14-hour ride to Washington. Jean Gump, a local peace activist, offered a prayer asking God's forgiveness for what she called the country's "moral blindness" over war plans that will undoubtedly kill Iraqi civilians. She quoted Mahatma Gandhi who said that non-violence is an inherent quality of women and that men should learn to cultivate it. Borrowing again from Gandhi, Jean said, "Leaders often react to protesters first by ignoring them, then laughing at them, and then fighting them, before they give in. We're in the next to the last phase right now, so keep it going."

Tobi Hanna-Davies dressed all in pink for the occasion. "I am outrageously in pink because I'm outraged," she said. She explained that the "Code Pink alert"—a spoof on the

27

color coded system used by the Department for Homeland Security to signal the terrorist threat—signified extreme danger to all the values of nurturing, caring and compassion that loving women and men have held. "We choose pink, the color of roses, the beauty that like bread is food for life, the color of the dawn of a new era when cooperation and negotiation prevail over force."

Several women shared their concern and determination to make a stand for peace that night. While some people in the crowd thought a war may still take place, others were sure their presence in Washington would make a difference.

"I feel a sense of urgency about preventing this invasion [into Iraq]," said Jackie Schmitz of Middleville, who was on the bus with her son, Nathan, a student at Western Michigan University. "We need to put on the pressure now to avert it."

Holly Benjamin, 21, who talked her mother, Sue, into going on the march said: "If we don't do anything, nothing will be done and war will happen."

Flanked by her husband and two sons, Janet Wiley of Battle Creek brought a placard her family helped her make which said: "War will *not* make us safe."

Janet said she feared "thousands of terrorists" might emerge if war breaks out. "We're attacking another country that hasn't attacked us. That's not what the United States is about. Lots of people are operating out of fear. They think war will protect our country. I think it will harm it."

Wiley, like many others going to the march saw the Saturday demonstration as a way to "stand up to say what I thought." She was distressed that few politicians were speaking out. "These issues need to be debated."

Many of the Kalamazoo women had never marched in Washington before, including Ann Gepert. During the Vietnam War one of her sons was in the Navy and the other son was at home as a conscientious objector. She wanted to keep peace in the family so she didn't take sides. But this time was different. "I speak as a mother and a grandmother," Ann said in the pre-departure send-off. She likened the Bush administration's handling of policy toward Iraq to that of a "bully in the neighborhood." Donning a blue and white button with the message, "Peace is the Church's business," she remarked: "It's time to reach down and pull up whatever is the best in us."

The bishop of the Episcopalian Diocese of Western Michigan, Robert Gepert, was among several husbands who came to the send-off service to support their wives' resolve to bring a message of peace to Washington. He shared his stand on the war in a private interview. "My opposition to the war is based on the teachings of Jesus Christ which I profess to follow," said the bishop. "As Christian people, the answers to life's problems are in the Gospel. The message is there and it's easy, it's not complicated. Jesus was a radical pacifist and I'm called to be a radical pacifist like him."

Wade Adams accompanied his wife, Sandy for the send-off rally as well. The former pharmaceutical scientist served as an officer in the U.S. Army's Chemical Corps during the Vietnam War to conduct research on weapons of mass destruction. He also worked on the detection of nerve agents in American and Vietnamese soil samples as well as binary WMD, a weapon in which two relatively non-toxic agents were mixed while in transit to the target, producing a very toxic nerve agent upon impact. He later sought Conscientious Objector status to his military activities and, after six months of federal court trials, was granted it.

"We want to make it clear we're against war and that we should abide by the decisions of the United Nations," said Wade. "Disarmament is working and I don't see the need to rush off to war. We should use non-violent methods to solve the problems of the world. Militarism is being ratcheted up.

But it is not something we need in the twenty-first century, not with the weapons that are currently available, weapons that indiscriminately kill innocent people, and not just combatants."

"Saddam Hussein is not a good person," said Wade, "but he's not the only dictator in the world. The cost on life is too much for a solution by military means. It will fuel terrorism in the Middle East and all over the world. I hope every march and every voice against war will help and I would call on all people to let their voices be heard. Until war breaks out, hope is eternal."

Upon their return from Washington, Kristy Pagan, 21, a junior at Western Michigan University, said she was impressed by the women's march for peace. "It was a great experience for women coming together to make an anti-war statement in the nation's capital."

Likewise Erica, 19, first year Kalamazoo College student, "came away feeling hopeful and encouraged by the sense of peace and community" the march engendered.

Lisa Dallacqua said she found the high security capital city "scary," especially around the White House. "It's kind of sad that they have to raise the level of security when there's a peace rally because you know no one there is going to do something violent." Nonetheless, she said that the trip to Washington gave her a more concrete understanding of the level of fear the Capitol city is experiencing.

The CodePink march was the last national demonstration to be held before the president gave the order to start the war. It was the culmination of a week of women's anti-war events called "Celebrating Women as Global Peacemakers" sponsored by several peace and women's groups including Global Exchange, CodePink for Peace, the National Organization for Women, Women's International League for Peace and

Freedom, United for Peace & Justice, Unreasonable Women, Peace Action, D.C. Asians for Peace and Justice, National Women's Health Network, Gray Panthers of Metro D.C. and the Sisterhood Is Global Institute.

The CodePink rally featured authors Alice Walker and Maxine Hong Kingston who were both arrested with 23 others on charges of crossing a police line in front of the White House. Among other women in attendance were Nobel Peace Laureate Jody Williams, musician Michelle Shocked, author-activist Dr. Helen Caldicott, feminist theologian Hyun Kyung, physicist/ecologist Vandana Shiva, Pacifica Radio host Amy Goodman, and peace activists Rania Masri, Starhawk, and Doris "Granny D" Haddock.

CodePink had made an anti-war presence in front of the White House since mid-November. It also sponsored the first all-women's peace delegation to Iraq. In December, CodePink conducted an anti-war Christmas caroling event in front of U.S. Secretary of Defense Donald Rumsfeld's house and a "wake-up call" gathering in front of Democratic Senate Majority Leader Tom Daschle's house.

NEWS SUMMARY OF
EVENTS LEADING TO WAR

Tuesday, February 4, 2003

Secretary of State Colin Powell addresses the United Nations to give the world the evidence that will justify a war with Iraq. He doesn't sway many delegates, however. Powell requests that the painting entitled "Guernica," which hangs in the Security Council as a reminder of the atrocities of war, be covered during his speech. The French ambassador also speaks to the U.N.

and he receives wild applause while Powell is noticeably miffed.

Wednesday, February 12, 2003

CIA Director George Tenet issues a warning that the U.S. will probably be attacked this week. He suggests various preparations of food and protection (plastic sheeting and duct tape) as a precaution against bioterrorism.

President Bush tries to cancel the peace march in New York City this weekend. City officials re-route the march. (Kalamazoo sends a van-load of people to attend the march.)

Saturday, February 15, 2003

People around the world denounce the U.S. attempt to wage war on Iraq. American troops continue to pour into the region, but not all their equipment has arrived yet.

Wednesday, February 19, 2003

It appears that even worldwide protests fail to move President Bush and he seems more adamant than ever to go through with this war. The U.S. reputation in the world is sinking, especially as the president says he is willing to make a pre-emptive, unilateral strike on any nation that misbehaves—and he has a 70 percent approval rating from the American public.

Tuesday, February 25, 2003

Saddam wants to talk to President Bush, who refuses to oblige. Political commentator Molly Ivins says that the administration is not taking this conflict with Iraq seriously enough and that any moves toward diplomacy are sorely missing.

Wednesday, February 26, 2003

Millions of Americans participate in the Virtual March by calling their two senators and the White House to express concern over going to war with Iraq. Win Without War (www.winwithoutwarus.org), a coalition of 32 national organizations that advocates alternatives to war with Iraq, organized the event.

Tuesday, March 4, 2003

The Turks refuse to allow U.S. troops to land in their country, which will prevent the Americans from launching a northern attack on Iraq as part of its squeeze on Baghdad. Some believe this development may delay war until mid-March or early-April. Other people are concerned that this delay may make it difficult for soldiers and Marines to survive the desert heat, especially since they will be in protective suits for possible biological/chemical warfare. There is some hope that war will be averted.

U.S. cities and states are talking about their troubled budgets and plan to reduce services like senior centers, swimming pools, police and fire protection, schools, roads and infrastructure. This is happening at the same time the United States is offering countries billions of dollars for permission to land our troops on their soil. The Bush administration is projecting a $100 billion price tag on the war and it aftermath.

Monday, March 10, 2003

Jim Wallis, editor of *Sojourners* magazine and others meet with Britain's Prime Minister Tony Blair in an effort to find a peaceful resolution to the conflict with Iraq—and a way for President

Bush to save face by not waging war. The effort fails.

Tuesday, March 11, 2003

It looks as though the U.S. will not get the nine nations it needs to defeat U.N. Resolution 1441. France and Russia vow to veto the resolution even if it passes. The resolution of the U.N. Security Council, passed unanimously on November 8, 2002, offered Iraq "a final opportunity to comply with its disarmament obligations" that had been set out in several previous resolutions (Resolution 660, Resolution 661, Resolution 678, Resolution 686, Resolution 687, Resolution 688, Resolution 707, Resolution 715, Resolution 986, and Resolution 1284), notably to provide "an accurate full, final, and complete disclosure, as required by Resolution 687 (1991), of all aspects of its programmes to develop weapons of mass destruction and ballistic missiles."

Resolution 1441 threatens "serious consequences" if these are not met. It reasserted demands that U.N. weapons inspectors should have "immediate, unconditional, and unrestricted access" to sites of their choosing, in order to ascertain compliance (http://en.wikipedia.org/).

More of the world's people are protesting in the streets against a war in Iraq. People posing as human shields are moving into Iraq in an attempt to avert war. Many of them are discouraged that they are being placed near military installations instead of near the civilians they want to protect.

Pakistan says it is helping to crack the Al Qaeda network. It has handed over the mastermind of

9/11 and says it is hours away from capturing
Osama bin Laden.

Some Europeans and Middle Easterners who
oppose the war have threatened to boycott U.S.
products if war breaks out.

Wednesday, March 12, 2003

The U.S. is poised for war, which could occur
next week. On the other hand, because the
U.S. can't get the nine-vote majority on the U.N.
Security Council on Resolution 1441, we are
willing to delay and withdraw the vote. The
soldiers in the field are getting antsy and the
sand winds are getting more intense. 130,000
U.S. troops are waiting for something to
happen—or not—and then go home. A few
reports outline the risks of chemical attack to
Americans soldiers and Marines should the U.S.
invade Iraq. There are also reports that some
officers in the field are already demoralized, but
this news is minor and not well publicized.

Peace organizers are circulating a petition to get
the Pope to go to Baghdad and settle this
conflict between Iraq and the U.S. They are
trying to obtain a million signatures from all over
the world.

Another national peace march is scheduled for
this Saturday in Washington and San Francisco
as the U.N. moves to avert a war. Many
Americans are angry at the U.N. for getting in
the way of a war, according to a *New York
Times* poll. They want to get on with it.

Pakistan reiterates that it's hot on the trail to
Osama bin Laden.

Saturday, March 15, 2003

President Bush holds a 50-minute press conference to tell Americans that the only thing we have to fear is Saddam Hussein himself. He also says that he is working for peace and democracy. Bush has so far amassed 130,000 U.S. troops outside the borders of Iraq and in the region.

Sunday, March 16, 2003

This week it has become clear that we will probably go to war with Iraq. The polls show that the majority of people 65+ years agree that they do not want war, however, a majority of people under 30 years favor a war.

Wind and dust from the desert are blowing hard as soldiers and Marines stand poised to invade Iraq. The sand is clogging the equipment and blinding military personnel in the field.

Press reports are coming in about faked evidence on the uranium yellow cake report that Secretary of State Colin Powell submitted to the U.N. as evidence that Saddam was in material breach over U.N. Resolution 1441.

The New Republic has written a story about the president's fundamentalist religious leanings and his belief that he has a hot line to God. Mainline churches have denounced this war (*see* Appendix B) but fundamentalist churches side with the president in favoring it.

In financial news, the AARP Bulletin has announced the collapse of our health care system. Last week, Michigan's Governor Granholm and governors across the country are slashing millions of dollars from state service programs. The Federal Reserve is scheduled to

reduce interest rates lower than 1.24%.
President Bush wants another tax cut.

The World Health Organization announces that
the pneumonia virus, SARS, is killing people in
Asia without warning.

Monday, March 17, 2003

At 10 a.m. the U.N. dropped the second
resolution and the door to diplomacy is quietly
and regrettably shut. President Bush will speak
at 8 p.m. to tell the world that Saddam has 48
hours to leave the country or war will
commence.

It is clear now that the president has
successfully provided adequate justification for
this war on Iraq because the majority of
Americans polled believe that Saddam was
behind 9/11. The support for the war and the
call to give up on the U.N. jumped from 50
percent on March 3 to 71 percent last night.

Wednesday, March 19, 2003, 10:45 pm

President Bush gives the order to begin the war
on Iraq.

Peace marches have begun in other parts of the
world and today the WMU student KNOW group
has encouraged students to cut classes in
protest over the war and to attend a 5 p.m. vigil
at the Federal Building in downtown Kalamazoo
tomorrow.

President Bush is calling for $70–100 billion to
fight the war and repair Iraq afterward. He now
warns people that there will be death, apparently
a prospect most Americans didn't anticipate.
Meanwhile, he is proposing the following: drill
for oil in ANWR, pass an anti-abortion bill,
appoint ultra-conservative judges to the Court of

Appeals, cut Social Security and Medicare and push a $700 billion tax cut.

A columnist in the Toronto Star has said that Bush is an insecure person who needs public attention and affirmation. That's why he is pursuing this war.

By midnight, TV programming is back to normal with trash comedy and late night shows. Only ABC features the war by interviewing military experts.

II.

WAR BEGINS

MARCH–APRIL 2003

Heroes of a Different Stripe

FIRST DAY OF WAR

Thursday, March 20, 2003

> Homeland Security Director Tom Ridge has devised a program for school children to take precautions in case of a terrorist attack. All over America police are securing bridges and ports. Washington government buildings are all closed and the city is being protected like an armed camp.

> American troops are carrying the largest burden in the "coalition of the willing" with 130,000 troops. Other nations have committed about 50,000 ground troops.

KNOW Candlelight Vigil

As the bombs drop on Iraq during this Lenten season of Christian rebirth and renewal, 700 peace demonstrators gather on both sides of Michigan Avenue in front of the Federal Building for an hour-long candlelight vigil on this second night of the new war. People light their candles and hold them in paper cups to protect the flames from the wind and their hands from the hot, dripping wax. They huddle together just simply to be together. Not much talking. Not much sound. Even moving cars mirror the mood as they slowly pass the crowd with only their headlights marking their presence. Not much horn honking. Not much noise on this dark and cold night.

After the vigil people from all age groups who comprise the crowd, walk two blocks to Bronson Park to sing a few songs, hear a few short reflections and perform a couple "Dances of Universal Peace" which Tom Holmes has been teaching for decades to people all over the world. The music and singing aptly provide people with some comfort, and the dances engage their whole body with an outlet for their pent-up energy, fear and uncertainty. The horror and grief of "the inevitable," as the president called it, seem to unite the people here this night. Even in their sadness, they hold on to a glint of hope that the death and destruction they imagine will be minimal.

"We are part of a worldwide movement that is not going to stop," Tom Small reminds the crowd. "As news reports show, hundreds of thousands of people are showing up to protest this war tonight. Millions throughout the world are there."

Many of the people who have been attending peace vigils for the past six months feel defeated. Many think they have wasted their time standing for peace. After all, they joined millions of people around the world and could not stop this war from happening. KNOW leaders encourage the crowd not to give up on peace. After all, everyone tonight is here for peace in the biggest vigil Kalamazoo has ever held.

SECOND DAY OF WAR

Friday, March 21, 2003

The assault on Baghdad begins with a new military strategy called "shock and awe." It attempts to rain down such horrible fire power that Saddam and/or his army will surrender, the war will end quickly and coalition troops will be protected from harm.

The Turks are invading northern Iraq, which the Americans call disruptive.

France says it will not allow the U.S. and Britain to work a rebuilding program through the U.N. in their way because France, which has opposed the war and not provided any coalition troops, does not want to legitimize this war in any way.

The president's proposed $700 million tax cut has been trimmed in half.

Prayer and Meditation in a Time of War

Tonight the leaders of the Kalamazoo Inter-Faith Coalition hold a "Service of Prayer and Meditation in a Time of War" at the First Presbyterian Church across the street from Bronson Park (*see* Appendix C-1). As 200 people file into the church, the soft, meditative recorder music soothes the numbness and sick hopelessness at the new political turn of events, at least for a little while.

Before the service begins I see Dr. Luqmani, a trustee of the Islamic Center, a native Pakistani and a business professor at WMU. I feel the need to go to him and ask if he is OK and if members of the Muslim community are OK. He assures me that all is well but he seems to appreciate my asking. He is a gentle, thoughtful soul that way.

I met Dr. Luqmani last fall when I was doing a story on Ramadan for the *Gazette*. As spokesman for the Islamic Center he works with the media to provide information about Islam and the Muslim way of life. He spent well over an hour with me explaining this sacred time and its meaning for Muslims. I then went to his home to take photos of him and his wife. They showed me various prayer rugs they had collected and we watched a cable TV program that showed Muslims prayerfully circling the Kabba in Mecca during this holiest of seasons.

The Luqmanis later invited me to attend the Eid-al-Fitr service (commemorating the end of Ramadan) at the mosque where I prayed with his wife in the women's section. Going to the mosque was a rare opportunity—and a different kind of prayer experience. I especially liked the practice of bowing on my knees, covering my face with my hands, holding up my arms and hearing the holy Arabic words. Such prayer engages the whole body in an attempt to experience and honor the presence of God. I was very moved and felt pretty comfortable with this way of prayer; I had learned it from the Jesuits years before.

The Luqmanis also invited me to the Eid holiday party held by one of their Muslim neighbors. It was much like the holiday celebrations of my own Sicilian family where people dress up, visit with one another and eat a lot of food while the kids play games or watch TV together. The women talk with the women and the men talk with the men. Many of the Muslims I met are professionals in town and despite the fact that they have lived in Kalamazoo for 20 to 30 years they tend to remain among themselves with their own families and friends. But September 11 changed that as many of the Christians and Jews in my town reached out to the Muslims in friendship and support. My experience with the Muslims has allowed me access to their community for subsequent *Gazette* stories because they trust that I will write about them honestly and fairly. I realize now how trust among strangers is what a multicultural society is all about.

Dr. Luqmani impresses me with his faithfulness to God and his gentleness and kindness toward others. Five times a day he stops whatever he is doing, closes his office door, kneels on the floor facing east and prays the holy prayers of Islam. At this night's prayer service, two days after the war begins, Dr. Lugmani reads a selection from the Qur'an in Arabic. As he reads, the church seems to well up in a silent remorsefulness at the thought that we are indeed at war not just with Iraq but with the Muslims.

As the prayer service begins, representatives from the various faiths file into the sanctuary to take their seats. It is very moving to see Catholics, Buddhists, Jews, Sikhs, Quakers, Unitarians and several Protestants all taking part in this solemn service by offering a reading, a discourse or a prayer. (It is typical of Kalamazoo to acknowledge and be inclusive of differences among people, but it hasn't always that way. Over the past 40 years the town has struggled with accepting ethnic and racial minority groups. Now we are trying to overcome religious differences.) This strong ecumenical display of unity that includes both men and women, gives those of us in the pews a vivid example of what it takes to make peace in the world: tolerance for differences; respect toward all people; concern for all individuals' fulfillment, growth and creativity; a constant search for truth and meaning, human well-being and individual responsibility; and the desire to make a better world for ourselves and our children.

The service, intended as a witness for hope and a guide for people to remember in the midst of war, opens with the following Statement for Peace (recited together by members of the congregation):

> As people of conscience and abiding faith, united by a concern for human dignity and justice, we call our nation and our world to peace.

> The situation between the United States and Iraq has drawn us together and it demands that we speak out. The people of Iraq have suffered under tyranny and sanctions. War only adds to their suffering. They deserve a

nonviolent solution. The United States has the power, resources, and democratic tradition to build lasting bonds of peace. As people of faith, we see the harm done to anyone as harm to everyone and we have a responsibility to speak out.

We support the people of Iraq and not its leaders.
We support diplomacy and not aggression.
We support inspections and not unilateralism.
We support democracy and not domination.
We support the U.N.'s efforts to promote the rule of law.
We oppose war as patriots seeking liberty and justice for all.

Now is the time for each of us to let this message be heard by our elected representatives and other decision-makers. As the role of the United States becomes that of the aggressor, we not only diminish ourselves as a people, but also neglect the pressing needs of the nation and the world. The strength of our faith and the courage of our convictions unite us in the belief that we can steer our grand nation from the darkness of war to the light of peace.

For me, one of the most poignant moments of the service is the rabbi's reading of Psalm 120, which he says, Jews typically recite in difficult times. It seems to capture the mood of the moment.

> I call on the LORD in my distress, [14]
> and he answers me.
> Save me, O LORD , from lying lips and

---

[14] This is a translation from the *New American Bible.*

from deceitful tongues.

What will he do to you,
    and what more besides, O deceitful tongue?
He will punish you with a warrior's
    sharp arrows,
    with burning coals of the broom tree.

Woe to me that I dwell in Meshech,
    that I live among the tents of Kedar!
Too long have I lived among those
    who hate peace.
I am a man of peace;
    but when I speak, they are for war.

Raelynn Joyce, a Quaker, gives a short reflection about how the cause of peace is creating a new consciousness in the world where people *are* demanding peace (*see* Appendix C-2). Participants are so moved by her words that several of them ask her for copies of her speech after the service.

All in all, the prayer service provides us with a time and a place to pray as a community. It helps ground us despite the disquieting realities of the war and to realize that we are indeed making a new world for peace. Many of us, as many people from all over the world, believe war and conquest are part of the old means of settling conflicts and no longer tenable or legitimate today. Therefore, in this service prayer leaders encourage the community to remain strong and focused and avoid veering from the vision of peace and community with all peoples.

As a resident of Kalamazoo for over 20 years, I feel very proud of the way my community responds to the war during these first two nights. In Grand Rapids, Mich., only 25 people assemble to pray. In Portland, Ore., war protesters create traffic jams. In San Francisco people chain themselves to buildings and are arrested. Clearly, Kalamazoo has some solid leadership about a vision for peace.

FOURTH DAY OF WAR

Sunday, March 23, 2003

> U.S. soldiers and Marines are in the desert amid the winds and the approaching intense heat. About 10 have been killed. Two Apache helicopters are shot down. There's been friendly fire. A missile hit a bus and killed five Syrians and injured 10. Saddam sent a TV message and appears to be alive—even though the message was taped. Coalition troops are fearful over the prospect of urban warfare since it is the most dangerous and most dreaded kind of fighting. The U.S. military has been working on strategies for handling this sort of war now that the world is becoming more urbanized.
>
> Today we strike the 100th hour since the war began—the same amount time the first Gulf War ended. We're half way through the intended territory we wanted to cover.
>
> Some American troops have been captured and President Bush and Secretary of Defense Donald Rumsfeld are now calling on Geneva Convention rules that our soldiers be treated fairly and humanely.

People's Church Sunday Service

I attend the pre-service talk at People's Church (Unitarian Universalist) and decide to stay for the morning service afterward. The war is four days old and the mood among the people is very somber. Church seems to be a good place to be right now. Any church.

Rev. Jill McAllister's sermon focuses on ways of handling the war as a people of peace. She then invites members of the congregation to express themselves. Their responses range from anger to sorrow to hope and I soon realize they encapsulate the feelings of Americans utterly distraught over this war. Individuals step up to the microphone in the front of the congregation, take a candle, light it and say their piece as Rev. McAllister stands next to them in empathetic support. Here are excerpts of their comments:

> *"We now have two superpowers: the United States and public opinion. Write your congressperson and Bush to express your opinion of this war."*

> *"I've been gloomy since the beginning of 2001. Last August this war was all scripted. The one thing that wasn't scripted were the millions of people who stood up in protest over Bush's actions. There is something slowly emerging here—and I want to be a part of it."*

> *"I have been writing letters to Congress and the president and I have been participating in peace marches. I didn't realize how devastating it would be to start the war. But I try not to be discouraged and won't give up on fighting for peace."*

> *"For the last several months I have been writing letters, attending vigils and looking at my computer for news. Now with war upon us, I feel an ambivalence that is difficult to get in touch with. Today I got a letter from my daughter. She said she needed the war to take an activist stance, to go into action. She has been involved in San Francisco peace activities. I need to take the next step and I need to take it now."*

"I will continue the journey to let go of selfishness and help others every day."

"How can we explain to the rest of the world what a democracy is now?"

"I'm concerned about the precedent we are setting and what the future will be. What if Iraq is followed by Iran and then others. Will we take them on unilaterally? I will work against this U.S. policy of unilateralism. I will listen to the opinions of people around the world. But we must avoid unilateralism in our own lives."

"Kids shouldn't receive toy guns," says a little girl. "I believe this."

"Before the war, I had hoped for a global way of thinking and believed that we were on the edge of something different. After hearing the sermon, I think it's still true and I had forgotten that. I was surprised. I thought I was in the minority before, but not now. I'll keep believing we're in a global community and will be more active in bringing it about."

"I'm a pacifist who grew up in a military family where I learned compassion. At work I know a woman whose son is overseas. It is wrong to support the war. It's what got us in this mess. We need to have conversations not to feel superior, but to be who we are."

"I have some concerns that if we depose Saddam Hussein, who will we attack next?"

"I had four daughters between 1951–61 and I thought it best to take care of my own little corner of

*the world. That doesn't work anymore and it has
made me frustrated. This administration is not
listening. We have to come out of just taking care of
our own corner of the world."*

*"I encouraged my 15-year-old son to stay informed
and discuss his thoughts and feelings about the war."*

*"'How smooth must be the language of the white man
when he can so clearly make right so wrong, and
wrong so right.' This is a Native American saying. I
try to teach my daughter about language and how to
think critically. There are lots of young people who
don't know how to think critically."*

*"What's happening can be a moment of clarity for all
of us. Before the war, we allowed Saddam Hussein to
do his thing. We let Palestine and Israel fight each
other. Something is broken and the situation has
changed. This is an opportunity to move into what
seems like chaos and make something different. With
Vietnam, it took us a long time to get it. We can't be
impatient any more than we can tell Bush to be."*

The service includes a number of songs and readings.
Here is one selection that seems to fit the mood and yet move
the congregation out of the depths of defeat to a higher
ground as a faithful people advocating peace in the world.

READING FROM THE *DHAMMAPADA*

Never does hatred cease by hating in return;
Only through love can hatred come to an end.
Victory breeds hatred;
The conquered dwell in sorrow
    and resentment.
They who give up all thought of victory

> or defeat,
> May be calm—live happily at peace.
> Let us overcome violence by gentleness;
> Let us overcome evil by good;
> Let us overcome the miserly by liberality;
> Let us overcome the liar by truth.[15]

On this first Sunday of the war, the pianist presciently played a musical interlude, "On a Clear Day, You Can See Forever." This happy tune from the play of the same name will become especially appropriate as Americans become used to seeing the searing images of burning wreckages and their accompanying thick, black clouds of smoke rising up into the desert's blue and sunny skies. As the war drags on into its second year, it will also become evident to more and more Americans that the motives ascribed to this war were less than noble and that the Marines, soldiers and weekend warriors of the National Guard are stuck in Iraq with extended tours of duty, stop-loss orders and recalls to continue the fighting.

Peace Vigil

After attending the People's Church service I go to KNOW's first vigil since the start of the war to get a glimpse of the mood there. About 200 people meet at the open-air stage on the west end of Bronson Park as leaders excitedly announce upcoming events and activities and introduce newly-formed groups. Interestingly, the peace activists have escalated, not diminished their resolve to promote peace.

Noah Dillard, one of the young voices of KNOW, stands up to the megaphone as several people distribute a handout

---

[15] The *Dhammapada* consists of 423 verses in Pali uttered by the Buddha on some 305 occasions for the benefit of a wide range of human beings.

that summarizes the Project for the New American Century (PNAC) platform (*see* Appendix D-1). PNAC is a neo-conservative think tank that sought to contend with rogue nations that threatened the post-Cold War world with terrorism. Iraq is regarded a rogue nation. PNAC suggests that the United States as the only remaining superpower assert its global dominance through the military in order to attain a *Pax Americana*. The "neocons" first suggested overthrowing Iraq in 1997 to then-President Clinton (*see* Appendix D-2). Apparently, the administration had adopted PNAC's suggestions judging from Bush's bellicose actions in the Middle East and some people refer to PNAC's strategy as the Bush Doctrine, although this term is not widely used. The Kalamazoo peace activists first learned about PNAC at Professor Gary Dorrien's February 23 speech at Kalamazoo College's Stetson Chapel (*see* Appendix E).

Dorrien has long posited that the neoconservative advisors to the President Bush encouraged him to invade Iraq and to keep Iran, Syria, Saudi Arabia, Hamas, Hezbollah and North Korea in mind as targets as well. They were looking for a "new Pearl Harbor" to justify doing that. September 11 provided that opportunity. As a result, Dorrien has called the war with Iraq fraudulent in its conception and justification.

"Make sure you know this document!" Noah tells the crowd in a firm but gentle voice as people peruse both sides of the handout. Some look appalled while others blanch with worry.

A beautiful, well-dressed, olive-skinned woman with an accent announces that Kalamazoo now has a Women in Black group that will join the Sunday vigils. Several women all dressed in black and donning black veils, accompany her. They hold large, white foam-board signs with the message: Women in Black mourning all victims of war and violence. "Our purpose is to mourn the loss of all human life," says organizer Shadia Kanaan. (The women will stage numerous demonstrations at KNOW events and vigils as well as on heavily-trafficked street corners near local shopping malls and theatres.)

Another women's group, Kalamazoo CodePink, announces its first planning meeting on Saturday, March 29, at 2 p.m. The group is to be a "place for every ordinary outraged woman willing to be outraged for peace," says spokesperson Marti Faketty. "Our purpose is to raise consciousness and passionately engage people about the issue of war and peace and about whether war is legitimate at this point in human history." She says she expects the group to do creative, intelligent and meaningful projects. (CodePink will hold several ceremonial rituals denouncing war and its accompanying waste of billions of dollars from human service programs. It will create a *papier maché* Peace Momma puppet that will turn up at various KNOW events.)

KNOW vows to continue its work for non-violence by educating citizens and elected officials. It will also lobby for U.S. Rep. Dennis Kucinich's bill (H.R. 2459 introduced July 1, 2001) to establish a cabinet-level U.S. Department of Peace.

Guitarist and performer Allison Downey unveils a new peace song she wrote about the war on Iraq entitled, "Not in Our Name."[16] She sings it through and invites the crowd to follow. The song is an instant hit and people learn the refrain quickly. They strain to hear the words of the verses and often react at poignant parts. Here is the song, "Not in Our Name":

> Don't put me on a plane bound for Baghdad
> Don't put me on a plane bound for war
> Don't jeopardize our lives to make widows of wives

---

[16] Words & Music by Allison Downey, © Addy Music, 2003 www.allisondowney.com

Don't put me on a plane for your war
Don't put my money into weapons.
Don't put my earnings into war
Don't put my name on your war game
Don't put my money into war

[REFRAIN]
> *Not in our name*
> *Not in our name*
> *Your war game is not in our name*

Don't put me in a hole in the ground
Don't put me in a box with flowers all around
Don't put me below to make your empire grow
Don't put me in the ground for your war
Don't tell me that I'm not patriotic
Don't tell me that I don't support our troops
Don't tell me not to say I want them
    out of harm's way
Don't tell me that I don't support our troops

[REFRAIN]

Don't tell me that I don't love my country
Don't tell me that I should not disagree
When you defy human rights with pre-emptive strikes
Don't look like my country to me
Don't tell me that my voice doesn't matter
Don't tell us our protests are in vain
Don't tell us we are wrong, 'cause we will vote
    and you'll be gone
Don't tell us that our protests are in vain

[REFRAIN]

In closing, Tom Small clarifies for the crowd that the goal of KNOW is broader than just the war in Iraq. Its purpose is to "oppose the culture of violence that our material civilization has given rise to, and to promote and to educate and to stand for a culture of peace." Even this unwanted war can't dampen the activists' desire for peace and justice and KNOW has essentially set the stage for continuing its mission of peacemaking—however long that may take and for whatever that may mean. The crowd then disperses with much enthusiasm and hope.

FIFTH DAY OF WAR

Monday, March 24, 2003

> The *Gazette* prints an article about the draft that indicates that the American people wouldn't stand for it so it will never happen. Military databases are ready, however, to call 11 million men between the ages of 18 to 26 if need be.

SIXTH DAY OF WAR

Tuesday, March 25, 2003

> The newspapers are starting to admit that Americans at home are surprised the war is lasting this long and that our troops are meeting resistance. Stock markets are going down and oil markets are going up now that uncertainty looms over the war's end. Troops may have found a chemical weapons plant in Iraq.

> American troops have crossed the Euphrates River and they remain positioned outside Baghdad. A threat looms over Saddam's possible use of chemical weapons should we enter the city. In the south, the city of Basra's

utilities are not functioning and the humanitarian aid that we are bringing as a show of peace to civilians can't get through.

EIGHTH DAY OF WAR

Thursday, March 27, 2003

The war is not going well. The Iraqis are threatening street-to-street fighting. So far casualties have produced 25 American deaths and 4,000 Iraqi deaths. The bombing continues.

Richard Perle has resigned his chairmanship of the Defense Policy Committee, but he will remain a member of this body. This change is prompted by his involvement in Global Crossings. The independent provider of undersea fiber optic telecommunications to the U.S. military has declared bankruptcy. Perle is reportedly scheduled to receive $700,000 for selling Global Crossing to a foreign firm and then get a $600,000 bonus for the sale.

NINTH DAY OF WAR

Friday, March 28, 2003

Supply lines to soldiers are at risk. Top brass are admitting that they never anticipated the fight the Iraqis would mount. The high tech surgical bombing strategy of "shock and awe" hasn't broken the spirit of the Iraqis; they fight amid women and children. The urban war is upon us—and President Bush says the war will take longer than we expected. Supplies still cannot get through for the Iraqis or the

> Americans and retired generals are now
> predicting starvation among the Iraqis. Some
> U.S. soldiers are down to one ration a day.
>
> Syria is threatening to get involved in the war
> with Iraq and Secretary of Defense Donald
> Rumsfeld says they better not.
>
> A U.S. general in the field says we're going to be
> in Iraq for a long time. No one expected the kind
> of resistance the Iraqis have mounted. It's not
> going according to the war games, says the
> general.

A Visit to Congressman Fred Upton's Office

It is Friday at noon on the Kalamazoo Mall and Sara Wick
has just come out of Rep. Upton's office after presenting
staffers with a six-point written proposal (*see* Appendix F).
Sara is one of 200 people scheduled to visit Upton's office this
week at 30-minute intervals. Organized by KNOW, these
visitors are here to voice their concerns over a 70-page
document produced by the Project for the New American
Century entitled: "Rebuilding America's Defenses: Strategy,
Forces and Resources for a New Century." According to Ron
Suskind in *The Price of Loyalty: George W. Bush, the White House,
and the Education of Paul O'Neill* (2004), the document was
endorsed by several members of the Bush foreign policy
advisory team and adopted by the president two months
before the 2000 presidential election. It calls for an aggressive
and historically unprecedented foreign policy of U.S. global
dominance.

"We didn't win or lose the argument over the war," says
Sara. "We're still for peace and need to keep the pressure on
to change the mindset that war is an answer to global conflict.
We have to keep planning and be a presence for peace as long
as it takes."

KNOW's visits to Rep. Upton's office were precipitated by a 90-minute town hall meeting held on March 1, 2003, in Parchment, a small town north of Kalamazoo. At that meeting the congressman said he was unfamiliar with PNAC and Sara Wick, who was there that day, promised to provide his staff with three copies of the PNAC document and Gary Dorrien's February 23 speech.

Sara has been working for peace in Iraq since last October. Prior to that, she protested against the bombing of Afghanistan. She is a regular at the Sunday vigils and frequently attends KNOW planning meetings. She has also participated in a couple pre-war Washington marches. However, all this time and energy have taken a toll. "Give me my life back, President Bush," she exclaims mournfully to me with her hands raised high.

Sara is disgusted with the media and "very sad for our country and the rest of the people of the world." She regards the "entertainment war" on television with "in-bed newsmen" distressful and not an informative or accurate portrayal of the full picture. As much as Sara dislikes Bush policy, however, she strongly opposes any efforts aimed at impeaching the president, a movement currently promoted by former Attorney General Ramsey Clark (1967–69) under President Lyndon B. Johnson. "This is not good for the cost or the emotional toll it will take on the American people. Besides, then we'll get Vice President Cheney." Sara hopes Bush will step away from the 2004 election and allow other Republican candidates to run for president. "He should do this gracious and unselfish thing."

Every day this week a small group of KNOW people has demonstrated on the Kalamazoo Downtown Mall outside Rep. Upton's office. Occasionally, passers-by stop and talk to the members of the group as they distribute anti-war literature, but most people just walk on by without comment.

"Thanks," says one older man to them after he spends some time talking with a couple women. "Stick with it, good goal."

"Hope you die choking on your own spit," says an older man.

"There's other countries you can live in," says another.

"Send more troops and kick their butts," says a 30-something man as the woman he's walking with pulls at his arm and pleads with him to refrain him from saying anything further.

"We're getting such thick skins, it just rolls off us," says Sandy Adams to me as we make eye contact following these comments from passers-by. She is one of the members of Kalamazoo Women in Black who is holding vigil on the mall this afternoon. The women have been choosing public places to convey their message of "mourning for all victims of war and violence." Their stark presence undoubtedly unnerves many people who do not like political demonstrations and do not like women dressed in black out on the streets.

Other KNOW people carry signs protesting the war such as: "Fasting for Peace" or "Fasting for Compassion and Peace." Tammy Williams is on her eighth day of what she calls a "Ramadan fast" which involves refraining from food sun-up to sun-down. "I think killing is wrong," she explains as her reason to fast for the duration of the Iraqi War. "A lot of religious leaders have chosen this style of protest. It is something that can be taken seriously."

Tammy tells me that the war has placed many people in difficult or uncomfortable positions socially. For example, Tammy swims with a woman whose son is in Iraq and she has been disturbed by the woman's comment that soldiers like her son fight to give Americans like her the right to protest. Tammy disagrees that the "violence done by our government" through war protects American freedoms. "I'm here for her son, too," says Tammy. "I want to bring him and all the soldiers home now. Get them off the TV set…it's so awful to see bombing and killing."

What Tammy fears most, however, is that the Iraqi war will develop into a world war. She also recounts some people's talk about Armageddon where Jesus returns at the end of the world and chooses only a few to go to Heaven with him and leaves the others to perish. "I don't want the world to end," she says sadly. "What the world needs to do is protest war."

Maria Wong Ogston, a psychotherapist, is also fasting as a prayer for "freedom and richness of life" through her advocacy of peace. "We teach our children to dialogue and not to fight," she says. "And then we have the worst examples of adults waging war." Like Tammy, Maria stresses that she supports the troops—by wanting them to "come home alive."

Supporting the troops becomes a blurred issue between those who promote peace and those who support President Bush. It is an example of one of the lessons of Vietnam where returning troops were faulted for the war and publicly humiliated. Thirty years later in this new war, pro-war and anti-war advocates are conscious of honoring the troops and almost regarding them as innocent bystanders of policy. So the real fight between the two sides will come to be defined in ideological terms as left vs. right, liberal vs. conservative, Democrat vs. Republican, and in personal loyalties to the baby boomer generation's presidents, Bill Clinton vs. George W. Bush.

Maria is originally from England and she is "very disappointed" with Prime Minister Blair who went to war with Iraq while 80 percent of the British people were against such a cause. She says that neither England nor the United States listened to the world's objections to this war and that Bush was intent on taking out Saddam *before* 9/11. He used 9/11 as an excuse to pursue this desire. Maria's attitude toward war has been shaped by the many Vietnam veterans she treats in her practice. "They are absolutely messed up from that war," she says. She also thinks that watching the war on television traumatizes people who believe that the world is stymied by unstoppable chaos and terror. She adds that she was impressed with candidate-Bush during the 2000 election when he said he wasn't interested in nation building. However, she sees through that stance now and quotes a recent issue of *The Guardian*, a British newspaper, that comments that Bush is not nation-building, he is "planet building."

Maria has been standing for peace since last October when she went to the first peace march held in Washington, D.C. She joined the February march in New York and has been attending the KNOW vigils every Tuesday and Sunday. But despite the start of the war, she still doesn't believe her effort and those of the millions of peace advocates to avert war are unsuccessful or ineffective. Instead she has her sights on the future where "diplomacy rather than destruction and terror" will bring peace to the world.

On Friday, April 4, a week after the demonstration at Representative Upton's office, I telephone Sean Bonyun, Upton's press secretary in Washington. He says the congressman received Sara Wick's package, has not yet read it, but will be briefed on it soon. Sean adds that the congressman knows William Kristol, the executive director of PNAC and one of the authors of the document.

Upton's district service office received 65 to 70 letters or emails regarding PNAC and recorded nearly 100 visitors to the Kalamazoo office during the week of March 24–28, according to Sean who adds that the KNOW people were polite and courteous and that daily business at the office continued without interruption. He says, however, that some of the

KNOW people "didn't fully appreciate" the fact that the staff was busy working on several other cases, some of which were time sensitive including one older woman who needed help with her prescription drugs. Some KNOW people had also apparently demurred about putting their concerns in writing, even though this is Upton's standard office procedure.

When I ask Sean if the peace activists' lobbying effort will have much influence on the congressman, he reiterates Upton's support for the president and this war in Iraq and says that the war shouldn't be politicized now that it is in progress. "The purpose of the war is about freeing individuals in Iraq," he says. "Those against the war don't realize the dangerous threat of chemical weapons." Then he excitedly tells me that he has just learned that WMDs may have been found. He promises to email me the story, which he did that night. Here's the www.MSNBC.com story:

> . . . [There is] evidence of the deadly toxins ricin and botulinum at a laboratory in a remote mountain region of northern Iraq allegedly used as a terrorist training camp by Islamic militants with ties to the Al Qaeda terrorist network. The U.S. Central Intelligence Agency is conducting its own tests at the same area, but has not yet released the results, according to officials in northern Iraq. (April 4, 2003)

The report turns out to be a false alarm. WMDs in Iraq are not found—and at press time they have yet to be found.

Sean says that even though the "protesters' letters carry the same message, every letter will be read, responded to, and treated in the same manner as any letter" Rep. Upton receives on any issue. He also says that the congressman will phone those people he knows personally and talk with them about

PNAC. According to office logs, Upton received only a few letters and phone calls from constituents in support of the war with Iraq. Nevertheless, Sean claims that 70 percent of Americans support the president while "it's the 30 percent who are making a lot of noise." However, Rep. Upton aims to keep the dialogue open among all constituents. He also plans a visit to Kalamazoo in April when he will spend time with families of troops.

ELEVENTH DAY OF WAR

Sunday, March 30, 2003
Peace Vigil

It's been 11 days since the war started and 400 people show up for today's peace vigil. They stand in front of the Federal Building and their line extends half a block down on Michigan Avenue. The Women in Black, 13 of them, stand silently across the street, kitty-corner to the rest of the group. Five people with signs and a drum continuously walk across all four corners of the intersection of Michigan Avenue and Park Street chanting: "No blood for oil" and "Drop Bush, not bombs."

Hildy Kerney sees me approach and grabs me. "I'm madder by the minute," she cries in her grave, high-pitched voice. She is disappointed that the war she had protested for the past few months has come to pass. People like Hildy are used to seeing me with my notebook and they know about my book project. They seem to want to share their views, as if it will help them endure this war through the recorded word. Another man stops me to say he heard that after giving the order to start the war, Bush said: "I feel good." Feelings of disappointment and anger that the president deliberately started this war pervade the crowd and the demonstrators' posters say it all:

> Shocked and devastated, not awed
>
> Thou shalt not kill
>
> Stop this unjust war
>
> Imperialism is not liberation – no PNAC
>
> May God forgive us
>
> War is not the answer
>
> Live for peace. Die for war
>
> Blessed are the peacemakers
>
> War is evil
>
> Let us not become the evil we deplore
>
> Stop state-sponsored terrorism
>
> At a loss for words
>
> Cowboys belong in movies

Frankly, I'm surprised that so many people still come to the peace vigils now that the war has begun. Many people say they expected it to be over soon, like the 1991 100-hour Gulf War, but that is not likely in Iraq. There seems to be more at stake this time in the administration's quarrel with Iraq.

"We have to keep protesting that the war is unnecessary, illegal and immoral and then demand it to stop," says Ron Kramer.

"What's next?" I ask him.

Ron reiterates what other KNOW leaders have stressed from the beginning: that KNOW is committed to educating people on how this war got started by focusing extensively on the Project for the New American Century (PNAC). The sociology professor refers me to a book by Paul Lobe entitled: *Hope in Hard Times*. Written in the 1980s as part of a movement for change, it includes an article by Jonathan Schell who discusses how the United States could move toward disarmament if it dropped the paradigm of having to defend ourselves before the world. This "hypocrisy" has led to a greater proliferation of weapons and war, says Ron.

One other KNOW leader, Rick Stahlhut, points out to me a young Spanish woman standing at the corner who told him that 99 percent of Spain's population were against the war, yet Prime Minister Jose Maria Aznar supported Bush by providing 2,000 Spanish troops to the U.S.-led coalition. Young Spaniards have refused to support their leader because he was acting like Franco, past dictator of Spain, who assumed the role of patriarch and promoted the idea that it was unseemly to "question the father."

I don't have an opportunity to talk with the young Spanish woman but her assessment of her country's feelings toward the war lean toward truthfulness or at least insightfulness. In spring 2004 the challenger for Spain's leadership, Jose Luis Rodriguez Zapatero, unseats Aznar because of his support for the war. Zapatero promises to withdraw troops if elected and says his country's presence in Iraq is illegal because it lacks a mandate. He is indeed elected and Spanish troops leave Iraq shortly after his April 17, 2004 inauguration.

Across the street next to the Women in Black, Jack Emmons (a pseudonym), 22, blasts out the song "Proud to be an American" from his car stereo so that he can "provide an opposition to the anti-war protesters."

"Saddam is a monster," says the tall and clean-cut young man, "sometimes war is the only way of getting rid of such people." In fact, Jack believes Saddam should have been done away with 20 years ago as he refers to the photo of Donald Rumsfeld shaking hands with Saddam after an arms deal. "That was sick."

The Air Force veteran (1998–2001) says he is concerned about "the poor guys in chemical suits all day." Although he never experienced combat, Jack believes it would be an honor to serve his country against a tyrant like Saddam. He admits, however, that life in the hot desert climate would indeed be miserable and that he wouldn't like the inconvenience of taking only one shower a week or getting only one ration a day. Yet he supports the war because he believes Saddam must be "taken out."

The peace activists upset Jack because he thinks they should do something rather than just complain about the war. "Why don't they adopt a troop?" he asks. Frankly, he is skeptical of the protesters' commitment to the cause of peace and thinks that the young people who protest are doing it because their parents were protesters during the Vietnam War. "They do it because it's cool," he says. His image of the young protesters is that they "play bongos and smoke pot." Jack concludes our talk speculating that he would have probably marched with the peace groups had he lived in the 60s, but for this war, "there's no reason to protest." (Jack never shows up again for any other vigils, nor do any other Bush supporters. During the Bush rallies, however, there are a handful of peace people who stand across the street from Michigan Avenue to stage a counter-rally.)

After every vigil, a KNOW leader holds a short meeting on the steps of the Federal Building. Usually Tom Small conducts these meetings by providing news, information, announcements and recognitions.

Tom stands tall in his scraggly, gray beard. The ends of his curly hair poke out from beneath his Tilley hat. He usually wears a green vest with many pockets and khaki trousers. He and his wife, Nancy, who usually sits on a boulder next to the steps during the meeting portion of the vigil, are both retired WMU English professors. They started a business out of their hobby of growing and reseeding wild flowers. I have seen them working on their hands and knees in the high grasses of a client's yard or on a roadside flowerbed. Here is a sampling of today's announcements:

* KNOW plans to send a bus to the next peace march on Washington scheduled for April 12. The cost is $70 for the 36-hour trip. Grant Murray (a pseudonym), 25, is organizing this trip. It's his first attempt at community organizing and he's quite excited. (He manages to fill a bus.)

* Wade Adams thanks the people who participated in last week's visitations to Rep. Fred Upton's office.

* Bishop Desmond Tutu of South Africa will visit Grand Rapids on March 25.

After the announcements, Allison Downey leads the group in song with "Not in Our Name." People join in as they concentrate on learning the words. Tom then ends the meeting with an inspirational message to keep up everyone's spirits and to focus on their cause. This week he quotes Mother Teresa:

> Give whatever it takes not to harm other
> people....if we have no peace, we have
> forgotten how to seek God in one another. If
> we saw God in one another, do you think we
> would use bombs and guns?

Tom ends this vigil in the same way that he ends all the vigils: "Thank you for standing for peace. Peace be with you. Go in peace."

As the crowd disperses I talk with a few more people about why they attend the vigils. Suddenly, a woman rolls her car up along the curb. "I wanted to see what was going on," she says. "I don't want to protest or support the war in public." The twenty-seven-year-old tells me that she, like most of her friends, oppose the war but that she wants to support the government and she wants peace. Her mission in coming today is to "take what I can to understand." Actually, I later discover that she represents the sentiments of a majority of citizens who feel caught in the delicate dilemma of supporting the government and supporting their desire for peace.

Another man, Ray Thomas (a pseudonym), married to a pacifist Mennonite woman, spells out his dilemmas and discontent to me. "I was supposed to be Catholic, but my daughter got raped. Then the church has this pedophilia scandal....The war has challenged [U.S. Rep.] Upton to take a stand but at a recent hometown meeting, Upton seemed more concerned about abortion than about the United States at war." Ray has been a Democrat but he has not appreciated the Democrats' passive response to this war. He is thinking about becoming a Green Party member.

As the group disperses, someone shouts from a passing car: "Remember September 11—God bless America."

TWELFTH DAY OF WAR

Monday, March 31, 2003

News correspondent Peter Arnett is fired by NBC because he reported that the U.S. has a faulty war plan. A U.K. station hired him, however, so he'll be able to continue reporting.

THIRTEENTH DAY OF WAR

Tuesday, April 1, 2003

There are more anti-war protesters arrested for civil disobedience in Washington D.C. and San Francisco. People are on edge, even in Kalamazoo. (The tension seems worse to me than 9/11. There an unfathomable sadness as well as fierce emotion.) The media is interviewing families of dead or missing soldiers and Marines—and the families consent to these intrusions.

This morning U.S. officers in the field report that the war strategists shorted them the necessary personnel to fight this war. On Sunday Rumsfeld is questioned about these accusations after a *New York Times* report claimed he trumped the generals in planning this war. Yesterday the president defended the war plans and said everything is going well. Today, General Myers, chairman of Joint Chiefs, defended Rumsfeld.

Saddam hasn't appeared on TV lately but one of his generals did yesterday. He called on all Muslims in Iraq to wage jihad or holy war, in defense of their country.

FOURTEENTH DAY OF WAR

Wednesday, April 2, 2003

The Americans are pressing in on Baghdad where they say there's risk of a chemical weapons attack.

The news is coming out that the framers of the Project for the New American Century who advocated perpetual war and American global dominance, are defenders of Israel and Netanyahu's regime. Ironically, Israel, like Iraq, has repeatedly violated U.N. resolutions only it has not been punished.

The *Christian Science Monitor* reports that two-thirds of Americans now support the war and that the peace activists are not getting in the news anymore. Since selling newspapers (and advertising) is the main goal of profitable media outlets, it is now untenable to show the opposing side of the war. (The *Gazette* is getting more Letters to the Editor by people who support the war, however.)

Jessica Lynch, who was captured, has now been rescued!

Colin Powell is warning Syria and Iran to back off from any involvement with Iraq. Meanwhile, world opinion is still strongly against the U.S. starting this war.

SIXTEENTH DAY OF WAR

Friday, April 4, 2003

The Marines take the Baghdad Airport and kill many Iraqis. The *Washington Times* quotes a soldier who talks about all the death and how wasteful it was and that he hoped he wouldn't see any more; he also questions the reason for starting this war.

Some U.S. generals are leaking information that Secretary of Defense Rumsfeld overruled top military leaders and created an ill-conceived war plan. Meanwhile, Americans are surrounding Baghdad—with no protection of their rear flank.

(It will later come out that there weren't enough troops to execute this war.)

Americans find a stash of what may be chemical weapons, but they're testing them. So far they have found no weapons of mass destruction, the presumed reason for starting the war.

Film footage shows Saddam unexpectedly appearing on the street and President Bush says that whether we kill Saddam or not, we're taking over Iraq. Critics point out that this is another change of mission, something that's become a common characteristic of this war.

Mary Anne Wright, deputy chief of the Mission in Mongolia, resigned her post on March 19, the day before U.S. air strikes began on Iraq because "she could no longer represent a government whose foreign policy she found indefensible." Wright is a retired Army colonel who joined the Foreign Service in 1987. In her letter to Secretary of State Colin Powell, she told him how bad our reputation is all over the world.

There is talk that Syria is next on the list of countries to be invaded with Iran after that.

Bush and Tony Blair are meeting in Ireland to talk about post-war Iraq.

Eighteenth Day of War

Sunday, April 6, 2003

Mention of Syria as our next target comes up on "Meet the Press" as Tim Russert interviews Deputy Secretary of Defense Paul Wolfowitz, one of the architects of the Project for the New American Century. PNAC is getting more exposure in the mainline media.

Peace Vigil

As the troops advance to Baghdad and apparent victory, the tension at home is increasing. During this past month I begin talking with people from both the peace side and the Bush side and have discovered that we are fast approaching an impasse in our ability to communicate with each other or to debate the issues of our day. Each side believes it is right and the other side is wrong. The pain of the 2000 election still weighs heavily on the peace activists and Bush's use of 9/11 to advance his power—and curtail Americans' civil liberties—has disheartened them to the point that they believe America's democracy is at risk.

On the other hand, Bush supporters point to the disgrace of the Clinton administration as justification to sneer at Democrats and liberals (also called "libbies" or "librotards") and now peace activists. Name-calling, vicious accusations and a resistance to cooperation have become *de rigueur* in Congress and over the airwaves and those who disagree with the president or the war are openly called "traitors" and "un-American."

Over the next 12 months the divisiveness will increase, become more embittered and gradually result in a high-pitched exercise of vilification during the 2004 presidential election. Neither side can conceive of its candidate losing. For the peace activists, the election results will be cause for great consternation as well as feelings of hopelessness, shame and defeat, however, their greater passion for peace will endure through their religion and through their community service. For the pro-Bush constituency it will mean greater strength and a validation of the president's policies and practices. Here are a few of the stories I collected at the Sunday peace vigil to illustrate.

JACK MCKINLEY (pseudonym) IS DISMAYED at being pegged "un-American" but some people's responses to his opposition to the war are making him feel that way. Here's a case in point. A deputy from the Kalamazoo County Sheriff's Department recently stopped Jack for obstructing the driver's view of his back window with a blue KNOW peace sign. He took a photo of the position of the sign after the deputy accosted him. The sign lay on the shelf below the back window of his car and not attached to the window in any way. He received a $75 ticket and two points for his offense. When he sees me coming with my notebook, he breaks the vigil line and takes me to his car to show me his sign and back window, which, he says, are in exactly the same position they were when the deputy ticketed him.

Jack is a high school government teacher. His principal recently sent out an e-mail reminding faculty that school was not a political institution and that teachers may not share their views about the war—for or against. "I pride myself in not teaching my political views," says Jack. "When students ask me about my political affiliation, I don't tell them. I want them to make up their own minds about politics." Jack is especially miffed by these recent affronts because he has exercised his patriotic duty by volunteering at the VFW's Disabled Americans program for the past 18 months. He has responded to 9/11 by helping those less fortunate.

DRIVE-BY HECKLERS WHO STARTED making nasty remarks from their cars last week are more vicious this week with remarks like:

"Why don't you support Hitler?"
"Fuck off"
"The Bible says there's no peace and will always be war."
"Go home, you're wasting your time."

☮

RON SOWERS, 51, ATTENDS the rallies every week in his white shirt, blue coat and tie with a large metal cross around his neck. He holds a different placard each week. Today he has a Greek icon of Jesus that reads: "Blessed are the peace makers" (Matthew 5:9). "The character of God is one of peace," says Ron who is known as a holy man by his friends. The health care administrator who grew up in the South during the Civil Rights era, started attending KNOW's peace vigils last October. "My own study of international religious communities leads me to conclude that this war doesn't fit the criteria of a just war. The message of the Sermon on the Mount expresses the deepest sense of being a Christian. It's not a statement you can make an argument against."

☮

A BIG MAN WITH THICK, WAVY HAIR and a full-face beard stands at the very end of the line of people right on the corner waving peace signs to passers-by. He wears an off-white church alb but the ends of it have been shredded. I've seen him several times before and finally approach him to find out why he has chosen to dress this way.

"When the bombing started I tore my vestments as an act of humility and grief for the suffering the U.S. is causing," says Rev. John Fisher, pastor of Sunnyside Methodist Church who has since been re-assigned to another church in another town. "I include myself in this act because I'm an American. We have failed as a church to teach a viable alternative to war. We haven't done our part."

John tells me that his congregation, which is mostly a World War II generation, agreed with him after 9/11 that retaliation with war and violence would only lead to more violence. "I was pleasantly surprised at my congregation who supported me in that view," he says. When the war with Iraq began, the congregation split as some people wanted to support the troops and others wanted to advocate for peace.

"I gave them my family history," says John. "My stepsister lives in Kuwait and said Saddam is awful. Her youngest son is a Marine in Iraq. His mother has me here and a grandson there and is appreciative of both. But there is better resistance to Saddam than the violence of war to remove him." In fact, John sees this war as immoral and compares it to what a second century Roman historian perceived about the invasion of Britain: "You created a wasteland and call it peace."

"I fear that's what we're about to do with this war in Iraq," says John. "It's good to end oppression but we've gone about it the wrong way. Winning peace is more difficult than winning battles. We need active resistance not passive resistance. We have to change the way we live. That's what has kept me here in the peace movement. Waging peace has brought invigorating diversity here."

John is also concerned that the administration has not been truthful about Saddam or Iraq and that it will have lasting effects on the country. "Before the war there was hype about what would happen," he says. "After the Superbowl it went a different way. I don't know but I fear this administration has fallen in love with war as a tool and it has withdrawn from the world community and placed itself in a position that right makes right."

When I ask him about the danger that Saddam might possess weapons of mass destruction he takes a view that reinforces his skepticism about the administration's justification for war with Iraq—and the war on terrorism in general as it affects this country. "Saddam probably had WMD, but he's not the only one," says John. "It wasn't a great threat to us; rather it was a justification for war. If we don't use that one, we'll find some other justification. But what worries me is PATRIOT Act I and II and how quickly people are willing to give up their rights [because of their fears]. It changes the tenor of the nation."

☮

The vigil ends with everyone singing the song, "Not in My Name." They have already learned the words well and the song encapsulates the feelings of solidarity that envelop the group today. Even the cold weather and nasty remarks from passing cars fail to dampen the demonstrators' enthusiastic commitment to peace or their resolve to come back to the vigil next week and the week after and the week after that. I still wonder why this is so and when I see John Flynn, a long-time peace advocate, I ask his opinion on this matter. "People come to the vigils because they feel a need to stick together against an administration that is scary, crazy and arrogant," says John. But as he talks, a woman walks past us and begins shouting to herself in a piercing, desperate voice, "I'm sick of the killing. Sick of the killing. I can't take it any more."

"You see, that's what wears you down," says John turning back to me after our alarm at this outburst. "The war is dividing the country and people have no way to talk with each other about our policies. Some people believe in Manifest Destiny and others believe in *noblesse oblige*."

TWENTY-FIRST DAY OF WAR

Wednesday, April 9, 2003

Baghdad has been captured and thankfully the U.S. has suffered no casualties.

TWENTY-THIRD DAY OF WAR

Friday, April 11, 2003
Women in Black Demonstration

I am at Bronson Park this evening, the center of the Kalamazoo's downtown. Churches of many protestant denominations surround the park as does the city hall, county court house, public library, and Civic Theatre. Our town's founder, Titus Bronson, insisted that this rectangular non-commercial strip of land remain so in perpetuity and he insured that in the 1829 town charter. Retail space is a block away on Burdick Street, once the home of the nation's first downtown pedestrian mall built in 1959. The mall has been reverted to a street, shop faces and interiors have been refurbished and developers have built loft apartments above the storefronts. This is part of the city's downtown revitalization plan, a program that has been initiated in old cities throughout America.

The park's artifacts record much of Kalamazoo's history. The Indian Mound, a grassy knob on the southwestern side, recalls the "Mound People" who lived here before the white settlers. It presumably served as a gravesite for the area's first residents. A green, Michigan historical site sign notes that an obscure, anti-slavery politician named Abraham Lincoln spoke here on August 27, 1856. Two water fountains, still dry from the winter season, run through the center of the park. One, designed by Alfonse Ianelli, commemorates the brutality of white settlement toward the Native Americans in the area. The other, designed by Kirk Newman and installed as a bicentennial memorial on July 4, 1976, features individual life-sized sculptures of children with an accompanying plaque that states: "When justice and mercy prevail, children may safely play" (paraphrased from Zechariah 8:1–8).

There are many memorials in the park that recognize veterans of America's wars. On the northeast corner stands a bronze cavalry soldier of the 1898 Spanish-American war who "guards" the park. Opposite him rests a 10-inch, 15,204-pound Columbiad canon that honors the soldiers and sailors of Kalamazoo who fought in the Civil War. Huge boulders with bronze plaques are scattered around the park noting the valor and patriotism of various people and commemorating the deaths of those caught in horrific events, like the September 11 attack and the sinking of the U.S.S. Maine in the Havana Harbor on February 15, 1898, the provocation of the Spanish-American War. One boulder honors "the memory of pioneers and patriots of this county who by their deeds of heroism voiced the 'spirit of liberty.'" Another (dedicated on September 11, 1913) honors the 50th anniversary of 11th regiment of the Michigan Volunteer Cavalry that left for the Civil War. A black, granite Korean War memorial occupies the south-central portion of the park while a Vietnam War memorial sits on the north-central part, almost opposite. Across a small street in front of the county building, the Kalamazoo County Disabled Veterans have erected a memorial to the men from all the services "who risked their lives and spilled their blood to keep [America] free." The figures wear World War II uniforms.

A permanent stage, donated by the Kalamazoo Rotary, towers over the western end of the park. It was built to celebrate the new millennium and to replace the old, roll-away trailer that had been used as a stage for years. Tonight, a couple roller bladers practice their jumps and flips on it. Sometimes they skate along the stage's narrow edges making a metal-against-concrete scraping sound, the only sounds on this splendid evening in this docile setting.

Bronson Park remains a popular gathering place for summer concerts, festivals, rallies, lunch breaks, general lounging and walking. During the holidays the city sets up the

Christmas crèche for families to visit and the 10-foot high red and white arches of Candy Cane Lane that both kids and adults enjoy walking through. Recently, the city purchased green metal benches to replace the old wooden ones as part of its downtown revitalization program. New 1890s-style lanterns located throughout the park light up the new cement walkways that have replaced the crisscrossed asphalt-paved paths. Tonight, a few couples sit quietly talking to each other on the benches.

We're on daylight savings time now, which started last Sunday. We have a delicious extra hour of light left for the end of the day that goes as late as 9:45 p.m. at the summer solstice. I came here tonight to talk with peace activists who will gather for yet another bus trip to Washington for yet another march against the war. The send-off is scheduled for 9 p.m. instead of 8 p.m. as it has been in the past. I'm here at 7:30, but my early arrival is not wasted. I encounter a Woman in Black demonstration in front of the Civic Theatre whose performance tonight is the musical, "Footloose."

A petite woman arrives for the demonstration dressed in a black top, black slacks, and black shoes. She stops in front of the theatre about 20 feet from the entrance. She takes the black veil laying on her shoulders and gingerly positions it over her head. She then secures the veil that is around her neck by whipping the cloth over each shoulder. With her eyes still downcast, she methodically takes her sunglasses out of her pocket and puts them on. She picks up a white 20"x 30" foam-board sign that has been resting at her feet and holds it up in front of her chest with both hands. The sign reads: "Women in Black: Mourning All Victims of War and Violence."

The woman stands there silently, alone. She just stands there with her sign, expressionless and somber, yet fully engaged with the crowd that quietly gathers outside the entrance of the theatre. I marvel at her nerve to stand there by herself as people walk by. I strain to listen to the comments of passers-by.

"I support you," a woman whispers as she passes by the lone Woman in Black.

"Thank you," the Woman in Black replies stoically.

"I'm glad you're here," says another woman quietly and reverently. The Woman in Black nods.

A second woman dressed in black from head to toe arrives, takes out her white sign, and stands next to the first woman. They recognize each other's presence with a nod and a brief smile. A minute later a third woman silently joins them. Not long afterward, an elderly passer-by says hi to this third woman and notes with surprise "I didn't know you did this. Good, good."

The theatre-goers are dressed casually, although several people, mostly women, dress up in evening wear. Ironically, many of these women are in black, too, but they pay no attention to the Women in Black. Many of the men wear white or khaki-colored clothes, signals of the annual push for spring in Michigan. It is easy to pick out those who are on dates tonight.

Upon seeing the Women in Black, many of the theatre-goers' faces are blank. A few of them grit their teeth. Some glance at the Women in Black's signs, mouth the words as they read or they peek over their shoulders to get a look at the austere presence before them. Almost all the passers-by walk past the trio without a word and instead look straight ahead as though the Women in Black are not there. But, of course, everyone knows they're there.

I find the theatre-goers' reactions tonight strange. Some of them are probably nervous, angry, confused, fearful over the war, fearful over terrorism, fearful over making any kind of response. So maybe that's why so many people just ignore the Women in Black. Of course, Americans are taught as children never to talk about politics or religion. Kalamazooans in particular utterly avoid ever bringing controversy out into the open. But these days how can anyone avoid it? And some people are still so traumatized by September 11 that they don't know how to respond to anything anymore. The Women in Black aren't afraid and tonight, in their silence, they know they are making an important political statement against the Bush administration's advocacy of war.

A tall, lanky middle-aged man steps up to the women: "I'm with you all, ladies." A young girl inquisitively calls her mother's attention to the scene. "I know, I know," says her mother quietly as she moves her daughter along through the theatre door without any further comment. A couple people see the Women in Black and just shake their heads either in disapproval or disgust; it's hard to tell the difference these days. Still, the Women in Black stand silently without expression.

A man I don't know sees me off to the side in a crouched position making notes of this demonstration. "God bless you for being here," he says to me as he shakes my hand. I guess he thinks I'm in the media.

A woman stops before the Women in Black and grasps the shoulder of one and says: "I read the article about you (*Gazette*, April 7, 2003). I appreciate what you're doing." Then she moves on.

Sadness comes over me as I watch this street theatre. I think about the war. I think about the death and destruction. I think about this demonstration and the courage it takes to stand there in public making a statement. I think about people's inability to discuss this war, to feel this war, to disagree with this war. It's as though we live in some other reality where the war is being waged with fluttering flags on car doors, bumper stickers, political loyalties, invective letters to the editor and public demonstrations such as this one while our soldiers and Marines risk their lives in Iraq.

With five minutes to go before the start of the performance, Jim Amos, a retired WMU student advisor, delays going into the theatre and instead stops to talk to me. He has a new TV show at the Community Access Center where he "challenges people to think about issues in Kalamazoo—everything from the war to parking policies." A short, white-haired, energetic man, Jim is genuinely friendly almost all of the time but tonight he seems agitated and anxious to talk with me. He says he is angry about the looting and death of Iraqi citizens who were supposedly liberated. Then he switches to the city's financial situation, which he is particularly hot about tonight. The city announced recently that it would increase traffic and parking fines to help raise more money for services. City commissioners must continuously juggle the delicate balance of enticing businesses to Kalamazoo through tax incentives, avoiding levying a city tax on residents (especially on non-city residents), and finding enough money to support the city's elaborate infrastructure. Part of the city's problem are the 26 tax cuts our previous governor imposed on the state during the go-go 90s. Now we don't have enough revenue sharing funds for the infrastructure and services we have become accustomed to having. And the implementation dates of these tax cuts will continue!

"So what do they do?" Jim asks me rhetorically. "They hire two more parking police to fine more cars. They should have the police catch people for smoking in the wrong places and charge them $200. That will raise money." Jim is one of the few people I've met who is beginning to question the money raised for the war and the money cut for services in the homeland. That question, though, will have to wait until September 2003 before people catch on. That's when the president proposes $87 billion more for Iraq's reconstruction—with calls for more money to come after the November 2004 election. We have already spent $63 billion on this war.

A few people are still milling around outside the theatre when the house manager announces curtain time. Jim shakes my hand and hustles off to the show. This evening's stint for the Women in Black is over now, too. The first woman of the group reminds the others about tomorrow night's demonstration at Miller Auditorium, the Sunday afternoon vigil at the Federal Building and the Wednesday noon hour demonstration on the downtown street mall. They all nod, promise to be there and silently leave.

☮

The Kalamazoo Women in Black are part of an international, grassroots effort of women witnessing the violence and killing in the world, and demanding that it stop. The organization began in 1988 in Tel Aviv, Israel, by Palestinian and Israeli women as a protest against Israel's occupation of the West Bank and Gaza. Their idea migrated to the United States and Europe in 1991 to protest the wars in the former Yugoslavia.

The Women in Black is not a membership organization. Rather, it is an international peace network that has spread by word of mouth and, of course, through the Internet (www.womeninblack.org). Of particular concern for the group is the women and children who become victims of war and violence, defined as rape, discrimination and indignity. The Kalamazoo Women in Black made their first appearance at the Sunday, March 23, peace vigil in Bronson Park. "We should have started our group long before the war," says Shadia Kanaan, organizer for the local group. "Our purpose is to mourn the loss of all human life during this war with Iraq."

The Women in Black do not align themselves with any partisan group nor do they claim to be for or against the war in Iraq, but the Kalamazoo women usually show up at KNOW peace vigils and events. As political activists they demonstrate in public and call for a change in policies supporting war and violence. In March 2003 I saw a small group of Women in Black stand in silence outside an auditorium in Grand Rapids when South Africa's Episcopal Bishop Desmond Tutu came for a visit. In October 2004 several Women in Black groups from all over Michigan met in Ann Arbor for a massive demonstration against the Iraq War.

"Our presence is an appeal to people's conscience," says Shadia. "Many people don't feel the misery and suffering of the world. So it's our statement, we are mourning for all the victims."

The 50 or so Kalamazoo Women in Black are comprised of mostly white, middle-aged and elderly women, although younger women sometimes show up as do a few Muslim women from town. They usually gather five, six or seven women to stand for an hour at the Sunday vigils and at noon on Wednesdays on major highways near shopping malls. The women maintain contact with each other mostly through e-mail and occasionally they meet to talk about future activities and demonstrations. In June 2004 they celebrated their commitment to peace by holding their first annual potluck picnic at Shadia's house. They marched in the Kalamazoo Memorial Day Parade in 2003, 2004 and 2005.

The Kalamazoo Women in Black exude a spirit of solidarity during their vigils, even though they remain silent during that long hour when hundreds of cars pass them. As the cars go by the people in them often stare at the demonstration before them. Sometimes passengers mouth the words as they read the signs. Children in the cars turn to their mothers undoubtedly asking who the women are and what they're doing. A few people honk their horns in support. Others shake their heads or sport an obscene gesture. I saw one deeply upset man in a huge semi-truck take both his hands off the wheel and give the Women in Black two thumbs down. Another man in a dress suit stuck his tongue out at them. Then there are those who rev up their engines as they go by.

What is utterly apparent about the silent presence of the Women in Black is that they upset many people. One man objected to their presence at the Civic Theatre that night in a LETTER TO THE EDITOR (April 27, 2003). Shadia answered him with her LETTER TO THE EDITOR by refusing to apologize for mourning the loss of life. Such responses to a public event illustrate the political nature the war in Iraq has taken on as loyalty and allegiance to one's side has become a dividing line among the citizens in our town.

Actually, I think people are upset by the Women in Black because they *don't* want to think about the war. They prefer to shield themselves from the issue of death and destruction that comes with war and dismiss the possibility that the Bush administration (and the congressional Democrats and Republicans) may have committed this country to a war that will cost thousands of lives and billions of dollars. People seem to prefer ignoring all these things so they try to quash all efforts to bring them out into the open. The Women in Black—and the peace activists in general—do not let them forget. [17]

---

[17] This issue resurfaces in April 2004 after the *Seattle Times* publishes a front-page photo of flag-draped coffins in a cargo plane in Kuwait. The photo is posted on the Internet and in newspapers across the country and the public then questions the Pentagon's policy of prohibiting the press from photographing the coffins' arrival at

For a number of months I have watched people's reactions to the Women in Black. Their stark, haunting presence is an unusual sight and a potent reminder of what is ultimately at stake when nations pursue war as a means of settling conflict. In the summer of 2003 I decide to stand with them for an hour on Wednesday afternoons. Part of my reason for doing this is that I desperately need a *public* way of expressing my grief, sorrow and outrage at what my government—and governments everywhere—do and have been doing.[18] Standing with the Women in Black also allows me to experience what it is like to hold a vigil.

Dover Air Force Base (Delaware) as well as the military funerals. During the week of June 21, 2004, the U.S. Senate refuses to change this policy by a vote of 54-39.

Senator John Warner, Republican chairman of the Senate Armed Services Committee and spokesman on the subject believes that the ban assures the privacy of the families, which he claims is "the most important priority." Nevertheless, people feel a need to grieve and a *Christian Science Monitor* (June 16, 2004) article entitled "Homegrown Memorials Used as Tributes, Antiwar Protests" note that communities across the country are honoring the dead through makeshift memorials despite the Senate's ban. KNOW also participates in this unorganized trend with a silhouette display that asks the question: Iraq—How many deaths? (*See* The Silhouettes, page 375.)

This practice of banning press and public access to the military coffins, according to the AP (Nov. 3, 2003), began during the 1991 Persian Gulf War and continues to the present. The Bush administration lifted the ban for a short period during the Afghan War.

[18] In the twentieth century alone, between 167–258 million people are killed as a result of war and violence, depending on how one counts. For a more comprehensive view of the estimates of death through war, see http://users.erols.com/mwhite28/warstat8.htm#Total

Not surprisingly I find that standing with the Women in Black doesn't change a thing in Iraq or other parts of the world in conflict, but it does give me the ability to make a public statement that war and violence are simply no longer legitimate or justifiable in our world because it's too easy to kill soldiers and civilians on a massive scale. (The actions of terrorists, random acts of violence by individuals and not nation states, is especially problematic today because terrorists hide and they do not play by war's rules of conflict.) Until enough people believe that any kind of violence and killing is not OK, the Women in Black will mourn. And mourning *is* definitely doing something.

The Women in Black demonstrations also represent a new style of protest different from the Sunday peace vigils and vociferous national protest marches: a group of women gathers in silence with each other as a grassroots *non*-organization whose cause is irrefutable and whose witness is a publicly expressed feeling of sadness. These elements provide an opportunity to stimulate serious thought and discussion about the human costs of war and violence. As other parts of this book will show, the Number One problem of America, especially after September 11, is our tendency to narcoticize ourselves from the world's realities—even as we are affected by them.

Below are statements by the Kalamazoo Women in Black who explain why they participate in these silent demonstrations.

> *I began standing with the Women in Black in March before the war began. It became an extension of my participation in the peace rallies. As a Woman in Black, I feel encouraged in the cause against war, especially when someone nods approvingly at me. When someone issues a rude remark, I consider it sort of sad. The men fight wars and start them. I think it is important that women stand*

and show the rest of the world that bombing Iraq is wrong. The Women in Black are not condoning violence and war, rather, we want to show great compassion and sympathy for those suffering from violence and war.

— Helen Bray

It's the most important thing I can do to try to make everyone think about the consequences of war and violence. It's not saying one side or the other is right or wrong or that I have all the answers. But war and violence are self-perpetuating.

— Pat Hollahan

It needs to be done so people at least have opportunities to think about the issue of violence whether they are drive-by shootings, rape, plague, whatever. Our presence gives people an opportunity to think about the role violence plays in their lives and the lives of others. Some of us write, some of us march, some of us stand.

— Jo Jacobs

It's important to make a visible witness of what I believe in. I stand with KNOW but the Women in Black has a broader mission and statement than just being opposed to war. We are opposed to violence—wherever it occurs. This is near and dear to my heart. It is part of my faith and a way for me to be a Christian in the world. Women and children are issues most pressing for me because they are the voiceless ones left out and ignored in the political agenda. I am able to be a voice for them. The present administration is promulgating a great erosion in the quality of life for children in the United States and women and children across the globe. I get distressed, however, that the Women in Black doesn't have hundreds of women out there.

— Lois Schmidt

I was looking for something women could do. Women could be a big influence on the election. The Women in Black is a group in solidarity making a stand for all victims of war and violence. We can show other women what we can do.

— **Sandy Adams**

The statement on our sign is such a good statement! It is inclusive and true. It expresses my feelings. I heard Israeli and Palestinian women started the group, and I liked the idea and started to stand with the Women in Black. Also, Sandy invited me. That was a powerful invitation to do this work.

— **Dru Carter**

TWENTY-FOURTH DAY OF WAR

April 12, 2003
Peace March in Washington, D.C.

Sandy Adams has just finished demonstrating with the Women in Black for the past hour in front of the Kalamazoo Civic Theatre. She rushes home to change clothes and pick up her husband, Wade, who has been working on the couple's income tax. They are going on a bus trip to Washington to demonstrate against the war. It is Sandy's third trip over the past seven months. Like the Adamses, several of the 47 people going on the bus bound for Washington are driven to do this one more time. However, now that the war is on and nearly all the cities in Iraq have been taken by coalition forces, the marchers have a new motivation for wanting to participate in this demonstration.

"I'm worried there will be other wars," says Bob Schellenberg, who went on the CodePink trip in March. He cites the Project for the New American Century as his impetus for joining this march.

Tammy Williams and her daughter do not like the government's plunging American soldiers into Iraq. "We're like an evil dictatorship trying to take over the world," observes Tammy.

"War is still not the answer," says Maria Ogston, who went to Washington in November and New York in February. She's on the bus again because she wants to "let the Bush administration know we're on to them. You've got to put your money where your mouth is. If you support something, be present at it." Maria admits to being tired of the long trip and she laments the cost of the bus, "but I feel I should go." A native of England, she has never protested against a government policy or program before because she was busy with children and graduate school. But nothing stops her now.

Maria's husband, Walter, is seeing off his wife tonight with his blessings because he regards the protest as an important religious witness. "If the peace movement stops demonstrating, it is giving in to the administration," says Walter. "They may try to start another war, especially since they succeeded in pulling off this one. That's scary."

Pat Klein, a retired WMU science studies professor, attended the October and January marches in Washington. She says she supports the troops and feels terrible about sending men and women to war, especially a "made up war like this." She is sure that if the troops knew about the PNAC strategy they would feel terrible about fighting for this brand of foreign policy.

"America is asleep and being totally duped by the line of rhetoric of the Bush administration," says Valerie Groszmann, a Quaker pacifist. She went to Washington in January and New York in February and regularly attends Kalamazoo peace vigils and stands with the Women in Black because "it's important to stand up and be counted." In fact, hundreds of thousands of Americans have stood up and been counted. According to estimates from various news sources and march organizers, the marches have drawn the following numbers:

Jan. 18	Washington, D.C.	300,000–500,000 people
Feb. 15	New York	500,000 people
Mar. 8	Washington, D.C. Code Pink	10,000 people

The bus riders admit that the war is largely over—but not quite. They are concerned about the looting and the lost civilian lives as well as the resentment American presence and firepower will engender among the people in the Middle East.

"The war is not over," insists Pat Klein. "It's not going to stop with Iraq." She cites PNAC and the Bush Doctrine as evidence that the policy of the Bush administration is to vanquish Iraq and then send troops to other countries in the Middle East.[19] "That means more slaughter and a lot of money spent on war-making."

Maria Ogston is concerned the administration may try to beat up on Syria next, one of the countries targeted by PNAC, especially since Bush officials have this month begun talking about Syria in the same way they talked about Iraq in the run-

---

[19] Pat obtained her information about PNAC from Professor Gary Dorrien, whose claims were backed up by General Wesley Clark, former NATO Supreme Allied Commander, who wrote *Winning Modern Wars: Iraq, Terrorism, and the American Empire.* In his book Clark noted that "he was informed privately by a top Pentagon colleague that the war on terror was part of 'a five-year campaign plan, he said, and there were a total of seven countries, beginning with Iraq, then Syria, Lebanon, Libya, Iran, Somalia, and Sudan.'" (Source: "Democracy Now!" host, Amy Goodman in her book, *The Exception to the Rulers*, p. 38.)

up to war. "No more wars," she says, "this is not the way to deal with conflict."

"We are creating more terrorists by our action in Iraq," says Valerie Groszmann who believes Bush is using the successful outcome of the Iraq War as a justification for starting it in the first place. "Homeland security measures are ridiculous. They can't protect anybody."

"Iraq will be the next Palestine," says Grant Murray (a pseudonym), organizer for this trip. "Only we'll be the occupiers." Grant believes that the majority of Americans are actually choosing to ignore the war in Iraq. "All the more reason for the peace movement to continue," he says. Some anti-war protesters have resorted to civil disobedience, some of it violent, but Grant defends the protesters' right—and duty— to make a statement and question the government "especially in times of war." This was a mistake the German people made 70 years before with Hitler, he says. "Yes, we should support our troops, but the government should be questioned." In fact, as Grant sees it, just going along with Bush without questioning him on war is treasonous. "It's not a matter of being right or wrong. It's a matter of principle. I despise Saddam and Osama bin Laden. They are dictators. But I put them and George Bush in the same boat." This bus trip, Grant's second, gives him a good feeling "to have like-minded people around. Being together helps us know that we're not crazy."

The April 2003 march organizers estimate that between 50,000 to 100,000 people show up in Washington, which actually makes the Kalamazoo participants feel rather upbeat since they didn't expect such a high turnout. Additionally, people from 60 other countries held concurrent marches that day.

"Although there were no significant incidents, Washington, D.C. was tense and police were on the alert for possible trouble," according to Wade and Sandy Adams who gave me this eyewitness report on the march. At one point on the parade route soldiers, in Israeli uniforms and holding Israeli and American flags, taunted the marchers. Of course, security was heaviest at Lafayette Park, which lies across from the White House; police wore riot gear.

Speakers at the demonstration objected to the one-sided media coverage of the war and pointed out that news about Iraq consistently leaves out reports about the looting going on or the Iraqi casualties. Instead, the news features generals and colonels commenting on the progress of the war.[20] The peace march was routed past several places that have been significantly connected to the promotion of the war including Fox News, Halliburton, and the Washington Post. The crowd booed these institutions as they passed them. As the crowd dispersed after the march, participants were prevented from using the subway, presumably as a security measure.

TWENTY-FIFTH DAY OF WAR

Sunday, April 13, 2003
Peace Vigil

It is a beautiful, sunny Palm Sunday with daffodils shooting up, grass greening, and the delightful, 60-degree spring air jolting people into the belief that warm weather is indeed ahead. In Michigan, we're never really sure it is spring until late May, although people push it in April. A couple of

---

[20] A year later, in June and July 2004, several journalists admit and regret their one-sided coverage.

young women strum guitars on the lawn and a few dogs that are tied to trees, bask comfortably in the shade. Four or five bikes are parked on the grass—their appearance is another sure sign of an enduring spring. This setting at the Federal Building, however, is hardly serene. The tension after nearly a month of war mounts as 200 people gather to stand for peace today. About nine Women in Black position themselves at the top of the steps of the Federal Building. They usually take the southeast corner of the intersection but today they decide to be closer to the group. Maybe it's getting a little too tense for the women to be separated from the group.

Drivers react to the peace activists in different ways. One white-haired man jeers and scowls at them from his pick-up truck and then flips the bird. The older woman riding with him just looks straight ahead in silence. Here are today's negative remarks from drivers in passing cars who are more virulent than ever:

"Traitors."

"You weren't out here one day when Clinton was president. Not one day!"

"Go home, commie."

"Go home, hippie."

"Nazis."

"Hey, what about the twin towers, uh?"

"Hey, the war is over."

"Get a fucking life."

"Fuck you."

"Anti-Americans"

"We're winning."

A car with two young men in it is stops at the traffic light. As they wait they look over the crowd with smirks on their faces. It is obvious they are going to do or say something. "You suck, you suck bad. Take a shower," says the driver as the light changes and his car begins to move. As they drive on their way, he and his companion give the crowd a thumbs down and laugh scornfully at them.

"Why aren't you over there in Iraq?" yells back Jason Roberts (a pseudonym), a high school student in the vigil. However, Tom Small is on top of this interaction and in his low, slow voice he tries to re-coup the situation by reminding the whole group on his megaphone that everyone must be peaceful in order to make the vigil effective and true to its purpose. "If someone makes a bad remark, avoid arguing or fighting back," says Tom.[21]

☮

Today I ask people if the tensions we see on the street are occurring in their neighborhoods or work places. Art Orzel says he created a stir in his apartment building when he passed out the blue and white KNOW peace yard signs. A woman whose son is in the Marine Corps won't talk to him as a result. Art never wavered, however. He was a combat Marine in Vietnam in 1968.

Judy Templeton (a pseudonym) says most of the people at her workplace are friends and share a stance on peace, but in

---

[21] I didn't see these kinds of negativities coming from passing cars during the pro-Bush rallies. Drivers did show their support, however, with horn honking.

the break room, after someone posted an anti-war flyer on the bulletin board, one man put up some pro-war materials. This was countered when someone put up more anti-war items. Now the company doesn't allow people to put up any political items.

"A lot of people are worried about speaking out against the war," says Tobi Hanna-Davies. "They are not un-supportive of our troops but feel policies that put troops in Iraq are wrongheaded, juvenile and dangerous. Why don't they speak out? Well, most churches have, people on various sides of the issue at work and in the neighborhood have, but they don't want to offend each other. Those against Iraq policy are not against troops. They don't want to be misunderstood."

The meeting at the end of vigil is more animated than usual with more people speaking their minds about current events and their meaning. Marianne Houston who has not been to the Sunday vigil before, decided to come out today not only to stand for peace but to speak against a reader's opinion column in the *Gazette* that calls those against the war "traitors."[22] "The hate I felt for the man who wrote the "Viewpoint" got me here, but now I am holding that poor man in the light. We can all feel down; it's like a steamroller going over us." Marianne encourages the crowd not to give up on peace and then concludes with a quote from Gandhi who

---

[22] The writer of the "Viewpoint" article refers to the "peace zealots" in San Francisco who try to block traffic in the city streets to protest the war. He concludes that they could not accept the war or Bush's election victory. (This is an example of the close connection between support for the president and support for whatever he does.)

advises peacemakers about handling their anger, hatred and frustration: "Be the change you wish to see in the world."

Wade Adams, who has been monitoring the activities of the Project for the New American Century, speaks about the 2005 sunset law on USA PATRIOT Act I. Congress will take up the issue of removing the expiration date completely and therefore extend its effect. He urges the crowd to call their representatives and senators *not* to remove the date.

Aijaz Turk, a native-born Pakistani, says that U.S. troops are trained to secure the oil fields but not the schools, hospitals and streets of Iraq. He also objects to the media's censorship about looting and anarchy going on in Baghdad. He is especially angry that the National Museum in Baghdad, which houses artifacts from the region, the Cradle of Civilization over 5,000 years old, was not protected.[23] The post-vigil meeting includes a number of announcements on upcoming events:

* CodePink will meet after the rally at a nearby coffee shop.

* A United Nations meeting will be held at 3 p.m. in the downtown Methodist church.

* PBS will air a program with Walter Cronkite reporting on weapons of mass destruction.

---

[23] The National Museum "was a virtual repository of treasures from the ancient Mesopotamian cultures as well as early Islamic culture, many of the 170,000 irreplaceable artifacts were either stolen or broken (later found safe and well in a vault). On April 14, Iraq's National Library and National Archives were burned down, destroying thousands of manuscripts from civilizations dating back as far as 7,000 years." These reports were later disproved and expurgated, according to Bruce Feiler in *Where God Was Born* (William Morrow, 2005).

* The WMU Student KNOW will have a demonstration this Wednesday from 12–6 p.m. Bands, poets and food will be on hand. (Last week the group formed a living peace symbol on the grassy area outside the library and stood in silence for three hours.)

* The video presentation of "Truth and Lies of 9/11" will be shown at the Kalamazoo Public Library.

"We're here because the peace we want has not been gained," says Lyn Bartley, a retired WMU professor and leader of the vigil today. He encourages the group to tell other people and correct the common misperception that the war is over. "People across the world want peace, dignity and a sense of wholeness." Then he quotes George Orwell: "War is not peace. We'll know peace when we feel it in our hearts."

☮

Some peace people told me last week that inside the Federal Building two men dressed in black shirts, trousers, caps and big boots stand at the doors guarding the building. After the vigil I see them for the first time and mention it to Father John Grathwohl, one of the activist priests in town. He says the men are supposed to keep people off the building's steps but they don't hassle anybody because there's no property destruction or litter left after the vigils. (Tom Small spends an extra 10–15 minutes after each vigil to make sure that the area is absolutely clean.) "They're very understanding," he says. Gosh, it's become easy to be paranoid these days.

TWENTY~SIXTH DAY OF WAR

Monday, April 14, 2003

The media is filming incidents of violence committed by peace activists.

TWENTY~EIGHTH DAY OF WAR

Wednesday, April 16, 2003

President Bush has a clear majority of voters on his side, according to a California pre-election poll for next year's presidential race. He is coming close to calling an end to the war. So far we have lost 125 soldiers with 500+ wounded. Saddam has disappeared.

THIRTIETH DAY OF WAR

Friday, April 18, 2003

Tens of thousands of Muslims overseas are protesting the Americans' presence in Iraq. However, our victory over Saddam makes 73 percent of Americans wary about the prospect of having to stay in Iraq as an occupation force.

THIRTY~FIFTH DAY OF WAR

Wednesday, April 23, 2003

The Department of Homeland Security announces a three-tiered warning system for the airlines: red is very dangerous, yellow is possibly dangerous and green is safe. Airport security guards will profile Arabs and Muslims as red. Citizens have no recourse to change this system. Meanwhile, a U.S. Olympic athlete is rated red and can't board a plane to participate in a competition.

THIRTY~SIXTH DAY OF WAR

Thursday, April 24, 2003

American soldiers have indulged themselves in the spoils of war, including helping themselves to the relics from the National Museum in Baghdad. They have also found millions of dollars that Saddam had stashed away, which they return to military authorities.

Weapons of mass destruction have not been found and neither has Saddam, although several of Saddam's officials have been captured. Secretary of Defense Donald Rumsfeld says that the U.S. must find these people; Saddam and the WMD are not what's important. The U.S. mission has changed again.

The war summary in the *New York Times* has suddenly stopped this week and stories from Iraq about "freedom of speech" and "freedom of religion" have appeared even as Shiites from Syria and Iran have been infiltrating into Iraq. *Gazette* coverage of the war seems to have been supplanted by the dramatic dissolution of Kalamazoo's largest company. Pfizer is down-sizing the research division of the former Upjohn Company. The city stands to lose hundreds of people with high-paying jobs and millions of dollars in tax money.

THIRTY-NINTH DAY OF WAR

Sunday, April 27, 2003
Peace Vigil

Many people think the war will end soon. Most of the troops remain in Iraq, but some have already returned. This war has lasted a month longer than the first Gulf war but with victory imminent, people are beginning to feel a sense of relief for they are sure the troops will soon be home.

"The war isn't over," says Art Orzel, a combat Marine in Vietnam in 1968. He comes regularly to the Sunday vigils—and will attend the vigils *every* week for the next year. "I expect we'll go to North Korea, they will re-establish the draft, and we will be dangerous as the only Superpower in the world....I don't foresee us having peace and I blame the media and us absorbing the information. This causes hate and aggression of the whole world. I just threw out the TV and don't read the newspaper anymore. I only listen to the BBC or WUOM (the Ann Arbor NPR station whose signal is strong enough to reach Kalamazoo). There's just as much propaganda but they give more details."

With the war coming to a close the Bush supporters have ceased holding rallies after seven weeks. After seven months, the peace activists continue their vigils, only now people are in shirt sleeves instead of their heavy winter coats. Between 150 and 200 people are here today with no indication that they will stop coming. Last week, on Easter Sunday, I'm told that 150 people showed up.

The car horns of passers-by are honking quite a bit today only with the war's end in sight, the activists' signs have changed in theme. Now the messages are about tax cuts and derision over the spoils of war. Someone has created a 10-foot display illustrating where our tax dollars will go as a result of the Bush tax cuts. Leaflets are passed out about how the administration spends "the people's money," as Bush called it in the 2000 campaign.

In order to keep interest going for the cause of peace, KNOW plans several events: a Mother's Day celebration in Bronson Park, a plea to boycott oil and gas products as a protest against the war and documentary film showings about 9/11 and the Florida 2000 election. The Kraftbrau, a local brewpub, will feature musicians and bands that play for the cause of peace.

Drive-by shoutings, which by now have become quite routine, continue with the following comments of the week:

"Get a job."

"Go home."

"Move to Iraq so we can bomb you, too."

Still, the peace activists feel a sense of mission and solidarity. And they do small things for each other. Today, someone brought several boxes of doughnuts. The sun melted the glaze on them and left many sticky fingers. Nevertheless, the war is also beginning to take a toll on the demonstrators. "I'm tired of being scolded for taking a stand," says Janet Jones, a long-time peace activist. "Why is it that the Left has to do it all the time?"

III.

BUSH SUPPORTERS

BUSH SUPPORTERS

I did not vote for George W. Bush in 2000 nor did I want the United States to go to war against Iraq—or against Afghanistan for that matter. However, half of the nation did and many people in my town took the time to demonstrate for this point of view over a seven-week period from March to April on Saturday mornings in front of the Federal Building and Wednesday nights in Bronson Park. My curiosity about their views and my desire to balance them with my peace activist conversations allow me to find out what they believe about America and the U.S. role in Iraq.

The following accounts share my interactions with the Bush supporters during their rallies. Sometimes I am able to record whole conversations, which help provide a more authentic flavor of their attitudes and beliefs. For three weeks in April I survey people from both sides and ask the same questions of both groups, given the constraints of time. The results are compiled in Appendix G.

In deciding whom to interview I use my intuition, look for friendly faces and bank on luck to engage demonstrators in a conversation.   I also keep my ears open for indirect conversations, like when I overhear a man speak about "soldiering" and mentions his father who "lost an eye in war and never complained about it." Then there are a few people who approach me, like Deb Buchholtz-Hiemstra, chairperson of the Kalamazoo County Commission and vice chair of the Kalamazoo County Republicans.   Actually, she is a little surprised to see me, presumably because she remembers me as the chair of the Kalamazoo County Democrats a few years earlier and is curious about why I am attending a Bush rally. Deb insists, however, that the rallies are not sponsored by the Kalamazoo County Republicans. "We don't even know the names of some of the people here," she says.

Sometimes, however, people don't seem to want me around. During one rally a couple Vietnam veterans (their garb and age gave them away) gave me a hard, square-jawed look as I wander among the crowd. I want to speak to them, so I talk to other people and eventually engage one of the vets who was a combat soldier in 1968–69. When I thank him for serving, he seems surprised but grateful for the acknowledgement all in one second and it helps to break the ice between us.

In general, the Bush supporters come to the rallies in defense of the president, his policies and the war. The local news has covered much on the peace activists' vigils and activities but virtually nothing on the Bush supporters. When they organize their rallies the *Gazette* does give them front-page coverage on Sunday, March 23, 2003. Essentially, the Bush supporters have no voice as a group as much as the peace activists do. So when they see me with my pen and writer's pad, they seem very willing to tell me what they think, perhaps because they feel they are being heard.

The main gist of the Bush supporters' position is that Americans have a responsibility to be loyal to the country when war arises. Soldiers should serve without complaint as both an important duty and a great honor. In a time of war the people back home should support the troops and their president—with no objection. The purpose of this war is to bring freedom and democracy to the Iraqi people who have been oppressed and tyrannized by Saddam. Casualties are to be expected in a war and since this war is a retribution for

September 11, the price the nation must pay in blood and dollars is justified. In conducting a "war on terrorism," war is different from other wars because there are no rules. International law and United Nations resolutions are not binding.

The Bush supporters are passionate about their beliefs and they feel hurt and dismayed that the peace activists discredit them. The "peaceniks and hippies"—people whom they regard as soft, naïve, unrealistic, uncaring and cowardly—are in effect denying freedom to the oppressed Iraqis and allowing a dictator to commit genocide on his own people. The peace activists by their resistance to this war with Iraq are also trying to prevent the United States from defending itself from the terrorists who are trying to kill us.

While the Bush supporters believe they are fighting the terrorists, I discover that some of their underlying attitudes carry yet another belief: America can do no wrong. Neither Bush nor his supporters can be dissuaded from these notions and when the president shares his intentions to wage a pre-emptive, unilateral strike on Iraq, he acts as though it is his right to do so as the leader of the only superpower in the world—and his supporters believe him.

The Bush supporters also assume a worldview that there are dangerous people out there who want to see America destroyed. This same view was used during the Cold War era, which also justified a strong military build-up including a vast stockpile of nuclear weapons.

After September 11 President Bush says that the reason the terrorists attacked us is because they "envy" America and its way of life. But this attack is unlike any other and it presents new problems. The Japanese attack on Pearl Harbor, for example, was one nation attacking another. The terrorists, on the other hand, are *individuals* attacking our nation. At first the president goes after Osama bin Laden—an individual—

whom the administration almost immediately identifies as the perpetrator of September 11. Since bin Laden lived in Afghanistan, we invade that country. After a year goes by without successfully finding him,[24] Bush then pursues Saddam Hussein—another individual, "the evil one," as he calls him. Bush claims that Saddam harbored the 9/11 terrorists. Many Americans, so overwhelmed by the fear of terrorism, believe the president. To this day half of the American people still believe this claim, despite the 9/11 Commission's report that confirmed no link between Saddam and 9/11.

Before the war starts, 43 percent of Americans do not favor war with Iraq. After the president begins the war, however, many of these people switch their position. Approval ratings for him reach 82 percent. For a long time after May 1, the polls steady around 50 percent.[25] All in all, however, throughout his first term, Bush governs a divided America where half of the people question even his legitimacy in the 2000 election. The November 2004 election wins him the popular *and* the electoral vote but the tone of the country is no different. This points to yet another characteristic of the

---

[24] Reuters reports on December 5, 2004, that Pakistani President Pervez Musharraf says the trail to Osama bin Laden has gone cold. The three-year hunt will continue but critics say it is impeded since the U.S.-led coalition does not have enough troops in Afghanistan to carry out the mission of finding bin Laden.

[25] According to a Zogby poll of July 18, 2003, "Support for war in Iraq has eroded. When asked if the country had to do it over again, nearly six in ten (59%) say they would support a war against Iraq, while 40% say they would oppose it. In April 2003 polling by Zogby International, 75% supported the war then underway, while 22% opposed." The president's overall approval rating on September 23, 2001, is 82%. A year later it slips to 64%. In the pre-Iraqi war period (March 16) Bush reaches 54% approval and three months later (June 10) it is at 58%. www.zogby.com/news/ReadNews.dbm?ID=721

Bush supporters: they put great trust in the Office of the President—now that it is in Republican hands. They expect their leaders to be strong, moral and honest and Bush delivers, especially as an avowed Christian. However, in talking to his supporters, they seem almost mesmerized by him, despite the bad news coming from Iraq, which they either don't hear or they deny and dismiss. Their accompanying trust in the president signals a more visceral issue: in this time of crisis and great social and economic upheaval, they *are* fearful and they *are* searching for a leader who will protect them from the dangers of the world and keep them safe. Bush knows how to do this, which accounts for his sustaining popularity—and power.

RICHLAND TEENS

Wednesday, March 26, 2003

Downtown Richland becomes *the* scene for an impromptu rally to support President Bush and U.S. troops in Iraq when 25 Gull Lake High School students jump into the political fray waving placards and cheering loudly as passing drivers approvingly honk their horns. As I approach the students who are hauling homemade signs out of their cars, a couple of them run toward me gleefully when they notice my pen and notebook. They have succeeded in attracting a reporter's attention! I am likewise interested in finding out what they think about this war.

In planning this event, the students notify the media and post signs in gas stations inviting people to join their rally. The *Gazette* and one radio station announce the rally but only Channel 41 (the ABC affiliate) turns out to film it at the intersection of M-89 and M-43 in this otherwise quiet village.

The students are quick to give me their views about the president and the war.

"In a time of war, it's sad when people don't support the country, whether or not they agree with the decision to go to war," says senior Jerry Holt as students chant "We back Bush" and "Freedom isn't free" in the background.

"I'm overwhelmed by the support of this community," says Sandy Varner, a junior and one of the organizers who produced the signs that read: "We love Bush" and "Fight for freedom; down with Iraqi tyrant" and "War is justified to destroy evil."

Ray Silvers, a senior and another organizer, is also pumped by the turnout of demonstrators and by the response of auto passers-by. "Polls show that since the war started, 70 percent of the American people are backing Bush. That's up from 43 percent. This shows how much support the country is giving the president."

On the other side of the village intersection a handful of students who represent a peace agenda carry on a counter-demonstration. Two adults join the small group as it huddles together and quietly displays its signs. Hardly any car horns honk for them. Gary McCleary, a senior, heard the announcement about the Bush rally on the radio so he called friends to come to demonstrate. April Adams, a junior, says that she loves her country and is exercising her First Amendment rights by not agreeing with the war. Opposing the war has been a struggle for peace activists at the local high school who represent a minority of Democrats in this largely Republican town of 600. Consequently, those who may have supported their side of the issue are reluctant to go public.

One of the adult peace demonstrators, Marsha Majors, says that there have been "some ugly and violent things said at school" against students who oppose the war with Iraq. Meanwhile, Gary's mother, Mary McCleary says that she attends the Sunday peace vigils in Kalamazoo and is here today because "it's important to make our voices heard in this little community as well."

The pro-Bush students also have adult supporters present, only they remain seated at a nearby picnic table in the town's central park abutting the intersection. That makes it easier for me to talk with them. Annalisa Cepod, aunt to two of the young Bush demonstrators, and Greg Varner, father of Sandy, say they are proud of their kids and glad they are demonstrating for their side of the issue.

"The anti-war protesters are out on the streets all the time because they don't have jobs and we do," says Greg. The peace activists are "missing the truth" and "naïve about reality" with regard to Saddam's regime. "He pays suicide bombers. That he bombs Israel is a known fact."

"He has no respect for his own people," says Annalisa.

"Oil is in our national interest and for a tyrant like him to control so much of it is not right," says Greg.

"We want to free the Iraqi people from Saddam," says Annalisa.

Annalisa finds it objectionable that a lot of Hollywood celebrities are Democrats against Bush and the war, and that they are not as highly educated as Bush and the members of his administration. "People want the best decision makers they can get," says Annalisa. Both Greg and Annalisa say they are Republicans.

Candlelight Vigil in Bronson Park

The night is misty, warmish and calm as 30 people quietly gather for the first of five candlelight vigils held in Bronson Park. The war is on and the group wants to express its support for the troops in a prayerful way. After organizers distribute printed "Support the Troops and the President" yard signs, they pass out candles. The service starts out with what would come to be identified in Kalamazoo as the Bush theme song, "Proud to Be an American" by Lee Greenwood. As the song ends, people raise their candles over their heads in an emotional tribute to the country and to the soldiers who are serving in Iraq.

Christy Nance nervously but courageously thanks the group for coming. She asks the people to take 5 to 10 minutes each day to stop and pray for the troops. "Even with the problems of our own lives, think of the troops."

Deb Buchholtz-Hiemstra announces that the gathering is not a political event or an activity sponsored by the party. (My sources tell me that the Clear Channel contacted party leaders to hold the rallies and supply them with a website and red, white and blue placards with the message "Support President Bush and the Troops." The national radio corporation apparently helped many local communities across the United States in this way.)

"We're here to support the troops and the president and to show our love of country," Deb says. "It's never easy to go to war. War is not a failure of diplomacy. It's important to support our troops so that they can make it safe for us here. There will be casualties, it's what's going to happen, but we must be vigilant and come out to rallies like this, and show our unwavering support for our troops." She encourages the people to bring their families and friends to the next vigil as well.

Tim Jacobs, organizer of the evening vigil and the Saturday morning rallies, proudly reports that 15 people showed up at the first rally two weeks ago (March 15) and that 160 people showed up last Saturday (March 22). "It's been a week since the war started and we'll have these Wednesday night vigils until the war ends." Tim stresses that the night vigils are meant to be more somber than the boisterous Saturday rallies but that they both represent "the voice of people who support the government and our troops."

Deb asks that everyone also pray for the POWs, MIAs, and those killed in action. Afterwards, the group stands for a moment of silence followed by the singing of "Amazing Grace" and "God Bless America." While the songs and speeches go on, a young woman talks on a cell phone to her soldier friend who is in an Army base hanger awaiting deployment. She tells him about the vigil and refers to it as "this amazing thing happening here." He expresses his appreciation, which brings her to tears.

The vigil ends and the group quietly disperses, but several people share their thoughts and feelings with me about the war. Their comments reflect what they understand about the purpose for the war (removal of a tyrant and finding WMD) and their sense of patriotism (support the troops and the president unequivocally).

I believe in human rights in Iraq. Iraqi schoolbooks have pictures of Saddam in them and it's wrong. His beliefs are being forced on the people. I believe in freedom of speech. The Iraqi people are living under his reign and they must be terrified having troops in their homes. It's unbelievable to me that they can live under someone's power like that and not be able to express their own wishes, beliefs and desires. It's great for us to show our support to the people of Iraq. It's important to talk about the war. I had misguided beliefs before and talked to a counselor who helped me understand where we're coming from. I definitely think it's important for the younger generation to talk with the older generation. I grew up with misguided truths and have learned to recognize fact from fiction.

— Hanna Weld

I support the troops, the president, and do what little I can to show support. There are probably a lot more people who support the troops but they tend not to get out like the peace activists who have a louder voice.

— **Jim Louden**

I've always been patriotic and supportive of the troops. My uncle died in Vietnam and I still cry when the national anthem is played. I think of our guys over there protecting our freedoms. This war should not be politicized. No matter who's president, we've got to support him. He's our only president—elected by the people. We never organized these rallies as Republicans or Democrats. We are supporting our troops. Now that we are at war, our troops are protecting our freedoms. Young kids don't realize what we're fighting for (referring to this and past wars). If you're not involved, you can't complain. People ought to be involved in political issues whether it's fighting for a city ordinance or running for office.

— *Pat Fine*

BUSH RALLY

Saturday, March 29, 2003

Seventy-five people attend the pro-Bush rally this morning in temperatures ranging in the mid-30's. They carry many signs with the following messages:

> We've not forgotten terrorism [Red X through last word]

> We thank God – Liberty found such great defenders.

One's still standing – Freedom will be defended
[picture of Statue of Liberty]

Proud to be an American

God bless all of our troops.

God bless President Bush–I proudly support

Appease Saddam? No!

3 out of 4 support this war

Freedom, slavery, religion, Hitler, persecution,
independence

If you enjoy your freedom, thank a vet.

At times war is necessary to have peace
in the future.

No one loves peace more than a soldier

Support our President

Be on your guard, stand firm in faith; be men
and women of courage, be strong.
Corinthians 16:13

Freedom isn't free [followed by names of
dead, MIAs, POWs]

I support the coalition of the willing. God bless
the troops. Let freedom ring.

To our Troops, thank you

Support Bush and our troops

As I mingle among the demonstrators, I meet three women from the same family who have two young men in the Marines, one in North Africa and one in Iraq. One woman holds up the same photo display that I saw a couple weeks ago on a car window with the caption, "Our Son." She is putting together a Marine scrapbook. I realize that there is another side to this war besides those who are for it and against it: the families of soldiers and Marines. They worry about their sons and daughters yet they are extremely proud of their taking on the responsibility to defend the nation.

At first it puzzles me that military families would align themselves with the Bush supporters. After all, the president is endangering their children by sending them off to war. Nevertheless, the military families seem to feel more comfortable at the Bush rallies not because they want their children to fight a war but because they believe the nation is at risk to terrorists and their children are helping to protect the country. In their minds, September 11 is a just cause for the war, the president indicated as much and they want to support their leader. That's what loyal Americans do to defend their nation against enemies. Moreover, they don't perceive the peace activists as offering a solution to terrorism because they don't believe in fighting back even though our country has been hit by a foreign enemy.

Suddenly, it occurs to me that America is replaying the Vietnam War and trying to correct its mistakes. There is much evidence for this. Many of the people I meet *from both sides* readily associate this war with Iraq to the Vietnam War of 30 years ago, including those who weren't alive at the time. They are motivated to participate in public demonstrations based on what they did or did not do at that time in history.   Bush supporters characterize the peace activists as dirty, pot-smoking hippies while the peace activists talk about the fear tactics past administrations used against war protesters and suspect it is being used against them now. In fact, they shy away from even calling themselves anti-war protesters and instead label themselves and their mission more positively: they are advocates for peace. They are also scrupulous about avoiding acts of violence and behaving in a peaceful manner no matter what is done or said to them. They are wiser from the last war in trying to convince the president not to start it.

This is an unprecedented action. They remember the long, dragged-out war in the rice paddies that had no exit strategy, killed 58,000 Americans, millions of Vietnamese and wounded many more.

Even presidential candidate John Kerry bases his campaign on his service in the Vietnam War as he ushers in the men who served under him to the convention platform. Bush campaigners counter Kerry with the Swift Boat Veterans that question Kerry's role in the war and de-legitimize his medals. When CBS news reporter Dan Rather (a former Vietnam War correspondent) runs a special magazine report on the president's military service in the National Guard (one of the avenues many men used to avoid going overseas), he is soundly criticized for using fake documents. Rather apologizes and in December 2004 he announces his retirement to take effect in March 2005.

Most of the people at these demonstrations are Baby Boomers. They remember the Vietnam era when anti-war protesters blamed and openly chastised the soldiers calling them baby killers and murderers. The military families are parents who want to protect their soldier sons and daughters from a repeat of the shame and dishonor lodged against soldiers. The nation, too, wants to avoid that mistake, which would account for the tremendous hype to support the troops with flag lapel pins, bumper stickers, red-white-blue magnet ribbons and yellow ribbons,[26] only the Bush supporters have an edge on this tactic since they started it. Meanwhile, the Bush supporters complain that the protesters treat the president unfairly and disrespectfully, especially in a national

---

[26]The yellow ribbons refer to a 1973 hit song by Tony Orlando and Dawn entitled "Tie a Yellow Ribbon Round the Old Oak Tree" (Levine and Browne). It was associated with support for troops returning home from Vietnam. It was later used for the return of the 52 hostages held in Iran in 1981.

emergency. The Baby Boomer generation wants to correct the mistakes of the former era. Last time out, no one demonstratively backed the administration in public rallies. What is not corrected, however, are the deepened tensions and divisions.

☮

Today's *Gazette* has an article in the Faith and Spirituality section which reminds readers that Iraq is the land of the Garden of Eden, the Cradle of Civilization, the home of the Jewish patriarchs, the Tower of Babel, the Hanging Gardens of Babylon, the place where the wheel and writing were invented and the place where the presence of good and evil were first recorded. How ironic it is that we, a modern democracy, fight a war in that ancient and holy land.

BUSH RALLY

Saturday, April 5, 2003

Probably the weather is a factor for the poor showing of Bush supporters at the Federal Building today. It is a bitter 31 degrees with an annoying wind and slight hail-like snow. Only about 35 to 40 people show up. The wind whips and crackles the American flags that many people bring with them. One man proudly displays his Marine Corps flag. Clearly, the Bush supporters have identified themselves with the flag. Only a few carry hand-made signs now; most of them hold red, white and blue printed signs with the message: "Support the troops and President Bush." A couple of new, homemade signs appear as well. One is a large sheet mounted on wooden poles and held by two men. It reads: "We support our troops. We value our freedom. We support President Bush." Deb Buckholtz-Hiemstra tells me she made the sign and worked on it late last night.

A 15-year-old girl stands on the southeast corner of the intersection with her own sign: "Praise the Lord and pass the ammunition." She is with her father who waves a large American flag. "It's a reference to an old World War II song," says Bob Keanes, 48, it implies that the "ammunition will keep the soldiers safe against enemy fire." Bob tells me he is here at the rally for political reasons, not religious ones like his daughter yet he expresses his purpose for being here in this way: "I humble myself before God's will. We're warriors on His behalf. I hope that what we're doing in Iraq will serve God's purpose." He is very concerned about the troops and the "danger and Hell the men are going through."

On the opposite side of the street stands a lone peace advocate with his blue and white peace yard sign on the trunk of his car. He also holds a new sign: "600 Iraqi civilians killed." Last week his sign said "God forgive America." This protester's comment illustrates a point the *Christian Science Monitor* makes about people in the peace movement: people think they only care about the Iraqis and not the U.S. troops. This is one more reason why military families and supporters of the president can't abide the peace activists. Worse yet, the peace activists don't understand the nature of this dynamic because they don't know many Bush people and don't talk to them. Consequently, there is little chance of bridging the chasm over the great divisions in America

BUSH RALLY

Saturday, April 12, 2003

People are really getting into these rallies and a few of them bring some colorful props. Luckily the TV cameras (ABC and FOX) are here and the most obvious person they go to for their story is Terry Hunt, 46, who waves a replica of the head of Saddam upright on a silver platter. He has poured theatre blood on the head to make it look more gory and then attached the platter to a rope on a pole. He swings it victoriously.

This is Terry's third week at the Saturday rallies. He says he isn't someone who looks for war but he recognizes that sometimes it is needed to make the peace. The Iraq War is one of those times. Terry says he feels good that the war is nearly over and he is sorry about the U.S. casualties—at least they are light. "I support the government and overall I support our troops. They're our kids, our loved ones."

Betty Wilson, stands next to a cassette recorder that plays various patriotic songs including "Proud to Be an American." She passes out red, white and blue ribbons to the demonstrators and passers-by. She made these same ribbons during the Afghanistan invasion. "At least it's something I can do," she says.

Doug Hagger is perched on the Federal Building steps with another woman holding a 12x18-foot flag formerly flown at the building where he works. He waves it vigorously at honking cars. "I support the troops 100 percent," he tells me, "and I'm here to show support for the country, the troops and the president."

This is Doug's first rally. He is a volunteer fireman so it's more difficult for him to take a Saturday morning off to come to the rally, but he is glad to be here today. He particularly finds the reactions from the passing cars to be "pretty encouraging. No one has given us a thumbs down."

Doug doesn't agree with the peace activists that Iraq will be a mess because of this war. Instead, he's keeping his eyes focused on the faces of grateful Iraqis, like the 40-year-old Iraqi man he heard interviewed on TV who said he could start living his life now that Saddam is gone. According to Doug, the outcome of the war, is the justification for it, but he says we should have taken care of Saddam 12 years ago. Since that time Saddam has lied and refused to follow U.N. resolutions, he should be taken out of power. Doug admits that even though we haven't found chemical weapons, we *have* found missiles that were barred; a couple of them were fired at Kuwait. That proves that Saddam had WMD. Doug would like to see Saddam tried in court for crimes against humanity but he regrets that we have not been able to find him. "At least Saddam is out of the picture," he concedes.

Doug is especially concerned about the post-war looting because troops have not been trained to handle such chaos. "The U.S. military police are coming in but the poor guys are trying to stop the looting while they protect themselves from snipers. They can't do everything." During the Vietnam War era, Doug was 4-F and missed being drafted into service.

Roger Woodson is a great, big man. He wears a red Marine cap and t-shirt and proudly waves his Marine Corps flag. He served the Marines in the United States during Vietnam. Standing close to him is Jenna Casey, the mother of a 24-year-old Marine who, she presumes, is in Iraq, maybe Baghdad. "The only thing tougher than a Marine is a Marine mother," says Woodson. Jenna's shirt bears the same message: "If you think being a Marine is tough, try being a Marine Mom."

A scraggily-looking middle-aged man walks down the street. He doesn't seem to be a part of the rally, but he stops for a minute to talk to us. "I've got a son over there," he says to us with impaired speech.

"Me too," says Jenna. "He's my only son, Ron."

"Being a Marine is like being a member of a brotherhood," Roger Woodson tells me. He is "heavily involved" in working at the Veterans Administration hospital in Battle Creek. One of the many tattoos on his arm is the Marine motto: Retreat is not an option.

"If you join the Marines you know it's the toughest group in the military and that a lot of responsibility is heaped on to Marines, more than in the other services." Woodson has taken me on like a student as he lists the qualities and values of the Marines: "You honor the flag, the president, never dishonor yourself—or your mother."

"That's why my son was so nice to me," quips Jenna.

"You know that the fellow next to you will take a bullet for you," Woodson continues.

A man wearing a combat-colored hat and jacket, passes by and signals Woodson with a "Semper Fi" and a "See ya next week." He was a combat Marine in Vietnam, Woodson tells me.

"In the Marines," Woodson continues, "you carry its values with you for the rest of your life, values like honesty, helping others, always being faithful to other Marines, taking care of your own."

"It's a community?" I asked.

"It's a brotherhood," he corrects me.

When it comes to combat and death, Woodson switches to more practical terms. "Nobody wants to take a life but if the enemy shoots at you and you refuse to shoot back, what do you think is going to happen?"

"So it's more a defensive stance than an offensive one," I ask.

"Yes," says Woodson.

Woodson has been at the rallies since they began. "I need to support our troops, like this lady's son," he says as he points to Jenna. "You won't find veterans that believe in war, but you'll never find a vet who doesn't believe in his country."

Woodson tells me about the insight he had this week after watching television and "seeing our babies fighting in a war." He suddenly starts to tear up. When he enlisted in the Marines in 1969, he was a baby, too. "I guess my mother was really worried. She had four sons in the service at that time." Woodson says that during his youth there were protests much like what we're seeing today, but that he expects the reception the Marines and soldiers get when they return home will be different from his homecoming. "All the people will say thanks to them—and that includes the protesters, too.

"I got spit at and had drinks thrown at me in bars because I was a military man." Nevertheless, throughout all these years, Woodson has remained firm of purpose, regarding the Vietnam War. He contends that he and his fellow Marines did their duty. Yet, he showed some sympathy and understanding for those who treated him and his comrades badly: "They were just taking it out on us because we were in the military."

"If our military guys didn't fight for us, we'd be speaking Japanese or German," says Jenna referring to the Marines' role in World War II. "We'd all be driving the same colored car."

"If we had a car," says Woodson.

Then Woodson speaks about the Baghdad takeover on Wednesday. Even though it makes the end of the war more imminent, Woodson isn't so sure. He thinks Baghdad will retain "pockets of resistance" from the Iraqis, whom he regards as "fanatics who were raised that way." Woodson expects that the fighting will end in three or four months and reservists will return home first. Then it will take another year before all the other military return and some time before "democracy gets going" in Iraq.

He compares the Iraqis to the Vietnamese, who were communists and trained to abide communism and think that capitalism was bad. "Once the Iraqi people see what democracy is, they will adopt it willingly," he says. Woodson goes on a tangent about democracy but he concludes that he has little patience with Americans who don't vote in elections. "They have nothing to say about how the country is run. Many people are 'down' on Bush, but Bush can only do what the Congress lets him do. Of course, the president can send in the Marines without congressional consent. To commit the other services to a war needs approval. And the Marines are ready to go and do whatever it takes. You earn the title 'Marine.'" (Soldiers, on the other hand, are members of the army, quite a different breed from the Marines, he says.)

Woodson reiterates that U.S. Marines wouldn't be in Iraq as a police force. "That's not what they're there for nor did their training prepare them for such work. They are in Iraq to help and support the Iraqis until democracy is established."

After the rally as people gradually disperse, I have a chance to talk with Jenna privately. She tells me that her son joined the Marines three years ago after talking about it with his high school wrestling buddies. He left the States for the Middle East in January. She received a letter from him last week and heard his voice on the phone six weeks before that. "You look in the mailbox every day and pray there's a letter," she says. "But no news is good news." She forces out an optimistic attitude during our conversation despite the worry she carries in her heavy voice and wincing face.

Jenna says she is not as much a "mess" as another mother she knows. Instead, she keeps her mind off the danger her son is in by staying busy. She has family, friends, and a four-year-old grandson, and she works out at the gym to relieve her anxiety and frustration. "I'm very proud of Ron, mostly because before he joined the Marines he just wandered." The Marines gave him direction, self-esteem and pride, something she didn't think he had before he joined, she says.

Jenna becomes noticeably agitated when we talk about the peace activists. "It's time they show some support for the troops. They keep getting arrested for riots. How can they be for peace?" She contrasts the activists' behavior with that of the Bush rally which has been peaceful. "That's the way it should be," she says.

Jenna favored the war before it started because she felt something had to be done about Saddam and Osama bin Laden. However, in the back of her mind she worries about something Saddam said, that the Americans would never leave Iraq. "What do you think he meant by that?" she asks me. I shrug my shoulders in a non-committal way. I have my suspicions about what it means but I'm certainly not going to share it with the mother of a Marine who is probably in Iraq. Yet, Jenna seems resigned that the United States will be in Iraq for "quite a while." Woodson says reservists will probably be the first ones to return. However, Jenna's son is a full-time Marine. She probably wonders when she will see him back in the U.S.

BUSH RALLY

Saturday, April 19, 2003

It is the day before Easter, 55–60 degrees and sunny. About 25 people show up for the rally and they are quite subdued. Maybe it is because there aren't as many people here. Of course, the war has quieted down quite a bit since the Marines have pulled out of Baghdad. Nevertheless, the faithful few, some who have been here since the first rally, feel just as strongly about their presence today as they did when they started. And a lot of car horns are honking today in celebration for the end of the war, even with this small group.

As I interview a woman for my survey, an on-foot policeman stands next to us conversing with her husband. I become a little worried that the policeman might tell me to leave. He might confiscate my data! I snap out of this little paranoid fantasy, though, when I realize he is probably just curious about what I am doing. So I tell him before he has a chance to ask and add that I want to talk to the man he is talking to. He obliges and walks away.

There are no peace activists present at today's rally.

BUSH RALLY

Saturday, April 26, 2003

Only a handful of people are at the rally today. Tim Jacobs, organizer for the rallies, does not show up at all. As I conduct my survey, Marine reservist Derek Brown makes the most interesting—and the most ominous statement:

> *There may be some problems if we don't find WMDs. That was the justification for going into the war. We'll look foolish in eyes of rest of world. We'll look more belligerent than we need to come across.*

TIM JACOBS, BUSH SUPPORTERS ORGANIZER

Tim Jacobs couldn't stand the "angry slogans of the peace protesters" he saw on the corner of the Federal Building on his way home from work. However, the sign that really got to him was "Not my vote, Not my voice."

"Government leaders are elected for their guidance and wisdom," he says, "but to shun democracy like that [with such protest signs] is a slap in the face." Another message he finds equally infuriating is "Not in my name."

Tim is a tall, clean-cut man and a rather unassuming self-described "guy that sits in an office." His reaction to the impending war and to the peace demonstrations at the Federal Building in particular causes him to step out of his ordinary private persona and move into a more public role as an organizer of the Wednesday vigils and Saturday rallies.

We speak on the steps of the Federal Building after one of the April rallies and he provides me with a comprehensive view of how one Bush supporter and former military man sees the world. This mild-mannered man doesn't really mind that people protest against the war or express their opinions before the war. He draws the line, however, once the decision is made to go to war. "Citizens ought to support their government and their president," he says. So he decided to start the rallies. As an Air Force veteran of the '80s, he knows intimately what it is like to be away from home and family.

"I'll be out here as long as possible," he tells the group of 30 gathered at the first candlelight vigil held in Bronson Park on March 26. "People need people at times like this."

Actually, Tim believes he is part of a "silent majority" that supports the war but which is over-shadowed by the peace demonstrators who manage to obtain much press coverage. Those who support the president don't feel comfortable expressing themselves publicly, he says, but when the war began and 75 to 80 percent of Americans polled supported it, they have "less chance of feeling ostracized" if they demonstrate.

Tim, who voted for Bush in 2000, consulted his friends in the Kalamazoo County Republican Party about what he regarded as a lack of support for the president. Party leaders encouraged him to get involved and do something, so he decided to organize the rallies and vigils. And people responded! The first rally attracted 15 people while the second rally had 160 participants. April 5 and 12 each brought 75 people to the rally site. Although the April 19 rally attracted only 25 people, Tim believes that this Easter weekend is a factor for the low turnout.

Tim speaks excitedly and proudly about the military's expert and speedy handling of the war. That they are able to do this after years of military cutbacks is "amazing," he says. Technology, of course, plays a key role with more "streamlined" weapons since the first Gulf War. "There were half as many men for this war and three times as much firepower," he says.

Military strategy has also changed since the first Gulf War and psychology is now used as a tactic. Commanders in the field are allowed to make decisions instead of waiting for Washington to gather intelligence, discuss strategy and give orders. Too often the intelligence they gather is old news and not "place sensitive," he says. Now forces are "able to cut through previous bottlenecks." "Thunder Row" is an example of this new psychological strategy, Tim explains patiently. Around the third week of the war when troops were getting ready to enter Baghdad, a commander ran a couple tanks in and around the downtown area and then got out. He did this a few times and thus provided a presence of American troops while he checked for retaliatory fire. The commander didn't have to call headquarters to do these maneuvers either. He knew the strategy and made the decision to go in when he thought it appropriate—and it worked. U.S. troops took over Baghdad on April 8.

Tim and I talk a bit about the pre-emptive strike, a new war policy the administration is employing against Iraq. Even though he says he is not familiar with the Project for the New American Century or the Bush Doctrine, Tim says that terrorism has changed war. Consequently, he defends the president's move into Iraq because the United States is at risk.

"U.N. resolutions give its members permission to do just that," he says. "In striving for a Middle East peace, the United States is both justified in what it did and it was able to do it." Many Middle Eastern nations hate the United States and are breeding anti-Americanism in their people. U.S. foreign policy has already shown that it will use economic pressure when necessary but it is also willing to use the military as a deterrent. "We can be looked upon as a bully but never do we have to negotiate from a position of weakness," says Tim.

Tim also explains the administration's need for tighter control over information: "So many people are involved in foreign policy formation. They need more accurate information about how the government is involved, what the foreign policy is, and what America's role is."

I ask Tim how he regards the "peace protesters" or "peace demonstrators," as he calls them. He thinks they have lost their way over this war because of their hatred of President Bush and his policies. They are still influenced by the 1960s when the press and the government misled the people. "This is unfortunate, whether by choice or by design. They are highly educated…they have a basis for protests but those are not founded on a factual basis. Rather, their positions and views are based more on fundamental beliefs."

Another problem Tim has with the peace activists is that they only focus on particular things and not on the broader struggle in the Middle East. During the second week of the war, for example, he points out their concern about a little girl who was run over by a tank and later about a boy who lost both of his arms. "These things happen in war," says Tim. "The soldiers did everything they could to avoid civilian casualties and we have to believe that. What we are doing is to save lives overall. We can't focus on one thing. We have to look at the implications further down the road." He points out that what we did made us safe and if that involves looking like the "bully on the block" as opposed to the "big brother" who helps other countries, then we have to do it.

"We need to look at what brought us to where we are," he says philosophically. Besides increased government spending and military cutbacks, other pertinent considerations are the impact of foreign oil, the benefits of a free market to the Iraqis, occupation and liberation.

"Our experience is that if we liberate, we'll be there a long time. That's one of the reasons the commanders didn't want the Marines to hang U.S. flags on Saddam's statue in Baghdad. It was never intended that Iraq be the 51st state," says Tim. "We need to get trust back into Iraqi government and put the right people in office."

Neither Tim nor the Bush supporters have had any significant confrontations with the KNOW people other than "a few stragglers" who jostled for the corner in front of the Federal Building one day. The Bush supporters just left. Since then they have locked in Saturday mornings for their rallies while the KNOW people stick to Sundays and Tuesdays. And despite Tim's obvious disagreement with their positions, he says he still "admires them for making a show."

Tim calls his group the "Kalamazoo Area Supporters" and says that many of those who show up to demonstrate are moderate and conservative Republicans. He insists, however, that the rallies are not about politics as much as they are a way of showing support for the troops. He regards himself "pro-USA" and likewise, the Supporters are a grassroots group of people unaffiliated with party politics. "If we had a Democratic president, we'd have the same support for the troops," he says.

Tim wants me to be clear that his support for the war doesn't stem from liking of war. "Nobody likes war," he says. And unlike the Vietnam War where soldiers faced "man-to-man conflict full of treachery and in-the-dirt fighting," this war is technologically oriented, so the Iraqi army did not put up as much resistance as the United States expected. Consequently, hundreds of thousands of Iraqis have not died.

"War has changed. It is more surgical and there isn't as much death," he says. "It's unlike past wars, like World War I, where machine gunners mowed down lots of people all at once. Those wars were futile wars where bones and flesh clashed against metal." Tim adds, however, that he has not seen any statistics of Iraqi casualties, damage assessments or the impacts of the war.

On this day, according to the U.S. Department of Defense, 94 Americans have died in hostile situations and 43 in non-hostile situations with 542 wounded by April 30, 2003. According to Iraqi Body Count (www.iraqbodycount.net) death among Iraqis is between 5,329 and 6,881

.

IV.

OCCUPATION

MAY–DECEMBER 2003

NEWS SUMMARY: MAY–DECEMBER 2003

May 1, 2003, may have marked the end of major hostilities in Iraq as far as the White House is concerned, but it begins a new phase of the war that no one anticipates: the Occupation. On this day President Bush declares a victory after 43 days of fighting, which is much longer than anyone expected of the world's most powerful military force—peace activists and Bush supporters alike. Indeed, we have become accustomed to short wars since the 1991 Gulf War, which some pundits will call an exception to the rule.

The Occupation begins with an eerie, seemingly orchestrated program of PsyOps—only it works against us as the Iraqis kill one U.S. soldier a day, sometimes two. Our response is to bear down harder on the enemy, only we can't tell the difference between those we seek to liberate and the terrorist insurgents we seek to kill. Much American and Iraqi blood is shed as a result; most of it is Iraqi civilian blood. The president requests billions more from Congress as the Pentagon consummates several no-bid contracts to favored corporations like Bechtel, General Electric and Kellogg, Brown & Root (Halliburton).[27] It soon becomes apparent that the Bush Team has "no exit strategy" for troops to return home, especially since the United States has been building 14 permanent military bases in Iraq. Worst of all, troops must

---

[27] Center for Public Integrity, "Windfalls of War" (www.publicintegrity.org) provides a complete list of contractors and their cumulative contract amounts.

conduct an "urban warfare" campaign, the Army's most dreaded and most dangerous form of conflict.

In April 2003 there is talk of going after terrorists in Syria. By the end of June the administration wants to stop Iran from developing a nuclear capability, which 56% of Americans favor because they believe that terrorism is spreading. Meanwhile, six Brits die in Majar al-Kabir on June 24 and Prime Minister Tony Blair is on the carpet in London for overstating the need for war against Iraq.

The front page of the July 4th *New York Times* signals a new turning point: wives of soldiers at Fort Hood, Texas, who have been wearied by worry, are now angry that their husbands have not returned home despite the president's May 1st declaration. At Fort Stewart, GA, a colonel meets with "800 seething spouses, mostly wives" who are "crying, cussing, yelling, and screaming for their men to come back." Besides dealing with children who want their daddies, the women's work life has become more demanding and less supportive. One woman tells of her experience:

> *When my husband was first deployed the people at work were so sweet giving me days off, saying take whatever time I need....But it's not like that today. Now they look at me kind of funny and say, 'Why do you need a day off now? Isn't the war over?'*

According to a July Gallup poll, 42 percent of the public thinks the war is going badly, a rise from 13 percent in May; those who think the war is going well has fallen from 86 percent to 56 percent. Soldiers' morale is also plummeting as many have been given orders for extended stays in Iraq. Insurgent attacks on coalition forces in Iraq continue through fall 2003 as U.S. soldiers become more public about their distaste for the war. Troops are fighting 17 battles a day throughout the country and an average of three soldiers are killed each week. So while the U.S. death rate has declined, the intensity of fighting increased. As a result, about 36 percent of reservists say they plan to leave the service once their tour of duty ends even though the military reports a rise in recruitment large enough to satisfy its needs.[28]

Word has also circulated that the president hasn't attended one soldier's funeral and the media are banned from photographing flag-draped caskets "out of respect for the families," according to Senator John Warner, chairman of the Armed Services Committee. To get around this rule, however, the media show death from war in other ways. The *Kalamazoo Gazette*, for example, pictures the faces of families mourning the death of their soldier son (November 9, page A-12). Then on page A-13 it prints a story about military families in San Antonio who speak out against the war as their patriotic duty and their right to dissent. The media that have so far given the president a pass on the war are now starting to question him. Soldiers themselves then leak photographs to the press of military coffins on cargo planes coming home to Dover Air Force Base. The Internet, which becomes a kind of "underground press" and a bane to the administration's increasing cover-up of bad news about the war, pre-empts the mainstream media in distributing these photos. This tactic will occur again when soldiers release pictures of the Abu Ghraib prison in April 2004.

Throughout 2003 the American people contend with intermittent alarms of terrorist threats thanks to the Homeland Security's color code system (which consistently ranges between yellow and orange). Americans also witness designated areas of high security in public places (especially airports and government buildings) and the diminishment of civil liberties through the USA PATRIOT Act. Nevertheless, public support for the war remains at 64 percent in December

---

[28] www.insidedefense.com, June 17, 2003

and people continue to see Bush as a strong leader who unrelentingly stays the course and takes necessary precautions against the terrorists. Bush's approval ratings continue at 50 percent. [29]

The economic picture is improving with the summer quarter seeing 57,000 new jobs and a 7.2 percent up-tick on the economy in mid-November. Bush claims his tax-cut plan is working and the economy is on the mend. The U.S. debt, however, reaches $7.1 trillion and the deficit skyrockets to its highest levels yet at over $400 billion. The U.S. government is spending about $1 billion per week on the war and Bush wants another $87 billion for Iraq, which Congress approves in October.

Whatever people feel about the president, these critical and fast-changing events seem to lull them to sleep. *New York Times* columnist Paul Krugman notes that America is in a state of denial:

> There is no longer any serious doubt that Bush administration officials deceived us into war. The key question now is why so many influential people are in denial, unwilling to admit the obvious....In particular, there was never any evidence linking Saddam Hussein to Al Qaeda; yet administration officials repeatedly suggested the existence of a link. Supposed evidence of an active Iraqi nuclear program was thoroughly debunked by the administration's own experts; yet administration officials continued to cite that evidence and warn of Iraq's nuclear threat. And yet the political and media establishment is in denial,

---

[29] Source: Bill Moyers' PBS show, "Now!" August 20, 2004.

finding excuses for the administration's efforts
to mislead both Congress and the public
(June 24, 2003).

Examples of this denial are at work in Kalamazoo. One
summer morning I scan the headlines of newspapers in the
newsstands with a couple older men outside the local YMCA.
The top fold of *USA Today* features the black smoldering
smoke of a downed U.S. helicopter. My companion onlookers
just stand there commenting on the football scores in a half-
dazed, slow talk. They never mention the dead soldiers. The
war has also left the front pages of the *Gazette* and now
regularly appears on page A-3, unless there is a big story that
moves it to the front page. The paper used to provide photos
and some background on fallen troops; now there is no photo
and the lists of the dead are located deep inside in the paper.

The Kalamazoo peace activists, however, haven't ignored
the war, in fact they remain quite obsessed with it. They
continue their Sunday and Tuesday vigils, plan more activities
and provide more opportunities for study on the issues of the
war, the USA PATRIOT Act and nuclear weapons. They also
draw connections between our actions in Iraq and the Israeli-
Palestinian conflict, which the media largely separate.
However, paranoia among some activists is also setting in as a
few remember how the FBI intimidated anti-war protesters
during the Vietnam era—they believe it is happening again.

Although the Bush supporters no longer hold rallies, they
don't suppress their sentiments entirely. Instead they express
themselves in random "drive-by shoutings" during the peace
vigils or in the *Gazette's* Letters to the Editor. While they
continue to support the president, it appears that some of
them, in effect, blame the peace activists for the deteriorating
situation in Iraq and then vent their anger at them.

By September 11, 2003, just two years since the attacks on
America, people in Kalamazoo are apparently so weary of all

the discord and upset that they are not up for remembering the second anniversary of the fateful event. The peace activists hold an evening candlelight vigil on September 10 and one at WMU. St. Augustine Cathedral holds its annual Blue Mass for public safety officers and St. Luke's Episcopal Church holds a prayer service. WMU and Kalamazoo College provide academic discussion circles on international affairs topics. It seems as though the feelings of unity this country experienced of just two years ago are forgotten. Now people must be alone in silence with their anger, their fears of terrorism and the deepening divisions among their neighbors. People from other nations, the same ones who mourned with us two years ago, are now disgusted with the United States over its bold actions of pre-emptive and unilateral strike against Iraq. Much of world opinion goes largely unreported in the U.S. mainstream media.

Note that the center of all of this division and derision is President Bush himself, and battle lines are again drawn between those who support him and those who do not. Policies and issues aren't discussed, his character is. This trend continue as the 2004 presidential election gets closer both sides become desperate to win as they both remain locked in fearful dread over the outcome.[30]   Even the capture of Saddam

---

[30] After the November 2004 election people who voted against Bush feel utterly defeated, angry and ashamed at the outcome. Commentators struggle to find explanations for Kerry's loss. Historian Chalmers Johnson, author of *The Sorrows of Empire: Militarism, Secrecy, and the End of the Republic,* puts the onus on the American people.   In the Dec. 13, 2004, issue of *In These Times* magazine he says that the re-election of Bush in November has now made Bush's war, America's war. "The last significant check on the imperial presidency was the electorate, and on Nov. 2 it failed. Neither the Congress, nor the courts, nor the federalist system of state governments is any longer able to balance the presidency and the forces of militarism" (p. 17).

Hussein on Sunday, December 14, fails to allay these intense feelings on either side, perhaps because the occupation has dragged on and troop deaths persist. By year's end, 491 troops are dead.[31]

The other center in this drama is the media. People constantly complain about the media's coverage because they doubt they are getting a complete picture of what is happening in Iraq—the good and the bad. For the peace activists, the alternative media serves their information needs with news sources like "Democracy Now," Common Dreams, the Alternet, the Guerrilla News Network and England's left-leaning newspaper, *The Guardian*—all available through the Internet. The scarcity of news also leads to the rise of book-length journalism, such as Bob Woodward's *Plan of Attack*, Ron Suskind's *The Price of Loyalty: George W. Bush, the White House, and the Education of Paul O'Neill*, Richard A. Clark's *Against All Enemies: Inside America's War on Terror*, John Dean's *Worse Than Watergate*, Kevin Phillips' *American Dynasty: Aristocracy, Fortune, and the Politics of Deceit in the House of Bush*, Justin A. Frank's *Bush on the Couch*, Chalmers Johnson's *The Sorrows of Empire* and films like "Fahrenheit 911" and "Outfoxed."

By the end of the year the credibility of the administration starts to teeter as "the liberal media" questions Bush's justifications to rush to war. Then in November the Senate Intelligence Committee subpoenas a stalling Bush administration to hand over intelligence documents pertaining to NORAD and its 20-minute delay in flight response on September 11. The Committee also questions why important Saudi families living in the United States are shuffled out of the country when all U.S. planes have been grounded.

---

[31] World Messenger website: www.worldmessenger.20m.com/uscasualties.html#dead

The world continues to mistrust the United States as it heaps shame and disgrace on the United States' invasion of Iraq. That comes back to haunt Bush when he tries to enlist our allies and the United Nations with aid for Iraq in October and receives very little in return. The administration's response is defensive while most Americans remain ignorant of the world's opinion of our country's actions in Iraq.

From what I've been able to garner from interviews, conversations and events in Kalamazoo, Internet message boards and the above books and films, people divide themselves along the lines of two major narratives. The pro-Bush people maintain that the president has accomplished a great victory in bringing down a tyrant, an opponent of freedom and a threat to the United States. They want to see Iraq adopt a democratic form of government. They extol Bush's effort to make America look tough and believe that this will keep the terrorists at bay and cause Arabs and Muslims to fear us, and consequently, desist in their terrorist activities. They appreciate the Bush tax cuts as well and assure themselves that a promising economic recovery is on the way after the recession that President Clinton caused. They also admire Bush for his religiosity and the fact that he doesn't change course. The peace activists do not buy these arguments and the Bush supporters are exasperated at the "liberals" naiveté.

The peace activists, on the other hand, gasp at the idea that victory has come to Iraq or that the economy is improving, and they fear another Bush win in the 2004 election. Their held-over anger from the rancorous 2000 election pales in comparison to their belief that Bush is threatening the presidency and American democracy itself with policies that endanger education, health care and the environment; reduce public services; and stain the reputation of the United States among our allies in favor of a bellicose foreign policy. The

Bush supporters do not buy these arguments and the peace activists are exasperated at their naiveté. In other words, Americans are unified in their feelings even though they are disunited over the issues. The stories in this section recount the activities of the KNOW peace activists and their reactions to the war, the USA PATRIOT Act, September 11, nuclear weapons and the capture of Saddam.

KALAMAZOO ADDRESSES THE USA PATRIOT ACT

Thursday, May 1, 2003

Just a couple hours before President Bush announces the end of major hostilities in Iraq, local civil liberties leaders hold an information session on the USA PATRIOT Act. The purpose is to urge citizens to persuade city commissioners to pass a "resolution of non-cooperation" with federal authorities who may attempt to enforce the PATRIOT Act on area citizens. Already 137 U.S. cities have passed such a resolution. Jim Rodbard, local attorney and president of the local branch to Michigan's ACLU affiliate, has helped to spearhead the effort in Kalamazoo (*see* Appendix H).

The meeting takes on an educational tone but as speakers explain the uses and implications of the USA PATRIOT Act and other executive decisions and directives, the 150-person audience is shocked into alarm and disbelief. Several members of the Muslim community attend, too, which adds particular immediacy to the speakers' concerns.

In actuality, two-thirds or more of the PATRIOT Act had already been drafted before September 11, says Rodbard. As a U.S. Senator, Attorney General John Ashcroft was among those who pushed for hard-core law enforcement enhancement, a kind of Department of Justice (DOJ) "wish list" that became the USA PATRIOT Act. The initial House version of the bill was negotiated with compromises addressing civil liberties concerns that allowed DOJ excesses and violated several Fourth Amendment rights.[32] However, Ashcroft and the White House, who both saw the bill as a top priority in concert with the House leadership, substituted the negotiated version with a final version in the middle of the night before the final up-or-down vote. And the leadership curtailed debate. This happened just 45 days after the September 11 attacks. The bill passed in the House 357-66. Because the U.S. Senate was locked out of its offices due to the anthrax scare, few of the senators or their staff even saw the bill, so there was no debate among senators and the bill passed 98-1 with only Russ Finegold (D-Wisconsin) dissenting. It was later discovered that most legislators hadn't even read the 342 pages of the proposal.

"Not all of the PATRIOT Act is bad," says Rodbard, "but there are some things in there which loosen the requirements to show probable cause before searches and seizures can occur." Nevertheless, the PATRIOT Act is like the Talmud, that is, it doesn't read in a straightforward way and requires a variety of texts to understand what it is doing. In a private interview, Rodbard demonstrates this to me by reading one section that refers to several other sections that refer to other sub-sections.

What is also frightening about the USA PATRIOT Act are the ambiguous definitions of domestic terrorism that have the potential of limiting First Amendment speech rights, says Rodbard. Section 505, for example, requires the issuance of a

---

[32] The Fourth Amendment provides for "The right of the people to be secure in their persons, houses, papers, and effects, against unreasonable searches and seizures, shall not be violated, and no Warrants shall issue, but upon probable cause, supported by Oath or affirmation, and particularly describing the place to be searched, and the persons or things to be seized."

National Security Letter for a records search, which before September 11 could be used only very narrowly. Now the FBI can issue the letter without judicial or a third-party oversight.[33]

In 1975 the U.S. Congress passed the Church[34] Co-Intelligence Provision, a response to the abuses of protesters during the Vietnam War that prohibited domestic surveillance without a criminal investigation. [35] However, the DOJ now allows agents to infiltrate and spy on people in protest groups, mosques, churches and synagogues (as illustrated with the Fresno, California, peace group in Michael Moore's film, "Fahrenheit 911"). The new rules for the Federal Bureau of Prisons also allows the monitoring of attorney-client discussions in national security cases.

According to Rodbard, the most controversial part of the USA PATRIOT Act is Section 215, which has to do with search warrants. The FBI may gather information on citizens without probable cause using warrants issued by special federal

---

[33] In April 2004 the ACLU filed suit in the U.S. District Court in New York, challenging Section 505's constitutionality. It is currently under review.

[34] Frank Church (D-Idaho) served the U.S. Senate 1957–81.

[35] "In 1975, few Americans had even heard of the National Security Agency (NSA). Created in 1952 as part of the Defense Department but with no written charter, the NSA's primary mission is electronic intelligence gathering. Gathering intercepts of foreign electronic communications required an NSA staff of thousands in the 1970s. The Senate Select Committee's questioning revolved around the use of this capability to target American citizens, particularly dissidents. The NSA's Project MINARET, created in 1969 to spy on peace groups and black power organizations, was the subject of some focus. At issue were Fourth Amendment rights against unreasonable search and seizure." Source: http://www.aarclibrary.org/publib/church/reports/vol5/contents.htm).

courts created under FISA.[36] This provision essentially lowers the threshold of what the FBI shows to the courts and allows for the search of any tangible thing from anybody, including records from a person's bank, library loans and bookstore purchases. Notification of the search does not have to be disclosed to the person being searched.

After U.S. Attorney General John Ashcroft's Justice Department finished drafting the USA PATRIOT Act, Ashcroft lobbied congressmen with the caveat that not passing the Act would result in their taking the blame for the next act of terrorism, says Noel Saleh, an immigration attorney and member of the Detroit American-Arab Anti-Discrimination Committee and the ACLU of Michigan's Safe and Free

---

[36] "FISA is the Foreign Intelligence Surveillance Act, which establishes a legal regime for 'foreign intelligence' surveillance separate from ordinary law enforcement surveillance. Foreign Intelligence Surveillance Act of 1978, Pub. L. No. 95- 511, 92 Stat. 1783 (codified as amended at 50 U.S.C. §§ 1801-1811, 1821-1829, 1841-1846, 1861-62). FISA is aimed at regulating the collection of 'foreign intelligence' information in furtherance of U.S. counterintelligence, whether or not any laws were or will be broken. *See* 50 U.S.C. § 401(a)(3) (defining 'counterintelligence' as information gathered and activities conducted to protect against espionage, other intelligence activities, sabotage, or assassinations conducted by or on behalf of foreign governments or elements thereof, foreign organizations, or foreign persons, or international terrorist activities). Department of Defense (DOD) guidelines state that the purpose of counterintelligence collection is to detect espionage, sabotage, terrorism, and related hostile intelligence activities to 'deter, to neutralize, or to exploit them.' In short, counterintelligence and criminal prosecution are different." Source: Electronic Frontier Foundation www.eff.org/Censorship/Terrorism_militias/fisa_faq. html

Project. He is one member of the panel of speakers in tonight's program.

"It destroyed the whole concept of separation of powers between the executive and legislative branches of government," says Saleh. "The Congress should not be a rubberstamp of the Executive Office to enforce the laws." The result is that the PATRIOT Act began a "gradual erosion" of the Constitution. What Congress had essentially done in passing the PATRIOT Act, says Saleh, was to authorize the president to do whatever was necessary to respond to the 9/11 attacks. The president interprets this power as a "declaration of war" that allows him to suspend parts of the Constitution by cutting through the requirements of probable cause and short-circuiting the rights of due process as provided in Fourth Amendment.

"We're in for some difficult times," says Saleh. "Many people are not aware of these events or actions of our government that are tearing away at the fabric of what makes America unique." He then lists some highlights of the actual repercussions resulting from the USA PATRIOT Act:

* Through the Foreign Intelligence Surveillance Act (FISA) federal authorities can open up secret courts to hear requests by the FBI for secret wiretaps and search warrants. No other party is permitted to appear and the courts are closed.

   While DOJ officials claim these activities are aimed only against international terrorists for intelligence gathering purposes, U.S. citizens and green card holders are not exempt from FISA surveillance under the USA PATRIOT Act. In the past when the FBI requested a secret search warrant, the FISA court scrutinized it to verify that the sole purpose for the search was related to the activities of foreign governments or their agents. Now the FBI only has to certify that the search is in connection with an investigation of terrorism. At that point, the court *must* issue the warrant.

* The USA PATRIOT Act changes the definition of terrorism. Before September 11 a $100 donation to an orphanage in Lebanon would go unheeded. Now, it can be the basis for a charge of material support for terrorism. If convicted, a person can be sentenced to 15 years in jail as a terrorist. Because of this provision, over 5,000 Arab and Muslim men in the United States have been questioned about their donations to the Middle East and Southeast Asian charities; many have been held without charges or access to an attorney. DOJ authorities have not acknowledged who these men are nor where they are being held.

When Congress asked the DOJ for information about these men, it has rebuffed because of national security concerns. The Attorney General designated such matters as "special interests" and closed them off from public scrutiny.

"Not all of the men were designated as terrorists," says Saleh, "but people like Rabih Haddad, a Muslim cleric who lived in Ann Arbor, was charged with overstaying his visa." They held him without bond for 19 months and did not charge him as a terrorist or a national security threat. During his trial in U.S. District Court, his family was not allowed to attend— not even his wife. Nor was the press permitted in. The ACLU, representing Haddad, Congressman John Conyers, and the *Detroit Free Press* filed suit against the U.S. Attorney General claiming that Haddad had a right to an open hearing in court under the First Amendment. The court agreed, and on appeal, the U.S. Sixth Circuit Court of Appeals Judge Damon Keith in his opinion upholding the trial court remarked that "democracy dies behind closed doors." However, in the DOJ appeal, the Third Circuit Court in New Jersey ruled against this case affirming the government's right to closed hearings in immigration cases.

The case went to the U.S. Supreme Court to settle the matter but the Justice Department considered Haddad a closed case and said it opposed any further rulings. The U.S. Supreme Court declined to review the case without comment (see Case No. 02-1289). The Sixth Circuit Court ruling prevailed for Haddad because he lived under its jurisdiction while similar cases tried in the Third Circuit Court were bound by its judge's ruling. Subsequent to his trial, Haddad was still deported for overstaying his visa.

* In 2002 in Moscow, Idaho, 120 FBI agents in riot gear arrested a Saudi Muslim graduate student early one morning and charged him with visa fraud and "unauthorized employment." His visa did not permit him to earn money while in the United States. Studying to be a computer engineer, the student had *volunteered* his time to design a website for a charitable organization. During the investigation he was accused of lying about his employment and providing material support to terrorists. The case was tried before a jury and he was pronounced not guilty.

* Members of Doctors Without Borders witnessed a raid by agents of the Immigration and Naturalization Service (INS) while they dined in a Southeast Asian restaurant in New York. The agents rounded up the employees and checked their documents to make sure their papers were legal.

"These examples illustrate a trend of injustice," says Saleh. "All of us need to be concerned about it. If it is happening to

Arabs, Muslims and Asians, it could happen to any of us."
Now that the government is requesting broader powers in the
co-called "PATRIOT Act II," these investigations could
increase.[37]

But the purview of the PATRIOT Act is not confined to
visitors, immigrants or green card holders. Access to public
information provided by the Freedom of Information Act
(FOIA) is also at risk, says Saleh. For example, under the
Clean Water Act of 1972,[38] corporations must provide a toxic

---

[37] Due to vast public outcry, the Domestic Security Enhancement
Act of 2003 or the "PATRIOT Act II" was never introduced in
Congress. Instead, it was piecemealed into a variety of other bills,
and in some cases enacted as the Intelligence Act of 2004.

[38] According to the EPA, "the Clean Water Act (CWA) is the
cornerstone of surface water quality protection in the United States.
(The Act does not deal directly with ground water nor with water
quantity issues.) The statute employs a variety of regulatory and non-
regulatory tools to sharply reduce direct pollutant discharges into
waterways, finance municipal wastewater treatment facilities, and
manage polluted runoff. These tools are employed to achieve the
broader goal of restoring and maintaining the chemical, physical, and
biological integrity of the nation's waters so that they can support 'the
protection and propagation of fish, shellfish, and wildlife and
recreation in and on the water.' Starting in the late 1980s, efforts to
address polluted runoff have increased significantly. For 'non-point'
runoff, voluntary programs, including cost-sharing with landowners
are the key tool. For 'wet weather point sources' like urban storm
sewer systems and construction sites, a regulatory approach is being
employed.

"Evolution of CWA programs over the last decade has also included
something of a shift from a program-by-program, source-by-source,
pollutant-by-pollutant approach to more holistic watershed-based
strategies. Under the watershed approach equal emphasis is placed on
protecting healthy waters and restoring impaired ones. A full array of
issues are addressed, not just those subject to CWA regulatory
authority. Involvement of stakeholder groups in the development and

chemicals report. Under the proposed PATRIOT Act II, many of these documents will no longer be available for public examination. Also, sensitive information such as the name of the company and the location of the plant that produces the chemicals can be removed. If a whistleblower releases the information, that person may go to jail for 10 years.

"These are small instances that just keep on coming and coming," says Saleh. "There is a possibility that our civil liberties are gradually being taken away by the Justice Department and the administration." He also noted that while the impact of the denial of access to FOIA documents is not directly related to the PATRIOT Act, the Justice Department has been answering FOIA requests as little as possible.

One member of the audience describes his experience of "having a file" and the importance of be able to access it through FOIA. As a 60's activist, he was "indexed" because he spoke out against the Vietnam War and carried a sign for peace. At no time did he ever have a chance to define what he was doing. "It was a shameful position," he says, "I had done nothing illegal. Someone out there kept track of what you wrote and said." If it had not been for FOIA, he claims he would never have known what was in his file. "Inform others about the PATRIOT Act," he says. "Never let our children live under this set of violations. This country belongs to us....We're not going to let this [the dragnet on citizens] happen."

Saleh also implores members of the audience to speak out in one voice and work to get the Kalamazoo City Commission to pass the resolution against cooperation with federal authorities invoking the USA PATRIOT Act. "This is not just

---

implementation of strategies for achieving and maintaining state water quality and other environmental goals is another hallmark of this approach." Source: www.epa.gov/region5/water/cwa.htm

about our individual rights, it is about our collective rights," says Saleh who is also concerned about national security—but with limits. "We want to be safe, but we also want to be free."

Bettina Meyer, assistant dean of the Western Michigan University Libraries, shares her recent experiences with the USA PATRIOT Act regarding the Department of Justice's recent request that depositories of government documents on health, energy (including nuclear energy) and the environment be removed. The request indicated that all U.S. libraries would be audited to make sure this order was carried out. Recently, the DOJ tried to remove some documents from university libraries, including WMU. "But we refused to comply," says Meyer flatly, to the applause of the audience. Complaints from the American Library Association and other university libraries who depend on government documents for research created such a flurry, that the DOJ rescinded the order. The WMU Library is a "selective repository" for government documents, says Meyer, meaning that it houses 70 percent of the government documents published.

"The American Library Association aims to protect the intellectual freedom of our patrons," says Meyer, noting that the library does record the books patrons read and borrow as well as the articles they photocopy. "However, in order to maintain each patron's privacy, we delete these records once the materials are returned."

Meyer says the library staff contemplated putting up a sign in the library that the government may be watching what patrons read. But they nixed that idea because they didn't want to scare students, especially WMU's international students.[39]

---

[39] According to the Office of Academic Planning & Institutional Data, WMU had a total fall head count of 29,732 with 1,921 international students in 2002. In 2003, the total head count was

"I don't want to let that happen or allow FBI agents to approach students without helping them out," says Meyer. On the other hand, she acknowledges that librarians would be at risk of apprehension for refusing to cooperate with federal agents. "The WMU Libraries and member American Library Association institutions have been at the forefront of fighting against invasions of privacy for both national and international students. The ALA has been very adamant in protecting people's right to read whatever they want to read.[40] It is

---

29,178 with 1,725 international students. In 2004, the total head count was 27,829 with 1,487 international students.

[40] ALA News Alert (July 9): "As you may know, the House has been debating the Commerce, State, Justice appropriations bill on the House floor today, July 8th. Rep. Bernie Sanders (I-Vt.) introduced an amendment earlier today that was a permutation of his bill, H.R. 1157, the Freedom to Read Protection Act. With vigorous floor debate, Sander's amendment failed in a tie vote 210 to 210. After the initial 15 minutes for electronic voting, the vote was approx. 219 to 210. However, the vote time remained open until enough had changed their votes to create the tie. (Not the first time that the majority leadership has used this tactic.)

"We're researching who changed their votes and will get final vote counts to you as soon as possible (probably about 12 R's and 4 D's changed their votes.) Remember, the actual H.R. 1157, the Freedom to Read Protection Act, still remains on the list of bills before the House. This amendment was a version of that bill put on as an amendment to the appropriations for Commerce, State and Justice departments prohibiting the expenditure of funds to enforce Sec. 215 and effectively make it as if HR 1157 had been passed at least for the length of this appropriations bill."

"But it is not all over. This is just another battle in a very long and very tough war. Our thanks to all of you and our other colleagues who have worked so hard on the local level and done great grassroots lobbying with House members. We couldn't have gotten this far

against any and all banning of books." She added that there have been attempts in the past to ban books on the subject of homosexuality and racism.[41]

The USA PATRIOT Act includes provisions to access library records because one of the terrorists used a library computer to carry out the September 11 attacks. Meyer ends her talk by encouraging members of the audience to support their public libraries, the "symbol of intellectual freedom in the United States."[42]

Metropolitan Detroit comprises the largest Arab population outside the Middle East with 400,000 people. Mohammed Abdrabboh, an attorney who serves this population, shares stories of his experiences with the USA PATRIOT Act that leave the audience with bone-chilling concern over its meaning to Arabs and Muslims in the U.S.

without your efforts. Keep it up. There will be other steps and more information. Stay tuned." Source: www.ala.org/ala/washoff/WOissues/civilliberties/theusaPATRIOTact/usaPATRIOTact.htm

[41] For a list of 100 most frequently challenged and banned books in 1990–2000, *see* the ALA website: ala.org/ala/oif/bannedbooksweek/challengedbanned/challengedbanned.htm

[42] "What people read, research or access remains a fundamental matter of privacy. One should be able to access all constitutionally protected information and at the same time feel secure that what one reads, researches or finds through our Nation's libraries is no one's business but their own. There are many privacy bills that have been introduced into recent Congresses relating to business, health, student and other records. The expansion of e-government, e-commerce, and other forms of electronic transactions, including library services, raises serious questions for the library community in protecting individual privacy, especially the privacy and confidentiality of library patron records." Source: ala.org/ala/washoff/WOissues/civilliberties/privacy/privacy.htm

After 9/11, the Justice Department sent a letter to thousands of non-U.S. citizens inviting them to participate in a voluntary interview. Abdrabboh sat in on 30 interviews and soon realized that the people who appeared were being racially profiled. Among the recipients of the letter were all men of a certain age who entered the United States during a certain time and who came from 23 Arab countries and North Korea. The Immigration and Naturalization Service (INS) fingerprinted the men and took their photos.

"This goes against our Constitution and what it stands for," says Abdrabboh. "It doesn't enhance security but it isolates and angers the people."

In other actions, the INS deported 300,000 people including 15,000 from the Middle East, who were sorted out first. The INS asked the Iraqi nationals for information that could help the United States with the war against Iraq. Abdrabboh worked on a case of one Yemini man who lived in the U.S. for 40 years, worked at General Motors and didn't even have a speeding ticket. He recently opened a postal service center and convenience store. On December 18, 2002, during Operation Green Quest, a cooperative program of the FBI, INS and Secret Service, this man was arrested, all his assets frozen and he was charged with failing to register his money when he transferred it over to his new business. He was under investigation because for years he had sent money overseas to his family, a typical practice among immigrants in America.

In five different U.S. cities Operation Green Quest also rounded up many other people of Middle Eastern descent under the guise of "fighting terrorism." The media reported this event as "busting terrorists" for sending money overseas. Some of the money went to orphanages, but the money now cannot get to those operations. As a result, many Middle Easterners have come to Abdrabboh to consult him about their contributions to family and charities overseas, which rely on their help.

Abdrabboh, who received the 2002 National Arab-American Discrimination Committee Pro-bono Lawyer of the Year Award, has also seen Middle Easterners' freedom of speech violated. As a result, these people have reduced their political activism and become less vocal due to their apprehension of federal authorities. They are also afraid to be seen as opponents of the war in Iraq or in favor of Palestine because they don't want to look like terrorist sympathizers.[43]

Unfortunately, many Americans are not getting much information about these civil liberties violations so the national Bill of Rights Defense Committee (BORDC) and the ACLU have been working hard to educate and encourage people across the country to lobby their states and local governments

---

[43] These profiling incidents may affect the vote of Arab and Muslim citizens (comprised of 2/3 Christians and 58.5 percent Muslims) in the United States in the 2004 presidential election. While 45 percent of this voting block voted for Bush in 2000, polls in mid-July 2004 show that their support for the president is at six percent (*Financial Times*, July 15, 2004). This poll was based on 500 voters in each of the battleground states of Florida, Michigan, Ohio and Pennsylvania.

On November 29, 2004, *Central Florida Future* (University of Central Florida) cited a Project MAPS/Zogby International poll that "found that while 42 percent of the Muslim vote supported Bush in 2000, largely because his emphasis on family values fit nicely with their conservative leanings, in the 2004 election 72 percent of Muslims supported Kerry, often citing opposition to Bush's handling of Iraq. Another poll, conducted post-debate by the Washington-based Coalition on American-Islamic Relations, showed that 80 percent of likely Muslim voters planned on supporting Kerry."
Source: www.pluralism.org/news

to pass a resolution "to encourage communities to take an active role in an ongoing national debate about the USA PATRIOT Act and other antiterrorism measures that threaten civil liberties guaranteed by the Bill of Rights," as the BORDC website (www.bordc.org) states.

Kalamazoo formed the Task Force for the Defense of the Bill of Rights, a collaboration of community organizations and individuals from the ACLU Southwestern Michigan, Kalamazoo American-Arab Anti-Discrimination Committee (ADC), NAACP, Hispanic American Council, Interfaith Coalition for Peace and Justice, League of Women Voters of the Kalamazoo Area, and Kalamazoo Trial Lawyers Association. Jim Rodbard, a member of the Task Force for Defense of the Bill of Rights, says the task force first met in March 2003 after 30 U.S. communities passed a resolution to protect local citizens from Department of Justice inquiries allowed through the USA PATRIOT Act. As of April 30, 2003, a total of 97 communities have passed a resolution including Ann Arbor, Michigan; Madison, Wisconsin; Cambridge, Massachusetts, and Honolulu, Hawaii. As of July 20, 2004, the totals have grown to 337 communities and 4 states that have passed resolutions to protect citizens' civil liberties, with hundreds more in process.

The original resolution for Kalamazoo called the City Commission to guarantee the following uses of city resources:

* Decline to expend city resources for surveillance of individuals or groups based on activities protected by the first amendment without further suspicion of criminal activity.

* Refrain from voluntary compliance with federal requests for expenditure of city resources in the secret search of any resident of the city whose property is the subject of the search.

* Require that the Kalamazoo Department of Public Safety *not* voluntarily engage in the enforcement of federal immigration laws and affirm the City Commission's strong support for the rights of immigrants.

* Decline to expend city resources, including the use of personnel, for the detention of individuals without charge and without access to an attorney.

* Seek actively the revocation of the USA PATRIOT Act, or any other federal legislation, order or directive which limits or violates the fundamental rights and liberties of persons as found in the United States and Michigan Constitutions, and to restore the checks and balances inherent in our constitutional tradition.

After months of wrangling, the City Commission finally passed a modified resolution to support "rights and liberties guaranteed by the state and federal constitutions," but not to "withhold cooperation in federal investigations unless those activities are declared unconstitutional by the courts" (5-2). On October 6 Kalamazoo becomes the 184th community in 32 states to resist automatic compliance with the USA PATRIOT Act (*see* Appendix H).

In 1999–2000 the Commissioners set a precedent of separating federal issues from local issues with the Living Wage proposals. The proposals required that employers who obtained city contracts adopt a living wage of $8.79 with benefits or $10.55 without benefits. Commissioners perceived that this measure was tantamount to superseding national policy and would put city contractors under an unfair disadvantage. It was seen as a local attempt to change federal law. "If you want to change the minimum wage, lobby the U.S. Congress," said one opposing commissioner to the proposal. This approach was applied once again with the resolution on the USA PATRIOT Act until a compromise was struck.

"What we were trying to do was to get Kalamazoo on the map among those who did not support the PATRIOT Act," says Rodbard who admits that the committee was unable to get all it wanted. The city's endorsement of parts of the proposal is "one more brick in the wall."

The task force attempted to pass a resolution at the Portage City Council in December 2003. After council deliberations in February 2004, the measure failed.

In September 2003 Attorney General John Ashcroft goes on a 30-city tour defending the USA PATRIOT Act and reiterating his commitment to protect the American people in the "war against terrorism." He also shares some of the successes of the PATRIOT Act. Here is an excerpt of his remarks in New York City on September 9, 2003:[44]

> To address all of the issues surrounding the PATRIOT Act would require more time than we have here. It is critical, however, for everyone to understand what the PATRIOT Act means for our success in the war against terrorism. I encourage Americans to take a few minutes and log on to a new website, www.lifeandliberty.gov. There, you can read about the PATRIOT Act and discover how it is keeping our nation safe and secure.

> The painful lessons of September 11 remain touchstones, reminding us of government's responsibility to the people. These lessons

---

[44] www.usdoj.gov/ag/speeches/2003/090903nycremarks.htm

have directed us down a path that preserves life and liberty.

Two years after Americans fought in the skies over Shanksville, we know that communication works. The PATRIOT Act opened new lines of communication between intelligence and law enforcement agencies. To shut down this communication now would limit the effectiveness of those we entrust with our security. It would make America more vulnerable to attack.

Two years after Americans died at the Pentagon, we know that cooperation works. The PATRIOT Act helped create new, enhanced teams dedicated to protecting American life and liberty. To prohibit intelligence officials from working alongside prosecutors and law enforcement would take us back to the days when our left hand did not know what our right hand was doing. It would increase the risk that more Americans will die.

Two years after citizens of more than 80 nations died at the World Trade Center, we know that prevention works. The PATRIOT Act gives terrorism investigators many of the same tough tools that criminal investigators have always had. To abandon these tools would place law enforcement at a disadvantage. It would senselessly endanger American lives and American liberty.

According to the ACLU, during Ashcroft's visits to these cities, protesters voiced their opposition to the PATRIOT Act. As a result, 28 more communities passed resolutions of non-cooperation. Here is an excerpt from its report:

> During the first half of his 30-city tour, protesters gathered outside to voice their opposition to the un-American law, and at each stop, the news media gave at least as much coverage to the demonstrators as they did to John Ashcroft.... The second half of his tour was completely stealth; the Department of Justice gave no notice of his appearances until after they were over. Clearly the protesters during the first half had a huge impact (www.bordc.org/Ontheroad.htm).

Senator Orin B. Hatch (R-Utah), with the Bush administration's blessing, wants to eliminate the December 31, 2005, sunset provision of PATRIOT Act and expand the PATRIOT Act with the Domestic Security Enhancement Act of 2003 (PATRIOT Act II). Tremendous protest from the ACLU, the BORDC, and hundreds of communities across the United States and all across the political spectrum scuttle Hatch's plan.

PEACE VIGIL

Sunday, May 4, 2003

On May 1st in a dramatic show of military strength and public relations acumen, the President Bush "lands" a fighter jet on the deck of the U.S.S. Abraham Lincoln and later declares that the "major combat operations in Iraq have ended."[45]   The liberation of Iraq is "a crucial advance in the campaign against terror," he says. "We have removed an ally of Al Qaeda and cut off a source of terrorist funding."   A banner posted behind the president declares "Mission accomplished," which meets with some criticism.   White House sources claim the sailors of the ship put it up there and not the administration.   Kalamazooans at the Sunday peace vigil have other assessments of Iraq.

"The war is not over," insists Sharon Hobbs (a pseudonym) who is concerned about the administration's plan for global domination.   She cites an article from *Harper's* October 2002 issue that features Vice President Dick Cheney speaking about the Project for the New American Century. She is also pessimistic about the president's "victory" in Iraq. "There is a different view of what happened and is happening in Iraq and Afghanistan," says Sharon, "but it's not going to be heard in the mainstream media."   She gets most of her news from "Democracy Now," an hour-long alternative news program aired through the Community Access Center every Monday through Friday at 8 a.m. and 12 midnight.   "Too many people confuse nationalism for terrorism," says Sharon.

In order to find out what is going on, Melissa Hopkins (a pseudonym) doesn't turn to the mainstream media either.   She resorts to the Internet where she reads the websites of CNN, Al Jazeera, *Hindustani Times*, *Swiss Times*, ACLU and Amnesty International.   "I take comfort that the U.S. media believes the war is over, but I wonder how the troops feel."   In looking toward the future, she cites the past and is sure the Iraqis don't want an American occupation force in their backyard.   Melissa fears that the "war on terror," as the president calls it, will extend to East Asia and that Americans will lose more of their civil liberties through the USA PATRIOT Act.   Already the

---

[45] www.cnn.com/2003/WORLD/meast/05/01/sprj.irq.main/

courts are discussing a reversal of the Miranda rule regarding the questioning of terrorists.

"The Iraq War will be just like Afghanistan, it will bear out nothing," says Louise Malthus (a pseudonym) 44, who also claims that the war has not ended because Americans and Iraqis are still being killed. Fifteen-year-old activist Halle Downs (a pseudonym) agrees with her. "We went there [to Iraq] and had no business there. How can the war be over when the troops are still there and the mission has *not* been accomplished: neither Saddam nor the WMD have been found."

David Macleod, a life-long peace activist and a regular at the Sunday vigils, looks more toward the future and outlines what Washington could do:

* Support Rep. Dennis Kucinich's proposal for a U.S. Department of Peace.

* Divert dollars from the military budget to Americans' health and welfare needs.

* Emphasize individuals' interests, not corporate interests.

* Replace our country's militarism with a more democratic national government.

Lauri Holmes is focused on the war in a more personal way: she has a son-in-law and a grandson currently serving in the military. She says she refuses to be called disloyal to the United States or a simple-minded, fuzzy idealist, either. In fact, she says that the people who continue to stand for peace every Sunday afternoon "are loyal, heart-broken Americans" who want the war to end. She particularly disdains Bush's decision to conduct a unilateral war, which she deems a mistake. "Unless we support the U.N. leadership to clean up this mess in Iraq, we alone will pay the price of this misadventure for generations," she says. "My loyal heart is breaking for the troops in Iraq and at the loss of dignity of our leadership, and at the legacy we give to the world's future generations."

Finally, the demonstrators' posters also continue their unwavering resistance to the war with the following messages:

"There is something you can do – Stand for peace"

"I support troops, not Bush administration"

"Imperialism – Democracy"

"War is still not the answer"

MEMORIAL DAY

Monday, May 26, 2003

For a Memorial Day parade, there is an uncanny lack of military presence this year. The Navy Sea Cadets, a youth group, leads the parade and the Southwest Michigan Young Marines, another youth group, wears combat garb and carries a "God bless our troops" sign. The soldiers, many of them from the local National Guard or the Reserves, are not here. They are in Iraq—and they are missed.

American flags, which have lined the main streets of town since September 11, 2001, are still here. Usually they are up only for national holidays but now the city keeps them up all the time. They provide a sobering reminder of that dark day.

Roger Woodson, the Vietnam Marine veteran I met in the Bush rallies is here. He rides in a 1920's-era car with the Marine Corps League. Company C Infantry is here with World War II and Korean War veterans. The banners on the sides of their vehicle read: "September 11 – Remember" and "United We Stand."

A few Humvees drive by with young, black-bereted soldiers in them. The soldiers distribute candy to anxious kids on the curbsides. A huge camouflage truck passes while an old soldier walks along side of the truck and gives away postcards.

A couple of bands march—Kalamazoo Central High School and Hillside Middle School. There are not many floats, but parades these days always seem rather sparse to me compared to the elaborate 90-minute parades my hometown had in the 60s. Several African-American organizations are here, mostly women, as well as the Navigator Academy[46], a Northside charter school.

The Shriners whiz around on their motorized scooters and then, to add muscle to the parade, comes the McDonald's tow truck, an earthmover, a car dealer's automobile and the perennial, horn-blasting, bright red fire trucks. All are here.

About 20 Women in Black participate this year. They come in their black clothes and headscarves and carry their white placards. The crowd gives them mild but respectful applause as they pass. I watch the entire parade on the shady south side of the street and stand behind some people who have Clear Channel bumper stickers pasted on the backs of their chairs. I listen as they ask each other who the Women in Black are. The best they can figure is that they are related to the Men in Black rock group.

The Veterans for Peace march in the parade just before the Women in Black, and they receive a wild round of applause. People have no trouble recognizing who veterans are and they show them not only proper respect but also admiration and gratefulness.

While I heard that the Bush people from the rallies planned to be a major presence, their effort turns out to be minimal. They have one float that featured Korean War veterans, a group that has received more and more recognition over the years since people started calling that war "the forgotten war." Several veterans ride trucks and vans that are decorated with "Support the Troops" signs on the sides of their vehicles.

Kalamazoo's Memorial Day parades typically focus on the veterans, so organizers discourage politicians from using the event as a campaign tool by barring all political advertising. Of

---

[46] The Northside is identified with Kalamazoo's African-American population. On June 30, 2004, the Navigator Academy announced it would close its doors due to financial difficulties.

course, many elected officials come to the parade; they just can't bring "vote for me" signs. This year U.S. Representative Fred Upton, State Representative Alexander Lipsey, and City Commissioner Sean McCann show up. Only Sean receives significant applause from the crowd. As Upton walks by, onlookers refrain from giving him their usual cheers. He doesn't get any boos but his reception is uncharacteristically cool. People in the city of Kalamazoo tend to be Democratic but they are fairly supportive of Upton. As a Republican candidate he regularly reaches out to people in both parties with the slogan: "Upton for all of us." Since 2001, however, the congressman has been sticking with whatever policies President Bush wants. For example, he says he voted for the war on the basis of some "secret evidence" he was privy to examine as a U.S. congressman. However, this seems to be a typical response for Upton as I have learned by attending his "town hall" meetings. He also used it when he voted in favor of Bill Clinton's impeachment.

I was truly apprehensive about coming to this parade because patriotism has been such an issue since the war. I expected boos for the peace activists and wild cheers for the Bush people. None of that occurred. Instead, there is quiet recognition and respectfulness for both groups. I feel proud of my town for that, but I am more relieved that no ugly incidents occur. After the parade Amy Anderson, whose World War II husband, Rob, marches with the Vets for Peace, says she has the same apprehensions I do about the parade. She says she is especially proud of the Women in Black for doing what she considers a "courageous act"—getting out in front of Kalamazoo. What may have spared the Women in Black negative comment, however, is that most people are ignorant of who they are. (That is not to be so in the 2004 parade when a few people give the Women in Black a thumbs-down or a scowled turn of the head. Kalamazoo parade marshals also play a little politics with the Women in Black by placing them right in front of the horn-blasting, bright red fire trucks.)

All in all, the crowd is pretty subdued today. Perhaps the surprise of this unfinished war has something to do with it. Those who support it may suspect a longer-term commitment than they expected. Those against it are turning out to be right in their assessment of the war's unintended consequences. Nevertheless, polls still show nationwide support for the war at 60 to 70 percent. What Americans are left with on this Memorial Day, however, is one American soldier dying each day in Iraq, a divided population at home, and an adamant president determined to "stay the course" until the job is finished. In another month, the media will report soldiers in the field saying they want to return home.

SPOOKS AND SPIES

July 2003

Spooks and spies? Well, no, not really. But paranoia and anger begin to rear their ugly heads this month in more pronounced ways. The first instance occurs at the June 29 Sunday vigil when Dave Becker sights a car with a man in it stationed half a block away from the peace vigil. As he walks over to the car he notices that it has U.S. Government license plates. Dave returns to the picket line, exasperated as he tells people what he sees.

"Yeah, I've seen that car before," says a man next to him.

"FBI?" asks Dave.

The man nods at the possibility.

I ask Tom Small if he has any knowledge about infiltrators or federal agents at the vigils. He says two agents were present at the demonstrations that drew 400—500 people. They were also at the candlelight vigil when the war started and 700 people showed up. City police were also present at many of these early demonstrations.

"They want to make sure we don't damage federal property or put up graffiti," says Tom. "Technically, we're not supposed to be on the lawn or the steps of the building because that's government property." The agents also told Tom that the demonstrators can't have any signs that insult President Bush or place anything there that is provocative or controversial on the steps of the Federal Building. Tom told them that he couldn't control what people say, and the matter was apparently dropped.

When the Women in Black decided to stand on the top steps of the Federal Building, the agent approached Tom again, but didn't want to approve or disapprove of their action. Tom thinks that the agent wanted *him* to make the decision about the appropriateness of their standing there, so Tom didn't pursue it. Occasionally on unusually hot and sunny days the Women in Black go across Michigan Avenue to catch the shade, but typically they use the top steps and stay close to the rest of the demonstrators.

Earlier in the year the city police got "excited" about chalk messages written on the sidewalk, which they considered "destruction of city property," says Tom. Federal agents checked out this complaint the following week and the matter was apparently dropped, especially as the crowds thinned out by May. In the world of crowd control in public assembly, it appears that size matters. "We have a good understanding of the ground rules," says Tom. "We haven't had any real messages about what we can or cannot do."

I participate in a Women in Black demonstration on the southwestern corner of Drake and West Main on Wednesday,

July 8. Halfway through the demonstration, one of the women notices a young woman in jeans and a red top taking pictures of us with a small camera. She is across West Main, a street with seven lanes of traffic. As the woman snaps a picture or two, her flash goes off.

"She's probably an FBI agent," one woman jokes.

I laugh at first, but as I think about it, the thought intimidates me. I watch the young woman as she drives off in her car. Maybe she is a tourist and just taking photos of interesting sights, I try to tell myself. About 10 minutes later this same woman drives right in front of us. As she rounds the corner where we are standing, she takes another photo and scowls at us.

This incident alarms a few more of us because we think the woman might be a government agent. We all know about the federal agent who shows up at the Sunday vigils. That and discussions about the USA PATRIOT Act don't lend us much comfort or security. This picture-taking incident makes some of us ripe for paranoia.

When I tell my husband, a former police reporter, about this incident, he assures me that someone is probably just trying to intimidate us. A federal agent wouldn't allow himself to be out in the open like that. And even if the woman is an agent, what is she looking for? What can she do with the photos? We were conducting a peaceful demonstration on public property and hadn't violated any laws.

As I stand with the Women in Black ruminating over our suspicious photographer incident, one of the women mentions that a local man takes pictures of the peace vigils and posts them on his website accompanied by nasty remarks. I check out his website which is, actually, nicely done. "Web Man," as I call him, has been photographing and commenting on peace vigils in Kalamazoo and Ann Arbor since fall 2002, but his comments mostly focus on the messages of demonstrators' signs and their readability from a car. He frequently links what he sees at the vigils with articles on the Internet. His site counter doesn't register many reader replies but he generously allows his viewers to borrow any his pictures as long as they give him a photo credit.

My Women in Black companion is quite disgusted with Web Man. She says his wife doesn't like his hobby but just lets him "do his thing" because she doesn't feel she can do anything to stop him. Besides, she is too busy rearing two small children. I admit it was a little disconcerting to see photos of people I know on the Internet when I looked at his site. As I scroll through the pictures I held my breath and hoped that mine wasn't there. (It wasn't.)

Web Man does not identify or interview the people in his photos so all in all, his site is quite harmless. I guess this is what Freedom of Speech is about: anybody can say anything about anybody in any way at any time. Democracy does demand quite a bit of tolerance from us all! I meet Web Man at the Sunday vigil, July 13.

Web Man is taking photos from across Michigan Avenue so I engage him in conversation, dying to find out why he puts up this website. A self-described "disaffected leftist" who became a "qualified supporter of the war," Web Man loves his computer and the website allows him to "satisfy his obsession to comment on everything." He documents events like the peace vigils because "the *Gazette* is never out here to record them."

"I used to be a hard core leftist," he says again. As a WMU student, he was against the first Gulf War and worked with Professor Don Cooney at the protests. He became discouraged with the Left over the past decade and felt compelled to point out its contradictions. "I'm here because I think the leftists have derailed. I don't disagree with everything going on here [at the peace vigil], but when I saw a demonstrator's sign that asked 'Who is next—Syria?' it boggled my mind that another dictatorial regime might be undermined."

I mention to him that the sign may have been provoked by the activists' study of the Project for the New American Century which names Syria, among others, as a potential terrorist threat against the United States. According to the Bush Doctrine, that would justify the United States going into that country and "taking them out." Web Man is unfamiliar with PNAC. "If Syria fell, regardless of how and who did it, it would be universally celebrated," says Web Man. "Syria is more brutal than Iraq."

What disturbs Web Man more than Syria or Iraq is the anti-Americanism of the United States—on the left as well as on the right. There is no middle ground. "Yes, the United States is involved in immoral acts [against nations], but the left makes it impossible for the U.S. to do anything positive or constructive in the world," he says. Web Man adds that Bush should NOT have used the WMD argument to go to war, which he contends was "oversold." At the same time he finds the Left lacking an adequate argument against Bush and his policies. "There are no credible anti-war critiques from the Democrats and no McGovernites."

PEACE VIGIL

Sunday, July 13, 2003

Tempers flare a bit today. An older man stops his car in front of those who hold Veterans for Peace banners and he initiates a curbside conversation with them. They talk about service in the Armed Forces during World War II and how it relates to this war, but their talk soon becomes tense. The man in the car thinks he hears someone tell him to shut up, which offends him until one of the bystanders tells him that no one said any such thing. He demurs and then rushes away. Of course, there are the usual drive-by shoutings:

> Go back to Russia.

> Get a job.

> Freaks.

> Don't you have anything better to do on Sundays?

A couple peace demonstrators yell back at passers-by who hurl obscenities at them. During the post-vigil meeting, Tom Small addresses all these tensions by reminding the demonstrators that "as people for peace, we have to be peaceful. Just smile or wave or give a peace sign," he says in his deep voice. "Don't respond with hostilities."

During the post-demonstration announcement time, Tom continues with another advisory—and a long list of activities that illustrate how the peace movement is spreading throughout the city. Some of the activities are connected to KNOW and some are not.

* The Kalamazoo Chamber of Commerce asks the peace demonstrators not to park in their lot (located across from the Federal Building on the east end of Park Street) because it might deter business. "We do, in fact, bring business downtown every Sunday," Tom quips.

* Young people from the Edison Neighborhood are holding a Peace Jam fundraising event at Hays Park on July 26. They want to provide children with a safe

place to play and a beautiful park with flowers. They are selling t-shirts for $10.

* The City Commission will put the USA PATRIOT Act on its July 21 agenda. Currently, 137 American cities, including Ann Arbor and Philadelphia, have passed some kind of resolution not to cooperate with federal authorities who want access to information about citizens. Local organizations supporting the resolution include the League of Women Voters, ACLU, and Arab Anti-Discrimination Committee.

* Kraftbrau, a local brewery and club, is holding a potluck fundraiser for KNOW today 4:30–8:30 p.m.[47]

* On Monday, July 17, at 7 p.m. KNOW is sponsoring an open forum to plan activities for the coming months.

* On Saturday, July 26, at 11 a.m. CodePink is organizing a demonstration at the Federal Building in honor of the three Dominican nuns from Plowshares (a group favoring nuclear disarmament). The nuns were sentenced for destroying federal property at a Colorado nuclear missile site. (For their story, *see* page 235.) Books on the history of Plowshares are on sale for $5. In the foreword, historian Howard Zinn praises Plowshares' "spirit of resistance."

* KNOW is writing thank you notes to the people who display the blue and white peace yard signs on their front lawns. In their notes they also invite people to

---

[47] In summer 2004, Kraftbrau will offer the "Be-in-the-KNOW" film series as well.

attend the July 26 CodePink demonstration
that honors of the Dominican nuns

Finally, Tom reads a statement from Gary Ashbeck of
Jonah House, a member of Plowshares, the same
community as the three Dominican nuns who have been
jailed for civil disobedience. On March 19, Ashbeck and
26 other peacemakers were arrested in front of the White
House for crossing a police line while holding a sign that
read, "My brother is worth more than cheap oil." He was
fined $10 plus $50 victim's fund assessment and refuses to
pay. Upon conviction, the judge refused to allow him to
speak, so Ashbeck has been circulating a statement around
the country. Here it is in full:

> I would like to make it clear that I respect the
> people that sit in this court as fellow people.
> However I cannot respect these courts. There
> is a gap between Law and Justice, and some
> courts I have seen do not follow either law or
> justice.
>
> Today in Iraq 100% of the people rely on
> food rations as opposed to the prewar level of
> 60%. Over 1/3 of the American casualties
> from the undeclared war in Iraq have
> occurred after Bush declared the war over
> with hostilities mounting. All of our brothers
> and sisters, sons and daughters, fought a war
> specifically protecting oil infrastructure while
> homes, universities, museums and stores were
> looted and ransacked. Respected world
> leaders such as Nelson Mandela, whom Bush
> is refusing to meet with, have condemned the
> actions in Iraq by the U.S. as illegal in
> accordance with international law. Bush

recently claimed God directly speaks to him when he causes war. This is his actual quote:

"God told me to strike at Al Qaeda and I struck them, and then He instructed me to strike at Saddam, which I did, and now I am determined to solve the problem in the Middle East. If you help me, I will act, and if not, the elections will come and I will have to focus on them."

In this country over 2 million people are in jails or prisons, one of the highest percentages of incarcerated citizens in the world. Too much money is spent on putting nonviolent people in jail. Rehabilitation in prisons is unheard of. Occasionally a token corporate criminal goes down. All the money the U.S. government obtains from the people goes to perpetuate this system. Our states are going bankrupt and many people are without healthcare, welfare and jobs. People who come to our door for our food program and those I meet in the neighborhood would do anything for a job or money to help their family. Many end up in and out of venues like this.

I am here today because I was convicted of a peaceful protest and given a fine. I have chosen to live a life of voluntary poverty and simple living dedicated to community service using the college education I have attained. I have discussed it with my community and I cannot in good conscience give community money to that which I cannot pay, a fine, no matter how small, to perpetuate this system. I would rather our money go to the source and the roots. We would be willing to donate to the House of Ruth in Baltimore, a domestic abuse shelter, $50 as they are victims, or better yet survivors, of violent crime.

I accept the penalties that come with my decision although I do not look forward to what that could mean. I plan to spend the time in prayer and fasting. I cannot in good conscience, allow my community's money to perpetuate a morally bankrupt system.

The vigil ends at 1:30 p.m. and the crowd disperses. A few people help take the extra picket signs to a KNOW organizer's car where they are stored until next week's vigil. Some people meet for coffee and/or lunch at the café half a block away, but most people leave.

Leaving a KNOW vigil has become a real downer for me. I usually walk to the Federal Building from home and making that short trek after spending time with the KNOW activists is comparable to ending a joyous family holiday party—it has an anti-climatic quality to it. Seeing the same people every week, looking forward to seeing them, catching up on important news about each other, and working together on a cause, these are the marks of a community. I've noticed that as I keep going to the vigils, even though I'm there writing about them, a sense of community keeps evolving to new levels. Once the vigil is over and everyone is gone, however, a feeling of emptiness comes over me. What makes it worse is that Michigan Avenue is impersonal and sterile with its seven lanes of traffic and its lack of trees, grass or people. Walking home after "being in community" is a very lonely time.

CODEPINK RITUAL OF ACKNOWLEDGMENT, DISARMAMENT AND REDEDICATION

Saturday, July 26, 2003

The women of Kalamazoo CodePink are intent on eliminating U.S. weapons of mass destruction for the cause of peace in the world. They conduct a ceremony today to promote their agenda and point to the Old Testament prophet's call to "beat swords into plowshares and spears into pruning hooks" (Isaiah 2:4) as the source of their beliefs. Ceremonies all over the nation are being held today in solidarity with Sisters Ardeth Platte, Jackie Hudson and Carol Gilbert who were sentenced to federal prison for 41, 30 and 33 months, respectively (*see* page 235). In October 2002 the nuns entered a Minuteman III nuclear missile site in northeastern Colorado, hammered on its concrete top and poured their blood over it. They are members of Plowshares, an international disarmament group that protests nuclear weapons proliferation in dramatic ways, usually as an act of civil disobedience.

"The current U.S. missile program contains 10,635 warheads that equal the force of 120,000 Hiroshima bombs," says Marti Faketty, one of the CodePink organizers who delivers an eloquent speech on the steps of the Federal Building to a crowd of about 70 people. Next to her stands an upright, 12-foot cardboard replica of a missile painted dull gray. "We are gathered in solidarity with people all over the U.S. to expose the enormous, costly, misconceived, suicidal/homicidal nuclear weapons program in the United States, which our government has built and is proposing to enlarge, even to the reaches of outer space."

Marti defends the three nuns' actions because they "wanted to expose the fact that the United States is the world's principal arms dealer, selling every kind of weapon imaginable to 150 countries, from the components of nuclear weapons to the shock batons used in torture chambers around the globe….Military spending has so consumed national governments that with each minute that ticks by, military institutions around the globe spend $1.7 million while during that same minute, 30 children [in the world] die hunger-related deaths." Marti concludes her speech by saying that the ceremony today is an opportunity to "raise our voices in mourning and in rage and in the hope that we will finally transform our sorrow and anger into meaningful acts that will move this country closer to enacting the vision of a world of peace and justice."

Four CodePink attendants stand next to Marti in white Tyvek suits with "Disarmament Specialist" printed on the front and the letters, "C.W.I.T." (Citizens' Weapons Inspections Team) on the back. They are wearing the "vestments" the nuns wore when they conducted a "liturgy" over the N-8 missile silo. They carry the "missile" from the Federal Building to Bronson Park, as the group follows them in a silent procession. Once everyone reaches the park, they form a circle around a black cloth on the ground. The attendants place the "missile" on its side on a black cloth. The group then turns its attention to three empty chairs.

An attendant calls attention to the first chair, which represents "those labor and civil rights activists and peacemakers who, whether alive or dead, continue to inspire us with their courageous deeds as they work for a world where justice reigns and peace smiles on everyone." Participants are invited to invoke the names of various peacemakers. Their responses include: Martin Luther King, Mother Jones, Dorothy Day, Paul Wellstone, Mother Theresa, Jimmy Carter, Joan Baez, Nelson Mandela, Helen Caldicott and Eleanor Roosevelt. A second attendant recognizes the second chair, which represents "all those who have sickened or died because of nuclear testing, bombs and accidents" as well as those American veterans who have been exposed to radiation and depleted uranium. A third attendant acknowledges the third chair, which represents people who could not attend the ceremony as well as those unaware of the problems associated with nuclear weapons. "We claim them all as brothers and sisters," say the attendants in unison. "May we find the wisdom to respond adequately to their fears and concerns."

The next part of the ceremony is the "mourning." One of the CodePink attendants leads participants in "mourning" over the "travesties wrought by humans' love affair with militarism and war." She does this by asking participants to name their sadness. Among the responses from the crowd are:

* War as a part of all the young lives of the soldiers in Iraq.

* Destruction of human life and creatures of other species and their habitats upon which they live, and the entire Divine Creation.

* Violence that has now gone to the federal level against the three nuns who work for the cause of peace.

* Iraqis who are now experiencing cholera and starvation due to the United States' war there.

* American children who now have a world where safety is a question.

* Spending $1 billion a day on the military while the country's social needs go unmet.

* Those who make a religion of killing.

* The terror of global warming and the depletion of the world's resources.

* Children who now ask what war is.

* Institutional violence as a way of life.

* Too few people who question our country's actions.

* A way of life that perpetuates war and leads to death and starvation around the world.

When the "mourning" ends, several participants, one-by-one, take a "hammer of justice" to the "missile" in order to "smash militarism" and "liberate" billions of dollars worth of military programs that could be "rededicated" to social programs like education, day care, environmental protection, Medicare, senior citizens services and famine relief. Drums beat and tambourines jangle as the group cheers for each program. Each program is noted by a three-foot long, green and white "bill" that is then hung on the clothesline tied between two trees. When the ceremony ends, Peace Momma "dances" to the music of a flute, drums and tambourines and "invites" others to join her. As the "dance" continues, the CodePink attendants pass out baskets of silver "peace kisses" (Hershey's chocolate kisses), which symbolically transform hatred to love.

According to figures gathered by the Kalamazoo CodePink, the U.S. military industrial complex has cost this country $5.8 trillion from 1940 to 1998. The military budget for FY 2003 is $396.1 billion or 17.8 percent of the nation's entire budget and 53 percent of total discretionary spending

($755 billion).[48] The Iraq War has so far cost taxpayers $48 billion.[49]

HIROSHIMA REMEMBERED

Wednesday, August 6, 2003

KNOW uses the 58th anniversary of the dropping of the atomic bomb on Hiroshima as an opportunity to call for the dismantling of all nuclear weapons. Such a prospect seems unfathomable but the peace activists remain firm in their conviction that war, especially nuclear war, is untenable to the survival of the world. It is a low-key evening as about 150 people gather in Bronson Park tonight for music, readings, origami paper crane making, a few speeches and a lantern float of remembrance.

Since 1980 Kalamazoo has held some sort of remembrance of Hiroshima and Nagasaki, the second city bombed by the Americans in an attempt to bring World War II in the Pacific to a close. The local Physicians for Social Responsibility first sponsored the event and different groups have subsequently planned it. This year KNOW took charge and co-organizer, Joe Gump, outlined the purpose of the evening in his welcome speech.

"The United States continues to develop new and more powerful nuclear weapons and it plans to use them in combat and to deploy them in space for control and domination of the world," he says. "KNOW is committed to pursuing

---

[48] Source: Dan Koslofsky, Council for a Livable World, an arms control organization and lobbying group.

[49] By June 30, 2004, the cost of the war is $120 billion. By December 2004, the cost is $148 billion and the president was getting ready to ask Congress for $100 more for 2005.

nonviolent solutions to domestic and international problems. August 6 gives all of us the opportunity to pause and take time to reflect on the devastating consequences of nuclear weapons." Joe knows a lot about nuclear weapons. He used to make them. Later in life he committed an act of civil disobedience at a nuclear silo and went to federal prison as a result (*see* his profile on page 329).

My mission tonight is to talk with a few people to get a sense of who they are, why they are there, and what they think about the Hiroshima commemoration. I'm also trying to discover how they relate to such a seemingly abstract notion as nuclear power and nuclear weapons especially in light of the Iraq War and the threats of the small-time nuclear power, North Korea. This section contains a series of vignettes of my encounters with a few participants.

One of the first people I see is Raelyn Joyce, a Quaker and a member of KNOW's leadership team. The short Philippino native wears a white t-shirt with tiny red dots covering a map of the United States. The dots represent the hundreds of missile silos we have in our country standing ready for launch. Her shirt brings me to some astonishing realization of the potentially destructive power we have—and it doesn't make me feel more secure or comfortable. "It's interesting to think about that and to know what we're facing today, says Raelyn, referring to the volatile North Korean situation. "Our missiles today, however, have 20 times the power of the Hiroshima bomb. We should remember what happened at Hiroshima!"

Steve Senesi brings a thick rope 560 feet long to the park with him tonight and then stretches it the length of the park. "Meditate on the destructive power of one Trident nuclear sub," says Steve to a crowd gathered around him. "This rope is the same size as that sub." He cites some statistics about the extremely sophisticated killing machine:

* A Trident sub has 15 to 16 officers and 140 to 156 crew members supervising 24 missile silos laying in its broad and menacing body.

* Each warhead carries 100 kilotons of destructive power.

* The Hiroshima bomb had 13 kilotons and killed 140,000 people.

* Over 70,000 people died in Nagasaki, site of the second bomb drop.

* The United States has 18 Trident submarines in the U.S. fleet including most named for states: Michigan, Georgia, Alabama, Alaska, Nevada, Pennsylvania, Kentucky, Tennessee, West Virginia, Maryland, Nebraska, Rhode Island, Maine, Wyoming, Louisiana, Ohio and Florida. Only one is named after an individual, Henry M. "Scoop" Jackson, former U.S. senator from Washington

"I don't bring this news to scare you," Steve tells the crowd, "or to make you fearful of the fire power we're capable of unleashing. I just want you to get a sense of the destructive power we have."

Steve, 57, first used this rope 25 years ago during the nationwide freeze on nuclear weapons proliferation campaign. He brought it to the Mackinac Bridge Walk on Labor Day[50] and once he took it to a Washington, D.C. peace event. Steve, an avowed peace activist who grew up during the Vietnam era,

---

[50] Every year Michigan citizens follow their governor to celebrate the joining of the Upper Peninsula with the Lower Peninsula by walking across the Mackinaw Bridge from St. Ignace south to Mackinaw City.

had a "gut feeling" as a young man that war was wrong. However, because he was a seminarian for the Catholic priesthood, he had a deferment. In 1969, at age 23, he left the seminary, was never reclassified and thus avoided the draft. "Not that I'm proud of it," he says, "but I was not ready to make a stand at that time."

As far as the Iraq War is concerned, Steve doesn't understand what Bush is trying to do, especially as large contractors have made billions of dollars off the war and the reconstruction of that country. "It's a little like what's happening in Kalamazoo," he says referring to the 1,500 scientists recently cut from Pfizer & Company, the most recent transformation of the century-old, homegrown Upjohn Company. "The upper end of the financial spectrum has been able to find jobs, but we lost three times as many industrial and manufacturing jobs [from other companies merging or moving] and the city didn't make the same outcry."

Howard Sissler (a pseudonym), 70, served in the Army during the Korean War. He came to the Hiroshima demonstration tonight because he is curious to learn what kind of people are against the bombing that ended World War II. "It was the right thing to do," Howard insists. "The war cost the lives of many Japanese and American GIs. I lost a friend at Pearl Harbor and it still hurts." Howard is concerned about North Korea's nuclear capability, however, and he recognizes that that country has been a threat for the past 50 years. "If we can't negotiate with them, they'll attack South Korea." He also recognizes that North Korea is more of a threat than the Arab countries. "I fear more for my family and not myself. I could cope, but I don't want something drastic to happen to them."

September 11 shocked Howard. It took the second plane crashing into the World Trade Tower for him to realize that the United States was under attack. Hearing about the lost lives made him very upset, especially since it happened on U.S. soil. Nevertheless, Howard is tired of hearing about 9/11 because he doesn't think it compares at all to the trauma the Japanese attack on Pearl Harbor caused. As for the Iraq War, he says he was for it because Saddam was killing his own people. "As long as we're there, we can provide the Iraqis with good government and maybe cut down terrorism." While it bothers him that one American soldier is killed each day, he believes that the Iraqis just "don't seem to understand our way of life."

On the whole, Howard is convinced that America has lost its way. Maybe that's because of his own experiences. After high school graduation Howard worked at a lumber yard until he was called to service in Korea to be a combat soldier. When he returned, he got his old job back but later worked as a technician at a manufacturing plant until he was layed off after 17 years. He then worked at a robotics company for four-and-a-half years and was offered early retirement at age 62. Now he works in parts delivery at a local car dealership where he says he's happy. He regrets, however, losing his retirement home, which occurred when his first manufacturing job fizzled.

Jana Wilder (a pseudonym), a native Japanese woman, has visited Hiroshima many times. Her sister who still lives there survived the bombing 58 years ago. On Monday, August 6 at 8:15 a.m. just before the glass of her house shattered into tiny pieces, her sister's baby started crying and screaming. She looked out the window and saw the mushroom cloud hanging in the air over the city. Shards of glass covered her scalp. Upon looking outdoors, she saw people running around begging for water. Later on as her sister looked for relatives among the piles of bodies and animal carcasses killed by the intense, radioactive heat, she saw buildings and concrete streets with vaporized shadows of human figures etched on them.

"Hiroshima is a place like no other," she says. "The scars of devastation are still there." And even though she has been to the city several times, Jana still can't fathom the destruction that ended the war. The Peace Memorial Museum provides a tangible record of the grim reality of that day and about the powerful impact that weapons of mass destruction have on a city and its people. The first half of the museum gives visitors a sense of life before the bombing; it showcases children's toys, books and magazines as well as a model of the city in tact. The second half of the museum holds shocking wax figures of the victims: their clothes burned right off of them, their skin hung in strips like tattered rags, flesh burned raw and sometimes exposed down to the bone, their eye sockets gouged out.

Many pregnant women delivered deformed babies and women who carried eight-week-old fetuses bore children with smaller heads and lower intelligence. Children were also muted, that is, their bodies stopped growing. As a result, many young women exposed to the radiation vowed never to marry or to have children because they feared what they might produce. The message of the museum is "Ban nuclear weapons and make peace in the world."

Every August 6 the city of Hiroshima holds memorial ceremonies to remember those who died from the bomb. The mayor usually gives a speech and tens of thousands of people attend. The memorial ceremony begins with a march from the Peace Cathedral to the Cenotaph, the central monument of the whole complex and the site of the stone coffin that holds the Register of A-Bomb Victims.[51] During the ceremony the name of each victim is read. At night the city holds a lantern float on the river and people buy candles for every family member lost to the bomb attack.

Peacemakers all over the world have adopted the lantern float as a memorial of this day in their towns and cities. They insert prayers, thoughts and messages of peace in their lanterns. In Kalamazoo the small, concrete pool at the west end of Bronson Park serves as the site for our lantern float. Appropriately, it has sculptures of children playing and a bronze plaque that recalls Zechariah 8:1-8: "When justice and mercy prevail, children may safely play."

Tonight, one by one the candles of the paper lanterns are lit and launched into the pool. The participants are very subdued, except for a little boy who sends out his lantern with a splash. Luckily, the flame doesn't go out. A little girl pokes at people's backs as she watches them launch their lanterns. She then splashes her hands in the water as if to be totally enmeshed in the significance of the ceremony. After all 58 lanterns are afloat everyone just looks at them in silence. Eventually, one by one, people quietly leave the park. A half moon brightens the darkening blue sky, complements the warm but somber air of the lush and green August night. Peace in the world—if only!

"Little Boy," the nickname given to the first bomb, was dropped at 8:15 a.m. from the Enola Gay, the B-29 bomber that flew over Hiroshima. Upon impact, the bomb generated an enormous amount of air pressure and heat and a significant amount of radiation (gamma rays and neutrons) that

---

[51] Source: www.pketko.com/Hiroshima/historic1.htm

subsequently caused the deaths of 140,000 civilians by the end of the year. Another 60,000 people eventually died from the bomb's effects. A strong wind generated by the bomb destroyed most of the houses and buildings within a 1.5-mile radius. When the wind reached the mountains, it ricocheted and hit the people again in the city center. Three days later "Fat Man," a second atomic bomb, was dropped on Nagasaki resulting in the deaths of approximately 70,000 people by year's end.

The July 24, 1995, issue of *Newsweek* recounted the event:

> "A bright light filled the plane," wrote Lt. Col. Paul Tibbets, the pilot of the Enola Gay, the B-29 that dropped the first atomic bomb. "We turned back to look at Hiroshima. The city was hidden by that awful cloud...boiling up, mushrooming." For a moment, no one spoke. Then everyone was talking. "Look at that! Look at that! Look at that!" exclaimed the co-pilot, Robert Lewis, pounding on Tibbets's shoulder. Lewis says he could taste atomic fission; it tasted like lead. Then he turned away to write in his journal. "My God," he asked himself, "what have we done?"

PEACE VIGIL

Sunday, August 10, 2003

Tobi Hanna-Davies stands at the very end of the line of 45 people who have gathered in front of the Federal Building this Sunday afternoon. She holds a bamboo pole with a big, blue, Planet Earth flag attached to it. The flag waves in the wind as she vigorously flashes a peace sign and a smile to passing cars.

When the people in the cars honk, nod or jeer at her, she thanks them, waves and smiles. Tobi has taken this new approach over the past few weeks. Today she started counting the cars that honked for peace on her hand-held counter: it will be 167 for the hour.

"I feel joyful being here," she says. "It makes me feel energetic." Tobi exudes energy despite her short, slight, middle-aged body. Her long gray hair, with streaks of black and white, often flies onto her face, but she gently pulls the strands back with her fingers. She is fully and tirelessly engaged and totally focused on the passing cars, trying to get a reaction from them, but then Tobi has been fully and tirelessly engaged and focused on the cause of peace for nearly a year since the question of war with Iraq surfaced. She participates in both the Tuesday and Sunday vigils and has been an organizer for KNOW. She attended four peace marches in Washington, including the CodePink demonstration at the White House in March, and then the February march in New York. She plans to attend the October 25 march on Washington to push for an end to military occupation in Iraq.

Tobi has no plans for stopping her cry for peace. She is part of a core group of people in Kalamazoo demonstrating not only for peace in Iraq, but for disarmament of U.S. nuclear weapons—and the dumping of the Bush Doctrine.

"I think we will succeed in abolishing war," says Tobi. "I really and truly believe we will do it this time."

"Why don't you go home," yells a man in a passing car.

Tobi laughs off the comment, shouts out "Peace" and waves an enthusiastic peace sign with her two fingers. "Margaret Mead says that it is only when small groups of people get together to change the world, that it can actually happen," says Tobi. "Look what happened when people opposed slavery. The Quakers and other abolitionists had the whole economic system turned against them. The church was against them, too—both in the North and the South. Obtaining votes for women in this country was a struggle. Susan B. Anthony and Elizabeth Cady Stanton worked for women's suffrage and didn't even live to see it. But it happened. Why can't this?"

A carload of young men rounds the corner in front of Tobi. They have two American flags attached to the sides of their car. I assume they are Bush supporters—until they wave a peace sign. "Peace and thank you!" Tobi shouts pointing out to me that cars with American flags are not necessarily pro-Bush cars. "This is a new development," she says. "See, our message is getting across to all kinds of people."

"Why do you continue to come out here?" I ask. "The war was declared over on May 1. Iraq has left the front pages of the newspaper. There are American deaths, but not too many. Why are you still here?"

"Someone says that collective action is good for your health," says Tobi. "And I need it."

Art Orzel brings his black Labrador, Kara, to the vigils every week. He ties the dog by her red leash to a tree in the shade as he stands in the hot sun waving at cars on the street and shouting "Thank you for peace" at honking cars. Art was a combat Marine in Vietnam from September 1968 to April 1970. He has nothing positive to say about war or the Marines.

"When you're 18 you think war is a big adventure," says Art who enlisted in the Corps right out of high school because he had no other direction in life and, "didn't know any better." It didn't take long, however, for the reality of war to affect him. "When you get there, you find out they are shooting real bullets."

Art and I were classmates in high school. We knew each other but didn't run in the same crowd. We discovered each other at a local bakery downtown four years ago. We talked about politics and Melvindale High. When I ran for public office in 2000, Art generously supported my campaign. Over the past year we've gotten to know each other through the Sunday vigils and I have appreciated him and valued his opinion and insights because of his experience in Vietnam.

Art says he started questioning the idea of war in the spring of 1969 when he first went into combat and his life changed forever. He arrived in Vietnam just after the Tet Offensive and was assigned to a clean-up maneuver in the northern-most province of South Vietnam near Da Nang. He encountered many small skirmishes, but the happy-go-lucky extrovert soon adopted a cynical outlook on life. "A certain feeling overcame me when people started shooting at me. It put me in a reflective mode. I began to lose my life and ask about the nature of our existence in this world."

Art doesn't claim to be a spiritual or a religious man, at least not in organized religion, but when he was in intense combat he had a "mind-out-of-body experience." As he fought, he saw the battle below—and realized he could have died there. "I came to appreciate the gift of life that God gives us and realize that it's a shame that we squander it in conflicts."

Art is especially concerned about the psychological damage done to young men in war and how it affects everyone around them: their family, spouse, kids, co-workers. He knows Vietnam vets who have struggled with lifetime repercussions because of that war. "Why should we send the young in harm's way?" he asks. "They have no sense of risk and they're not old enough to reflect on the value of the life they have been given. They think they will either be heroes or dead men, but then there's a gray area they don't think about: what if they get wounded?" (According to www.wikipedia.org, 153,303 men were wounded in Vietnam and 58,226 were killed in action or classified as missing in action for a total of 211,529 casualties.)

September 11 moved Art. He recalled scenes of men he saw who were maimed in Vietnam. However, he resisted the idea that Iraq was a war that needed to be fought in retaliation for that day. Art, a gentle but cantankerous fellow, doesn't argue from the position of policy. He thinks about those who will fight the war itself and how they will be affected. "In religion you're bound to a code, a set of values and a certain community. I'm not sure about the spiritual existence after this life, so I appreciate the life I have here and now. I savor the moments. It makes war and killing so senseless."

When Tom Small calls the group together at the conclusion of a vigil, he usually starts at the farthest end of the line and quietly invites the people to gather at the steps of the Federal Building where he presides over a short meeting. Tom counts the number of people present so he can report it to the whole group—and apply the multiplier effect. "We have 45 people here today, which means that each of you is standing for 10 other people," chuckles Tom in his characteristic straight face. "That means that this Sunday we actually have 450 people who would be here with us today if they could." Tom then invites the activists to share announcements.

Grant Murray, who is organizing a bus trip to Washington on October 25, solicits people who want to participate. The march will be part of an international call to end military occupation in Iraq.

Ineke Way from the pacifist Skyridge Church of the Brethren alerts the group that her church and the local Quaker congregation will hold information sessions on Conscientious

Objector status in November. This program is being planned in anticipation of a possible reinstatement of the military draft.

Tom reads a recent letter from Noah Dillard who is visiting Gaza this summer with the Michigan Peace Team. Noah, one of the young KNOW organizers, had planned to be in the Middle East for three weeks but then decided to extend his stay for six months. He will delay the start of his Ph.D. program. In his letter Noah describes the horrible conditions Palestinians must live under and the many ways the peace team is helping to allay some of the stress.

"Did I give you the videotape on Father Zebelka?" Sara Wick whispers to me. (Zebelka was the priest who blessed the men and the bomb of the Enola Gay before they dropped it on Hiroshima. Since that time he has become a peace advocate. His hometown is Niles, a small town southwest of Kalamazoo.)

"Yes, but I haven't watched it yet. I'll get it back to you by next Sunday's vigil," I reply.

"Here's my friend's editorial from a California newsletter that I promised you." It blasts the Democrats' reluctance to criticize what the U.S. did and is doing in Iraq and in much of the rest of the world. Sara also gives me "Vision 2020," the U.S. Space Command's plan for warfare in space.

"They've taken down this website," says Sara. "But I copied the materials on it and I have them."[52] Sara is a university librarian and one of KNOW's information disseminators. She has been with the local peace movement since fall 2002. She marched in the January demonstration in Washington, attends KNOW's planning meetings, participated in alerting Rep. Upton to the dangers of the Project for the New American Century and just organized the annual Hiroshima Day memorial observance. She was thrilled that

---

[52] The website address now takes a surfer to the economic development program of Peoria, Illinois.

150 people showed up and the *Kalamazoo Gazette* and Channel 3 covered it because the media haven't been attending the peace group's events lately.

"Are you going to the October 25 peace rally in Washington?" I ask.

"I want my life back," Sara whispers to me with a sigh. "I want to do my garden, a good cleaning of my house and read some books."

"Sara, you said this several months ago, and you are still here," I answer.

"Well, we must do this. How can we *not* do this?"

At today's meeting Father John Grathwohl, a retired Catholic priest back from a visit to the Upper Peninsula, speaks to the crowd about the vitality and energy he found in the peace movement Up North. Father John is one of a few clergymen in town who joins the peace vigils from time to time. "We have a need for one another in the energy we get— even from friends in the Upper Peninsula," he tells the group. "I get so much energy when I come here."

The people who gather for today's vigil clap and cheer for Father John as they try to balance their protest signs between their arms. Their signs today show such messages as the following:

> Army vets distrust Bush.
>
> Who is lying to us? Where are the WMDs?
>
> The rich start the war and the poor get
>   slaughtered.
>
> Patriot Act attacks freedom.
>
> Impeach President Bush.
>
> Peace is patriotism.
>
> Mother against depleted uranium.
>
> May God forgive us.

Father John concludes his report by inviting the crowd to sing what the people in the U.P. call the "Song of Peace for Baghdad." This song was originally called "This is My Song," and also "O Finlandia." It has become a peace anthem for the memorial services of 150 families who lost loved ones in the September 11 attacks. Sibelius composed the melody in the late 19th century and the lyrics were added after World War I to emphasize the common aspirations and dreams shared by all humanity[53]. Kalamazooans sang this song at the Friday memorial service held at the United Methodist Church downtown, three days after the September 11 attacks. Here are the penetrating words of the first verse:

"This is My Song"

This is my song, O God of all the nations
A song of peace, for lands afar and mine
This is my home, the country where
    my heart is
Here are my hopes, my dreams,
    my holy shrine
But other hearts in other lands are beating
With hopes and dreams as true and high
    as mine

During these post-vigil meetings the peace people's backs are turned away from the street so they can listen to the announcements. Occasionally, a passer-by honks his/her horn or gives a wave with the two-fingered peace sign. Many drivers stop at the light just stare at the demonstrators. It appears that they either haven't seen a peace vigil before or that they wonder why the peace activists continue to gather.

---

[53] Music by Jean Sibelius, Words by Lloyd Stone, Lorenz Publishing Co. (1962).

"Go get a fucking life," yells a man in a passing car who obviously knew why the demonstrators are there. A few activists react to him by looking over their shoulders or chuckling or smiling at each other. Then they all continue singing the third verse of the song—in louder more resonant voices. The song permeates the group into a greater unity and sense of purpose:

> May truth and freedom come to every nation;
> May peace abound where strife has
>   raged so long;
> That each may seek to love and
>   build together,
> A world united, righting every wrong.
> A world united in its love for freedom,
> Proclaiming peace together in one song.

Several people cram themselves under the shade tree on the green lawn next to the building's steps. The hot August sun is quite a contrast to the cold winter winds when the activists met here before the war. They will undoubtedly counter the heat again when the group huddles here at the street corner next winter. A chill runs down my spine just at the thought.

Under the shade tree is a woman I've not seen before who brings her nephew-in-law with her to the vigil. He is Lebanese and visiting the United States. During today's vigil she introduces him to various demonstrators who greet him cordially. It is almost as if people make a special effort to exhibit their warmth and support to him as they give him a sincere welcome. The woman has obviously briefed her guest about the Sunday peace vigils because he comes ready to hold up his own sign written on a cardboard box bottom: "Compassion for the world."

The 20-minute meeting ends with Tom's usual benediction in his usual low, strong, resonant voice: "Thanks for standing for peace. Peace be with you. Go in peace." The people quietly disperse until next week.

IN MEMORIAM

Thursday, September 11, 2003

Nearly 100 people show up for a candlelight vigil on the eve of the second memorial observance of the September 11 attacks. The vigil, organized by KNOW and held simultaneously with similar events in New York City, Chicago and throughout the United States, is sponsored by Peaceful Tomorrows, Not in Our Name and Families Together, groups comprised of 9/11 families opposed to the war with Iraq.

Kalamazoo mourners begin their silent hour-long vigil at the Federal Building tonight and then process to Bronson Park where they sing and dance the Dances of Universal Peace, led by Tom Holmes, a WMU professor who has been teaching these dances for many years all over the world. Tom Small leads tonight's small demonstration.

"We are among the millions who yearn for peace and nonviolence in this community all over the nation and the world," says Tom. "We recognize that there is no way to peace except through peace and nonviolence." He asks the group of 75 gathered there to offer any reflections.

Ron Kramer mentions that Western Michigan University has asked professors to take a moment of silence in each classroom in observance of the September 11 tragedy. He says he will comply with that request but that he will also memorialize those who have also paid the price for the tragedy like the victims of war and violence in the Middle East including the 7,000 Iraqis who have died during the past year, the hundreds of thousands of Iraqis (including half a million children during 1991–98) [54] who died during sanctions, and the countless Palestinians and Israelis killed in their conflict.

Several people also point out the first anniversary of KNOW's founding on September 1 as a response to tensions building over the possibility of war with Iraq.

Kalamazoo's 9/11 observance is quite minimal, which surprises me. While there is no city-wide service or memorial as there was on the days following 9/11, different groups have planned a few events including the following:

* Panel discussion on "The Aftermath of 9/11" at Western Michigan University, 4 p.m.

* Annual Blue Mass honoring area police, fire, military and emergency personnel and 9/11 victims at St. Augustine Cathedral, 5 p.m.

* Prayer service for all victims of terror at St. Luke's Episcopal Church, 7:30 p.m.

* Candlelight vigil for September 11 memorial at Western Michigan University, 8 p.m.

* Benjamin Barber, terrorism expert and author of *Fear's Empire: War, Terrorism and Democracy* at Kalamazoo College on Thursday, September 11 at 8 p.m., and Friday, September 12 at 9 a.m.

Frankly, I am surprised at Kalamazoo's lack of interest in commemorating 9/11. For all the talk of patriotism, the "Pearl Harbor event" of the 21st century has fallen flat under the weight of some ominous avoidance to understand who we are and what our purpose is in the world as a result of this event.

---

[54] The U.N. imposed sanctions on Iraq from August 6, 1990, until the start of the war with Iraq on March 19, 2003, according to the Global Policy Forum. www.globalpolicy.org/security/data/childdeaths.htm

It's as though our connections to the world around us—at the local, national and international levels—have been numbed or deadened. Maybe it's because we are unable to deal with 9/11 as a tragedy. Maybe we lack the strength and desire to unite. Maybe we are still terrorized by fears that we will be attacked again. Maybe our apprehensions about our future lead us to the unthinkable: that we are on the brink of World War III and will be annihilated if those nuclear weapons are used. Maybe we are worried that our young may be taken into service to fight such a war which we know isn't winnable—for anyone.

Whatever it is, we are definitely hiding from 9/11 just two years after the horrendous event. Not that we should remain stuck in the past, which is another kind of avoidance strategy that doesn't take the hurt away or keep us safe or unite us. Instead, what September 11 has become is provocation toward war against an enemy that fights in the shadows and is comprised of a group of extremist individuals with a twisted cause and a motive of revenge against us. Our response to these sordid individuals is to limit ourselves to vengeance and retribution. These attitudes also evolve into a generalized indictment against Muslims, Middle Easterners, immigrants, the poor and even our fellow Americans who disagree with us. After two years and two wars, we are embittered over the world's intrusion into our lives and have convinced ourselves that our attackers are jealous of our way of life. And in that, we have also revealed our greatest vulnerability.

Blue Mass at St. Augustine Cathedral

A lone bagpiper greets the 500 worshippers at Thursday's annual Blue Mass held at St. Augustine's Cathedral in the Catholic Diocese of Kalamazoo. It's not quite a full church. The Mass honors area police, fire, emergency service men and women as part of the diocese's September 11 memorial observance.

Accompanied by the Knights of Columbus with their red and white capes and white-plumed hats, firefighters in dress uniforms and fire helmets lead the procession in a quick-step march. They hold up high their shiny axes, a symbol of their service, as their eyes are solemn and riveted forward. Police and emergency workers follow while a young blond girl wearing a white alb and an American flag scarf wrapped around her head (like the Spirit of '76), carries the processional cross before the eight priests who are here to concelebrate the Mass. Several police, fire and emergency personnel—both active duty and retired—sit with their families in the congregation, made up mostly of elderly people. This haunting scene matches the equally moving opening hymn, "Sing with All the Saints in Glory."[55]

> Sing with all the saints in glory,
> Sing the resurrection song!
> Death and sorrow, earth's dark story,
> To the former days belong.
> All around the clouds are breaking,
> Son the storms of time shall cease;
> In God's likeness we, awaking,
> Know the everlasting peace.

Even though two years have passed since the horrors of that day, the work and sacrifice of those who saved lives and recovered bodies from the wreckage of the twin towers still resides clearly in our memories, says presiding celebrant and homilist, Father Robert Consani. "The twin qualities of love of God and love of country allow Americans to stand tall and strong and majestic against any aggressors at any time.

---

[55] Lyrics by William J. Irons, 1812-1883; music "Ode to Joy," Ludwig von Beethoven; arranged by Edward Hodges. (www.hymnsite.com/).

Americans take pride in professing their faith and patriotism in one nation under God so that they can find compassion for the victims and forgiveness for the terrorist perpetrators."

"The events of 9/11 remind us that we live in a violent world, but I had the opportunity to glimpse at how you stand ready daily with acts of bravery, courage and sacrifice to serve, protect and keep the peace," says Fr. Consani, who served as chaplain for the Michigan State Police from 1974 to 1990. "You have our undying admiration and respect. May God watch over you as you watch over us."

WASHINGTON NATIONAL PEACE MARCH

Saturday, October 25, 2003

Today's march coincided with protests in more than two dozen cities across the United States and around the world, including San Francisco, Anchorage and Paris.[56] The demonstrators represented a diverse mix of dissent, from suburban high school students to gray-haired retirees, from fathers pushing their children in strollers to Muslim American college students shouting through bullhorns. There were people from D.C. Poets Against the War, the Louisville Peace Action Community, Northern Virginians for Peace, KNOW (at least 44 of us) and Central Ohioans for Peace, among many others. Banners in Spanish, Korean, Urdu, Hebrew, Arabic and Tagalog decried the war.

The mobilization to End the Occupation of Iraq and Bring the Troops Home Now was broadcast live and then rebroadcast several times on C-

---

[56] This account was provided by the *KNOW Bulletin* on its website: www.kzoo4peace.com.

Span. It received major coverage by CNN over
an 18-hour period and was also picked up by
hundreds of local newspapers and received
widespread international press attention. The
Washington Post carried a photograph of the
demonstration on its front page.

Organizers estimated that 100,000 people
attended the march while police counted 50,000
and the *New York Times* reported 10,000. In
another shameful example of biased reporting,
the *New York Times* report of Oct. 25 gave a
lower crowd estimate than even the Washington,
D.C. police by a factor of five.

WHAT ARE THEY TEACHING IN THE SCHOOLS?

Saturday, December 6, 2003

The *Kalamazoo Gazette* bleeds with irony this morning. In
the Faith and Spirituality section the columnist calls for an end
to violent toys for Christmas. A story in the Local News
section then reports that fifth-grade students were treated to a
90-minute presentation by two U.S. Air Force reservists who
were stationed in Kuwait and Iraq earlier this year. The
teacher and a university intern (a teacher-in-training) planned
the visit in an attempt to bring "history to life." The students
have been studying aviation since September.

The airmen showed the students "artifacts of their time in
Kuwait and Iraq." Students also got a gander at an inert bullet,
a gas mask and a small replica of a 500-pound general purpose
bomb. After a slide show and two videos of American soldiers
in the Middle East, the room grew silent, according to the
article, while images of bombs, sand storms and convoys were
flashed before the students to the tune of "Proud to Be an
American." At the end of the presentation, the reservists led

all 19 students in the "Pledge of Allegiance" as they stood facing the American flag with their right hands resting over their hearts.

One eleven-year-old boy thought the airmen's visit was "cool" because he "got to see two people from Iraq that build bombs." Another boy said that he appreciated receiving his own 30mm empty bullet cartridge that the reservists provided each student. He also liked the movies.

This school is located in a sleepy but growing upper middle class exurb of Kalamazoo, a place people moved to in order to provide their children with safe haven from the city.

THE CAPTURE OF SADDAM

Sunday, December 14, 2003

No Saddam.

No weapons of mass destruction.

No connection between Saddam and the September 11 attacks.

The Bush supporters have been quite demoralized judging from their Letters to the Editor in the *Gazette*; still they maintain that everything will turn out fine, just as the president has promised. The peace activists, on the other hand, have witnessed their worst fears about the war's death and destruction—and they aren't happy about it.

After nine months of war, it has become almost a foregone conclusion of *both* the Bush supporters and the peace activists that Saddam and the WMDs will remain at large. Not only that but people have become inured to seeing Iraq as the top story in the news. Even notices of the slow but constant death counts of U.S. troops fail to move them. Word about the wounded goes almost completely unreported. No one on the street talks about the war in Iraq except the peace activists and this seems to anger Bush supporters who drive by and shout at them during the Sunday vigils.

This Sunday morning, however, brings a surprise to everyone: Saddam is captured. The peace activists dread that this turn of events might be used to justify the war.

"I have very mixed feelings," says Nancy Small:

> *Naturally, I'm glad such an evil man is no longer on the loose. But when I think of the propaganda the Bush administration will use. We must not allow ourselves to believe that it will be an automatic peace for Iraq or an end to warfare. It's going to be a long, hard slog.*

"I'm glad he's been captured and that he's alive," says Tom Small:

> *I hope he's turned over to an international court, but that probably won't happen. I hope we remember that we supported him for many years, which helped to maintain his power. I hope that we don't forget that there was no link between Saddam and 9/11. Today is a good day but it is also a day of remembrance of all those who are suffering and our own collusion with much of this. I pray for a more peaceful time rather than proof that war works, because the war is not yet over.*

Tobi Hanna-Davies expresses the most comprehensive view of Saddam's capture and how it links to 9/11:

> *I'm very glad he wasn't killed. That would have made him a martyr and increased terrorism. What's important to me is that we understand the reasons for people to fear and hate Saddam, but also for people to understand the reasons for people to fear and hate the government of the United States.*
>
> *On 9/11 people asked: why do they hate us? It was no surprise to me. I already learned (through the Peace Corps) about the U.S. involvement in nasty business around the world, military and economic nasty business. When the*

planes hit the World Trade Center and the Pentagon, these were the symbols of terrorism used by our government's policies all over the world. For example, our government funded Saddam and supplied him with huge amounts of weapons to fight against Iran. He was our ally and we looked the other way. We knew of his brutality. We made him strong. That is just one example of the many times we have supported brutal dictators. Our government has overthrown democratically-elected leaders in countries in every continent.

Our country needs to live up to its principles of freedom and democracy. The rest of the world knows we're not. Americans need to understand there are strong reasons for others to hate and fear the United States. We could be such a force for good in the world. We have the wealth and power. Instead, I'm afraid we're talking about greed. Our trade and military policies are all very greedy. There is huge disparity between the haves and the have-nots.

Shadia Kanaan points out Saddam's cowardice:

His capture means different things to different people. The news is like a small earthquake: it has to settle for a while before you can assess the damage. To me, if Saddam had dignity or sense of courage, he would have shot himself, but he's not like that. I had expected that someone of his stature would have committed suicide. Still, it's unfortunate for him that no one had a sense of loyalty to him, among his own people. The irony is that he built castles and they found him in a hole in the ground.

Some people are already focused on Saddam's forthcoming trial and how he will be treated then and during his imprisonment.

"Thank God he wasn't killed," says Walter Ogston. "I expected them to go in on a bombing raid. To be consistent, we must take him to Guantanamo where we will lock him up, give him no representation, drop him down a hole and leave him there.

"My wish is for a public trial," says Shadia. "Let all the dirt out."

"I tend not to get overly excited about political events," says Ron Sowers. "It doesn't take much of a view of history. We have many more tyrants in line. We need to change what produces them. I'm pleased to leave it in God's hands. I'd love to be excited and I'm glad he's been captured. It will make good TV and his trial will be a showcase."

"I hope they show him mercy," says Marti Faketty. "He shouldn't be let off, but he's still a human being even though he's done evil things."

Some people, like Ron Kramer, look at the broader view, the place of American foreign policy and the outcomes of this war with Iraq already:

> *Saddam was a criminal so it's good he was caught and will*
> *be given justice, but this is not a vindication of what the*
> *U.S. did: violate the law, start a war based on lies,*
> *commit death to Iraqis and American soldiers. The end*
> *does not justify the means. His capture will bring in huge*
> *propaganda, which will justify everything that's happened.*
> *Ten thousand Iraqis have been killed and 400+*
> *American soldiers. The ends do not justify the means.*

"It may seem very dramatic," says Raelyn Joyce, "but what effect will it have on the day-to-day lives of Iraqis under American occupation? There is a lack of safety and infrastructure. Terrorism has spread to other parts of the Arab world."

Some people are concerned about the progress of the war and view Saddam's capture as insignificant, like David Macleod:

> *I hope that it's good. I'm disappointed with the degrading*
> *way the media showed Saddam and the arrogant way the*

> *American commander says, 'We got him' and then added*
> *'God bless America.' This is not the end of the war. It's*
> *only a change. We still have to figure out a way to get our*
> *troops out and put other people in. That can only happen*
> *if we work with the U.N.*

Others remain stalwart in their position not only that the war with Iraq is the wrong thing to do but that war, in general, is an atrocity. "The Enola Gay, the airplane that dropped the atomic bomb on Hiroshima, will be enshrined in the Smithsonian Institution. There is no mention, however, of the consequences of that act," says Joe Gump.

The peace activists may be somber and apprehensive about Saddam's capture, but there is jubilation on the streets of Kalamazoo as a young man in passing car shouts, "Bush led us to victory today." Then again there is Andrew, an older man who walks past the peace activists every week after Mass at St. Augustine's; he usually scolds them for their lack of patriotism. This time he picks out one of the men standing with a sign and starts yelling at him: "Free Saddam. Free Saddam. I guess that's what you want to say now, you commie."

Within a week the excitement over Saddam's capture wears off. The press seldom speaks about him.[57]

---

[57] A year later, Reuters reports that hope of a new Iraq, a trial for Saddam and curtailment of Iraqi insurgency will occur, "but twice as many U.S. soldiers were killed by insurgents in the seven months after Saddam's capture than in the seven months before, and thousands of Iraqis have died. There are growing fears elections set for Jan. 30 could be derailed by the mayhem," (Dec. 12, 2004).

V.

RELIGION, WAR AND PEACE

WITNESSES FOR PEACE

The United States' action against Iraq fuels a debate over the war—and war in general—with justifications for and against it from a religious point of view. Many people question the efficacy of the Just War Theory that has been operating for 1600 years[58] while others cite the Book of Revelation and encourage its 19th century apocalyptic vision. Still others call for a complete end to war for moral and practical reasons, that is, today's advanced weapons systems, should they be used, are unsustainable for the survival of life on earth.

The war in Iraq has also become a religious war between Christians and Muslims—although people regularly skip over the role of the Jews and the State of Israel in this conflict. President Bush immediately frames the "War on Terror" in religious terms as he identifies the 9/11 hijackers' deeds as evil and then creates a narrative about how we are engaged in a great battle between good and evil. He also uses religious code in his stern warning to terrorists, rogue states and eventually to dissenting Americans when he says "you're either with us or against us." This is an allusion to Jesus' admonition to his disciples and their commitment to the Kingdom of God. What is interesting in all of this, too, is how religion mixes with politics in an already grossly-divided population and calls for unmitigated loyalty to the president as one Bush

---

[58] See an explanation of Just War Theory on pages 272-273

demonstrator's sign at a March 2003 rally states: "Be an American not a Democrat."

The media tell us that the president prayed for spiritual guidance over the war but, according to Bishop Thomas Gumbleton of the Archdiocese of Detroit, the president did not consult any religious leaders, including those from his own Methodist faith. Mainstream Christian churches urge the president not to invade (*see* list of endorsements, Appendix B). Pope John Paul II personally implores the president to avert war and after it starts, to end it—several times. Only the Vatican's Cardinal Pio Laghi, a friend of the Bush family, is allowed entrance to the Oval Office but that visit obviously fails to change Bush's mind. Consequently, the war in Iraq also pushes forward questions about peacemaking and whether and how it is possible in our world.

Several religious leaders come to the Kalamazoo area to speak on this issue favoring the cause of peace and nonviolence. I include them in this section as examples of those who have successfully applied Jesus' teachings on peace in their own remarkable journeys. They also illustrate that peace is not an absence of war but rather that peace is *deliberate* action and *commitment* toward dialogue, compromise, forgiveness, reconciliation and love. The Scripture they use as their guide is the Sermon on the Mount (Matthew 5–7) and the Golden Rule ("Do unto others as you would have them do unto you," Matthew 7:12).

The feeling I come away with after hearing what these peace activists have to say is hopeful excitement that peace IS possible. However, it is obvious that we as a people, we as a human race must see the world with new eyes and new attitudes about God and each other if we are to accomplish this great thing.

BISHOP DESMOND TUTU OF SOUTH AFRICA
Witness for Peace

GRAND RAPIDS. Perhaps it is serendipitous that after six days of war Nobel Peace Prize recipient, Bishop Desmond Tutu, takes the podium in one of the most pro-Bush areas in the country. Amid the reverberating cheers and standing ovations, the short, wide-grinned man stands before a near-capacity crowd in the huge VanAndel Arena and recounts not only how South Africa rid itself of apartheid, the most heinous of all modern governments' policies against its population, but how any nation can work through deep-seated hate and violence. It has been a mere 10 years since the pall of apartheid was lifted from South Africa after enduring 50 years of it and Bishop Tutu lived through it all. As he speaks poignantly about the last stages of the "nightmare" of apartheid, I gaze upon him and wonder how he could withstand the oppression and sustain the hope that justice and peace could ever come to his country.

"Violence seemed endemic," recalls the bishop. "Death was so frequent that when only five or six or seven people were killed, the living sighed with some relief. It was as ghastly as that. There were times when people doubted that there was a God. There were times when the people predicted racism would overwhelm the land in a devastating blood bath. There was a sense that the whole country was on the brink of the most awful catastrophe. But," and he pauses with the artistry of a storyteller, "it didn't happen. Instead, something approaching awe occurred."

Bishop Tutu notes the day with reverence—April 27, 1994—the day apartheid ends and the people vote in the country's first democratic election. Nelson Mandela, who has been released from prison after 27 years, 18 in solitary confinement, is elected South Africa's first black president.

"We won a great victory that day," says the bishop, referring to the long lines of South Africans waiting to cast their ballots. "A spectacular victory over the awfulness of a vicious system."

South Africa's victory did not occur out of a void. In fact, the bishop readily credits the change in his country to the efforts of the international community, especially from the citizens of the United States. "We are beneficiaries of quite extraordinary praying, for no other country had such a concentration or an intensity of praying like we had at that time." And then he pauses and lets his characteristic humor come through. "What, you were surprised? You prayed, didn't you? God listened to your prayers and South Africa became free."

The bishop speaks of his country's new freedom in a metaphor: "You are like a blind person who sees a gorgeous red rose for the first time or like a deaf person who suddenly hears this fantastic Beethoven symphony."

Although he has been a bishop of the Episcopalian Church in South Africa for 27 years and a priest for 32, I find it difficult to remember that he is, in fact, a clergyman. The clergy in my own church do not typically speak out firmly and unequivocally about peace and justice. Nevertheless, as I listen to his speech tonight, it is obvious that he is indeed not only a bishop but also a man who stands for the Gospel!

Bishop Tutu's story about his country only becomes more incredible when he speaks about the post-apartheid government's efforts to create peace and equality among the races. Actually, he says, many people throughout the world didn't think South Africa would be up to it. The secret of the new government's success is to extend a general amnesty toward those guilty of the crimes and atrocities of apartheid as long as they make a full disclosure of all the facts of their activities. Those victimized by apartheid waive their right to sue for compensation and instead accept reparations.

Reparations, then, become a symbolic gesture that the nation bares the victims' pain and trauma. This strategy is based on the assumption that peace in South Africa can only be won when the people admit that evil is present in everyone.

"How could you ever compensate a mother for the gruesome killing of her son?" Bishop Tutu asks his audience demonstratively. "We knew we could never replace her son. This was the first step toward forgiveness of others. We sat down and negotiated with our former enemies. We forgot the past, looked for the best in everyone, and came to terms with the ghastly things done by both sides." He illustrates how this system works by citing an "incredibly moving" inter-faith service he attended in Pretoria the previous week. Survivors who endured the killing of 11 people stood before the congregation—holding hands with the same police officer who gave the order to kill them and their family and friends. The officer had applied for and was granted amnesty through the Truth and Reconciliation Commission, but as part of the process, he had to make a public showing of his regret for his actions by going back to the community to ask its forgiveness. When he did, the community was at first hostile toward him and disbelieved his repentance, but he pressed them to move beyond the past.

"In that moment, barriers toppled," says Tutu, "and the community forgave him. We don't know how it can happen, but it happened. Former enemies were able to find one another in magnanimity, even after they experienced untold suffering. They all had good reasons for revenge, but by discovering their own capacities for evil as part of the whole picture of themselves, they were able to forgive and forget."

"Each one of us has an extraordinary capacity for evil," says Bishop Tutu. "None of us can ever predict that we couldn't do such things. We don't know how we will respond if we are exposed to the same factors or pressures. Yes, we have a capacity for evil, but we have a remarkable capacity for good. We are quite extraordinary. We are fundamentally good! We are created by God for love and for compassion, gentleness, caring and sharing. We are made as those who stretch out to the transcendent. We are finite creatures created for the infinite. And our hearts are restless until they rest in God. . . .We are made for laughter, joy, peace, reconciliation and goodness. We are all family!"

During the question and answer period, which is reserved to college students, the one subject most on the minds of the audience is the U.S. invasion of Iraq. Before the war Bishop Tutu opposed to the United States' proposed pre-emptive strike against Iraq and called it "an abuse of power." It is rumored that some people did not show up for his lecture tonight as a result. So, not surprisingly, it is the first question asked.

"Power can be a wonderful instrument for good. It can also be something that is corrupting. We drew considerable inspiration from your history. You fought against a colonial power and won. You fought for Blacks in the Civil Rights Movement. You are a generous people. Believe this of yourself—you are a remarkable people in many ways. But, if you have a legacy of helping people to become free non-violently, why tarnish it?"

A 22-year-old student asks what qualities a person must have in order to make a difference in society. Bishop Tutu answers that the idealism and dreams of the young always inspire him and that he hopes they will continue to dream and believe that it is possible for the world to be different and better. He cautions that not everyone will do spectacular things. Rather, it is important, that every individual makes a difference where s/he can.

Another student asks if the Truth and Reconciliation process might work in Iraq as it did in South Africa. "It can work anywhere and be suitably adapted," he says firmly. "If it could happen in South Africa, then it must be the case that it can happen anywhere."

Someone asks the bishop about the biggest obstacle he ever faced. Curiously, he says it is his need to be loved. "It is a most awful and excruciating thing to be regarded as an ogre that most white South Africa loved to hate," he says of his reputation during apartheid days. He overcame that hatred by identifying with the prophet, Jeremiah. "I want to use his words in what he says to God:

> *You cheated me and called me to be a prophet. All I do is denounce people I love deeply. I know if I speak on your behalf your word is a fire in my breast.*

Many times I felt: why don't I shut up, but I can't and I couldn't because God grabbed me by the scruff of my neck."

At the end of Bishop Tutu's speech, I am left with only one reaction: I have witnessed greatness.

Life under Apartheid

Life under apartheid was difficult for the non-white majority that amounted to more than 80 percent of South Africa's population. If you were black or Indian or a mixed race, you had no say in governance, little access to it and few choices to education, housing or career opportunities. You couldn't own land, you couldn't move outdoors without a pass and, at one point, you were told where you could live. Of course, you couldn't vote or have a voice in government. Life was defined in racial terms and the white government's policies created a system that constantly worked to divide the non-white population. Privileges were apportioned in ratios: four parts to the whites, two parts to the "coloreds" (Indians or mixed races) and one part to the blacks. If you weren't white, you lived in a society where suspicion, tension and competition for scraps was a way of life. A common jingle spelled out this reality:

> "If you're white, you're right.
> If you're brown, stick around.
> If you're black, stand at the back."

Several political movements sprouted to correct these injustices but, eventually they, too, were banned. Uprisings led to government suppression, which would fuel more anger, more division and more violence and hatred. Things became so bad in South Africa that by 1976, after the police massacre of children in Soweto, the entire world condemned apartheid and eventually divested their stock with companies that did business with the nation. Soon it became clear that the South African church remained the only institution left to do something about this hideous situation; however, the church had to overcome its history of racial preferences. In fact, the white church had even concocted a "theology of apartheid."

In 1985 progressive clergy and university intellectuals came together to create the "Kairos document" which condemned the "theology of apartheid" and its practices. Because active ministers comprised the Parliament, the body itself imposed, in essence, a theocracy and the "Kairos document" had a significant and deepening effect on change in South Africa. It opened the way for church organizations within the country and around the world to begin forming a movement intent on crushing apartheid. However, the movement also became more militant and was often accused of inciting and supporting violence. The Anglican Church emerged as the leader of this new push for freedom and Desmond Tutu, at the time a black priest from Johannesburg, began to speak out against the injustices of apartheid.

Tutu was eventually deported to England as a troublemaker. Even so, he became a voice for his country as he advocated non-violence and peaceful resolution. He received the Nobel Peace Prize in 1984.

SISTER HELEN PREJEAN
Witness for Justice and Mercy

On April 5, 1985, Patrick Sonnier was executed by three jolts of electricity, each one registering 1,900 volts. He killed two teenagers and was condemned to death in the electric chair at the Louisiana State Penitentiary. Louisiana is one of 32 states in America that has the death penalty. However, he does not die alone or without dignity. As he walks to the electric chair fearing his legs might not carry him, he appeals to the nun who has been his spiritual advisor, Sister Helen Prejean. "Patrick, just look at me and I'll be the face of Christ for you," she tells him. Then she watches him die.

On the way back from the penitentiary, Sister Helen feels so nauseous she asks her friend who is driving to stop the car so she can get out and vomit. "I was stunned and traumatized," says:

> *I kept asking myself, 'Did I see that? Did they really kill him?' It was done in the middle of the night, and I felt as though everyone else was asleep and I was the only one awake. That's what motivated me to be a witness about this process and speak out against it.*

Knowing nuns and their work for the past 35 years makes me wonder how Sister Helen who was a teacher for 25 years and a trainer for young sisters in her religious community, could get mixed up with Death Row inmates, Hollywood, and then lead the nation—and the world—toward a moratorium on the death penalty. The answer is that Sister Helen's work is clearly in line with God's call for reconciliation and mercy— even among victims and perpetrators of murder.

I first heard Sister Helen speak at Marygrove College in Detroit in May 2003 and at then at Nazareth, the motherhouse of the Sisters of St. Joseph in Kalamazoo in April 2005. The perky but forthright nun from New Orleans recounted her journey and the extraordinary inspiration she commuted to other people to join her in her cause. She was ministering to the poor at the St. Thomas housing project in inner-city New Orleans where most of the people lived below the poverty line. Someone invited her to participate in a pen pal program for Death Row inmates and she received Patrick's name. She found him distraught and miserable as he tried to face his eventual death alone, so she helped him to see his worth as a human being and to seek forgiveness from God for what he had done. After Patrick died, Sister Helen continued to minister to other Death Row inmates and to the victims' families, some of whom objected to her work. Nevertheless, she found a way to hear them in their "unfathomable" hurt and to reconcile them to God and to their loss.

Sister Helen also went to Oklahoma City to comfort families after the bombing of the Murrah Building in 1995. Reconciling their loss was difficult especially when some wanted to send the perpetrator, Timothy McVeigh, to the death chamber without a trial. Although she couldn't blame families for this predictable reaction, she tried to raise them to a higher level more aligned with Jesus' message of peace and forgiveness. The death penalty only emulates McVeigh's violence and in the end does not bring back their loved one. Instead she offered people a peace option: resist the temptation to strike back at their pain with more violence. On her website (www.prejean.org) Sister Helen includes a prayer that best sums up her approach and gives insight into the uncommon discipline one must take to deal with such extreme sorrow:

God of Compassion.
You let your rain fall on the just and the unjust.
Expand and deepen our hearts
    so that we may love as You love,
    even those among us
    who have caused the greatest pain by taking life.
For there is in our land a great cry for vengeance
    as we fill up death row and kill the killers
    in the name of justice, in the name of peace.
Jesus, our brother,
    you suffered execution at the hands of the state
    but you did not let hatred overcome you.
Help us to reach out to victims of violence
    so that our enduring love may help them heal.
Holy Spirit of God,
You strengthen us in the struggle for justice.
Help us to work tirelessly
    for the abolition of state-sanctioned death
    and to renew our society in its very heart
    so that violence will be no more.
Amen.

Sister Helen's ministry does not stop with Death Row inmates at the prison, however. She wrote a book, *Dead Man Walking* (Vintage, 1993), which describes her experience with Patrick Sonnier. After actress Susan Sarandon read the book, she wanted to make a movie out of it, so she persuaded her husband and partner, Tim Robbins, to write a screenplay and to produce and direct the film. She also convinced Sean Penn to play Patrick. Sarandon received the Best Actress Award at the 1996 Academy Awards for her role as Sister Helen and the film received nominations for Best Picture, Best Director and Best Actor. Ironically, Sister Helen doesn't know any of these Hollywood stars and finds out who they are by reading various celebrity magazines. Nevertheless, as the film was being made, she suddenly found herself on the set as a consultant working to inform a mass audience about her ministry to the most dangerous, most shunned and most hateful people in society. She light-heartedly quipped that people frequently confuse her with Susan Sarandon or that they want to see Susan whenever Sister Helen is slated for an event.

In probably the most unforeseen development of Sister Helen's remarkable story, Jake Heggie, a leading composer, decided to turn *Dead Man Walking* into an opera. It opened in San Francisco in 2000 and is currently on tour around the world. As the nun's website (www.prejean.org/Media/Opera-info.pdf) states: "This deeply moving [opera] has touched audiences across the country. It raises questions about ourselves, our society and our spirituality." Heggie also put Sister Helen's mediations to music in an album entitled "The Deepest Desire: Four Dramatic Songs of Praise."

Recently Sister Helen's ministry has taken her to The Moratorium Campaign (www.moratoriumcampaign.org), which is designed to stimulate citizens' discussion on the death penalty and to advocate for its elimination. Her second book, *The Death of Innocents: An Eyewitness Account of Wrongful Executions* (Random House, 2004), points out that many people on Death Row are either wrongly accused of committing murder, they do not have an adequate defense because they cannot afford a good lawyer, or they have a mental illness. "It's just that a lot of people are sleeping," says Sister Helen on her website. "They need waking up. I've been amazed at their good hearts, their decency. They really don't want the government to kill people but they've had no one to bring them close to the issue of the death penalty and wake them up."

Together with the Sant'Egidio Community and Amnesty International, Sister Helen has become part of a *worldwide* effort to ban the death penalty. These groups recently presented petitions with over 3.2 million signatures to the Secretary General Kofi Annan. A few years ago Sister Helen also appealed to Pope John Paul II to condemn the death penalty—and she won him over. At present there are 108 countries that have eliminated the practice. Her hope is that the United States will join this group, too, and soon. Several states are contemplating this and in January 2000, the movement made a significant breakthrough when Illinois Governor George Ryan enacted a moratorium on capital punishment by recognizing that the system is "fraught with errors." Governor Ryan received harsh criticism for his stand but Sister Helen congratulated him on his integrity, adherence to principle and his decency to fellow human beings.

The significance of what Sister Helen has done and is doing is not lost on other religious women, especially in the face of dwindling numbers of those interested in becoming nuns today. In fact, they say she is an emerging new breed of religious woman that is solidly focused on mission and ministry. I talked with Sister Susan Marie Maloney, SNJM, who teaches religious studies and women's studies at the University of Redlands in California about Sister Helen's work. "She's the future," says Sister Susan Marie, "especially as her influence on the Moratorium has made an impact for justice and love on millions of people through media savvy in a high-tech society." In terms of numbers of people impacted, this approach to ministry in the twenty-first century is comparable to the ministry sisters performed in the nineteenth century when they opened up schools and hospitals, she says. Long-time broadcaster and former president of the Leadership Conference of Women Religious (LCWR) Sister Camille D'Arienzo, RSM, agrees with Sister Susan Marie and sums it up this way. "Where is our place as women religious? In the works of justice and mercy. That's what it's about."

"Finding Peace in the Midst of Tragedy and Pain," by JOHN TITUS, Stetson Chapel, May 17, 2003

The morning of September 11, 2001, felt like a typical day from the onset. The bright sunshine filled the beautiful blue sky as I drove down North Territorial Road to Schoolcraft College from my home outside of Dexter. Except for a powerful dream about death the night before, life seemed to be as always. In my dream, family and dear old friends from childhood and well-meaning acquaintances came to give us comfort and help the family mourn. I observed all of this in my dream thinking, how sad that it takes a death to bring all of these beautiful people together in such a powerfully significant way, one in which all pretenses are put aside and true caring, a relating of the souls, was transpiring. I awoke thinking about how glorious life would be if we could relate to each other in such an honest and meaningful way, minus the games, the bullshit, the mundane, and the selfishness. If only we could remove the protective façade and relate from a soulful level all the time, wouldn't life be a heaven on earth?

I didn't dismiss the dream because it was so real, so poignant, so divine in its message of love and harmony. I thought that it was me who had died in the dream. People came from all over to offer love and support to the family. The feeling in the air was one in which love and truth came together in an act of charity and every heart was filled with goodness and compassion. Little did I know that it was a premonition, a glimpse into what was about to transpire.

I arrived at work around 8:00 AM and shifted into my work mode. I started preparing in my mind for what I needed to focus on for our upcoming staff meeting since I was leading it. As the director of counseling and student advisement, I had several agenda items to cover with the counselors and staff. During the meeting, Gail from the Registrar's Office came bursting through the door in an excited manner and said turn on the TV, a plane crashed into the World Trade Center. While the news commentator speculated on how this could happen, I remember thinking, this is a suicide/murder mission. Just then, the Boeing 767, United Flight #175 came into view on the TV heading toward the South Tower. A part of me refused to think of the possibility that Alicia could be on that plane that I witnessed crashing into that Tower. After all, I reasoned, there are a couple of thousand planes flying each day. What are the odds? I remember very distinctly feeling a deep sadness for all of those poor souls whose lives would be taken and for their families. My God! What has our world come to?

I watched the news for awhile and retreated to my office. My sister, Jodi, a flight attendant for US Airways, called and was very upset. She was Alicia's favorite Aunt Jodi (her only Aunt Jodi also, but they were very close). Alicia was a very intelligent, caring, giving, joyful and peace-loving soul who decided to become a flight attendant in between her careers in corporate marketing and her new chosen direction, teaching. Her plan was to work for an airlines, travel at her leisure, and go back for her masters and PhD in journalism. She longed to work with young folks and utilize her excellent people skills along with her love of learning.

"John", my baby sister said in a very guarded and caring voice, "do you know where Alicia was flying to today?" No, I replied, but I'm sure she's all right, Jodi, I found myself saying for me as much as to her. I felt a deep sense of helplessness and panic as the possibility made its way into my mind. Jodi went on to say that she thought Alicia was flying out of Boston and that there were two United planes missing. She hung up with, "I love you and I'll try to call her roommate to see if she knows". I found myself sinking into a deep abyss, one in which my greatest fears in the whole world were being bombarded, the forbidden and guarded fear that something bad would happen to one of my beloved children. I couldn't bear the thought. It was every parent's nightmare!

Alicia was my firstborn. She came into my life at a time when I needed divine intervention, I needed unconditional love to give and receive, I needed a prevailing wisdom to guide my life that was too carefree, too self-focused, and off of my true "path with heart". My wife, Bev, and now Alicia, dear sweet Alicia, gave me meaning, gave me purpose, gave me hope, and fulfilled my longing for love. She was a godsend and I loved every second of being a father, her father. Those endless hours of playing and hiking out doors, dancing for hours, learning and growing together, living life to the fullest, loving, hoping and dreaming of what was to be…all shattered.

Jodi called again trying hold back the tears and be strong for me, but I could feel the depth of her pain and the growing fear as she relayed to me that Alicia did indeed fly out of Boston and was headed to Los Angeles. At that point the planes were just being identified, but we didn't know her flight number. She suggested I call United directly but they were not ready to release any definitive information at that time. I was dying inside. The reality of what was happening had the impact on my heart that Alicia's plane had on the South tower. I could feel my whole being exploding into a pile of rubble. I desperately prayed to God that she would be spared.

I let my staff know what was going on and returned to my office to receive a phone call from my wife Bev. She had awoken in a start at 8:41 AM, the time that Alicia's plane lost communication with the control tower, the time that the plane was commandeered by terrorists. Initially she told me that she heard Alicia's voice in her dream, calling "Mom". Bev and Alicia were best friends. Their relationship was so very special. Bev called and told me that she had talked with Greg, Alicia's fiancé, and had talked with our other daughter and had called our son, Zac in Montana, and left a message on the answering machine. It was his 23rd birthday. Greg had told her that Alicia's flight, according to her roommate, was over Indiana. We breathed a sigh of relief but we were only grasping for any ray of hope. Bev said she would come over to my work so we could be together. When she arrived around 10:45, we decided to go home after several more attempts to contact United Airlines. Zac had called me prior to her arrival and we shared what we had heard. So, we headed home shortly before noon, not knowing for sure if Alicia was dead or alive. Our souls knew the horrible truth but our minds refused to give up hope.

When we arrived home about 12:45, the phone was ringing. I answered it and it was Zac. He was crying and through the sobs said that United Airlines had called him and confirmed that Alicia was on the plane that crashed into the South Tower. My body jerked in spasms of pain and I felt like I would surely be consumed by the relentless waves of grief and pain. But reality kicked in, I had to go get my son, Elijah, from Dexter High School. We had to get our family back together. We could not go through this apart.

The coming days were a blur. Everything seemed so surreal. Nightmares haunted our fitful sleep. We hoped that at any minute we would awaken from this horrific dream. Family and friends came from everywhere just as I had envisioned. But the journey of grief had only just begun, a journey that will last a lifetime and beyond to heal. A part of me died on that day along with my dear sweet Alicia. My life was shattered and will never, ever be as it was before.

So, how does one come to a place of peace out of such a life-shattering, horrific tragedy such as this? From whence comes the light that would shine on the path of darkness and the love to guide us through the mire of confusion, this pit of despair, this lonely place of pain and sadness? How could forgiveness ever be possible?

Grief is such an all encompassing and personal process. Although there are similarities in the actual process of grief, many factors come into play as it unfolds. Initially, shock and disbelief help protect you from the searing pain, a pain that has the power to destroy, a pain that reduces your life-force energy, destroys joy, laughter, innocence, trust and causes one to question everything that was heretofore sacred. Sadness and pain of this magnitude can send a person into a downward spiral of depression and desolation. Into a deep abyss whose walls seem impossible to scale. Many times you find yourself on the precipice and feel the powerful pull of the dark abyss that longs to consume. Yet, even in the midst of all of this, even in my deepest moment of despair, I could feel the presence of goodness and truth, I could feel the love that so many people were sending us, I could feel the power of God, and a glimmer of hope did flicker like a candle in the wind. I was not alone!

And through it all, I was absolutely certain that I would not want to be responsible for another father's grief of losing an innocent child to the political machinery of war and destruction. Compassion had found its way into my heart and I could feel a new hope coming out of the rubble; a new hope that goodness and truth would overcome hate and deception. A new hope that would arise because of what had happened! I could feel it all around. I had been given a precious gift and I could see beyond the hateful act of angry terrorists, beyond the need for revenge, beyond the fear and anger that seemed so prevalent, beyond my own pain of the worst loss imaginable. I had somehow been given a glimpse into the Divine and I could feel it in my soul. My purpose in life had now shone forth and made itself manifest. Alicia had passed me the torch of truth and love would give me strength to travel the road less traveled.

Alicia lived in peace with all of God's creation. She longed for a world in which we could all just get along. She openly embraced diversity and saw the world as a rich tapestry of people of differing shapes and colors all woven into one big beautiful creation. She never stood in judgment of others but looked beyond the appearance into the very soul of the other and touched their heart. She could see the presence of the Divine in others. Many people told us that she would light up a room with her mere presence and stated that her smile was one by which to measure all other smiles against. Her joy was effervescent. Her smile contagious. Her sense of peace was pervasive. Her friends, family members and acquaintances all described her as a wizened soul, an old soul.

I am not a pacifist. Although, I have sought to understand the principles of non-violence and have tremendous respect for those heroes who have used these means to overcome oppression and war, I have a hard time letting others run over me and have, in the past, struck back rather than turn the other cheek. As I grow in understanding and love, I've since learned that there are very effective nonviolent solutions to conflict and fully support that approach. I believe that the perpetrators of this heinous act of murder that killed my Alicia and 3000 others should be made accountable and brought to justice. But, I am totally opposed to the killing of more innocent children and families to achieve this. We must find a better way of resolving conflict and stop the senseless killing!

Throughout my grieving process, it has become abundantly clear that the cycle of violence must stop. That hate only produces more hate and violence begets more violence. In this day and age of advanced technology, we have the capability to destroy each other and to decimate our planet. But do we have the strength, the will and the spiritual understanding to overcome violence? If we believe that we are a part of God's creation, is it not possible to grow in love and in wisdom to a place that seeks out nonviolent means for overcoming our ideological differences? As the late and great Dr. Martin Luther King, Jr. stated, "only love can overcome hate". And, from my experience as a grieving father of a beautiful, loving, peaceful, gentle soul whose life was taken by forces of hate and violence, love guided by wisdom is the only solution. Our primitive ancestors reacted out of fear and ignorance. Killing other tribes because they posed a threat to their well-being was commonplace. Have we not grown beyond that mentality? Have we not evolved spiritually from where they were? God help us all if we haven't!

During the 20th century, 180 million people died as a result of war. Seventy percent of these people were civilian casualties. This breaks my heart! Have we learned nothing from our past only how to make greater weapons of mass destruction? Have we no compassion as a nation of people, the greatest nation on earth? What kind of precedent are we setting by waging a pre-emptive unilateral strike of a country clearly inferior to us in military might who posed very little threat to the United States? We used shifting justifications and a severe lack of evidence to justify our actions. Evidence that would not even stand up in a court of law! We scorned the United Nations and threw dirt in the faces of our former allies because we had something to prove. And what have we done to stop terrorism? We have only solidified the efforts of the Jihad and recruited more terrorists. God help us all!

I am very disheartened by the Bush administration for turning their backs and doing nothing prior to September 11th to prevent these acts of terrorism, when in fact the evidence was very conclusive and did include "specificity" about how, when, where, what and why. A cab driver in New York City foretold of the event one week prior to September 11; large volumes of stocks of companies that would be effected by the bombings were sold the week prior to September 11;

companies with middle east connections moved out of the World Trade Centers the prior week; the FBI knew of terrorists training to become commercial airline pilots in Phoenix, Arizona and Minneapolis, Minnesota; CIA and others had very specific information about the hijackers and their movements from an Al Qaeda training camp in Malaysia and back to the United States; the congressional committee on terrorism issued a statement to vice president Cheney in late August of 2001 about the imminent hijackings and attacks...the list goes on. The Bush administration, for whatever reasons, chose to ignore the obvious. And, the rush to war was on! Thousands of innocent children, entire families and villages were destroyed in a country that was already devastated and ravaged by a gang of terrorists called the Taliban and Al Qaeda, whom we had trained and given weapons to when it served our needs against the Russians in the late 70's and early 80's.

I could feel the pain of the Afghani people as they mourned their losses, innocent civilians, after our attacks. The biggest difference between them and me is that I had lots of support, love, family and friends to help me through the horrible grief. They had nothing. And, help would not be forthcoming for many days and weeks or maybe never. They were left to survive in the midst of the death and destruction with no food, water, shelter, medical care or caring people to help. Their cries for help to our government went unheard. And, the world witnessed it all. Our conciliatory efforts for aid were for political purposes, not out of compassion.

Compassion is a gift that comes out of tragedy. Yet, not all people are ready to receive it. Anger, a natural response to the pain of loss, often consumes people and drives them obsessively. In my grief, well-meaning people would tell me that I needed to get angry. But all I could feel was sadness and pain. I couldn't see how anger would help me heal and revenge seemed so pointless. It would not bring Alicia back and it would not make me feel better. I had searched my heart and looked to God to find forgiveness. I realized that forgiveness was not about condoning the actions of another, it was about me letting go of a cancerous growth that would soon destroy me if I let it run its course. Forgiveness was the miracle that allowed me to feel peace in my heart and compassion for my Afghani brothers and sisters who were suffering as a result of our misguided war that killed a loved one.

After the bombing in Afghanistan, after the killing of thousands of innocent people, I felt more pain and disappointment. What had we accomplished? What had we gained? We destroyed a country that was already devastated, we killed a lot of people, and we sent the Al Qaeda and Taliban on the run, but Osama bin Laden lives on. Rather than focusing our energies on rebuilding Afghanistan and networking with the rest of the world to guard against terrorism, we sought more destruction, more killing in Iraq while alienating those countries who had been empathetic to our cause. Hate produces more hate and violence begets violence! We couldn't have done more to recruit radical Muslims for suicide missions for the Jihad. To add insult to injury, our government, the Bush administration, deceived the American people and the world to justify an unjust war that had no connection with the events of September 11th.

I pray for peace. I pray for George Bush and his advisors. I pray for the leaders of the world. And, I pray for my enemies. I alone cannot change how they view the world or what motivates them to do the things they do. But if every person in the world who believes in a Higher Power, the one God who stands for goodness and mercy, the one God whose love is the very essence of life itself, we could find a way toward peace. We could stop the bloodshed! And, perhaps my remaining children, my grandchildren and your children could live on an "earth as it is in heaven" without the threat of being murdered, without hate and mistrust, without fear and avarice. Is this such a bad thing to long for? Is this unpatriotic? Or is this what God wishes for us all?

I will not allow the death of Alicia and the 3000 other victims of September 11th, nor the innocent victim's of Afghanistan or Iraq die in vain! I will not settle for a world in which distrust and fear create a widening chasm between my brothers and sisters, who happen to look, believe and think differently than me. I am my brother's keeper! And, "my brother" includes all of mankind: Iraqis, Afghanis, Syrians, North Koreans, Iranians as well as Americans. We are all interconnected through God. We are all part of the "Great Mystery" as our Lakota brothers call God. Until we accept that reality, we will always find reasons to justify any act of outrage including murder. Let us break down the barriers that serve to divide us, put forth efforts to understand and accept those people different from us, and join together in a state of peace that sees no need for weapons of mass destruction but a need for tools of mass construction. Let us learn from the tragedy of September 11 and the resultant tragedies that continue on today before we destroy all that is good and each other. Let us go in peace.

NUNS IMPRISONED FOR EXPOSING U.S. WMD
Witnesses for Peace

Sometimes peace advocates seek extraordinary means to make their point. In October 2002 three Dominican sisters from Grand Rapids, Michigan, went to northeastern Colorado, cut down two 32-foot high fences that enclose a nuclear warhead silo, tapped their hammers on the railroad tracks used to transport the weapon and sprayed six crosses in blood on the 110-ton concrete silo dome. Their blood had previously been drawn by doctors sympathetic to their cause and stored in baby bottles.

Sisters Carol Gilbert, 55, Ardyth Platte, 66, and Jackie Hudson, 68, were convicted on April 7, 2003, for interfering with the nation's defense and causing property damage amounting to more than $1,000. Their actions could have gotten them up to 30 years in federal prison, but the nuns were not concerned about prison. They wanted the American people to understand the dangers of war, especially as talk of war with Iraq was heating up. As they awaited their July 25 sentencing, they toured the country to tell their story.

"Today, war is so antiseptic," says Sister Carol, who speaks to 70 peace activists at St. Thomas More Student Parish. "We spilled our own blood as a symbol and witness of the messiness of war. Blood gives life and Jesus gives life. We follow the example of the nonviolent Jesus."

The nuns' protest was not an off-the-cuff act. They are members of Plowshares,[59] a worldwide peace organization that uses such tactics to call attention to the dangers of militarism and its weapons of mass destruction. Their hammers and wire cutters served as symbols of disarmament referring to the prophecies of Isaiah 2:4 and Micah 4:3 which read: "They will beat their swords into plowshares and their spears into pruning hooks."

Before the nuns met up with the N-8 Minuteman III missile silo, one of 49 in that area, they spent the previous nine months in prayer asking for guidance on what they could do to promote peace. They decided to expose the truth about U.S. weapons of mass destruction which, as they said at their trial, the United States never promised not to use.

---

[59] Plowshares website: www.swords-to-plowshares.org

The N-8 is a one-kiloton weapon with twenty times the power of the bombs dropped on Hiroshima and Nagasaki in 1945.   It can destroy everything within a 50-mile radius and have a ripple effect of over 100 square miles. The radioactivity expended by this single missile will endure "forever." The N-8 and all the missiles in the U.S. armory are subject to alert for launch only on the orders of the president. Missile silos stand in remote areas of Colorado, Montana, North Dakota and Nebraska where only the grass grows. Because there are so many sites, they cannot be guarded individually. That is the reason the nuns went undetected for 45 minutes.

Upon entering the N-8 silo, the nuns chanted the mantra, "Oh, God, teach us how to be peacemakers in a hostile world." They conducted a simple ceremony reading Scripture, singing songs and offering petitions of prayer. They wore white Tyvek suits, which they called vestments. On the front of their "vestments" they printed in black letters, "Disarmament specialists," on the back, CWIT, which stands for "Citizen Weapons Inspection Team." They brought a Bible, excerpts from international law that deal with weapons of mass destruction and Francis A. Boyle's book, *The Criminality of Nuclear Deterrence.*

Military guards who eventually accost them were 18-, 19- and 20-year olds.   The guards surrounded the nuns and shouted so loudly that the nuns found it difficult to make out their words. However, Sister Carol did hear one soldier say, "They're singing Christian songs."   Later, two Humvees arrived and crashed through the same fence that the nuns had cut. These soldiers stood before the unarmed nuns carrying M-16 rifles with attached grenade launchers. For the next 90 minutes the soldiers searched the nuns, confiscated their "liturgical materials" and made them lie face down on the ground while they awaited the local sheriff, the FBI and a bomb squad.

On October 21, after spending time in the local jail, the nuns went to the U.S. District Court in Denver and appeared before Judge Robert Blackburn where they were charged with injury, interference and obstruction of the national defense, as well as damaging government property, i.e., the fence surrounding the silo. Their trial took place before a jury March 31 through April 4. All 22 motions they made were denied, including one that claimed they were religious nuns operating under international law as prescribed by the United Nations, the Geneva Convention and the U.S. Army field manual. They claimed their actions were meant to stop an international crime. "We all have a responsibility to international law," says Sister Ardyth. "We left these documents at the missile site so that they would find us not guilty."

Judge Blackburn wanted to charge the nuns with vandalism and trespassing, but the prosecutor insisted they be charged with destruction of national defense materials and damage to government property. Jury deliberation lasted 65 minutes one day and two-and-a-half hours the next. At one point the jury asked the judge to charge the nuns with sabotage but the prosecutor objected. The nuns later learned that only one member of the jury had some misgivings about their case and the rest were passive, probably without an opinion. Although the nuns contend they "never received a straight answer of what they were charged with," the jury found them guilty. Here is an eyewitness account, reported by Mike McPhee and Kieran Nichholson of the *Denver Post,* April 8 2003:

The pronouncement of the guilty verdict electrified the courtroom.

"This is a kangaroo court," shouted Susan Crane, a supporter of the nuns who quilted during last week's trial. "Shame on this court." Two U.S. marshals hauled her out of the courtroom on orders from the judge.

Sister Platte, a former councilwoman and mayor pro-tem of Saginaw, Mich.; Sister Carol Gilbert, 55, of Baltimore; and Sister Jackie Marie Hudson, 68, of Bremerton, Wash., stood in their orange jail jumpsuits and began singing, "Rejoice in the Lord above, again I say rejoice."

Sister Platte faced the jury and made the sign of the cross. She did it again to the judge, to the prosecutor and to the approximately 40 spectators who packed the gallery.

Sister Gilbert shouted to the jury, "We will not be found guilty under God's law."

Jury forewoman Terrah McNellis, 25, of Denver, says the six-man, six-woman jury followed the law and not its collective heart.

"We all agree with their politics," McNellis says. "Nobody in the U.S. wants nuclear weapons, but you have to demonstrate lawfully."

During the trial Sister Jackie's lawyer, Walter Gerash, compared the nuns' act of civil disobedience to those of Martin Luther King Jr. and the American colonists who dumped tea into Boston Harbor. Judge Blackburn, on the other hand, regarded them "dangerously irresponsible," but he veered from sentencing guidelines that called for a six-year minimum term. In the end he ordered the following prison sentences: Sister Jackie two-and-a-half years; Sister Carol two years, nine months; and Sister Ardeth three years, five months. After serving their terms all three nuns would be on supervised probation for three years. "This is not a win-win, politically correct situation where everybody will leave this court feeling warm and fuzzy," the judge said.

The nuns' lawyers wanted to appeal the case because the jury comprised people who had some relationship to the military: jobs, relatives or parents in the service. The jury included three Hispanics but no African Americans or senior citizens. Peace sympathizers were eliminated from the 25-

member jury pool. President Bush had appointed Judge Blackburn less than a year before and the nuns' case was only his second federal criminal case.

In recounting their experience to the Kalamazoo audience, the nuns indicate their surprise at their conviction because they believed international law would prevail. Other citizen activists had done what they did in other parts of the world and were acquitted. They also expected only a charge of vandalism or trespassing which is what happened to them in 2000 after they entered Petersen Air Force Base in Colorado Springs and hammered on a communications satellite and a fighter jet during an air show there. They were there to demonstrate against the U.S. Star Wars plan that was meant to "dominate, own, and control outer space." In that election year both presidential candidates endorsed Star Wars, says Sister Ardyth.

Nevertheless, the nuns decided not to appeal this latest judgment because they fear that if they lose, they will create a precedent injurious to other peacemakers. "What is our responsibility?" Sister Carol asks the audience, "can we as a country go on as usual?" She says the sisters' intent was to "invite the community to see our weapons of mass destruction" and to "inspect, expose and disarm U.S. weapons of mass destruction."

"If we sisters can't do this, how can we expect families to protest?" asks Sister Ardyth. "We want war banned forever. We want the weapons of mass destruction dismantled." Sister Ardyth notes that the United States has spent $20 trillion on arms since 1945. Meanwhile, millions of people in America and throughout the world are poor and lacking a fraction of such resources. The nuns believe that the United States is on a self-destructive path in its quest to maintain its expensive military. As of mid-June, for example, the U.S. has spent $80 billion on Iraq alone with no end in sight.[60]

The nuns also appeal to the audience to look at the human cost of war. For example, although the 1991 Gulf War casualties amounted to only 148 Americans who died in battle and 145 more in non-combat situations, another 10,000 soldiers have since died from exposure to depleted uranium with 100,000 more suffering from the substance.[61] The nuns

---

[60] On July 22, 2004, the Senate approved a $416.2 billion defense spending bill with another $25 billion allocated in emergency funds for Iraq and Afghanistan (Reuters). On the same day, CBS news anchor Dan Rather reported that the military operations is Iraq were out of money, out of soldiers and out of supplies, including ammunition.

[61] The dangers of depleted uranium have been documented by several individuals and organizations including:

Col. Doug Rokke, military official in charge of several clean-up crews after the 1991 Gulf War. He, himself, was sickened by depleted uranium: www.ratical.org/radiation/DU/Duuse+hazard.html

Military Toxics Project, http://www.miltoxproj.org/DU/DU_Titlepage/DU_Titlepage.htm

Depleted Uranium Watch, http://www.stopnato.org.uk/du-watch/

World Health Organization (WHO), http://www.who.int/mediacentre/factsheets/fs257/en/

The Depleted Uranium Education Project, (www.iacenter.org/depleted/du.htm) reports: In this year's war on Iraq, the Pentagon used its radioactive arsenal mainly in the urban centers, rather than in desert battlefields as in 1991. Many hundreds of thousands of Iraqi people and U.S. soldiers, along with British, Polish, Japanese and Dutch soldiers sent to join the occupation, will suffer the consequences. The real extent of injuries, chronic illness, long-term disabilities and genetic birth defects won't be apparent for five to 10 years.

point out America's growing poverty and lack of health care and education services to Americans are being sacrificed in order to maintain a high-cost military. "We have a responsibility as the richest nation in the world to strip ourselves of this lifestyle while other people are in straits," says Sister Ardyth. "We want to bring a nonviolent presence to weapons of evil."

As longtime peace activists, Sister Ardyth and Sister Carol live in Baltimore's Jonah House, founded by the late Philip Berrigan (a former priest and social justice activist, like his brother Daniel Berrigan). Sister Jackie lives in a similar community in Poulsbo, Washington. The three nuns have been arrested at previous anti-war protests: Sister Ardyth, at least 10 times, Sister Jackie, five times; and Sister Carol, at least 13 times.

Audience members ask the nuns what they can do to help remove WMD from the U.S. arsenal. "We have to be leaders," says Sister Carol who predicts that change in government policies toward war will only happen through the people and not the politicians. "We have to expose our weapons of mass destruction and disarm. We have to get out into the streets and build a new world." She adds that Americans must also confront their fears, especially when leaders talk about national security.

Despite their prison terms, the nuns resist losing hope about their future and remain determined to follow the nonviolent Jesus as their ultimate mission. They anticipate that

---

By now, half of all the 697,000 U.S. soldiers involved in the 1991 war have reported serious illnesses. According to the American Gulf War Veterans Association, more than 30 percent of these soldiers are chronically ill and are receiving disability benefits from the Veterans Administration. Such a high occurrence of various symptoms has led to the illnesses being named Gulf War Syndrome.

the hardest part of prison will be, "the risk of dying to self and losing their comforts."

"We saw millions of people who took to the streets across the world before the Iraq War," says Sister Carol. "Our own story has gone around the world and we have received thousands of letters of support."

Actually, the nuns regard their time in prison as "sacred time" where they will "sacrifice" themselves for the cause of nonviolence. They remain astonishingly upbeat as they contemplate a ministry to the people they meet in prison. "This is a new time," says Sister Ardyth. "It is a time to end war, to expose weapons of mass destruction, and to let people take control. War will destroy us if it is allowed to continue."

Nationwide demonstrations in support of the sisters are planned for Saturday, July 26, the day after their sentencing, a point not overlooked by the prosecutor, Robert Brown, who drew gasps from people in the courtroom when he referred to local activists' plans to protest at various Colorado missile silos.[62] "Tomorrow all these people are going to go out and adopt a silo," he said. "But for probably 40 years these missile silos have adopted us and protected us because there hasn't been a nuclear exchange."

Kalamazoo CodePink plans a demonstration for July 26 (*see* page 180).

Was the nuns' action an extreme form of protest? Was it civil disobedience or just priggishness? Don Cooney, a long-time peace and justice activist, WMU social work professor and ex-priest explains why the three sisters engaged in such action:

---

[62] Details on the trial come from a report by Judith Kohler of the Associated Press and published in the *Denver Post*, July 25, 2003.

*It is the core of their being. They live by principles that
make them fully human and to make life worthwhile.
Through this action they are doing what we should be
doing. People have to take stands for the issues that they
care about. The nuns have no responsibility of family and
so are free to act in a way that others can't. For them it is
a fulfillment of their vows to the Church. No doubt this is
painful for them but they live by a higher vision and this is
what sustains them. They see that prison gives them a
chance for a new ministry. We wish they were not in jail
but we respect and honor them for what they've done.*

Phyllis Senesi has another view of the nuns' action from
her perspective as a life-long Mennonite pacifist:

*Some people feel so very strongly about their convictions that
they do not worry about what happens to them but rather
live for the statement that needs to be made. They care
about the rest of the world that much. I was raised a
pacifist and always believed in it. These nuns are similar.
In every step they take, every decision they make, every act
is planned. As people who want to work for peace, they
know they are in it for the long haul. For some it means
prison. For others it means standing here at the Federal
Building. For others it means staying home and praying.
The Mennonites have been working for peace all along.
Even during World War II some of us refused to fight and
instead took alternative service in camps.*

BISHOP THOMAS GUMBLETON
Prescriptions for Peace:

"The costs of the war on Iraq are not confined to the Iraqi people," says Bishop Thomas Gumbleton,[63] auxiliary bishop of the Archdiocese of Detroit. "War teaches people how to kill and it throws an upheaval on those who do the killing." Gumbleton speaks to an audience of 75 mostly middle aged and elderly people at Stetson Chapel as part of the Kalamazoo College campus ministry's Friday chapel service. "War takes its toll on the victors as well as the victims."

U.S. veterans have suffered from war, says Gumbleton who recalled Senator John McCain's admission in 2002 that hate sustained him in Vietnamese prison camp so that he could "devote himself to the complete destruction of the enemy." He also cites a Traverse City Marine who fought in the first Gulf War and related how violence had broken the human spirit within him at age 18. The bishop says that most of the 250 to 300 people who come for meals at St. Leo's Parish in inner-city Detroit, where he is pastor, are veterans of the Vietnam War and the 1991 Gulf War who have never recovered from war.

Gumbleton has been highly critical of the recent war on Iraq, which he says is clearly a war for oil and not the administration's stated purpose of ridding Iraq of weapons of

---

[63] Bishop Gumbleton is a longtime international peace activist. He is a founding member of Pax Christi USA, the current president of Bread for the World, and an outspoken critic of the sanctions against Iraq. He has appeared on numerous radio and television programs, and has published numerous articles and reports. He first became involved in the social justice movement after John Cardinal Dearden of the Archdiocese of Detroit assigned him to pursue a mission of peace and justice as outlined in *Pacem in Terris* (Peace on Earth) published in May 1963 by Pope John XXIII during the Second Vatican Council (1962–65).

mass destruction, which have never been found. "We could have contained Iraq without war," he says referring to the United Nations' efforts. "We wanted the oil wells." He notes that the U.S. military protected the oil fields after the first days of occupation and that the schools, hospitals and museums were left to destruction and looting. He also criticizes the media for making the war sound as though only buildings are destroyed while it minimizes the number of Iraqis killed.

As of May 9, 2003, Iraq Body Count, an independent non-profit organization, estimates that between 3,760 to 4,795 Iraqi civilians have been killed. This information has not been widely shared in the mainstream press. The United States and coalition forces have lost nearly 200 troops.

Gumbleton fears that another cost of the war is that we leave behind a "trail of hatred and resentment for many years to come" which may involve tens of millions of Arabs and Muslims. Peace is the only solution for settling conflict among nations. All religious traditions proclaim man to be made in the image of God where we love and are loved. Love allows us to grow into full humanness. Hate destroys this most profound humanness of what God wants us to be.

Gumbleton refers to examples of successful peacemakers. Mahatma Gandhi led his people to nonviolent protests against the British Empire's two centuries of colonial rule over India. In one instance Gandhi told Lord Louis Mountbatten, the last viceroy of India, that Britain would remain a friend of India and that the empire would not leave with a trail of hatred and resentment. In 1947 Britain finally left India and, true to Gandhi's prediction, the country has remained a member of the British Commonwealth to this day.

Nelson Mandela of South Africa spent 27 years in prison after committing violent acts against the government over its apartheid policy. Eighteen of those years were in solitary confinement. However, at his presidential inauguration,

Religion, War and Peace

Mandela stood next to his jailer, with whom he had become friends. "This extraordinary act symbolized the new government Mandela had sought to create as an 'artisan of peace,'" says the bishop.

Gumbleton cites Pope John Paul II's "palpable sadness" at the United States' decision to wage war against Iraq and its subsequent death and destruction of that country. During the pope's recent visit to Spain, a member of the U.S. coalition in Iraq, the pope expressed his concern about "a spiral of violence, terrorism and war" and beseeched an audience of hundreds of thousands this way:

> . . . [B]e artisans of peace . . . creative artisans building peace in the world. Respond to blind violence and inhuman hatred with the fascinating power of love—the message of Jesus. Return love for hate—goodness for evil—nonviolence for violence. Respond to blind violence, inhuman hatred with the fascinating power of love. Keep yourselves far from every form of exaggerated nationalism, racism and intolerance.

> I wish for everyone the peace that only God through Jesus Christ can give—the peace that is the work of justice, truth, love, and solidarity. The peace from which people can benefit when they follow the way of God—the peace that makes people feel like brothers and sisters.

Bishop Gumbleton challenges his audience to take up the cause of nonviolence as the only way to obtain peace in the world. "My hope is that the young people of the twenty-first century commit themselves to be 'artisans of peace' and to use the 'fascinating power of love'. . . .My hope is that not only the young, but all of us continue to work for change and say no to all war."

BRUCE FEILER
Witness for Peace through Writing and Conversation

Bruce Feiler had just published *Walking the Bible: A Journey by Land Through the Five Books of Moses* (William Morrow, 2001), the story of his 10,000-mile trek from Mount Ararat to Mount Nebo where he sought to understand how the three great religions could relate to one another without extinguishing one another. A fifth-generation American Jew from Savannah, Georgia, Feiler felt no particular attachment to the Holy Land, but once there, he "began to feel a certain pull from the landscape.... It was a feeling of gravity. A feeling that I wanted to take off all my clothes and lie facedown in the soil."

On September 11, as Feiler sat in his New Jersey office, he watched the World Trade Center Towers crumble to the ground. He realized that the struggles of the Middle East had finally come to America—and that Americans could no longer ignore this volatile region or avoid talking about politics and religion. Within two weeks he decided to go back to the Middle East and discover the legacy and appeal of Abraham, the man who was both the center of this religious conflict and the means of resolving it. What came out of Feiler's second journey was the book, *Abraham: A Journey to the Heart of Three Faiths* (William Morrow, 2002). I enjoy Feiler's books and his travel articles in *Gourmet* magazine, so like a literary groupie, I can hardly resist driving an hour north from home to hear him speak at the Fountain Street Church in Grand Rapids in May 2003. I am hardly the only groupie there that night as Feiler draws an audience of 600 people.

Feiler begins his talk by recounting the story of Abraham. God tells this 75-year-old man to leave his home in Ur (located in what would be the future Iraq 4,000 years later) and go to the Promised Land in Canaan where he will become the father of many nations. Even though Abraham doesn't know where Canaan is or how he will get there, he obeys God and takes his wife, Sarah, and Lot, his brother's son on this journey. Because Sarah is barren, Abraham marries the handmaiden, Hagar, who bears him a son, Ishmael. Soon afterward, Sarah bears a son called Isaac. She then jealously drives Hagar and Ishmael away. One billion Muslims will descend from Ishmael and 12 million Jews and two billion Christians will descend from Isaac. This is half of the people living in the world today, Feiler points out to his audience.

"Would you have the courage to leave what is familiar in your life and go in search of a promise because God tells you to do so? Abraham, who stands at the center of it all, contains the seeds of hope," he says pointing out the possibility that it is through Abraham that the world's Jews, Christians and Muslims can come together in unity just as the estranged brothers of Isaac and Ishmael did when they buried their father and prayed and wept for him. "This is Abraham's legacy of peace for all of us, but it has to happen in every neighborhood, every community and every heart."

Feiler's enthusiasm and engaging style provide the audience a much-needed call to a greater holiness. Dialogue, he suggests, is certainly one place to start. As a result, he has created an Internet salon on his website (www.brucefeiler.com/discuss/index.html) and people have surprisingly taken to it. He invites his audience on this night to participate as well.

FATHER ELIAS CHACOUR
Witness for Peace Through Education:

Father Elias Chacour visited Kalamazoo in September 2005. I include him in this book because of his outstanding witness to peace in one of the most troubled regions in the world. He spoke to 500 people during Western Michigan University's annual Peace Week. The next day he spoke to 300 more people at Kalamazoo College's Friday Chapel Service. This article combines both speeches. Fr. Chacour neither asks for money nor passes out donation envelopes for his projects. He neither wants pity nor accolades for his work. He just wants people to know the story of what happened to the Palestinians in 1947 and what life is like for them today. He only urges his audience to "get their hands dirty for peace."

"I am a Palestinian, a proud Palestinian, a Palestinian Arab," says Father Elias Chacour as he begins his speech. "My mother language is Arabic. I am also a Christian. I am a Palestinian Arab Christian—and a citizen of Israel. This adds confusion to those who think that Palestinians are Muslims and that they are bloodthirsty people born to violence." He opens his coat and exposes his clean grayish-white shirt. "See, I have no bombs." The crowd giggles but is already giving him its rapt attention.

"Slow down your prejudices and your preconceived ideas," he says. "Even though my identity looks like a lot of contradictions, take it on as a new challenge. I am here to prove to all that there IS a way to create unity with a respect for diversity that can co-exist in the Holy Land."

Father Chacour is a stout, animated man. His short, dark, spiked hair and long, white chin beard are framed in his wide smile and flashing bright eyes. He can listen quietly or switch to speaking vociferously about Palestine in a split second, depending on whatever the occasion requires. He wears a black suit and clerical collar and might otherwise be lost in a crowd—until he speaks. This is his capital. As I observe him I realize little by little how obvious it is that this "homeless Palestinian" was nominated three times for the Nobel Peace Prize (1986, 1989, 1994) and was awarded the World Methodist Peace Prize (1994) and the Japanese Niwano Peace Prize (2001).

What is wrong between Israel and Palestine? Father sums up the problem: two nations have identical claims for the same territory and each wants to impose its exclusive control over the land. The problem with exclusive control, however, is that one nation or the other will be finished off and that would be the great tragedy, even worse that the violent conflicts that have been taking place over the past 57 years.

"Jews are my blood brothers," he says. "Both are descendents of Abraham, an Iraqi citizen. Instead of reconciling to each other, they are each fighting to prove that the other has no right to exist." Father Chacour envisions Jews and Palestinians sharing the same land and living interdependently, but so many fundamentalists from both sides want a theocracy that is making democracy in this region nearly impossible. He believes that the only way for Israel to survive and for the Palestinians to have a future is to end the hostilities. He then explains how the conflict began.

Before 1948 Israel did not exist and there were no Palestinian refugees. The trauma of the Holocaust coupled with the Western world's guilt spurred the creation of the new state of Israel after World War II. The Jews wanted a homeland and the United Nations and the United States led the world in making that happen. "These nations wanted to do anything possible to repair the evil done to six million Jews," says Father, "but it was not their right to take the land from the Palestinians and give it to the Jews. Palestinians paid the bill for what happened." Father Chacour and his family lost possession of their home, farm and orchards and his book, *Blood Brothers* (Chosen Books, 1984, 2003) recounts this experience when the Israelis came to his small village of Biram in Galilee. He was eight years old at the time.

"We welcomed the Jews and offered them our beds. We slept on the roof of our house," says Father Chacour. This went on for 10 days until Israeli military officers asked the Palestinian families to move out of town and then they would be allowed to return after a few days. The entire village left and slept in their fields under their olive and fig trees for two weeks. When the fathers went back to town to ask the soldiers about returning to their homes, the soldiers put them on military trucks to Nablus where they were told either to cross the border into Jordan, Syria or Lebanon or be killed. Most of these Palestinian men never came back but Father Chacour's father did by walking through the northern borders. He appealed to the Supreme Court of Israel to return his family to its home. The army resisted his proposal but the court granted the Chacour family access to their land where olive trees planted in the sixteenth century were growing—only the family no longer owned their land; it was now Israeli land. Upon entering their village, the family noticed that all of it, including the church, had been bombed and burned to the ground. "But my father said not to use any violence against violence," says Father Chacour. "Violence can't bring you justice." His father's advice would shape the young boy forever.

As it turned out, the Israeli surge of violence killed tens of thousands of Palestinians and displaced one million of them from their homes. Some people went to Lebanon, Syria, Jordan or Egypt. Others went to Gaza or the West Bank and hoped that after a time they could return to their villages. Gaza, which had 8,500 inhabitants, suddenly swelled to 1.2 million people, most of them were refugees from the 460 towns and villages of Palestine that were taken over by the new Israeli government. A third group, the poorest of them all, stayed put on land that became Israel. They, in turn, became a "tolerated minority," exiles on their own land. Of the 1.1 million of them, 25 percent or 137,000 are Palestinian Christians—Father Chacour is one among them. "This is the reason I became obsessed since childhood to do something for my community," says Father Chacour.

Today the Palestinians are still refuges; they have no health care, no schools, no jobs and no future. Sixty-five percent of the men are unemployed. They must also endure daily humiliations, like waiting for five to seven hours at checkpoints in areas designated as high security zones. They have seen the destruction of their homes and mosques and they have witnessed the Israelis' uprooting of their orchards and olive trees. These trees are most sacred to them because they are hundreds of years old and have been cared for by their families over the centuries. "The only thing the Palestinians are free to do is to make children," says Father Chacour.

"This is the source of bitterness and hatred that has made some of them suicide bombers," said Father Chacour. "Their hope is gone and they find dying is better than living. However, suicide bombers commit three crimes: against themselves, against humanity and against God. There is no way to justify suicide bombings or manslaughter. To say so and do nothing, well, you are wrong. We must go much deeper to understand why they decide to terminate their lives. We must understand why the young who despair and have lost hope believe that dying is better than living. It is our responsibility to give these people hope and a reason to live."

At the same time he admonishes his audience: "For your own dignity, never accept prejudices and collective judgment from any group. Don't accept any collective judgment against Jews. Don't call them dirty Jews. That's what the Third Reich called them. At the same time, don't call the Palestinians terrorists. We are a terrorized people."

☮

In 1965 Elias Chacour was ordained a priest with the St. George Melkite Catholic Church. His first assignment was Ibillin, a small Arab village in Galilee where Christians and Muslims have lived together peacefully for many generations. He was only supposed to stay there a month but "bishops have short memories and mine forgot that he put me there," says Father. "And I forgot myself, too." He chose to repair the mosque as his first task as the village priest. Now, 42 years later, his work has evolved into planting untold orchards of peace and justice by educating the children of the Galilee region where 50 percent of the Arab population is under 14 years old and 75 percent is below 28 years old. "My life's meaning has been to give hope to my people," says Father who is also called affectionately, "Abuna."

For 25 years the Palestinians in Galilee lived without electricity or water and were restricted from leaving their village. So Father Chacour began collecting old books and distributing them and eventually built the first public library. This gesture helped the children "leave" their poor environment a little while through books. Father sought to make life better by sponsoring summer camps, which have always had more children than room to accommodate them. In the first year of camp 5,000 children registered from 30 villages all over Galilee. Father couldn't reject anyone so all were accepted, but he was stuck about what to do with all those children. He admits he was scared at first, however, "when I pray and abandon myself to God's hands, I give inspiration to others." He invited 10 mothers from among the campers in 30 villages to help prepare sandwiches and drinks for the children—and ended up with 300 mothers! Father is quick to point out that most of these mothers were Muslims. "It was a beautiful community," he says describing the success of the camp. "We Christians don't have a monopoly of doing good. We don't have exclusive control of the Holy Spirit. Even God is not a Christian."

As time went on, Father Chacour became a sly, patient man and he illustrated this in his story about building the high school. In 1981 Father realized that only 18 girls were enrolled in high school, so he decided to build one and provide this opportunity for everyone including girls. The Israeli government, however, denied him a building permit. He decided to build the school anyway and "que sera, sera." Three months later the police tried to stop him from continuing building and he subsequently went to court. The judge scheduled his hearing for Sunday at 10 a.m. but Father Chacour said that as a Catholic priest he didn't go to court on Sundays. The judge postponed the case for six months. Then Father received another letter announcing a new court date for Sunday at 10 a.m. Again he refused to appear and the judge again postponed the hearing for another six months. This went on six more times and the high school was completed— and never touched by the Israeli military. Established in 1982 with 80 students, the high school now has over 1,100 students.

"I invite you," says Father Chacour in a moral-of-the-story tone, "never condemn anyone to be good or bad. There is evil in every nation and in every human being. There is also good. Choose what to enhance. There is good in every human being and it is stronger than evil."

Building schools became Father Chacour's ministry and mission in Ibillin and his success went way beyond his own imagination. He believed that educating the young gives them hope and skills for the future. Before the high school was built, Father Chacour founded the The Myriam Bawardi Kindergarten in 1970; it now enrolls 220 students. The technical college (founded in 1994) has over 800 students. A regional teacher training center (founded in 1996) works with teachers of Arab children throughout Galilee with 1,000 teachers enrolled. An elementary school started in 2001 adds one class per year starting with grades one to four. About 130 students were initially enrolled. The school for gifted children was formed in 1998 with 120 students. All of these schools fall under the Mar Elias Educational Institutions (MEEI) where children and young adults of several faith traditions learn to live and work together in peace.

Father Chacour insists that every child in Galilee is admitted to school and no one is refused because he or she is poor or unacceptable due to his or her religion or ethnicity. He never recruits either. People are invited to integrate themselves with their neighbors and there are no attempts toward assimilating them. The MEEI schools currently enroll 4,500 students. Sixty-five percent of the students are Muslims but there are Christians and Jews, too. However, living out the mission of openness is not automatic. Father Chacour relates a story about the time Jewish children started coming to the school. He was glad they were there but he was scared there might be trouble. So on the first day he ordered some buses and took the students to Mount Carmel for a field trip. By lunch time the kids all forgot they were Jews and Palestinians and instead exchanged addresses, e-mails and telephone numbers.

"This is the only campus in Israel that has kindergarten through university and it is the country's only private institution," says Father Chacour. "We teach the spirituality of the Sermon on the Mount to all the students and they all live and work together. Children care little about labels and after a while, they don't know who is whom. My only wish is that they sit together around desks and write the future for their children. It can't be an isolated future for them. This is vital for human unity and dignity. Besides, they were all born in the image and likeness of God."

The next MEEI project, called the "new venture," is expected to bring together Arab-Israelis (Muslim and Christian) with Jewish Israelis. Next, Israeli-Arab and Israeli-Jewish students will be joined by Arab students from the neighboring countries of Jordan, Palestine, and Egypt. As the final phase of the plan unfolds, international students from the United States, Canada, the United Kingdom, and Europe will be admitted.

It would seem an impossibility to build these schools given the scarcity of resources, the breadth of the mission and the dream of peaceful coexistence among Jews and Muslims, but Father Chacour has not done this alone. He has been able to enlist many, many people to help him. One group actively responsible for providing subsidies for student scholarships and building projects is the Pilgrims of Ibillin (www.pilgrimsofibillin.org) based in Livermore, California. He also obtained the help of Secretary of State James Baker.

"I learned that the shortest way to Jerusalem is through Washington, D.C.," says Father. When he was having trouble getting the building permit for the high school, Father Chacour decided to pay a visit to then-Secretary of State James Baker. It was just after the Gulf War in 1991 and he went to his house and knocked on the door. The secretary's wife, Suzan, answered.

"Who are you?" she asked.

"Another man from Galilee," he answered.

"Do you have an appointment?"

"Sorry, we men from Galilee never make appointments, we only make appearances."

Mrs. Baker didn't want to let Father Chacour in but she found it equally difficult to turn him away. She brought him to the kitchen and offered him a drink of iced tea. He told her he needed help with the building permit so she also gave Father her husband's office phone number. She then bid him good-bye because she was holding a Bible Study Hour in her living room. Father asked her what the group was studying.

"The Sermon on the Mount."

"What language are you studying this in?"

"English."

Father Chacour knows 11 languages and speaks five fluently: Arabic, Hebrew, English, French, German and Aramaic. "I pity you but good luck," he said.

"Can you help us understand it better?" Suzan Baker asked, and he obliged. For the next two hours Father Chacour sat in her living room with some "gentle, loving ladies" and explained that the first eight verses of the Sermon had a different meaning in the Aramaic language of Jesus from the "be happy attitudes" the women were taught. The message in Aramaic went something like this: "Straighten up yourself, go ahead and do something. Get your hands dirty if you are hungry and thirsty for justice."

A week later Suzan Baker asked Father Chacour to return to her house so that they could pray together. Eventually the two struck up a friendship that included her husband as well and lasted over a decade. When Father wanted to build a college (the young Christians were leaving Galilee thus causing a brain drain there), it was James Baker who helped Father connect with the University of Indianapolis and establish a UI branch campus in Israel. In July 2003, after two and a half years of exchanging 264 letters with the Israeli government, the Mar Elias Campus was accredited by the North Central

Association and accepted by the Council of Higher Education in Israel. In one month 126 students—Arabs, Christians and Israelis—applied for the first semester that began on October 21, 2003. The university has three departments: Environmental Science and Chemistry, Computer Science, and Communication and is looking to add more.

The MEEI schools employ a 290-person faculty including 100 people with Ph.D.s and 92 with master's degrees. Twenty-eight faculty members are Jewish. Father's own nephew, who was graduated with a doctoral degree in mechanical engineering from Western Michigan University, also signed on to teach at the college after turning down a lucrative opportunity with the U.S. Marine Corps. "I promised him that he would not make a lot of money with us but that he would receive much love. For four years now he has been there."

Father Chacour pauses a moment at the podium and closes his eyes as if to contemplate the significance of these achievements. "If these schools did not exist, where would all the faculty be today? Certainly anywhere but Palestine. This gives me hope and courage and the drive to continue despite all the problems."

Then in a quiet moment, Father Chacour tells the audience that after he obtained accreditation for the college, he fell on his knees in his office and prayed: "Lord, now you can take your servant in peace." However, he did not receive an answer. Instead, he established the Mar Elias Peace Center, which will play a vital role in the schools' local and international outreach programs and serve as a peace research center. English has been adopted as its language of instruction.

These accomplishments are astounding, however, Father Chacour remains modest and faith-filled. "You are called to become God-like, not to be our size," he says. "We must set

God free from our concepts and poor understanding. God is Great!"

As the end of his speech draws near, Father makes a plea to his audience.

"I believe in you. You can make a difference. You love to make a difference. You are called to make a difference. On behalf of all Palestinian children, I beg you," he repeats, "I beg you to be in touch with the Jews you know and to continue giving friendship and sympathy to them and to respect them as human beings. They need this more than anyone during these times of big decision-making. Ask them to be more reasonable in their perceptions of Palestinians and not to be automatic enemies of them. And, know, too, that if you are friends with Jews, that does not mean that you are automatically at enmity with Palestinians.

"If taking our side, however, means that you accept everything we do and you become an enemy of the Jews, then we do not need your friendship. For us to find one more enemy in this horrible situation that has to stop is not what we need. What we need is one more common friend. Can you do that? Do you have the courage? Decide for yourself—and get your hands dirty for peace and justice. You can do it!"

Father Chacour receives wild applause and a standing ovation. Curiously, he just stands at the podium with his head bowed and his eyes closed. He is praying. When the applause ceases, he speaks again: "Don't applaud for me but for a corner of your own conscience that is awakened."

Before his speech at Stetson Chapel, Father Chacour sits on a bench in the narthex looking at the students as they enter the building. When I see him, I dart over to him anxious to obtain his autograph for my *Blood Brothers* book. He does not seem rushed or bothered by my move, even as "curtain time"

is about to begin. In this short encounter I realize the depth of his work. He never turns away an opportunity to promote his mission of love and peace, not for a book signing groupie, a small Palestinian child or a talk with the wife of the U.S. Secretary of State. He clearly lives as though he is guided by the Spirit. He does not plan things, he merely responds to the world and the opportunities it affords. Is this what he learned to do as a homeless Palestinian child of eight? Is this how he learned to survive as a second-class citizen of Israel? Is this what he sees as his priestly ministry? Or is he a messenger of God in his words and deeds? With a gentle patience, he flashes his eternally wide smile, takes my book and signs it with the message: "God does not kill."

VI.

PROFILES OF PEACE

Heroes of a Different Stripe

PROFILES OF PEACE

In this book I have presented the sentiments and activities of ordinary people in a medium-sized Midwestern town who have actively and passionately stood for peace and justice. This chapter profiles the more prominent KNOW activists to provide a more in-depth view of what inspires them to be peace advocates. The short answer to this question is that they discern how the world is and how it can be and then attempt to stand for the latter. They make a commitment to peace and justice at different stages in their lives and in different ways, but peace ultimately becomes their passion. They risk ridicule from family and friends and certainly they expect it from the public. Yet, once they acquire their vision for peace, which they develop through either religious conviction or humanist concerns, they cannot keep it to themselves. They must share it with others.

The people represented here advocate for peace in different ways. They do it through public rituals like Shadia Kanaan or acts of civil disobedience like the Gumps, through study like Rudi Siebert, Ron Kramer and Rob Anderson, through organizing like Amy Anderson or Noah Dillard, through acts of kindness like the Naglers or through strategic proposals for change like David Macleod. But they all participate in some sort of public demonstration of their conviction again, because, like Jeremiah, they cannot hold this passion within themselves (Jeremiah 20:7–9).

None of these people has become a peace and justice activist lightly or for personal, professional or financial gain. Many of them risk their own reputations by espousing what are considered counter-establishment ideas. All of them, however, come to their calling through careful study, discernment and a powerful experience that tips them toward peace advocacy. Then they make a commitment to do what they can with their talents, skills and time to advance the cause because they believe they are making a difference. For these reasons I call the people of Kalamazoo profiled here and throughout this book, "heroes." None of them has received accolades for such acts of courage. No medals. No parades. Yet none of them is able to desist from what they do. What they want most is to inspire others to work for peace and justice as a solution to conflict and war. In this way they know they are challenging the status quo in an effort to make the world a better place for their fellow human beings.

I believe all of these people are prophetic in their vision and in their witness to the Truth. They also represent a small sampling of what is happening in the peace movement throughout the world. As humanity struggles to be the best of what it means to be human, they are all aptly responding to the prophet Micah's call, "to act justly, to love tenderly, to walk humbly with our God"—and they inspire others to do the same in *their* own way.

RUDI SIEBERT
Scholar for Peace

I first meet Rudi Siebert when I visit him at his tri-level home, which he shares with three or four college students in one of Kalamazoo's westside neighborhoods. It was December 2002. As I approach his house, I see a peace pole in his front yard. The four-sided pole is white with black writing that spells out "peace" in several different languages. The prayer, "May peace prevail" is written in four languages (English, German, Spanish and Arabic) one of each side of the pole. In the 1980s many Kalamazoo churches and private citizens planted peace poles in their front yards as a sign of their commitment to peace.

It is unclear to me which door I should enter to get into his house: the one leading through the garage or the one with six icy steps. I choose the latter and am greeted by a young woman, one of the students who lives with Rudi. She takes me to Rudi's study located on the lower level of the house. Smells of chicken soup pervade the inside, which is quiet yet seemingly filled with activity.

As I descend the steps into Rudi's quarters, I immediately see a blazing gas fire burning in the fireplace and a cream-colored wrap-around couch sitting in front of it. It matches the cream-colored sculpted carpet. To one side is a comfortable, dark leather chair, which Rudi will soon occupy. On the opposite end of the room is Rudi's desk and computer. One wall is filled with books positioned with exactitude on the edges of the shelves. Before the wall is a large library-sized table that holds several file boxes all neatly arranged. He's very German, I think to myself.

As I enter his office, he immediately rises from his computer and greets me warmly and exuberantly by shaking my hand and smiling widely. Instantly I feel at home.

I first heard of Rudi from the Sisters of St. Joseph who had known him and spoken of him favorably over the years. I am curious to find out who he is because the sisters made him sound like the kind of person from which legends are made.

I have come to see Rudi to do an advance story on an adult religious education class he is offering in January at St. Thomas More, his home parish, entitled: "Why So Many

Wars: A Christian Perspective." After speaking with him for nearly two hours, not only do I decide to take his class, but I realize that he is one man I want to know more about.

Rudi is a big man with a full head of gray-white wavy hair that flops over his broad forehead and straggles at the ears and the nape of his neck. His smooth, pinkish skin bears only a few deep lines, the most prominent ones at the smile junctures. He wears a simple sweater over his white shirt and black trousers. He walks with a slight hobble and sometimes uses a cane for balance.

At 75 years old, Rudi is a professor of religion and society at Western Michigan University, where he still works full time. Every year since 1965 he has taught two six-week classes on themes pertaining to religion and contemporary society. This commitment is precipitated by his past: he was a Nazi resister before he was pressed into service as a fighter pilot, an infantryman, and later an American prisoner of war during World War II.

Religion Class

Rudi begins each class with a Scripture reading. Tonight, it's Luke's discussion of eternal life as illustrated by the Good Samaritan (Luke 10:29–32) and the Golden Rule:

> You shall love the Lord your God with all
> your heart, and with all your soul, and with all
> your strength, and with all your mind; and
> your neighbor as yourself. (Luke 10:27)

"In order to inherit eternal life," Rudi admonishes his students with the force of a wise master, "you put oil and wine into the wounds of strangers as the Good Samaritan did. Otherwise, if you make wounds, as in war, you have no chance for eternal life."

Rudi lectures with ideas and concepts spewing forth in rapid-fire from his German-accented mouth even as he keeps a relatively expressionless face. However, his words are packed with a concern for the world and the determination to expose what is going on in it.

"So many people wondered why they weren't told about what was happening in Germany in the 1930s and 40s," says Rudi. "They said that if they had known, they could have stopped the terrible things that happened there."

Rudi knows intimately what happened in Germany at that time—and in January 2003, he fears the United States might be headed in the same direction.

War Experience

In 1939 when the Nazis took over Germany, Rudi joined the Catholic Youth Movement headed up by a Roman Catholic priest, Father Georg Rudolphi. The priest who was at first pro-Nazi, became an anti-fascist when he saw the new regime beat and kill his own friends. He also became a father-figure to German youth and had a major influence on Rudi who had lost his own father when he was 11 years old.

In 1943 at the age of 15 Rudi was drafted into the German Air Force—at the point of a gun. The next day he saw his hometown, Frankfurt, fire-bombed by the allied forces. He had heard that other cities were being bombed as well, some killing 80,000 civilians in 45 minutes. He regarded this type of killing a crime and it led to his resolve to do what he could to defend German civilians in the cities. As an air force pilot, he shot down 18 allied planes.

"I do not feel guilty for shooting down 18 American planes," says Rudi. "We had a right to live and a right to defend ourselves. That is a principle of natural law. It is not the Gospel. It is one of Augustine's Seven Points of the Just War Theory."

Rudi tells me about the American veterans he met recently in Grand Rapids, Michigan, 50 years after the war. Some of them were involved in those bombing raids on German cities.

"When we talked about our war experiences, many of the men embraced me and wept," he says in a matter of fact way. "I think those things should come into the open if we want to finish war—the nonsense and meaninglessness of it."

The most striking thing about Rudi is that he is not bitter, embarrassed or shy talking about his experiences of war or religion or politics. Rather, his experiences make him more dogged than ever to engage others in discourse.

Rudi does not claim to be a pacifist, rather, he says he's "specific from war to war" citing that the United States has been involved in over 20 wars since 1945. That's why he keeps a peace pole at his home because, he says, after one war ends he knows there will be another. "If we only talk about the glory of war, we can't do something about it, huh? If the next generation hears about the horror and terror of war, then maybe we can change it and oppose it."

In late 1944 when the German Air Force ceased to exist, Rudi trained as an infantry lieutenant for the Russian Front. "That is why I am not afraid of the cold," says Rudi who wears only a sweater, even on a cold Michigan winter night. But he and his men never made it to the Russian Front. Instead, on their way there, they ran into General George Patton's tank division in a small town near Frankfurt. Seventeen-year-old Rudi led 250 men in a three-week battle. He survived but most of his men did not.

"Every year for fifty years after the war I visited the cemetery where the men were buried," says Rudi. "Their helmets were put on top of their gravestones and held by wire." Many villagers continued to visit the graves, too, until the cemetery was plowed under to make way for a park in 2002.

After this battle with Patton, Rudi was captured and made a prisoner of war. Eventually he was sent to Camp Allen in Norfolk, Virginia, his first trip to the United States.

On his way to a prison camp through Europe he remembers riding in a stuffy freight car. It stopped in Marseilles and when he poked his head out of a hole to get some air, an angry crowd outside threw stones at the car. One of the stones knocked him out cold.

When he regained consciousness, a Protestant minister on the train gave him some water, the last drops of water he had in his canteen.

"This has always made me feel friendly toward Protestants," says Rudi who had grown up only around Catholics. "I thought it was heroic. From this experience on, I became an ecumenist."

Soon after he arrived at Camp Allen, the war was declared over. As part of the peace effort, political science professors from Harvard and Yale trained POWs like Rudi in democracy education so that they could re-democratize Germany once they returned home.

In Germany, Rudi studied theology, philosophy, history and critical theory of society at the famous Frankfurt School. While still in Germany, he became a teacher and professor and later taught at St. Agnes College and Loyola College in Baltimore, Maryland. In 1965 he came to Kalamazoo to become a professor at Western Michigan University where he has focused on studying, writing and teaching classes about religion and society.

His class at St. Thomas More Student Parish has particular relevance on the Monday nights in January 2003 as the United States faces possible war with Iraq. Rudi wants to help his fellow parishioners understand war from a Catholic perspective "because that is the basis upon which we profess our faith."

Rules of War

One of the important lessons Rudi teaches is that war has rules—and that the West has followed these rules for the past 1,600 years. The rules of war were first articulated by St. Augustine (A.D. 354–430) who attempted to answer the questions "When is it permissible to wage war" (*jus in bello*), and "What are the limitations in the ways we wage war?" (*jus ad bellum*). Rudi gives a short history on how these rules came to be.

In 387 A.D. after Constantine made Christianity the state religion of the Roman Empire, the Christians, who had been enemies of Rome, suddenly became allies of the state. "This was the same state that had executed Jesus and hundreds of his friends centuries before!" he says.

As citizens of Rome, Christians had to deal with questions of war and Augustine tackled the problem by formulating his famous "Just War Theory." For Augustine, war was a logical extension of governance which was ordained by God, according to St. Paul in Romans 13:1–7. Leaders entrusted with the responsibility of governance, were answerable to God because they were responsible for the welfare of their people. When it came to war, the leaders could only commit their people if the war were morally justifiable. Augustine said such a war had to meet three conditions. First, a nation must have legitimate authority to declare war. Secondly, the aggressor-nation must take care not to hurt non-combatants or civilians. Third, a nation must consider a proportional means to achieve its goal. Even though these rules of war have been layed out, Christians have been waging war through the centuries, says Rudi—in truth, Augustine's Just War Theory runs counter to

Jesus' Sermon on the Mount, which preaches that we love our enemies.

This alliance between the church and state begun with Constantine, has resulted in the church's "horrible history of war, which we try to forget by re-interpreting the text," says Rudi. Hitler, for example, reinterpreted the text with the 1933 Concordat, a treaty he made with the Vatican in which he guaranteed the Church's right to regulate its own affairs in Germany while he proclaimed that Christianity was "the basis of our collective morals," the family, and "the kernel of our people."

Applying Just War principles to the twentieth century has become "very murky" says Rudi, because today's wars may involve weapons of mass destruction and they often include genocidal violence against civilians. Even so, for all his study and experience of war, Rudi admits that the ultimate paradox about war is: "All wars are bad even if sometimes some wars may be necessary." So, why so many wars? Rudi offers his students some explanations.

Economically, we fight over scarce resources. Culturally, we have movies that glorify war and killing. Psychologically, we have a death instinct "as if there were something biologically wrong with us."

"Even wolves have an instinct to stop fighting when it is clear that one wolf is vulnerable and defeated," says Rudi. "He opens his neck to the other wolf and the aggressor doesn't bite. We human beings don't have a mechanism within us to be against war—except the Sermon on the Mount."

Rudi also contends that religion has also been the source of much violence and war. "And when religion fails, what does that leave us?" The state with its laws and secular morality is one means of averting violence and war. International controls like the Geneva Convention, the United Nations, and NATO are institutions that foster restraint and discourse, the necessary vehicles to avert war. These institutions are rooted in the ideas and ideologies of the Enlightenment of the seventeenth and eighteenth centuries when modernism was born. But, says Rudi, these days even these institutions are losing their effectiveness.

Modernism

Modernism began when the bourgeois class emerged as the ruling class during the Enlightenment, thus superseding the Church and the monarchy. The European bourgeoisie were urban middle class merchants, financiers and intellectuals, as differentiated from the aristocratic, Church, or peasant (agricultural) classes.

As mercantilism took hold during the age of exploration and colonialism, society gradually became more secularized and science replaced religion as the primary way of constructing knowledge and reality. Knowledge and reality could be observed and puzzled out by anyone rather than only by a king or a priest—just as the Protestant Reformation allowed ordinary, non-clerical people to interpret the Scriptures. Science became the source for Truth rather than faith, superstition or obedience to an authority. Scientific rationalism provided a systematized decision-making process of critical analysis rather than inspiration or royal decree. These elements made straight the way toward mechanization and the industrial revolution when the machine became the new hegemon.

Government and economics adopted the scientific method, too, and saw society like a clock, the prevailing image of the Enlightenment, a device that is mechanical, measured and constant. Indeed, the framers of the U.S. Constitution and our Founding Fathers were all members of the bourgeois class. They used the principles of modernism to create a just society where everyone had an equal chance to "life, liberty, and the pursuit of happiness."

By the twentieth century, however, modernism's influence on Western society is one of fragmentation, complexity, technological advancement and economics. Urban lifestyles overtake rural lifestyles, which impact people's values and mindsets. The family also begins to disintegrate, communities become more impersonal and transient, and all the values associated with small town life and agriculture are replaced increasingly by a society that resembles a machine with its values of speed, mechanization, mass production, uniformity, atomization, and specialization. The bourgeois class then invents organizations to run society. These became known as corporations but there are other developments that emerge with this new, corporate, technological society.

As more and more people stream into the cities in greater numbers, ideas about tolerance surface, minorities and women win the full rights of citizenship, unions work to provide people a decent living, and education becomes available to all people as a right. The poor and infirm are taken care of by the state courtesy of such visionaries of the time as Franklin D. Roosevelt's New Deal and Adolf Hitler's Third Reich.

Rudi says that the 21st century is now seeing its bourgeois values and structures disintegrate before our very eyes—and there is nothing to replace them. The fundamental categories that we use to describe our lives and understand ourselves are no longer there. There is a lack of consistency, even in the language used. Here are some examples:

> * "Donald Rumsfeld says that he was taught in school never to attack other countries, but now he says that today is different and so he is planning a pre-emptive strike against Iraq. They are playing language games that they learned in the university. Actually, it's the Constitution that says we cannot conduct a pre-

emptive strike, but the watchmen are not there—the Congress and the Supreme Court who should challenge the president."

* "We pray for our heroic soldiers that they will keep out of harm's way. Yet, they use murderous weapons to kill other people."

* "We have our soldiers bomb civilians to pieces and then pray [our enemies] don't bomb us. This will weaken any moral existence!"

* "People say today: 'I trust my president.' Well, people trusted Hitler, too, some until the end of the war, even with rubble all around them."

* "We can't have a war against terrorism because the terrorists are not a state. So we attack a state. The first one was Afghanistan. Now we plan to attack Iraq. After that, we plan to attack Iran. Meanwhile, the object of terrorism, Osama bin Laden, is still at large."

The new world order that George H.W. Bush proclaimed after the fall of communism in the late 1980s has become the "new world dis-order," according to Rudi. And a possible war with Iraq will make that "dis-order" even more evident as members of bourgeois institutions are even more shaken, split or impotent.

"Once you break open the system, all the structures fall," says Rudi. "Bourgeois society is crumbling. There is no opposition party to replace it. Not even a new paradigm can do that. Consequently, in its absence what will we get? Germany in the 1930s got fascism." What the United States gets remains to be seen but some people already believe that we have inadvertently adopted a national security state where the checks and balances provided by our Constitution are ignored, the opposition party has been silenced, elections are fixed, and the Bill of Rights is compromised—all in the name of fighting terrorism. How did this happen to the most free, most powerful, most diverse nation in the world's history?

Core of the Problem

Modernity, itself, is one major reason for the "disintegration of the bourgeois brain," as Rudi calls it. It has come about because of the split between religion and secular society. Modernity emphasizes autonomy while it simultaneously promotes solidarity. An unfortunate consequence of this split is confusion over truth, especially when the search for truth leads to antagonisms, as we see among the major political, social, and economic factions today.

"How can you love your neighbor, as Jesus tells us, if you cannot see him?" Rudi asks bringing the issue to local land use policies that encourage local people to leave the cities and sprawl out in the country far out of sight of their neighbors. "It is an extreme autonomy at work here," he says. In fact, all of life has become "atomized" or separated down to its smallest parts. It is a consequence of machine-like thinking. The result is a disconnection among the parts and the people who are unable to feel solidarity with a larger whole, be it a family, a neighborhood, a country, or the world.

This breakdown comes from "discourse avoidance," says Rudi. People are simply not talking to each other. This can only lead to more isolation, the breakdown of communities and in its extreme, war among nations—or as the terrorists have shown, war with individuals against nations.

"Modern civil society is atomistic," says Rudi. "It has autonomy, but it has no solidarity, except maybe in catastrophes and shortly afterwards."

Rudi contrasts the unity of America and the world after the September 11 attacks. Eighteen months later, the world is rife with division between America and Europe, between the American people and their government, and between Americans.

Atomistic thinking has torn us apart from our religion, too, says Rudi. For example, when we pray the Lord's prayer and ask for our daily bread, we are confronted directly with the problem of modern society: our bread is mediated through the capitalist owners, workers, and supermarket chains rather than from our own hands. God, then, disappears.

"Modernism makes all religious activities complicated," says Rudi. "We get disconnected from nature as well as the processes that provide us with the most basic human need: food. Then, what we hold on to in order to keep our religious identity are the social antagonisms like the wars between religions, the sexes, the races, the classes, the individual and the group."

"September 11 radically opened up and deepened the antagonism between religion and the secular, the sacred and the profane, monotheism and modernity, faith and enlightenment," says Rudi. "The attackers represented religion but their target was the World Trade Center and the Pentagon, the financial and military centers of the most secular capitalist nation in world civilization!"

Osama bin Laden represents religion fighting modernity. Bin Laden, who lived for many years in Boston, perceived American women to be loose and the cause of failed marriages. He blamed this phenomenon on modernity as another outcome of the break from religion and the emphasis on the secular. To bin Laden, religion is integral to Muslim identity, a characteristic that he wants to preserve. However, the tension over religion and secularism has been aroused in our own country and not just in the Middle East. We witness the rise of fundamentalism, among the fastest growing religions in America, while progressive, mainstream religions continue to lose membership. Rudi calls this phenomenon the "theodicy problem." Indeed, the mainstream religions are united in their opposition to war with Iraq on religious grounds while many fundamentalist religions support the war. Bush, a fundamentalist, became their champion.

The "theodicy problem" addresses God's justice and identifies him as a vengeful God. It asks such questions as: Are we sick because of sin? Why did Job have to suffer the tests of his faith? Did six million Jews die because they were sinful? Rudi notes that this latter idea was Hitler's belief and justification for the genocide of the Jews even though the rich enterprising Jews who ran the banks had already fled Europe.

Bringing the question closer to home, Rudi says the "theodicy problem" asks: Who was being tested when 200,000 people died from the atomic bombs dropped on Hiroshima and Nagasaki in 1945? He points out that the American pilots who dropped the bombs each had different reactions in the aftermath: one went insane, one committed suicide, one joined a Trappist monastery where he took a vow of silence. Only one remained unphased by his action and even prided himself in it.

Then the "theodicy problem" asks the most basic question: What kind of God allowed Jesus to be crucified? Was it the vengeful God, the Old Testament God of the *Talion* (the "eye for eye" code of law) or the loving father-god of Jesus in the New Testament?

"Jesus brought the Kingdom of God and all that came was an institution, the Church," says Rudi, who remains a weekly communicant in the Catholic Church even though he is highly critical of it and its priesthood.

"Jesus had no 'theodicy problem,'" says Rudi, "because Jesus didn't believe that bad things happened to people because of sin. Bad things just happened. What should we do when bad things happen? Luke describes it in the action of the Good Samaritan: we put wine and oil on the other's wounds. And when disagreement leads us to the brink of violence and destruction, Jesus says that what we must do lies in the Golden Rule: 'Do unto others as you would have them do unto you.'"

For nations in conflict, the only tool available to resolve conflict is discourse. Keeping the discourse going is preferable to avoiding it. The U.N. inspections and the resolutions provided time for discourse in the run-up to war with Iraq. A collective solution among the nations would have been best. However, when President Bush said that the U.N. was "irrelevant," he caused a breakdown in discourse, says Rudi.

"The ultimate consequence of 'discourse avoidance' is immeasurable human suffering," says Rudi. "That is bad enough, but the all-pervasive knee-jerk reaction of *Lex Talionis*, the Law of Retaliation and Retribution, further separates people from each other. And when nationalism is combined with *Lex Talionis*," which Rudi fears the most, "you have a recipe for disaster."

Rudi's first experience of nationalism was in Hitler's Germany in the 1930s, but it emerged during the Yugoslav wars in the 1990s, too. Now he thinks the United States is going the way of nationalism, another victim of "discourse avoidance." The American refusal to regulate a dispute permeates all levels of our society and the world today. As a result, the problem then "goes deeper into the death zone."

America the Superpower

During the early 1990s, the United States found itself as the only remaining superpower in the world with the capability of unilaterally waging war against Iraq or any nation, has presented some predicaments, says Rudi, especially as millions of people from around the world have advocated for peace. Unilateral war against Iraq signaled a radical shift in American foreign policy and values, even though the administration tried to paint the situation as a coalition. America has traditionally pursued a multilateral or "cosmopolitan" relationship with its allies. This approach to foreign affairs includes gathering with our allies, consulting them, engaging in diplomatic and cooperative arrangements, and showing respect for differing interests.

After the September 11 attack on the World Trade Center and the Pentagon, it appeared as though the president would continue this "cosmopolitan" approach, observed Rudi. "It didn't look as though he were going the route of *Lex Talionis*. Instead, Bush formulated a policy change in our dealings with terrorists."

The war against Iraq represents a nationalistic agenda, says Rudi. Nationalism emphasizes American interests over the interest of allies. It carries such messages as "right or wrong, my country" and "my country—love it or leave it."

"Cosmopolitanism is what made the United States great and a much-loved nation," says Rudi. "America's turn away from it has led to a wave of anti-Americanism in Europe—and around the world." Cosmopolitanism is a kind of international law that makes governments accountable for war crimes. Expressions of this approach surfaced after World War II at the Nuremberg and Tokyo trials, when German and Japanese war criminals were prosecuted.

American cosmopolitanism emerged after the war when the United States became a dominant nation acting with its allies to contain the opposing superpower, the Soviet Union. Even after the break-up of the Soviet empire in 1989, the United States, as the remaining superpower, continued to work cooperatively with its allies. President Bush's father formed a coalition to execute the Gulf War in 1991. President Clinton continued to use coalitions throughout the 1990s when he called on other European nations to help stop the wars in the former Yugoslavia. However, something changed in America to make pre-emptive, unilateral war against Iraq a viable option, says Rudi. It started with the Nixon administration (1969–74) as the United States engaged in numerous invasions of places like Chile, Nicaragua, Panama. It continued in the Reagan administration (1981–89) when it traded arms to Nicaraguan Contras for the American hostages in Iran. It continued throughout the 1990s as the globalization of capitalism strengthened U.S. nationalism.

"I've never seen a healthy nationalist state anywhere in the world," says Rudi referring to Hitler's fascism in Germany as well as the "horrible wars" in the former Yugoslavia that were fought in the name of "ethnic cleansing." He has first-hand knowledge of the nationalist mania that gripped the people in Dubrovnik, Croatia in 1991 and continued in civil war for 10 years. Since 1975 he has spent his summers there working on a critical theory of religion with his international religion and society colleagues. Over the past decade he has seen his Croatian friends become nationalists.

"There is no justification for outrageous crimes and inhumanities that are produced by fascism, nationalism, racism or patriotism. One cannot condone the nationalism or racism of one nation or praise that of another," he says in his 2003 letter to the Dubrovnik conference membership. Rudi abhors and fears nationalism and racism and asserts that it should be rejected as a "source of the most outrageous evil."

One of the attractions of nationalism is that it sounds so sincere, says Rudi. It provides explanations while it instigates fear. Hitler, for example, had a justification for the slaughter of the Jews, Slavs, gypsies, communists, gays, and mentally ill people—and he continually identified with God in all these actions. However, it is hypocritical for us to condemn Hitler for his evil, which was rooted in nationalism and racism, if we ourselves do the same.

"Once Americans get mad, they can't get un-mad," says Rudi, fearing that a war in Iraq will stimulate "nationalistic blood lust" in the American people.

Countries are especially prone to embrace nationalism when they get in trouble, says Rudi. For Germany, economic depression brought on by the Allies' punishment of that country after World War I led to the rise of Hitler. As a result, 50 million people died during World War II. Russia alone lost 26 million of its people. In World War I, the "war to end all wars," 14.5 million military and civilians died.[64] In the 1991 Gulf War and its aftermath, 100,000 Iraqis died.[65] Ten thousand civilians lost their lives during the wars in the former Yugoslavia. Now terrorists haunt humanity with a new category of war that is difficult to define and even trickier to contain.

As a result of the experience of two world wars, Europeans have become opposed to war, says Rudi. This is why they were reluctant to go into Yugoslavia—and Iraq as well. The power of modern weapons has made war for them an unthinkable alternative to peace. Besides, they know their

---

[64] Death Tolls for the Man-made Megadeaths of the Twentieth Century (www.users.erols.com/mwhite28/warstatx.htm)

[65] "In June 1991, the U.S. estimated that more than 100,000 Iraqi soldiers died, 300,000 were wounded, 150,000 deserted and 60,000 were taken prisoner. Many human rights groups claimed a much higher number of Iraqis were killed in action. According to Baghdad, civilian casualties numbered more than 35,000. However, since the war, some scholars have concluded that the number of Iraqi soldiers who were killed was significantly less than initially reported." The Americans lost 148 soldiers in battle deaths and 145 non-battle deaths. (www.cnn.com/SPECIALS/2001/gulf.war/facts/gulfwar/)

economic interests will be crippled, especially since they have big Arab populations living in their countries.

"As long as the president chooses to go it alone in Iraq, he is striking a chord for nationalism. As a result, Europeans are disappointed with America because America has betrayed its cosmopolitan approach to world politics."

Actually, Rudi sees the president mouthing cosmopolitan values while he pursues a nationalist agenda. He did this when he tied 9/11 to Saddam and Iraq, defended the USA PATRIOT Act, and actively drummed up fear in Americans with warnings like: "If you're not with us, you're against us." Rudi contends that these trends toward nationalism, the disintegration of bourgeois structures and institutions, discourse avoidance, and Just War Theory itself require a critical theory of religion. And that's just what he's been working on these past years.

A Critical Theory of Religion

Since 1975 Rudi has worked with colleagues in Dubrovnik, Croatia, on the future of religion, which aims to reconcile personal autonomy and universal solidarity. This means that they are developing a "critical theory of religion" that aims to unite religion and science in addressing the problems and issues of today's world, which include conflicting ideologies over war, the over-institutionalization of society and humanity's inherent need for community and spirituality. Since 1998 Rudi has met with colleagues in Yalta, Ukraine, in developing an international course on "Religion and Politics."

The critical theory of the new Frankfurt School, of which Rudi was trained and educated, originated after World War I when Max Horkheimer, Friedrich Pollock, Erich Fromm, Herbert Marcuse and others "tried to make sense out of the senseless war experience" says Rudi. By exploring the writings of Immanuel Kant, Friedrich W.J. Schelling, Georg W.F. Hegel, Arthur Schopenhauer, Karl Marx, Friedrich Nietzsche, Sigmund Freud and others, they "hoped to discover the philosophical, political-economical and psychological causes of World War I, and later on, the different forms of nationalism and fascism of World War II, and of the following Cold War and restoration period."

Horkheimer saw a "crisis of religion" as a result of a contradiction between religion and secular society among the German and European bourgeoisie before and during World War I. This crisis affected the youth of the time such that they were loyal to their faith, devoted to justice and equality—no matter how much they suffered the loss of privileges. Unfortunately, this position had consequences. Youth developed an aggressiveness due to a conflict between the ideal and the real worlds. This aggression showed itself throughout the nineteenth century, in the early twentieth century. Again it emerged in the 1960s and expressed itself as personal autonomy, that is, separation from community. Something else showed, too: the will began to take precedence over the intellect as well as a "continual youthfulness over the resignation, cynicism and despair of old age."

"Critical theorists are deeply impressed by the great human suffering connected with the antagonistic character of modern society," says Rudi. "Therefore, the critical theorists try to fight through the painful antagonism of civil society toward an identity change after which it will no longer reproduce itself through a war of everybody against everybody nationally and internationally."

Rudi and his colleagues are looking for a new approach to society where personal autonomy and universal solidarity can be reconciled. The key to this reconciliation is discourse. For example, Habermas saw religion as a system of interpretation of reality and orientation of action. Religion is part of the "life world" that has a communicative quality and is steered by ethical and moral norms. In the twentieth century, economics and politics have been separated by the "life world" which is why protest movements (civil rights, feminism, labor, peace, anti-nuclear) emerged against the state's exclusive hold over power and money.

"These movements try to generate communicative power against administrative power, in so far as they tend to violate the 'life world' of the people in terms of a one-sided application of instrumental rationality," says Rudi.

With emphasis on the difference between "good" religion, which demands attention to these issues of the "life world," and "bad" religion, which maintains the status quo without the consideration of justice, Rudi and his colleagues also attempt to explore the dichotomy between religion and secularism where religion has lost its credibility against the scientific and political ideas fostered by the modern world of the Enlightenment thinkers. As such they have stressed a "religion of liberation against a religion of domination." A religion of liberation discusses the points missed by the hierarchical church that is more concerned with maintaining the institution and its structures than in providing guidance and inspiration for its followers who include the growing numbers of the poor, the down-trodden, the worker classes and the dominated.

Rudi and his colleagues have identified three possible futures or responses to these problems of the modern world. The first future is a retreat to fundamentalism out of disgust for modernity. The second future is the total secularization of society. The third and preferred future is reconciliation between religion and modernity.

This split between religion and modernity must and can be healed in two ways. The first way is to let the split heal itself, as will eventually happen. The second way is to insert religious themes into modern scientific themes where people work "toward a friendly living together." They create something new to address the world's problems of war, community, the over-institutionalization of society and spirituality. This effort is all aimed at concentrating and understanding what it means to be human. In this, Rudi again turns to Jesus as a guide: follow the Golden Rule.

And so when Rudi's students ask: what can we do to prevent a war in Iraq, Rudi provides a long and passionate answer: "Speak up. Point out the inconsistencies you hear people say. And do the enlightenment work. Why does it have to be that we have winners and losers? (or to use Hitler's terms, the predators and the prey.) When people fail to question what is going on, they become silenced. There will be no peace among the nations without peace among the world religions. There will be no peace among the world religions without discourse among them. There will be no discourse among the world religions without knowledge about their substantial teachings. Only the world religions and world humanisms together can form a world ethos, which will have a chance to resist successfully the worst disease of humankind: war. No matter how powerless we may feel sometimes we all are competent speakers. Out of faith and scientific knowledge we can speak to people and we can enlighten them about the meaninglessness of war and its causes and about ways to eliminate them."

Rudi and his colleagues hope to find a way to stitch together autonomy and solidarity that are behind the split between religion and science in order to reshape a global sort of morality. The search, they predict, will come from religion, which is the basis of all morality for solidarity and for autonomy.

For the sake of peace in the world, we can only hope that they succeed.

Shalom!!! Irenae!!! Pax!!! Friede!!! Peace!!!

BOB AND ELLY NAGLER
Activists for Peace

Elly and Bob Nagler grew up an ocean apart but their commitment to peace eventually brought them together and has continued to strengthen them during their 50-year marriage.

The couple exudes the beauty of a peace-filled life in their home, their world view and in the globally-conscious lives they lead. They are both introverted and unassuming, short and slight of figure. Bob's gray hair is thick and wavy and Elly's is short and thin. Bob speaks with an Iowa accent and Elly with a Viennese one. Neither of them stands out, particularly; you might even miss seeing them at the peace vigils, but they're there—every week, twice a week. And there is no mistaking their devotion to the cause of peace and the depth from which it comes in all that they do and say.

We sit in the Biedermeier Room, as they call the library of their home. It was named after the nineteenth-century table, chairs and chest of drawers they acquired from Elly's family in her native Austria. The bourgeois furniture style was popular during 1815–48, the same period as the Congress of Vienna, the world's first major peace conference that re-drew the map of Europe into nation-states and averted war for 65 years. Unfortunately, that Congress failed to anticipate the negative power of nationalism in its expanding and unquenchable thirst for land, capital and resources. Some people have attributed nationalism as the single-most contributing factor leading to World War I.

An odd-shaped, multi-colored vase sits on the Biedermeier table. It's a gift from Panamanian university students the Naglers hosted in the early 1990s. (One of the students later became the science advisor to his country's representative to the United Nations.) The students liked to visit the Naglers and they were especially interested in their 1962–64 slides of Nigeria when Bob participated in a USAID science-training program through WMU. Bob found it to be "the most fulfilling than anything I ever did." He worked with the top five percent of all students in a country that was so poor that one light bulb might serve 20 people. Most of the time students lacked adequate books or supplies and had to share what little they had.

"All the students were exceedingly motivated and highly intelligent," says Bob. "They all worked very hard, around 15 hours a day, because they knew that college was their only chance for a better life." Various Nigerian art works reminiscent of the Naglers' time in that country decorate their airy ranch home, which is surrounded by woods and gardens that make their home a welcome, calm and peaceful refuge to visitors and wildlife alike.

As we talk, we munch on *manner-schnitten*, special Austrian lemon- and hazelnut-flavored wafer cookies, and sip fresh elderberry juice the Naglers have just made from flowers soaked in water with sugar and citric acid.

"Bob is more Austrian than I am," quips Elly, who was born in London, England, but whose family hails from a small town near Salzburg. The couple has made countless trips back to her native land, which has helped shape their global view of the world. But their interests and sensitivities for peace that have occupied them over their lifetimes originated by the example of both their fathers who saw the destructive vagaries of World War I as a good reason to end all war—forever.

Bob grew up in Iowa City, the son of a famous hydraulics engineer who consulted on the Hoover Dam and several Mississippi River projects. Within 16 years he was awarded three professional medals for his research. In his career he always sought to make the world a better place, says Bob. Likewise, as a peace activist for the Methodist church he wanted to rid the world of war and to promote nonviolence as a peaceful solution.

In 1933 Bob attended the Epworth League's[66] summer youth camp on Clear Lake, Iowa. The theme that year focused on peace and the Oxford Pledge.[67] The children learned that the pledge was derived from the world's first peace movement started in England during the late 1920's and early 1930s as a response to the disastrous global conflict, World War I (1914– 1918).

Half of the 200 kids at the conference signed the pledge, Bob among them. Part of the reason the peace pledge "stuck with him" was that less than three months after he made it, his father died leaving the 10-year old and two siblings, ages three and seven, with his 32-year old mother. The pledge became his father's legacy to him.

"My father was my hero," says Bob who sought to remember him by emulating him. "I made the commitment to take any opportunity I could to be a part of a Christian peace movement." Eventually, as a teenager, he became a Quaker. Bob had good reason to be attracted to the Quakers. His

---

[66] The Epworth League is a Southern Methodist religious education program for youth formed in 1889 in Cleveland, Ohio, "to help develop godliness and loyalty to God and our Church among the young people," according to its website. It was the first denominational youth ministry in the history of the Christian Church. It typically met on Sunday nights. The name, Epworth, originated from the British boyhood home in of John Wesley, the founder of the Methodist movement. (www.southernmethodistchurch.org/id48.htm).

[67] Students at Oxford University in England had taken a "pledge" that they would "not fight for king and country" as their fathers had in World War I. That war had seen millions of men die on the battlefield for "nothing more than a lie," according to William L. Anderson of Frostburg State University in Maryland on his website: www.lewrockwell.com/anderson/anderson65.html.

father first became acquainted with them through the Cedar River flood control project in Iowa. The Quakers lived lives of peace and nonviolence and they helped people in need, like Bob's mother after his father's death. Bob also got to know the Quakers personally by working on their farms in the summer and then by deciding to attend William Penn College in Iowa.

In 1943, while in the middle of his junior year in college, Bob was drafted into the Army. However, because of his Conscientious Objector status, he was assigned to a Civilian Public Service (CPS) base camp in North Dakota under the direction of the Quakers. The summer before his induction he worked for the American Friends Service Committee in Mexico. He also volunteered for a starvation experiment in Minnesota, which didn't work out, and an infectious hepatitis project at the Pennsylvania Hospital in Philadelphia, which did. He worked under the direction of the U.S. Surgeon General and one of his colleagues, the senior physician and future U.S. Surgeon General, C. Everett Koop.

Because many of Bob's friends were in the war putting their lives on the line, including four of them who died because of illness, he, too, put his own life on the line when he volunteered as a human "guinea pig" in a hepatitis project. As a result, he contracted a mild case of hepatitis that would change his life once more. After he recovered, the CPS indicated that it needed people with science backgrounds for a project and asked Bob to stay an additional 18 months, which he did, until 1946. He discovered he loved chemistry and had a knack for research, so he went to graduate school at the University of Missouri and later at the University of Iowa for his Ph.D. "I changed my career objectives," says Bob who had planned to be a high school chemistry teacher. His first job as a chemistry professor took him to Purdue University. However, in 1956 he was tapped to start a graduate program at

Western Michigan College in Kalamazoo, which was in the process of becoming a university. He was just 33 years old.

In 1952 Bob and Elly met serendipitously in Iowa. Elly had completed her degree in Russian literature and history at the University of Vienna and had come to the United States at the invitation of an American girlfriend she made during vacation in Holland. She married Bob a year later and they would have four daughters and one son. In 1957 after Sputnik, Western Michigan University wanted to incorporate Russian language into its curriculum and Elly was able to oblige. Her native German language abilities came in handy as well.

Like Bob's father, Elly's father had converted to pacifism as a result of his experience as a Bavarian soldier and French prisoner of war during World War I. The war had bid him to kill, which dashed his hopes to become a priest when he returned. "He had blood on his hands," says Elly, "and didn't feel he could be a priest." He became a writer and a peace organizer for the International Fellowship of Reconciliation (IFOR), a newly-formed non-governmental inter-faith organization. IFOR was the first organization of its kind in the world to be committed to peaceful nonviolence. He served as secretary at IFOR's London headquarters and it was during this time that Elly was born.

IFOR recognized that divisions among peoples occurred mostly through conflict and violence between nation states. Founded in 1919 as a response to World War I, IFOR has consistently stood against war and in favor of healing and reconciliation. According to its website (www.ifor.org), "the founders of IFOR formulated a vision of the human community based upon the belief that love in action has the power to transform unjust political, social, and economic structures." Elly's father established a branch office for IFOR in Vienna and operated from there until 1938 when Hitler took over Bavaria. During the war, however, virtually all his work stopped. After the war as Europe rebuilt itself, her father re-established IFOR as well. Today it flourishes with a presence in more than 40 countries.

Elly's sister, Hildegard Goss-Mayr, later took over her father's work at IFOR and became an international figure advocating peaceful, nonviolent approaches to settling disputes among peoples and nations. A prolific writer and speaker, the Second Vatican Council asked for Hildegard's input for its important encyclical, *Pacem en Terris*. (Peace on Earth). She also conducted training programs on nonviolence in Latin America, Africa and Asia and served as a consultant to leaders like Cory Aquino of the Philippines. As a result of her work, Elly's sister was nominated for the Nobel Peace Prize three times. Twenty years ago Kalamazoo College honored her with an honorary doctoral degree.

"I was not as committed to peace work as my sister," says Elly modestly who spent much of her time raising her family and being a support to Bob. "But I learned about situations in the world through my sister." In comparison to her father and her sister, Elly doesn't consider herself a peace activist, but rather an "agitator" for change. "I'm just a human being," she says. "We should have a responsibility for each other and do all we can to make the world a better place." She thinks that the only way to settle conflict is through nonviolence and living up to our possibilities and helping other people. "We're all brothers and sisters. We have to be there for each other," she says.

In reality, Elly's no slouch when it comes to peace activism. In 1947 she joined the Quaker youth work camp movement in Austria, Sweden, Mexico and El Salvador to help rebuild houses in villages and to provide assistance in refugee camps that harbored Russians, Germans and Ukrainians. "I lost half of my heart in El Salvador," says Elly. It's probably one of the reasons the Naglers were so active in the Sanctuary movement in the mid-1980s when they helped harbor a Salvadoran family.

While the Naglers may seem to lead unassuming lives, their voices for peace and justice are unmistakable. Much of the way they see the world is couched in their experience of World War II. For example, they have difficulty with the Bush Doctrine, which is based on many of the tenets of the Project for the New American Century's (PNAC) advocacy of aggressive, pre-emptive unilateralism. They also have difficulty with the Bush team's penchant for equating Saddam with Hitler, 9/11 with Pearl Harbor and other allusions to World War II.

"Historically, the United States has been reluctant to go to war," says Bob. "In both world wars, we had to be pulled into it politically. The Bush Doctrine bypasses that tradition— dangerously so. My feeling is that Reagan and his team (Cheney, Rumsfeld, Wolfowitz and Perle) *made* Saddam in order to keep the Middle East revolution going his way."

"Saddam didn't want to conquer the world," says Elly. "He was not a good Muslim either. Saddam was concerned about his own position and the Kurds had given him trouble in that. So he took extreme measures to take care of them."

"World War II was an unjust consequence of World War I," says Bob. "It put Europe into economic cataclysm and hopelessness. Saddam did not quite have that kind of motivation as Hitler did, however. For him it was an internal quest for dominance over the Sunnis, Shiites and Kurds. Hitler had worldwide aspirations and he was psychologically crazy. Saddam never reached that state."

Bob also believes that Bush used September 11 as a justification for the war in Iraq and Al Qaeda's declaration of war on the U.S. It was the same tactic President Harry S. Truman used with Pearl Harbor to justify the bombing of Hiroshima and Nagasaki. "Over 200,000 people died in the blasts in Japan," he says. "How many will die in Iraq? Already 20,000 people have been killed" [by summer 2004].

"9/11 helped Bush pursue the plans he had already made to invade Iraq," says Elly. "His father didn't finish the job in 1991, so he took advantage of 9/11 to do it." While Elly saw September 11 as "horribly devastating," she mostly feared America's retaliatory response, especially with its "explosion of patriotism." All the waving flags everywhere reminded her of Hitler's appeal to nationalistic fervor, which ultimately ended up in war. "Patriotism is overblown emotionally in this country," says Elly.

Likewise, she finds it puzzling that so many Americans were surprised that 9/11 happened at all. "People all over the world live with this kind of danger all the time." Elly believes that the Muslims felt threatened that the United States was trying to take over their corner of the world. "We don't realize that the way we have treated the Muslims has left them feeling powerless and humiliated. This is what happened in Germany after World War I. The Germans felt humiliated and then fell to Hitler."

"The Crusades are still real to the Islamic community because their religion was threatened," says Bob alluding to a time when Europe descended on the Muslims in the Middle East in a series of wars between 1095–1291. "And now that the Cold War is over, the United States, as the only remaining superpower, feels it can tell the world what to do. This is sad. We could have been a powerful force to do good things."

☮

The Naglers have been showing up every Sunday and Tuesday for the peace vigils at the Federal Building since October 2002. However, they are not always comfortable with the Kalamazoo peace movement, which they see becoming more politicized as the 2004 elections near. They prefer to stick with the moral and Christian issue that war is wrong and immoral.

"Now most of the protest signs are political," says Bob pointing to messages like: "Bush lied" and "Down with Bush." The signs should instead read: "War is murder" and "Nonviolence can win" and "Peace is the way. The political environment is getting more and more nasty. These days people are reacting to half-truths and missed truths."

"Nonviolence gives us hope in the future and it can help convert the people who drive by and see the signs," says Elly confidently.

I ask the Naglers about their hopes and fears for the world, given their experience and long history of peace advocacy. Their responses are equivocal.

"I fear that Kerry may be just as bad as Bush," says Bob immediately.[68] "His acceptance speech at the convention was upsetting as it stressed the military position that 'no one is going to tell us what to do.' I also see us flitting into the direction of the Religious Right with a march to Armageddon moving the world to hatred. We're heading down an awful black hole. Military violence provokes more violence." (He points out that this message would make another good sign for the peace vigils.) Despite his bleak view, Bob remains hopeful. "Human beings are God's creatures who have the capacity to wake up to the light—eventually. If they have enough chance to think about it, there is hope."

"You can never give up on hope," says Elly, who has seen the total devastation of cities in her youth—twice, with two world wars. She points out that Austria lost almost all of its Jews in Hitler's genocidal campaign of "the final solution." Vienna now has a holocaust monument dedicated to hope. The Cardinal there regularly leads a candlelight march through

---

[68] This interview took place the summer before the 2004 election and just after the Democratic National Convention.

the city as a sign of hope for its 95 percent Catholic population. "However, anti-Semitism is beginning to rise again," says Elly who remains skeptical of her Catholic faith because the Church gets so bogged down by the Just War Theory[69] and allows nations to make a case for war all too frequently

Bob dreams that the United Nations will evolve into the meaningful peace organization it was meant to be. "A lot of what we are doing is threatening the U.N. out of its existence," he says referring to the United States' refusal to pay its dues and the world's refusal to do something about situations like Rwanda where one million people were killed. "I'm not discouraged or encouraged about the world's situation," he says pointing out that there are now hundreds of organizations all over the world working for peace, educating people, and publishing books on peace. "Some of this will rub off. Peace activists are responding to those who make war more readily. They know that violence escalates itself and they want to stop it. They realize that other people have rights and opinions and that peace is a constructive activity."

"But we Americans and Europeans need to come off of our superiority complex," says Elly. "We need to realize that human beings have value. We take it for granted that total inequality exists because we don't know how to go about making a world where we see people as our equals. This will take much education."

Despite the glints of hope that they see in the world's darkness, the Naglers continue to do what they can do to uphold their pledge of nonviolence in the world. For one thing, Bob writes a monthly letter to Rep. Fred Upton to convey his concerns about the war in Iraq "just to keep Fred aware because he doesn't have contact with European attitudes

---

[69] For a definition of the Just War Theory, *see* pages 272-273.

about the war and doesn't know how negatively they perceive the U.S." Upton always writes Bob back, but Bob is realistic enough to know that his representative in Washington will continue to support the president and his policies. Bob also writes Upton about science concerns, particularly those on the environment and stem cell research. After eight years on the Kalamazoo Environmental Council, as well as his membership in the Environmental Defense Council, the Union of Concerned Scientists and Physicians for Social Responsibility, Bob knows his own expertise and experience can help shape the congressman's positions.

What keeps the Naglers going after all these years? That's easy, they say: the consistency of their actions for peace and their concern about the world. "You can make an impact on the world with your persistence in doing what you think is right," says Bob. "It is symbolic of your conviction." Sometimes other people notice your effort, too, says Elly, and they support it, like when the passing cars honk their horns in approval at the peace vigil. "It is satisfying to you and makes you feel good."

ROB AND AMY ANDERSON
Everyday Servants for Peace

Amy Anderson's journey as a peace advocate was quite unanticipated. The petite, always smiling, always positive, wife and mother decided to go back to college in 1972 to pick up where she left off before she married Rob in 1948. She took a philosophy course at WMU, which stimulated her thinking and gave her an opportunity to talk about the philosophical issues of the day. And there were a lot of issues at that time: the Vietnam War, feminism, the environmental movement, nuclear weapons, and the changing configurations of the family.

Things began to change for her, however, when her class attended a talk by Peace Pilgrim, the original cross-country walker for the cause of peace.

"I was so inspired and overwhelmed by her," Amy says, "that I asked the woman next to me, my classmate, if we shouldn't invite Peace Pilgrim to lunch. She agreed and the three women met at the Anderson home for a lunch of scrambled eggs and green grapes. Throughout the afternoon they talked about Peace Pilgrim's adventures as a walker, how she got started walking and ways she spread peace from one person to another. At the conclusion of their visit, Amy offered Peace Pilgrim a bunch of grapes to carry with her, but she refused saying that she didn't carry food with her. Amy then offered Peace Pilgrim a ride to her next location, Allegan, 40 minutes away, partially by freeway. Peace Pilgrim usually avoided walking on freeways so she accepted Amy's offer, but only as far as the freeway exit to M-89 in Otsego.

"She got out of the car, thanked me and walked on her way. I never saw her again," says Amy fondly. "Peace Pilgrim affected my life a great deal. She was a blessing to me. I thought that if she could affect others like she affected me, then her life was a blessing to the United States and the world."

As we talk around the kitchen table, Amy shows me her paperback copy about Peace Pilgrim, which portrays a half-length portrait of the woman. Her face alone instantly draws me in and intrigues me how a single individual could to promote peace in the world—by walking. Amy handles her book reverently. She points to a quote on the back cover: "I shall remain a wanderer until mankind has learned the way of peace, walking until given shelter and fasting until given food." This was Peace Pilgrim's motivation that led her on a 25,000-mile journey during the last 28 years of her life.

"Actually, Peace Pilgrim's philosophy was rather simple," says Amy as she opened the book and read from the inside cover page: "This is the way of peace: overcome evil with good, and falsehood with truth, and hatred with love." Amy closes the book, heaves a sigh and shuts her eyes momentarily. "That's what affected my life, that woman and this statement. But I'm just an ordinary person who did what I could to make a difference," says Amy.

Ordinary, indeed. Amy grew up on a farm in Illinois and has been a Christian all her life, living by the watchword: "you reap what you sow" (Galatians 6:7–9). "I always believed in this. If you expect people to be nice to you, that extrapolates to the whole world," she says. Being nice for Amy has led her to a lifetime of service. As a wife and mother in the 50s and 60s she did all the usual things: PTA, church, hospital, Church Women United. She then assisted youth minister, Wayne Connors, for 11 years at her downtown Kalamazoo church, First Presbyterian. More recently she helped set up the walk-in health clinic there. Amy is always interested in doing different kinds of things and Peace Pilgrim took her to a new place where she could be "more brave" and less afraid of what other people thought about her activism. "Peace Pilgrim put a little starch in my spine," says Amy.

Amy's foray into the Kalamazoo peace movement occurred when she attended a Helen Caldicott film at the YWCA, then located on Rose Street, across from Bronson Park. She met different types of people she had never encountered before and she found them interesting and engaging, like Steve and Phyllis Senesi and Jack and Chris Payden-Travers, longtime friends who lived in a "commune" in the Vine Neighborhood, one of the historical districts in Kalamazoo. They were Catholics, and Steve had been in seminary for the priesthood. Amy recalled first meeting Ron Kramer in 1982 during the Nuclear Freeze petition drive when he dropped off his signed petitions at the Bread Box, a small soup and bread restaurant that later became headquarters for the Nuclear Freeze petition drive. "He came in and his mustache was frozen from the cold, like Dr. Zhivago. I have loved Ron since then," she says. "He's a remarkable man and a wonderful speaker." She met Sister Mary Bader of Nazareth, a Roman Catholic nun, when she was looking for places to house the cast of the anti-nuclear play, "Alice in Blunderland." The two formed a lifelong friendship.

Amy's peace work gave her a new sense of activism and it made her more curious and more engaged because the issues were far too important to ignore. She served as secretary of the Valley Alliance, Kalamazoo's antinuclear weapons organization, for nine years and then collected documents on everything this group ever did: posters, newsletters, letters, petitions, news clips, diaries on its activities, meetings and other events. She inadvertently became the Kalamazoo peace movement's historian.

"God made it just right that I could have a job," says Amy who always found that things just popped into her life when she was ready for them or when she needed them. For example, the opportunity to work with the Valley Alliance occurred about the same time her children were grown up and "leaving the nest." When the Valley Alliance needed larger meeting space, First Presbyterian offered its Guild Room, which Amy was able to procure since she was a member of the congregation. When Ernest Sternglass, a scientist, came to Kalamazoo College to speak on the dangerous effects of radiation from nuclear power plants, he inspired Dr. Dick Hodgman to start the Kalamazoo chapter of the Physicians for Social Responsibility, which often partnered with the Valley Alliance in sponsoring public projects and events. When the Valley Alliance needed a fundraising project, Steve Senesi was able to get his friend, Charlie King, a singer of protest songs, to put on a benefit.

But Amy is also a proactive woman. She and several others were concerned that too few African Americans participated in peace activities. So with her son, Dale, she arranged a bus trip for local blacks and whites to go to Washington, D.C., for the anniversary observance of Martin Luther King's "I Have a Dream" speech. "Doors have always opened up for me all the way along to help things progress," says Amy.

Rob grew up in a similar small town environment that Amy did, only on the northwestern Illinois prairie in the town of Monmouth, population 10,000. Everyone walked to where they were going, came home for lunch and knew everybody in town. His father was the assistant postmaster and the college he attended was three blocks away. Life would change drastically for Rob and everything he knew when World War II started. Little did he imagine that he would serve in transatlantic communications for General Eisenhower, become a research chemist at a prominent international pharmaceutical company and participate as a faithful and vital member of the Kalamazoo peace movement.

Tall, lean and brainy with a deep, resonant voice, Rob had already started college when the war began. Naturally, the draft became a popular topic of conversation among students. Eventually, Rob enlisted in the Army Reserve Corps and obtained a four-year deferment to finish his undergraduate degree. However, he got orders in February 1943 to report to Infantry Basic Training. The Army needed smart people like Rob for technical work both during and after the war, so he took a qualifying exam for basic engineering and won a spot at St. Norbert College in Green Bay, Wisconsin. After nine months his orders again changed and the Army sent him to the Signal Corps to train as a radio operator. In this work he learned how to type Morse Code translations for the high-speed radio teletype team. After one month's training at the Pentagon he was sent to New York City to board a troop ship in what turned out to be the last major convoy sent to Europe in 1945. "The sea was alive with ships as far as the eye could see," says Rob.

On May 8, 1945, Germany surrendered and Rob became part of the Army of Occupation. He handled transatlantic communications for General Eisenhower's headquarters. On April 17, 1946, he returned to the United States and picked up his education where he'd left off at Monmouth College, only this time he met Amy, a first-year student there.

"Rob swept me off my feet," says Amy. He was a hero, like all the returning soldiers, sailors, marines, and airmen of World War II. And like so many of the veterans, Rob went to college through the G.I. Bill, married and had a family.

Monmouth College, a small Presbyterian college, was bulging with war veterans. Space for married couples was limited, but the Andersons found a room in a single, older woman's house. By screening off the bedroom and sharing the bathroom and kitchen, the woman accommodated Rob and Amy—and one other returning G.I. and his wife.

Rob studied chemistry and Amy got a secretarial job in an agricultural extension office. Later they moved to the University of Illinois so Rob could obtain his master's degree in organic chemistry. Before he graduated, The Upjohn Company interviewed him on campus and hired him for the research unit in Kalamazoo. That was 1950 and for the next 34 years until his retirement Rob worked at Upjohn with his major responsibilities as a cataloguer and translator of pharmaceutical nomenclature.

Although Amy spent a lot of time with the peace movement beginning in 1972 and Rob was busy in the lab, the couple's interest in peace grew and merged. Rob's library is testament to the voluminous reading he did before his retirement, particularly on nuclear weapons and their dangers. Afterward, in 1984 Rob became an activist in the community. He started by learning how to work the cameras and editing equipment at the Community Access Center where he worked on the Peace Video Project starting in May 1986. He produced and edited 202 out of the 267 programs aired over a nine-year period. Later, the Andersons served on the crew for "People and Politics," a talk show produced over 10 years by the Kalamazoo County Democratic Party. Rob also joined the Veterans for Peace and he and Amy went to several annual meetings held all over the county. He regularly rides in the Vets for Peace float at the Memorial Day parades in downtown Kalamazoo. He also joined the Pushkin–Kalamazoo Partnership, which holds events and fundraisers for Russian citizens needing food and medical supplies, and he volunteers at the First Presbyterian Church's Health Clinic sorting the meds and doing other odd jobs.

In 1982 Betty Bumpers, wife of former Senator Dale Bumpers of Arkansas, started Peace Links,[70] a pen pal organization between Americans and Russians of the recently-fallen Soviet Union. After seeing an ad in the *Gazette* inviting

---

[70] Betty Bumpers founded Peace Links in 1982 at the height of the Cold War. She "realized that the survival of the planet was too important an issue to leave to the politicians, and that women, networking and learning together, could educate their communities about the threat and consequences of nuclear war and the nuclear arms race. The core of Betty's network was a group of congressional wives, who began to spread the word in their states." Teresa Heinz-Kerry, at the time the wife of the deceased Senator John Heinz of Pennsylvania, also participated in the program. Source: www.peacelinks.us/history.html

people to participate, Amy signed up and began correspondence with Galena, an English teacher from Spratov, Russia, on the Volga River. Rob also obtained a pen pal, a chemist in Kazakhstan. The two men still write to each other.

Rob turns out for the KNOW peace vigils every Sunday in front of the Federal Building. Sometimes Amy joins him. Every other week Rob and Amy go to the KNOW planning meetings. They also show up to help build the silhouettes (*see* pages 375–378) and to attend all of KNOW's major events.

"I never considered the possibility of not continuing this peace work," says Rob, 80. "War is a problem still there needing to be solved."

"As long as I have energy and the capacities, I will work for peace," says Amy, 75.

DAVID MACLEOD
Architect for Peaceful Futures

I speak with David Macleod one hot summer day as we sit on the granite steps of the Federal Building after one of the Sunday peace vigils. He is always ready to talk about peace, with anyone, anytime. His start in the peace movement turned out to be an astonishing story of what religious people might call divine intervention. It is probably the reason he has stuck with peace as his life's purpose. David, I think, is a prophet for peace.

A tall, lanky, graying red-haired man, David, 67, walks with a slight hunch and talks with a gentle, low resonant voice. He has spent a lifetime assiduously informing himself about the technical aspects of how wars are waged and how peace can solve conflict. The former professor turned handyman who sometimes brings his Model-T Ford with him to the Sunday vigils, David is currently studying how the Bush administration distorts scientific data in order to promote its agenda. He is also writing a book about the history of peace activism in Kalamazoo.

I first met David in 1985 at Nazareth College, a small, private, liberal arts college located on the northeast side of town.[71] He taught geography there as a part-time professor, one of many jobs he had stitched together to make a living. He seemed reserved and a little eccentric to me at the time, but I didn't really know him or understand his projects. Talking with him today about his tireless efforts for peace over the past 53 years sheds new light on him and the way an individual's call to be a peacemaker is often a lonely, yet enduring, vocation.

In 1950 at age 13 David attended the Boy Scout Jamboree held in Washington, D.C. On the night before the event, he and a group of boys saw the movie, "Forgotten Men." The film featured a history of World War I and how it led to World War II. "I was so appalled, horrified and upset that night, I couldn't sleep," says David. When he finally got some sleep he awoke from a nightmare quite shaken with the sun shining in his eyes. It took him awhile to adjust to reality. He had just dreamed that the atomic bomb hit Washington and that he was trying to escape his hotel that was in flames.

After breakfast, David attended the Jamboree with 40,000 other boys from around the world. The event proved to be a moving and influential experience for him as well. "We all got along with one another," recalls David. "Somehow, I thought back then, that we should all be able to avoid what the world was coming up against with war and nuclear weapons." Ironically, on the same day, North Korea invaded South Korea. "It was only five years after World War II and we were right back into war again," says David mournfully. It was on

---

[71] The college closed its doors in 1991.

that day, however, that he made a lifelong commitment to peace.

While some people regard David a hopeless idealist, others find him a steadfast advocate for peace. One of David's proudest achievements was his suggestion that the government institute an international peace program. This idea turned out to be the Peace Corps, which John F. Kennedy announced in his 1960 presidential bid on the steps of the Student Union at the University of Michigan where David was a student.

During the late 1970s David and his wife, Mary, returned to Kalamazoo. On the day after they arrived, the Fetzer Institute held a peace conference that featured Anwar Saddat, prime minister of Egypt; Norman Cousins, editor of the *Atlantic Monthly*; and Robert Muller, former U.N. undersecretary general and president emeritus of the University for Peace in Costa Rica. At the conference Mueller encouraged the audience to consider Kalamazoo an ideal place to establish a world center for peace that would offer conferences and serve as a think tank toward specific actions for peace. Besides, Muller said, Kalamazoo's odd name would attract the necessary attention for the cause.

"I was delighted to hear others reflect what I thought," says David who never forgot what Mueller said. Ever since David has worked hard to make that vision a reality. For example, David taught a course in peace education at Western Michigan University and wrote a pamphlet to accompany the class entitled "World Peace: A Positive Approach." Other professors across the country adopted it for their curriculum. In the pamphlet he advocates a five-point positive approach to peace that includes the following programs:

* a code of world law

* a democratic world government

* a program of peace education and world citizenship

* a way for people to become world citizens

* a military conversion program that adapts systems, hardware and personnel to peaceful uses.

But David doesn't just think up ideas, he works to implement them. For example, he developed a plan for a military-base conversion program in Michigan and, in 1976, came close to convincing the state to convert Kinchloe Air Force Base near Sault Ste. Marie into a global disaster relief project. The state seriously considered his plan until then-Governor William Milliken suddenly changed course and transformed the base into a state prison instead.

David also wanted to see the Fort Custer Army Base in Battle Creek converted into a world agricultural center. He submitted a proposal but this one, too, fell short of adoption. Part of the base did become an industrial park that welcomed several international manufacturing companies including Japan's giant auto supplier, Denso. In 1990 when Nazareth College announced it would close its doors, David proposed that the campus become a world peace education center, but authorities nixed that idea, too. Despite these setbacks, David has never given up on his vision for world peace. Actually, even today especially since 9/11, David still can't fathom why the world can't be peaceful any more than he could when he was a boy scout at age 13.

"We have computer networks that allow us to speak to each other. We have an awareness that the violence of modern weapons could have untold destruction of the whole world," says David. As an emergency preparedness coordinator for Kalamazoo Township, David also knows the tandem effects of nuclear weapons, that is, if one goes off, a whole system trips off a response for several other bombs to go off as well. "The first thing we *should* do about this nuclear weapons system is shut it all down," says David.

Still, despite his efforts and his optimism that peace is possible, David says he is quite discouraged with what the Bush administration has done with Iraq. He has even become a full-fledged pacifist as a result, which surprises even him. "I've found that various methods of violence are degrading to the human spirit and counter-productive," says David who defines the scope of violence as anything from interpersonal relationships to global military conflicts.

"The Bush administration seems determined to make Iraq a U.S. colony, when the country has the potential of being an example of what can be done globally," David says referring to the Iraqi Governing Council that wrote a democratic constitution. However, he maintains that Iraq presented no credible threat to the United States in the first place, at least, not enough to warrant going to war. He also questions why the administration saw such an immediacy to war with Iraq when it didn't see one with the more volatile North Korea—which *has* nuclear weapons.

"The rule is that if we threaten them with the bomb, they'll break down. However, North Korea's one weapon is enough to create a credible threat to us," says David. Consequently, David has made a stand for peace at the KNOW vigils since fall 2002 and shows no signs of quitting.

To David, today's geopolitical situation is as dangerous as it was in 1950. Back then he thought we were on the verge of World War III when he heard General Douglas MacArthur declare he wanted to use nuclear weapons to stave off the North Koreans. "I felt urgency then and I still do now," says David. "I feel an urgency to do something."

RON KRAMER
Scholar and Activist for Peace

Ron Kramer never intended to be a political activist or a professor. As a high school senior he knew he loved baseball and school and planned to be a teacher so he could do both. He went to college, the first in his family to do so, married his high school sweetheart, had kids, went to graduate school and obtained a professorship in sociology at Western Michigan University by the age of 27. Along the way, he had certain influences that steered him toward concerns about social justice and peacemaking.

"It all started with Sister Jane Connors' high school writing class in Tiffin, Ohio," says the 53-year-old sociology professor as we talk over a casual lunch at the University Roadhouse in between classes. "I knew I was against the Vietnam War; I just couldn't articulate why. I just sensed that it was morally wrong due to the religious and moral dimension of the people who influenced my thought."

Sister Jane gave Ron new eyes to see what was going on around him and the skills to analyze it, talk about it and do something about it. What was going on around him at the time were the turbulent 60s with the Vietnam War, youth counter culture, the Cold War—and the draft. Sister Jane introduced Ron to the importance of logical argument and the passionate activism of the Berrigan brothers, priests who played a prominent role in the anti-war movement and subsequently worked on social justice and nonviolence issues.

Then there was the weekend retreat program called Teens Encounter Christ (TEC). Ron had seen friends come back from this program completely changed so the intellectually curious and somewhat skeptical high school senior went to TEC just to find out what was going on. Then it happened to him: he had a dramatic conversion experience.

"I felt that for the first time I understood what it meant to be a follower of Jesus Christ," says Ron. As a cradle Catholic he knew the catechism, the rituals and the rubrics of his religion. On the TEC weekend, however, he learned that Christianity was about love, caring for people, working for justice and making things right. It was about dying to self and one's own selfish needs in order to be reborn as a follower of Christ. By extension, Ron attributes his introspective base and the greatest influence on his work as a political activist to his Roman Catholic faith.

"It grows out of a spiritual conviction that is against violence, war, and for peace and social justice," he says. "People can come to their religion in different ways—and from different faiths. What's important is that they reflect the true message of Jesus Christ, which is that we love one another."

The music of the 60s also helped shape Ron's emerging social consciousness. His favorites, "Look to Your Soul," "Crystal Blue Persuasion," "Sweet Cherry Wine" and "Instant Karma," talked about a vastly changing world and finding one's place within it. These songs, together with his faith, helped this highly introspective and intellectual young man make an important decision about the world and his response to it: war was evil and he wasn't going to allow himself to be drafted into the army.

Ron entered the University of Toledo in fall 1969 and was immediately confronted with one of the first big campus protests against the Vietnam War. In class he studied the history and politics of Vietnam and learned to articulate why he was against the war. The following spring he planned to visit Jane, his girlfriend and future wife, at Kent State one weekend. It happened to be May 5, one day after the Ohio

National Guard killed four students and injured nine others on campus during a noontime demonstration.[72]

Campus was consumed by a great anger, says Ron. On the towers near the football stadium someone had placed a big banner that says, "STRIKE." Carl Rowan of the *Washington Post* and the most prominent African-American columnist at the time, was scheduled to speak that day. From the balcony of the student union he, "ripped [President] Nixon up one side and down the other," says Ron. Afterward, students began to organize themselves in different groups and committees to protest the war in Vietnam.

In 1969 Congress reinstated a lottery system for the draft.[73] Ron had a low number and a student deferment—but he was determined not to be drafted.

---

[72] Governor James A. Rhodes had ordered in the Guard after students burned down the Army R.O.T.C. building on May 2. He appeared on campus the next day and promised to use "every force possible" to maintain order against the protesters who he claimed were worse than "brownshirts." Rhodes vowed to keep the Guard on campus "until we get rid of them [protesters]." The Kent State protest was part of the massive campus protests that erupted across the nation after President Nixon had ordered the invasion of Cambodia on April 30.

[73] "A lottery drawing—the first since 1942—was held on December 1, 1969, at Selective Service National Headquarters in Washington, D.C. This event determined the order of call for induction during calendar year 1970, that is, for registrants born between January 1, 1944, and December 31, 1950. Reinstitution of the lottery was a change from the 'draft the oldest man first' method, which had been the determining method for deciding order of call." Radio, film and TV covered the event as officials placed 366 blue plastic capsules containing birth dates of all men within the 18–26 age range in a large glass container. The capsules were then drawn by hand to assign the order-of-call numbers. The drawing continued until all the days of the year had been paired with sequence numbers. The first capsule—drawn by Congressman Alexander Pirnie (R-NY) of the House

"In the arrogance of youth I decided I wasn't going to let the government decide my life for me," says Ron, so he looked over his options. He would not flee to Canada because he was too close to his family and would not see them as often as he wanted. (Besides, once he crossed the border, he knew he would not be able to return to the United States.) Anyway, he didn't know anyone there. He also considered imprisonment for failing to report and Conscientious Objector (C.O.) status as well. Fortunately, the draft ended before his deferment was up so he wasn't forced to make a choice.

Ron described his first year in college as "really intense" and "so political." As a result, Vietnam, the Civil Rights Movement and the assassinations of Martin Luther King, Jr. and Robert F. Kennedy made a Democrat out of him. He joined Students and Teachers Opposed to War (STOW) and worked for Democratic candidate George McGovern in the 1972 presidential election. "I couldn't stand to watch Nixon on TV," he says.

Meanwhile, Ron's studies led him to sociology and criminology after he had taken a course by a "young, radical professor" who then encouraged him to go on to graduate school. He went to Ohio State University and got a paid teaching assistantship, an unusual feat for a doctoral student to obtain at the beginning of his course work. And, once again, his timing was perfect: a new kind of criminology had emerged out of UC-Berkeley called "radical" or "critical criminology." It was based on a Marxist analytical method of looking at societal structures and power relationships. This method, also called "critical theory," made its rounds in many

---

Armed Services Committee—contained the date September 14, so all men born on September 14 in any year between 1944 and 1950 were assigned lottery number 1. The lottery system continued 1969–1972." (Source: www.sss.gov/lotter1.htm)

disciplines throughout academe. "This was a time when students were extremely radical," says Ron.

However, as the war wound down, the fuel for student protests dissipated. Ron finished his graduate work in 1978 and obtained his first and only professorship at Western Michigan University. He soon became interested in white collar and corporate crime after reading a story in *Mother Jones* magazine about secret documents it had obtained showing that the Ford Motor Company had sold defective Pinto cars knowing that hundreds of people could needlessly burn to death in them. Ron soon became a specialist in this area and it coincided well with his predilection for social justice.

In 1980 Ronald Reagan won the presidency, started an intervention in Central America, increased the U.S. military budget and stockpiled bigger and more powerful nuclear weapons. Ron objected to these policies and became involved in the anti-nuclear weapons movement, which called on the U.S. and Soviet Union to "adopt a mutual freeze on the testing, production, and deployment of nuclear weapons and of missiles, and new aircraft designed primarily to deliver nuclear weapons." Kalamazoo's peace and environmental groups also responded to this new turn of events by forming a coalition called the Valley Alliance headed up by Sharon Froom, David Macleod, Robert and Amy Anderson and their son Dave. In March 1983 Ron, together with Don Cooney, professor of social work, and Rev. Don VanHoeven, campus minister, met at the Wesley Foundation on the WMU campus to plan a "Week of Education and Action to Prevent Nuclear War." The week featured films, speakers and a march from campus to Bronson Park. Ron became the campus leader, even though he didn't feel qualified to do it. "I wasn't as hard core an activist as they had been," says Ron, who admits that VanHoeven had collaborated with Cooney to get him involved.

As part of the week, the group also held the "March 21 Peace Coalition" with George McGovern as the speaker. "I picked him up at the airport, had coffee with him, and took him back to the airport after his speech," says Ron. "He then asked me whether he should run for President in 1984. I told him he didn't have a chance to win but that running in the primaries would allow him to raise some important issues, which is what he eventually did."

Peace Week, as it was called, had gone "spectacularly," says Ron and the money left over went to the United Campuses to Prevent Nuclear War (a.k.a. UCAM), a spin-off of the Union of Concerned Scientists. UCAM eventually dissolved but Ron and other activists at WMU kept it up only in different forms like the United Campuses Against Militarism until the late 1990s. Their issues included U.S. presence in Central America (which included the Iran-Contra scandal), the military budget and an ever-increasing military society. During the fall of 1983 the campus convened its second peace week and concentrated its efforts on the Union of Concerned Scientists' call to action for a November 11 demonstration against Ronald Reagan's proposal for a Strategic Defense Initiative (Star Wars).

When Howard Zinn came to Kalamazoo in the 1990s, Ron asked him about how he could maintain his optimistic attitude. Zinn decided that his answer wasn't adequate so he thought about it and then re-answered it in the first chapter of his next book, *You Can't Be Neutral on a Moving Train* (1994). In it he referred to his visit to Kalamazoo and Ron's question.

"I was a football linebacker and a young sociology professor. I came from a working class family and was once opposed the idea of the United Nations. Imagine the thrill of being in a bookstore and reading about myself in Zinn's book!" says Ron.

From 1987–1995 Ron helped produce "WMU Forum," a monthly Community Access television program. He and director and co-producer Harvey Stewart from the WMU media services taped 89 shows featuring professors and other experts talking about peace and justice issues. "The idea for the 'WMU Forum' was cooked up on the softball field," says Ron, who at age 53 still plays the game three times a week in various city leagues.

By the mid- to late-1990s life on campus became a rather quiet period for peace activists. The Cold War was over, people's energy had been "drained away" from years of demonstrations and the Peace Education Fund had dried up. Ron, too, had activist burnout. Besides, he wanted to publish more research about state crime and international law. In 1998 he co-authored the book entitled *Crimes of the American Nuclear State*, which discusses American nuclear violations of international law. He also wrote an article about the 1996–97 World Court decision that made nuclear weapons illegal. Peace Week continued with Don Cooney becoming the force behind it; still, every year Ron helps him with the planning. After 9/11, Ron's activism kicked in again. He became one of the leaders of KNOW and regularly attends the peace vigils and planning meetings.

"If you're going to be a peace activist, you must be in it for the long haul," says Ron. "There have been many ebbs and flows in this work, but I view it as a long-term commitment and a lifelong project." He likens peace and justice work to laundry: it's never done and there's always more to do. The work is often frustrating as well. You're never there and it's frequently one step forward and two steps back. He doesn't worry about that anymore because he knows, "it's the nature of society and conflict in our world."

I ask him the Number One question: what sustains activists and how do they know they're right? Ron heaves a deep sigh and speaks.

"Peace and justice are extremely important values and the right things to do. What Bush is doing, killing thousands of people, is impersonal and causing chaos around the world. You can fight evil but you also must think about the means you are using and determine whether it is moral and proportional to your reasons for doing it. Getting rid of Saddam was a good end but it happened through evil means. Bush says he was fighting evil but his goals are world domination with a *Pax Americana*. I don't believe we can liberate or bring democracy to the Iraqi people that way.

"Secondly, having a sense of history helps. Howard Zinn points to history to show that many things thought to be impossible have been overcome. The abolition of slavery was deemed hopeless but people kept at it and it was eventually defeated. Apartheid was another instance. Nelson Mandela was imprisoned for 27 years and yet when he got out he became president of South Africa. The Berlin Wall fell and the Soviet Union was dissolved. Gandhi finally convinced the British to leave India. These things all happened even though people never thought they could. Throughout history, social movements have been effective and they have brought down monstrous evils and structures of injustice."

Ron, who was inspired by Gandhi and Martin Luther King, Jr., frequently quotes King in his speeches and presentations. As an academic, Ron has also followed the activist model of the Berrigan brothers, Noam Chomsky and Robert J. Lifton;[74] but he also studies, writes, and he speaks

---

[74] Lifton is the Distinguished Professor of Psychiatry and Psychology at the Graduate School University Center at The City University of New York. He is also the director of the Center on Violence and Human Survival at John Jay College of Criminal Justice there. An

publicly. "Not many people have the privilege of doing that. I am privileged to be in a profession to do this and to have the time and resources to study these issues."

Ron's resources are websites and books that he buys by the hundred. However, he doesn't read newspapers because he doesn't think the media give a complete picture of how things work in politics. "I think the country is in denial and willful ignorance about this president," says Ron. "But it's hard work to keep yourself informed, especially if the media doesn't do it well. It's also hard to be actively informed if you think the United States is the best country in the world and without fault. You tend to filter out critique and criticism over policies and practices."

He calls this filtering out of bad news or reinterpreting bad news, "cognitive dissonance." It is a social-psychological dynamic that prevents people from changing their views about reality. People believe lies, especially when they are systematically given one at a time, one lie after another. Ron says that cognitive dissonance also occurs during the "fog of war" because leaders cannot resist the temptation to pass on lies and distortions. When one lie is exposed, they switch to another one. Ron believes this is happening in our country.

"We shouldn't underestimate the impact of 9/11 on our country. It has produced great fear, anxiety and anger in Americans. It allows us to think that anything we do in response is justified because we have been grievously harmed. As a result, the administration has skillfully exploited 9/11. The war in Iraq, for example, could not have happened without the emotions of 9/11, Al Qaeda and Saddam. And

---

expert on mass social trauma and the psychological after-affects from anger, rage and vulnerability, Lifton is interested in the relationship between individual psychology and historical change, and in the problems surrounding the extreme historical situations of our time. He helped found this new field of psychohistory.

although the administration never made a direct statement of the ties between Iraq and 9/11, they have associated them. Even today, 70 percent of Americans believe Iraq was responsible for 9/11. You have to wonder how people can be that misinformed! But this is also due to the media's failure to present the proper context of the war to the American people."

From a criminological point of view, Ron also believes that a 9/11 climate and culture have been created, which gives the Bush administration greater license to take action because it can cloak it all within the parameters of 9/11. He calls this a "cynical exploitation of the issue." As a result, he is currently working on a new book entitled *Crimes of Empire*. In it he discusses how Bush led an illegal invasion and occupation of Iraq and committed a "state crime." Ron believes the book can be an important contribution to discussion and analyses of this war now and in the years to come.

I am curious to know if Ron ever gets into trouble with his peace work. "No one at the university has ever said a word about my activism," says Ron, who holds a tenure track position as a full professor. Occasionally he writes viewpoint articles for the *Kalamazoo Gazette* and even then he gets only mild criticism. "I try to not to be a ranter," says Ron, "but to remain calm and analytical by presenting evidence in a logical manner. I also avoid speaking for shock value."

Ron has been able to cover a lot of ground with his peace and justice work in addition to his professional work through various partnerships he readily makes. It helps that he's an affable and positive fellow who seems to draw people to him, especially when they see his warm and gentle smile. He is reluctant, however, to admit that he has any serious process or trick to his work. He simply sees what he does as an essential part of organizing people to accomplish some goal or work for a good cause.

Ron has enjoyed working with KNOW because of people's commitment to the cause of peace and justice. He claims it's not a social group, although he has made friends with many of the regulars. "People trust each other and they carry out their responsibilities. Mostly this happens because they don't want to let other people down." Part of that commitment to each other is to attend the various events. Members look for each other's presence. "Sometimes going to the Sunday vigil is the last thing I want to do," says Ron. "But then I go and I see the people and it's a great thing to do for the day."

NOAH DILLARD
Next Generation Peace Activist

I first met Noah when I bought my bus ticket for the January peace march in Washington. I thought he was a hippie. He was young, he dressed simply, he lived simply with a group of students in an old house, and he had long, light-brown hair in dreadlocks rolled up under a green and orange knitted cap. If he was a hippie, Noah was a very organized and energetic one as he planned that trip for 224 people in four buses, obtained much publicity and served as an excellent spokesman for the media.

Noah's sharp features complement a benevolent crease of a smile that he carries most of the time. He walks fast enough on his crutches to keep up with others and to march in peace demonstrations side by side people of all ages and physiques. People instantly recognize him when he rides his hand-operated tricycle, another distinct trademark that accommodates his body. As he whizzes by without looking, people wave and shout excitedly, "Hey, Noah!"

I watched him once in a KNOW organizational meeting. The small room was filled with about 60 to 70 people, some even sitting on the floor for lack of chairs. The war had just begun and everyone was anxious to share ideas about what KNOW could do to respond. He listened, asked for volunteers, gave everyone a chance to speak, remained patient, and didn't let the meeting run too long. He did an expert job. From time to time he spoke to the crowds gathered at the Sunday peace vigils. Always eloquent. Always passionate. And always reasonable and forthright.

I am curious about this intelligent, articulate, and highly-informed 24-year-old and want to know more about him, so we meet for tea at a local café one afternoon. As we take our seats he pulls his heavy backpack off his broad shoulders and sets it down on the floor. It contains books, papers, a strange-looking spoon and his own special blend of fragrant tea that he carries in an air-tight tin can. He retrieves the can and with the strange-looking spoon scoops out some tea and puts it in a cup, careful not to drop any leaves on the table. He does this in a seemingly rhythmic way and establishes the beat of our talk together.

When I conduct an interview I usually gulp my coffee and furiously write my notes, but I am not like that with Noah. His internal calm slows me down and draws me in to listen to him from his heart as well as from his highly-developed brain. As we talk, it soon becomes clear how this quiet, soft-spoken and gentle man became a powerful advocate for peace and non-violence by reading and studying the issues, talking with others and connecting the dots as to what is going on in this country.

As one of the early leaders of KNOW, Noah shows a unique brand of commitment tempered by a principled life and a contemplative attitude over his words, thoughts and deeds. He is one of the most unusual young men in the peace movement and, without a doubt, one of the most beloved.

"It was how I was raised," Noah says without hesitating to credit his parents who instilled in him, "a love of something greater than myself, a love of humanity, community and social service." The cultivation of Noah the Peacemaker, however, grew out of his own life experiences and the choices he made.

As a child Noah developed a bone disorder and spent much time in the hospital. This drastic life-changing event curtailed his physical growth and confined him to crutches for the rest of his life. All his strength is in his upper body, as his legs are too weak to hold him up completely. Locomotion is no obstacle for him and neither is his incessant search for knowledge and truth. In fact, Noah's physical inconvenience has shaped his thinking and his way of seeing the world. Being laid up in the hospital for months taught him to be patient and contemplative. To Noah these qualities call on his ability to think things through logically in order to make sure that what he does and says is internally consistent. If he were sour or pessimistic about life, that would be understandable. Instead, he is one more member of the peace movement who is absolutely firm about the idea that organizing people toward peace and justice is the first step toward making it happen and he derives happiness and a sense of purpose from this quest.

As a high school student Noah went on a study trip abroad to Russia. He instantly sensed the tense environment of the post-Soviet empire and found that people lived without wages for six months at a time. Survival depended on their reliance of each other through sharing and through the strong bonds they developed as a community. However, violence and anarchy prevailed in that land and made life difficult. In the crossfire of this chaos, one of his young Russian friends was killed. Before he died, his friend told Noah that, "Life becomes precious when you know you can die easily."

"I found happiness and joy there," says Noah, who noticed that the real strength of the Russian people was in their handling of difficulties rather than the difficulties themselves. Consequently, Noah began to understand freedom in a new way, too.   Growing up in the Maine woods, he thought freedom meant that he could do whatever he wanted.   In Russia he learned that freedom meant *not* doing what you *don't* want to do.   In this way, the Russians taught him that nonviolence entailed restraint from anger and despair.

As a biology major at Kalamazoo College, a rigorous program at an equally rigorous small, private, liberal arts college, Noah found that he could search for truth and knowledge about the natural world and hone his analytical skills to examine, critique and explain it.   He began to see nature as a connection, an interaction and a communication between creatures, plants and ecosystems.

"I love biology so, so much," he says, "and would study it now if I weren't part of the peace movement."   The struggle of his dilemma hangs in his voice.   I can feel my own hope that he will stick around Kalamazoo, but it is obvious that this town is only his first stop of a long life's journey.   Noah's peaceful nonviolent approach to life does not mean that he shrinks from controversy or strong opinions.   He is an activist and the run-up to war with Iraq challenged him to do what he could to stand for peace and justice.

"From Day One this administration has set out to intimidate the American people in exchange for a more centralized, more powerful government," says Noah.   "Their interest in controlling oil in the Middle East is part of their plan to dominate the economies of the entire world.   September 11 gave them the excuse to execute this plan.   They said their aim was to go after the terrorists.   Iraq, which has the second largest oil reserves in the world, became their target.

"In their propaganda to stoke up support for a war, the administration said that Saddam was a brutal dictator with WMDs that threatened the United States and it was important that we stop him.   They said Saddam imported uranium from

Nigeria to manufacture nuclear weapons[75] and that he sponsored training camps for terrorists. This was all a public relations campaign full of lies and fabrications—and it worked to convince America to go to war with Iraq."

Noah sees the Kalamazoo peace movement as one part of the "millions of creative, active, and participating people" throughout the world who filled the streets of their cities and strenuously protested Bush's handling of the war on terrorism before it became apparent that the war was misguided and eventually regarded as a mistake.

"We have some of the same struggles going on and so we're connected. I'm working for them and they for me," Noah says.

Even though the news media hid the full extent of the worldwide peace movement for months, it was the knowledge that millions of people marched for peace that kept Noah buoyant and true to his pledge to work for nonviolence not only in Iraq, but in the broader world.[76] "When you see that you are in the same struggle for peace and justice with Latin American *campesinos*, Palestinians, and School of the Americas watch activists, you feel solidarity," he says. "Their victories are mine and my victories are theirs. This is very powerful."

However, when war with Iraq did break out, many people contended that the peace movement was irrelevant because it

---

[75] Joseph Wilson reported to the administration that there was no evidence that Saddam had a connection to Nigeria. As a result, Wilson says in his book, *The Politics of Truth: Inside the Lies that Led to War and Betrayed My Wife's CIA Identity: A Diplomat's Memoir* (2004), one of the administration's senior aides leaked the name of the former Ambassador's wife, Valerie Plame, to Robert Novak and other journalists. Plame was a CIA undercover agent.

[76] Noah spent six months in Gaza as a member of the Michigan Peace Team, a group that aims to help stop violence between the Palestinians and the Israelis.

had lost the argument against war. Americans were advised to accept the reality of the war and support the troops and President Bush. "To say that we were ineffective is wrong," says Noah, "the peace movement continues. Just because it is not covered by the media doesn't mean it isn't there." And, although Bush declared "major combat operations in Iraq have ended," Noah fears that the United States is only in the first stage of a long occupation in Iraq. "Peacemaking starts when inroads between countries can take place. There is none of that going on in Iraq," says Noah. As for his assessment of the war, he says he measures it by the loss of life.

"We lost the war because we lost thousands of Iraqi citizens' lives," says Noah. "For every human being that dies, it suggests that reason was lost." He adds that there is no justification for supporting a violent, aggressive massacre where one side takes all the losses, especially when in the rush to war the administration made no attempts to resolve problems with Saddam. The war instead would open up the floodgates for the United States to commit ethical missteps and to acquire a new, tarnished reputation in the eyes of the world. "Bush talks about peace and then holds a gun to people's heads," says Noah. "This is a humiliating position to hold and it doesn't make the world safer."[77]

The war is also affecting the people at home directly as efforts to fund the war cut into domestic spending and services, says Noah referring to the mounting number of Americans without health insurance coverage, the rising unemployment rate, the freedoms Americans are willing to give up because of fear and demagoguery, and the unraveling

---

[77] On July 12, 2004, President Bush defends the war against Iraq and says that his policies have made Americans safer since the September 11 attacks. He makes these remarks in the wake of revelations about intelligence failures at home and abroad.

of the local and state infrastructure through tax cuts. "I know they don't know what's going on and what it is they're supporting," says Noah about the Bush supporters. "They think they're supporting Bush without realizing he's making us into a third-world nation."[78]

Before 9/11 the United States was on the brink of an economic collapse, says Noah. Bush's ratings were declining. Then 9/11 changed everything. People followed him blindly and the media gave him a free pass. By the end of April peace activists were being called "traitors," by their fellow Americans. Noah regards such tactics as an angry response that will prove to be highly ineffective simply because they have not stopped the peace movement.[79] Rather, this kind of "name-calling" has strengthened peace groups' solidarity throughout the United States and all over the world. "Being a 'traitor' is probably the most patriotic thing to do," says Noah, citing the unpatriotic travesties of this administration in its handling of the Guantanamo prisoners, its use of the USA PATRIOT Act, its manipulation of the media, its lies and deceptions that led us to

---

[78] Thomas Frank (2004) published the book, *What's the Matter with Kansas?* to explain how working class people who are losing their middle class lifestyle still vote for the Republicans and Bush in particular because he strikes a chord with their values. The 2004 election will prove his point.

[79] Peace groups organized over 30 protest marches during the Republican National Convention, one of them drawing 500,000 people. The president of Spain who supplied troops for the war in Iraq was defeated in the 2004 election. On July 10, 2004, Reuters reported that Tony Blair has faced such criticism for his support of the Iraq War that he contemplated resigning from the office of prime minister in June. Many people thought Bush would lose the 2004 election as grassroots groups and 527 organizations worked to defeat him. Kalamazoo's "people's movement" continues and has remained active despite Kerry's loss.

war and its no-bid contracts to senior officials' friends in the defense industry.

Noah also questions the integrity of the news media, which has fallen in line with whatever "news" the administration provides them.[80] For example, at the time of this interview (late April 2003), rumor had it that the Marines found weapons of mass destruction. Fox News reported it, but then gave no follow-up on the story to prove or disprove the claim. So, although we still have not found WMD, 50 percent of the American people still believe we did.

Debate in this country is polarized and partisan, says Noah with concern. "People are not worrying about the country as a whole as much as whether they win their argument and carry out their position." In an era with an overabundance of weapons of mass destruction available to too many people, Noah believes that the same standards of ethics should apply

---

[80] In July 2004, "Outfoxed: Rupert Murdoch's War on Journalism," a new documentary by Robert Greenwald is released. The 75-minute film drew on weeks of compiled clips of the network's news to show how the Fox News Channel is anything but "fair and balanced." It features former Fox News staffers who describe the workplace environment of the Murdoch media empire. "We weren't necessarily, as it was told to us, a newsgathering organization so much as we were a proponent of a point of view," says Jon Du Pre, a former Fox News correspondent. The film is backed by liberal political groups and demonstrates what the filmmakers believe is a pattern of right-wing bias and support for the Republican agenda. Source: www.outfoxed.org

Books on Fox News practices include *The Oh Really? Factor: Unspinning Fox News Channel's Bill O'Reilly* (2003) by Peter Hart and Fairness & Accuracy in Reporting (www.fair.org), a national media watch group offering well-documented criticism in an effort to correct media bias and imbalance. Also, Al Franken published *Lies and the Lying Liars Who Tell Them: A Fair and Balanced Look at the Right* (2003)

to both Democrats and Republicans. While he admits he did not protest the injustices the Clinton administration lodged against Iraq with its bombing raids, Noah says that people were not aware of the atrocities committed. Clinton could have cut back military presence, but instead he escalated it with bombs and sanctions. Bush, however, is bolder. He sent troops into Iraq because his foreign policy is guided by the stated objectives of neoconservatives like Vice President Dick Cheney, Secretary of Defense Donald Rumsfeld, Assistant Secretary of Defense Paul Wolfowitz, and TV and *Weekly Standard* editor, William Kristol. Colin Powell and Condoleezza Rice have also signed on to the neoconservative agenda, which advocates unilateralism, permanent war and pre-emptive strike against any nation seen as a threat to the United States. [81] Sixty nations are on the list as potential threats.

"The threat to this country is the military industrial complex which began to gather strength in the late 1950s," says Noah. "The Pentagon has continuously gained control and leverage over the American agenda, just as President Eisenhower warned Americans it would do upon leaving office in 1961. The people with power are the multinational corporations that conduct weapons sales all over the world, including Iraq."

I ask Noah whether he supports the American troops, one of the major criticisms of the pro-Bush people. "I'm not advocating death for our troops, but what they're doing are crimes against humanity and peace. They are engaging in an

---

[81] Here is PNAC's statement of purpose: "The Project for the New American Century is a non-profit educational organization dedicated to a few fundamental propositions: that American leadership is good both for America and for the world; that such leadership requires military strength, diplomatic energy and commitment to moral principle; and that too few political leaders today are making the case for global leadership." www.newamericancentury.org

illegal action (invasion into a sovereign nation) by an illegal government (the 2000 election scandal) in an illegal war (pre-emptive strike runs contrary to the U.S. Constitution). There is no justification for an aggressive, invading and occupying show of force. This is not a war of defense at all."

Noah doesn't hold individual troops responsible unless they do ridiculous, inhuman things while they are in Iraq,[82] but ultimately, they have an obligation to answer to a higher authority. "Just following orders is not an excuse. Nuremberg answered that issue," he says. "I'm not against people who enlist in the service, especially when I realize that 70 percent of the people join the military because they want to earn some extra money or help pay for their college expenses."

JOE AND JEAN GUMP
Civil Disobedience for Peace

After the Sunday vigils I have often seen an elderly man pull up to the curb in front of the Federal Building in a gray, bumper-sticker-laden Honda sedan. He and his wife then load the trunk of their car with protest signs. They move slowly as their age forces them to sway back and forth when they walk, but that doesn't interfere one whit with their passion for peace. They are Jean and Joe Gump and they make it to the vigils every Tuesday and Sunday in Kalamazoo and every Saturday in Paw Paw, a town 30 minutes west of the city. They attend most KNOW events and gatherings held throughout the month. Jean participates in Wednesday noon Women in Black

---

[82] The revelation of the prison abuses at Abu Ghraib is the first known salvo of crimes against humanity. The July 12/19, 2004 issue of *The New Yorker* explains how soldiers are trained not to think of their targets as people so that they are able to kill them.

vigils near the shopping malls and Joe, treasurer of KNOW, attends the bi-monthly planning meetings.

A petite, woman with big, penetrating eyes, a round face, and a salt-and-pepper page-boy haircut, Jean has been on the picket line for some social justice cause ever since 1965 when she went to Alabama to walk with Martin Luther King, Jr., in the fight for African Americans' voting rights. Joe, bearded and slim, wears a baseball cap with the bill turned upward. It makes him look a little gawky, but he's nothing of the sort. He's a Korean War veteran and a retired chemical engineer. He's also a savvy social justice organizer, and like his wife, Joe has a sense of humor that complements his well-grounded but idealistic outlook on life and the world today.

Joe and Jean Gump are pacifists and local folk heroes for peace. They have long associated with the Quakers such that I thought they *were* Quakers, but they're Catholics who have lived their faith with such a devotion to peace and justice that they have willingly paid the price for it—which includes time in federal prison.

The consistent theme of the Gumps' life together these 45 years can be summed up as passion and conviction. They grew up in Chicago and were high school sweethearts. Avid jitterbug dancers, they became known as "jazz freak radicals."

As members of "the greatest generation" their lives were typical. Joe was drafted into the Army in 1946 where he spent 15 months training in the states and six months in Korea. The Army exposed him to a world totally different from his more parochial upbringing in Chicago. It was the first time he had close contact with African Americans, another culture, and Europeans (World War II veterans who emigrated to America and re-enlisted). After discharge Joe took advantage of the G.I. Bill and went to the University of Illinois to study chemical engineering. He saw college as a "good experience," especially since he "didn't have to kill anyone."

In 1958 the Gumps married and had 12 children over the next 14 years. Back then, says Jean, they led rather traditional Catholic lives of daily Mass, night-time fasting, meatless Fridays and confession on Saturdays. In the 60s they joined the Catholic Family Movement (CFM), a new apostolic group that engaged lay people in social action. Among their first projects was a ministry for civil rights program sponsored by the Archdiocese of Chicago, which tried to attract the black population to the Church. They and their brood also participated in the city's interracial program that provided weekend youth exchanges between black and white families and sponsored a Dutch family of 12 that left Indonesia after independence was declared in 1960. Many white, European families left that former colony and resettled in the Netherlands and other parts of the world. Jean and Joe are still in contact with the family they helped find a house, furnishings and jobs.

The Gumps also met people from other religious backgrounds, formerly a practice frowned on by the Catholic Church until the Vatican II (1962–65) reforms encouraged ecumenism. Through the Inter-Faith Human Relations Council and CFM they got to know many Jewish couples and worked with them on various projects like promoting fair housing. "We exchanged views about religion and broadened our religious tolerance," says Joe. "We also made lifelong friends with the Jews who were there to support Jean when she went to prison, something many people in our own parish refused to do."

As a result of their work with the CFM, they eventually became involved in local politics and sponsored a coffee for a young congressional candidate named Donald Rumsfeld who successfully unseated the incumbent in the 13th district of Illinois (Evanston and other northern suburbs of Chicago). "We were Republicans at that time," says Joe. "So much so that even though we were Catholics, we didn't vote for John F. Kennedy for president." Joe had good reason not to like Democrats; the Chicago Democrats were the most corrupt people around. Led by Mayor Richard Daley's political machine, "dead people" voted while some of the living cast their ballots more than once.

"Mom and Dad were immigrants from Germany," says Joe. "Dad was a Democrat. He voted for FDR." FDR's push to enter World War II convinced his father to switch his party loyalties, so he voted for Wendell Wilkie in 1940 and Thomas Dewey in 1944. "As a boy, I remember holding a campaign placard for Mayor Edward Kelly, the ward healer." Joe was very sick with scarlet fever and Kelly saw to it that constituents were well-taken care of when they were hospitalized. "It was a kind of grassroots organizing by Republicans in the face of a Democratic machine that was so strong." Such activities are akin to today's constituent service offices of state and national legislators. "These events shaped me as a Republican," says Joe.

Things began to change for the Gumps in the 1960s in the face of social unrest, the Civil Rights Movement and Vietnam. They became Democrats and Jean became a political activist.
"I always told my children that they should defend anyone on the playground who was being bullied," says Jean. One day the kids were watching TV and they saw news stories about Blacks' poor treatment in the South. "I was cooking dinner and my son, John, came up to me and asked what I was going to do about it. I was puzzled at first. Then he reminded me of my own advice about helping those hurt by bullies. I took the next available plane to Alabama and marched with Martin Luther King, Jr. from Selma to Montgomery."

During these early years of her activism, Jean also participated in her community serving as president of the high school PTA, a member of the League of Women Voters and

executive secretary of the township's Human Relations
Council. In 1972 she was a delegate to the Democratic
Convention. When Ronald Reagan stepped up the arms race
in the 1980s, Jean joined the Silo Plowshares, a social justice
group that works to rid the United States of its nuclear
weapons through acts of civil disobedience. One Plowshares
tactic is to break into a missile silo's chain-link fence with wire
cutters and beat the top of it with a hammer. The act alludes
to Isaiah 2:1–6, "They will beat their swords into plowshares.
Nation will not take up sword against nation, nor will they train
for war anymore."

On Good Friday, 1986, Jean and four young Catholic men
went to a Minuteman II missile silo near Holden, Missouri, and
carried out their mission. The Minuteman II is a first-strike
weapon with a single 1.2 megaton warhead (or 2.4 billion
pounds of TNT) that can decimate an area of 72 miles—and
all living things in it.

"These are my children and I love them," she says about
the motivation her actions that day in an interview with Studs
Terkel for his 1988 book, *The Great Divide:*

> But if they're going to have a world, we have
> to stop this madness....We have got to have a
> future for our children and we've got to make
> some sacrifices for it, okay? Call it a legacy, if
> you want to. What else is there? My
> grandchild, I want to offer him a life, that's all.
> We all had a crack at it, so I think it's fair that
> this generation should.

Authorities arrested and charged Jean and the others with
conspiracy and destruction of government property for her act
with the Minuteman II. She was sentenced to eight years at the
Correctional Institution for Women in Alderson, West
Virginia, and fined $248.49, her portion of the $745 worth of

damage done to the chain-link fence surrounding the silo. However, Jean refused to pay. The judge said she could be released in six years if she promised to be good. Jean couldn't make that promise either, but he reduced her sentence to four years. During that time she spent 63 days in solitary confinement for refusing to give a urine sample, a punishment comparable to shooting the warden.

"I was three years in the system and they suddenly wanted a sample," says Jean. "I was not there on a drug charge and could see no reason for it except that they were trying to punish me. So I refused. I didn't know the repercussions of my refusal, however." As she left for "the hole" one of her friends, a bank robber, gathered Jean's books, knitting and Bible to take with her.

Jean has no regrets for what she did with Plowshares but she doesn't advise activists to set themselves up for prison. It's not so much the punishment and confinement as it is the disruption it causes on the homefront. "Prison is a process that takes at least a year to prepare for," she says. "It's costly, it upsets the family, and you have to find someone to take care of your household." But Jean is philosophical about her reasons for accepting her punishment, again as recorded by Terkel:

> Oh, it's a hard spot to be in, but it's not an
> impossible one. It is saying to the people of
> the world that we have to give up a little of
> our comfort now, in a critical time, to point
> up the horrendous errors of a government. I
> always thought Joe and I had a lovely love
> affair when we were young. It's only gotten
> better. We're not going to see each other for
> a while—that's hard.

Joe was supportive of Jean's efforts even though, ironically, he was a chemical engineer who worked in the nuclear power plants that produced the materials for nuclear weapons. Despite the fact that he was familiar with the weapons' enormous power, he didn't make the connection that they might be used for war. This was the Cold War era when the United States feared a communist takeover by the Soviet Union and America protected itself by stockpiling nuclear-tipped missiles. As Jean became more involved in the anti-nuclear weapons movement, Joe began to take an interest in it, too, especially when Jean's trial finally "converted" him.

"I listened to the expert witnesses who testified on behalf of Jean and the other members of her Plowshares group," says Joe. American historian Howard Zinn spoke, even though the judge tried to muzzle him. Dr. Helen Caldicott spoke on the medical consequences of nuclear weapons (genetic mutation passed on to future generations and an atomic cloud drifting across the world affecting the world's populations). Dr. Paul Walker, a defense analyst, described the power of these weapons in their use and their after-effects. Then Joe acted.

On August 5, 1987, at 5 p.m., Joe and Jerry Ebner, a priest from the Milwaukee Catholic Worker, went to the K-9 missile silo in Butler, Missouri (near Kansas City), and performed the Plowshares ritual. Their act was timed to the 42nd anniversary of the bombing of Hiroshima: August 6 at 8 a.m. (Japan time). Joe ended up in the Oxford Prison Camp in Wisconsin for two years. During that time he refused to work on a beautification project for the staff quarters and was punished with 30 days of solitary confinement. He was then moved to the Sandstone Security Prison in Minnesota.

Joe says that prison isn't as bad as it's made out to be, especially federal prison. There is not much discretionary time and you have no responsibilities to attend to and no decisions to make. So he read books by Zinn and anti-nuclear weapons activist Dr. Helen Caldicott, Gandhi, Martin Luther King, Jr., Dostoevsky and "Civil Disobedience" by nineteenth century author, Henry David Thoreau.

Ironically, the missiles in Missouri were taken down as a result of the SALT II talks between President Ronald Reagan and Soviet Prime Minister Mikhail Gorbachev in the late 1980s.[83] "I'm one of the few people who experienced taking them down," jokes Joe.

Jean maintains that prison is not as bad as the probation period afterward. For example, when one of her children was preparing to marry out of state, the law prevented Jean from going to the wedding. "That was a bummer," says Jean, "but my family understood."

Jean met many "outstanding people" in prison. Some of the women helped make a peace quilt, which was unfurled at

---

[83] The last Minuteman II silo was imploded on December 15, 1997. The implosion of the Minuteman II was in accordance with the Strategic Arms Reduction Treaty signed by former U.S. President George H.W. Bush and former Russian President Mikhail Gorbachev on July 31, 1991. The treaty took effect Dec. 5, 1994.
Source: Federation of American Scientists, www.fas.org/

According to the Center for Defense Information (www.cdi.org/), the United States currently has a total of 10,455 nuclear weapons with 7,000 strategic weapons and 800 non-strategic tactical weapons activated. These missiles sit in underground silos 60 feet deep in the following states: Colorado, Montana, North Dakota, and Nebraska. Other land-based strategic weapons in the U.S. arsenal include the Minuteman III, a 350 kiloton weapon with three independently targetable warheads and the MX missile, a 300–400 kiloton weapon with 10 independently targetable warheads. The MX runs on railroad tracks to keep moving and avoid being targeted by enemy firepower. Richard Perle, one of the neoconservatives of the Project for the New American Century and currently on the Defense Policy Board for the Bush administration, helped to coordinate this missile system in 1986.

the CodePink demonstration at the White House on March 8, 2003. She also got to know the women as individuals through card games. An avid bridge player, she taught the women how to play. At one point she organized three tables. Among the players were convicted bank robbers. "We had fun," says Jean in her usual spirited chuckle.

Early in their marriage, bridge had been a big part of the Gumps' life. They played tournament bridge with such passion that they discussed specific plays on specific hands during their ride home from these games. Oftentimes a shouting match ensued between them over mistakes. "It got so bad that we had to decide between bridge and our marriage," laughs Joe. These were the days before they became social activists when they led comfortable, professional lives with home, church, family and friends as their priorities.

"I gave everything away," says Jean about that way of life, "because I knew I had to devote myself to working for justice and peace."

"Working for justice. That's what we do in our retirement," says Joe.

"Don't you tire of standing on street corners?" I ask them.

"You get used to it," says Jean off-handedly. "It's easier when you do it with a group."

"Yeah, you get energy from doing it with other people," says Joe.

The Gumps' energy, however, also springs from their spiritual commitment to the Beatitudes, which they first learned through the CFM in Chicago. That's when they put Jesus' teachings and political action together.

Iraq has been an issue for the Gumps since 1996 after the United Nations imposed sanctions on that country's oil exports for six years. That action resulted in strangling Iraq's economy, increasing the poverty of the people and causing death to thousands of Iraqis due to the lack of healthy living

conditions and inadequate medical care. Some people believe
that over an estimated 500,000 Iraqi children under age five
died as a result of sanctions—almost three times the number
of Japanese killed during the bombings of Hiroshima and
Nagasaki.[84]   In the mid-1990s, Americans were not paying
much attention to Iraq. It seemed that the 1991 Gulf War had
passed and the issue with Saddam was settled. Nevertheless,
the Gumps, Quakers and a few other local peace activists
deemed the sanctions abominable so they formed a group
called Voices in the Wilderness and stood in front of the
Federal Building protesting the sanctions. Between one and
ten people came to these demonstrations on and off for about
five years.

---

[84] "Since the U.N. adopted economic sanctions in 1945, in its charter,
as a means of maintaining global order, it has used them fourteen
times (twelve times since 1990)," according to Joy Gordon in the
November 2002 *Harper's Magazine*. "But only those sanctions
imposed on Iraq have been comprehensive, meaning that virtually
every aspect of the country's imports and exports is controlled, which
is particularly damaging to a country recovering from war . . .

"News of such Iraqi fatalities has been well documented (by the
United Nations, among others), though underreported by the media.
What has remained invisible, however, is any documentation of how
and by whom such a death toll has been justified for so long. How
was the danger of goods entering Iraq assessed, and how was it
weighed, if at all, against the mounting collateral damage? As an
academic who studies the ethics of international relations, I was
curious. It was easy to discover that for the last ten years a vast
number of lengthy holds had been placed on billions of dollars'
worth of what seemed unobjectionable—and very much needed—
imports to Iraq. But I soon learned that all U.N. records that could
answer my questions were kept from public scrutiny. This is not to
say that the U.N. is lacking in public documents related to the Iraq
program. What is unavailable are the documents that show how the
U.S. policy agenda has determined the outcome of humanitarian and
security judgments."

When the second Bush administration threatened war with Iraq in summer 2002, Voices joined with other local peace activists in Kalamazoo to form KNOW. The difference in this movement, however, is that a mounting mistrust of the Bush presidency fueled people not only in Kalamazoo but throughout the country and the world, especially when the president began talking about a war against Saddam. Still reeling from September 11, the Democrats, the media and the public at large remained largely mute and compliant to the president. In October 2002, Congress authorized Bush with the powers to wage war on Iraq, if need be. When Bush bandied about the idea of a unilateral, pre-emptive war against Iraq, millions of citizens in the United States and from countries all over the world began protesting in the streets. Kalamazoo joined these protests in September 2002.

One interesting and unforeseen trend during this time when politics became more separated from populist concerns is the emergence of citizen activist groups at the local and national levels. Many of the groups used the Internet to organize people to object to Bush's threat to Iraq through peace rallies and marches. KNOW met this need in Kalamazoo.

"If ever there is a change, it's through the grassroots," says Jean. That's why she and Joe go to the KNOW peace vigils to express themselves and to inspire others to the cause of peace—even if it's only one by one. The Gumps also conduct a peace vigil every Saturday in Paw Paw, a largely Republican and pro-Bush town about 30 minutes west of Kalamazoo on I-94. They stand near the U.S. Post Office, a high traffic area where people can stop and talk to them. Most of the time people ignore them. A few honk their car horns and a few sneer at them. In the days preceding the war Jean says 30 people used to show up in Paw Paw. However, by December

339

2003, only five or six people come regularly. Sometimes, it's only Joe and Jean.

One day in Paw Paw, a woman stopped to talk with them saying that their presence was "hurting" her because she had a son in Iraq. "We are every bit as interested in your son as we are about the Iraqis," Jean told the woman. The woman admitted that she never voted for Bush and that she tried to dissuade her son from signing up for the military. Jean listened to her and the woman left saying that the conversation was pleasant and that she had gained some insights. The woman's dilemma, it turned out, was having to go home and face her son's wife. The woman didn't favor the war, but she didn't know how to handle it with her family and this impasse only increased her concerns about her son.

Jean says that such conversations sustain her and help to divert her own worries of each day's sordid news on Iraq—as well as the administration's other domestic and foreign policies. "I always have anxiety when I listen to the news," says Jean. "We might have to soup up our activities for peace."

The gradual support for peace, even a year after the war started, remind Jean of the Civil Rights Movement in the 60s. Changing people's minds about an issue is a slow but constant witness, she says. It requires that people—usually one by one—be allowed to conclude a position on their own. When enough people "pile on to it" or "buy into" an issue, it eventually becomes a force all of its own.[85] Then change can

---

[85] Many activists refer to this dynamic as the Hundredth Monkey Syndrome, a classic story. Monkeys inhabited a group of islands in the South Pacific, "which experienced a severe drought. The monkeys were beginning to starve due to lack of food so a team of anthropologists visited one of the islands to try to help. They discovered that there were sweet potatoes on the island, so they showed one of the monkeys how to dig up the root and eat it. By the next day, all the monkeys had learned how to dig up roots and were

occur. Jean has stood for peace and justice in the world with this belief in mind. That's why she cannot stop her stand for peace.

However, the Gumps point out that forces countering the peace movement are also gathering. Things that may not have looked like terrorism in the past are now, in the post 9/11 era, deemed to be so. Joe points out that Timothy McVeigh's bombing of the Murrah Building on April 19, 1995, is currently referred to as a "terrorist action." New definitions of terrorism are also emerging and being leveled against citizens through the USA PATIOT Act. The Bush Doctrine calling for a "War on Terrorism"[86] and a state of "perpetual war," justifies

---

eating. The anthropologists went to the next island and to their amazement, they found the monkeys were already digging up the sweet potatoes and were eating them. In fact, as they visited each island, the monkeys were eating sweet potatoes. Somehow, the education they provided to the original monkeys transferred by some illogical means to all the monkeys on all the islands. Another example of a similar kind of phenomena is when the first track runner achieved the four-minute mile. Prior to this accomplishment, it was thought that it was an impossible feat. But after it happened the first time, suddenly many people were running four-minute miles." (Source: www.themessenger.info/MAR2002/WynnFree.html.)

[86] The *New Yorker* reported in its August 8 & 15, 2005, issue that the War on Terror has been re-named to "a global struggle against violent extremism." Author George Packer contends "the focus has shifted from a tactic to an ideology." White House officials wrote a July 23, 2005 Op-Ed in the *New York Times* indicating that the word change "is an ideological contest, a war of ideas that engages all of us, public servant and private citizen, regardless of nationality." Packer points to something more telling: "The Administration is admitting that its strategy since September 11th has failed, without really admitting it. The single-minded emphasis on hunting down terrorists has failed. The use of military force as the country's primary and, at times, only response has failed, and has stretched the Army and the Marines to the breaking point. Unilateralism has failed . . . Loading the entire burden of the war onto the backs of American soldiers,

aggressive, pre-emptive action against nations it deems threatening to the United States. Joe says this includes the greater expense and heightened activity of the Defense Department and the creation of the Department of Homeland Security, which was recently elevated to a cabinet-level status. "The war on terrorism can be continued forever," says Joe, "and our rights are being abridged as part of the process."

The Gumps have had their own personal experience with "the war on terrorism." They believe someone is watching their computer. A message recently popped up on their screen, "You're computer is being observed." The message appeared and disappeared so quickly that Joe was unable to print it. "The message came from our server company," says Joe, which meant that the company was cooperating with government surveillance, probably under the USA PATRIOT Act. Joe immediately called the company but it denied posting the message or cooperating with a federal agency.

"Are you concerned about this?" I ask.

"No!" the Gumps answered simultaneously with a laugh.

"If they *are* listening, they'll get a lesson," says Jean. "I get wonderful letters [from members of the peace movement]."

"Aren't you afraid your computer might be bugged" I ask.

"What is there to be afraid of?" says Joe. "If they want to monitor me and try to imprison me, let them go ahead. I've been to jail before. It's not so bad."

Even though the Gumps are not ostensibly fearful of such invasive tactics, they argue that snooping in their home is an invasion of privacy and "un-American." Jean compares such tactics to an interview she just heard on an NPR talk show (December 9, 2003) where a Russian-born woman told of her

---

while telling the rest of the citizenry to go about its business, has failed. . . .In a recent Gallup poll, only 34 percent of Americans said that we are winning the war on terrorism. The phrase has outlived its enormous political usefulness" (page 33).

experience of government oppression and her flight from the country with her father and husband. "The government came for people in the middle of the night," says Jean, recounting the women's story. "And that's what's going on in the United States right now over individual citizens' rights. This should alarm people."

"This administration is blatantly dishonest," says Joe. "We have never had such a bad group in office—unless I was too naïve to see it before. We are the most powerful empire in the world and certainly the most violent." Joe cites a story he heard recently about a couple of young people who had left the United States in protest over its policies. "I have felt that if I were their age I would leave, too. It's so hard to be optimistic about the direction our country is going."

Paralyzing fear and disbelief that these things are happening begin to grip me as I speak with the Gumps. Just that morning I had a conversation with a woman who grew up in Nazi Germany and was now beside herself with anger and disgust. "These shits are dangerous," she said, referring to those the Bush administration who "hunt down" terrorists in our country through government surveillance.

"Are their tactics like Hitler and the Nazis?" She nodded solemnly and added that such violations against citizens go by inches, unobtrusively. Worse yet, they seem justified as authorities seek the perpetrators of "crimes against America." Then, when people speak against such practices, they are attacked. Bush officials and supporters call objections to measures that aim to protect the population, such as the USA PATRIOT Act, hysterical and exaggerated. Yet, they deny evidence that these tactics against Americans are taking place. A country under terrorist attack must protect itself both inside and outside the country, they claim. This is why the "war on terrorism" must be waged, especially since no one can know who the terrorists are or where they lurk. The root of this belief comes from the fact that many of the 9/11 terrorists were integrated into American communities and no one suspected these men of plotting evil against the United States.

The post-9/11 era has created an unreasonable ethos of fear in the American people such that they go along with government tactics that attempt to identify terrorists at the expense of their civil liberties. These tactics appear to produce the same kinds of intimidation lodged against citizens during the McCarthy anti-communist era of the early 1950s and during the Cold War when Americans feared the Russian menace. We were supposed to hate and fear the Russians, even though most of us had never met any. Jean illustrates this in Studs Terkel's book (1988) as "state engineered" hatred in its citizens:

> When I started dating my husband, right after World War Two, my aunt says, 'Jean is going to marry a Hun.' I thought, What the hell is a Hun? My husband's of German descent. We had just gotten through a war and we had to hate Germans. They were bad people. We certainly had to hate the Japanese. They were bad people. Through these years, I found out there's a lot of people that I have to hate.
>
> We have to hate the Iranians, 'cause we have to go over there and kill 'em. I had to hate the Vietnamese people. I have to hate the commies. Everybody has to hate the com-mies. There is no end to my nation's enemies. But I don't think they're my enemies. I think, God help me, these are people.

The Gumps have found a comfortable place with KNOW and, although their conviction for peace comes from their Catholic faith, they realize that KNOW attracts many people who are of other faiths and some who do not practice a religion. "We all have the same feeling for peace regardless of our motivation for standing for it," says Jean.

That's why the president's expressions of religious faith through war is an anomaly to the Gumps. "I don't know the same God the president has," says Jean. "Jesus was nonviolent. Some people point to his throwing people out of the temple with a whip as justification for violence—and war. But Jesus didn't kill anybody. He just shooed people out of his Father's house." Jean says that people who use their faith to justify war tend to focus more on Old Testament morality rather than the Good News of the New Testament where Jesus demonstrates a new way of being.

"We don't believe in the Just War Theory either," says Joe, referring to St. Augustine's 1600-year-old treatise that created a compromise between the peace-loving Church and militant Rome in the fourth century. St. Augustine says:

> We do not seek peace in order to be at war,
> but we go to war that we may have peace. Be
> peaceful, therefore, in warring, so that you
> may vanquish those whom you war against,
> and bring them to the prosperity of peace.

"We're pacifists," says Jean. "We don't believe in taking human life through war. If people approve or disapprove of us, that doesn't affect us. We're actors, not reactionaries."

"We do this work out of a conviction that this is what Jesus would want us to do," says Joe.

"Our judgment may not always be right," says Jean, "but we leave it up to God to take care of the consequences. We have to be sure about what we do and say. This is our moral obligation."

Our conversation is just getting started, but sadly, we have to end it. The Gumps are on their way to the Tuesday 4:30 vigil.

"When Eisenhower was leaving office, he said, 'Someday people are going to want peace so bad, the government had better step aside and let them have it.' I think that's coming to pass," says Jean. [87]

SHADIA KANAAN
Founder, Kalamazoo Women in Black

I visit Shadia at her home on a snowy day in December. As I approach her house at the end of the cul-de-sac, she is shoveling snow on the pathway leading to her front door. I arrive before she finishes, so we enter her house through the garage, squeezing in between her family car and the wall lined with cabinets and shelves. On one shelf there is a stack of what looks like 15 pizza boxes. But they are not pizza boxes; they are containers for baklava from a bakery in Detroit. Shadia and her husband buy these tasty Middle Eastern treats in bulk and give them away as gifts or serve them as party favors for family and friends.

I usually see Shadia at the Federal Building or on a major city street corner standing with a handful of Women in Black, the group that she started in Kalamazoo. Today is different and we have the opportunity to sit and talk in the enclosed patio of her beautiful, well-appointed home. The patio is filled with plants and flowers sitting in stands, on window sills or hanging from chains. The rattan couches and chairs are inviting and comfortable. We sit in this serene setting looking

---

[87] Studs Terkel, *The Great Divide*. New York: Pantheon Books, 1988. p.439.

out on her whitened backyard. Shadia surrounds herself with beauty. She, herself, is a beautiful woman with big brown eyes; dark, shoulder-length hair; a soft, throaty voice; and long, well-manicured nails with lovely gold rings on her fingers.

She offers me some mixed nuts and hot green tea and moves swiftly but graciously to the adjoining kitchen to retrieve them. Shadia has a powerful presence that is engaging. And I have wondered about who she is ever since I met her nine months ago in Bronson Park when she announced the beginning of the Kalamazoo Women in Black. We are alone now, away from the crowds and able to speak deeply and seriously to each other. We will talk for the next five hours.

Shadia has a master's degree in political science, but there are other reasons why she is so articulate about politics. As a Palestinian, Shadia knows the politics of her native land not just because she has studied it and lived, but it is still a very important part of her. "Every Palestinian, whether Christian or Muslim, rich or poor, inside Palestine or outside, has a feeling for Palestine," says Shadia. "They see Palestine as an orphaned child that needs protection and nurturing. Every household in generation after generation breathes this love for the land and its people." To Shadia, Palestine represents home and she describes it as a peaceful and romantic place that still connects her to a land, a people, her family and friends, and a way of life.

Prior to 1948, Shadia's family owned farmlands and orange orchards that were rented out to farmers. However, with the establishment of Israel as a sovereign nation on 78% of historical Palestine in 1948, Shadia's family lost all the property they owned in these areas. As a wealthy family they also owned property in the areas that were not lost to Israel in 1948 and in the city of Nablus in the West Bank of the Jordan River; real estate, a soap factory and a home where they lived until now.[88] Many Palestinian families were not that fortunate and lost everything.[89] Then, because her family's income dropped so precipitously, Shadia's father had to find a higher paying job than the local Arab Bank that he managed. As a graduate of the American University in Beruit, Lebanon, and among the very few college graduates at the time, he was commissioned to establish the first Arab Bank in Riyadh, Saudi Arabia. He lived there until he died in 1970. The family united each year for only one month during the summer breaks. Since there were no schools yet in Saudi Arabia, which just discovered oil, Shadia attended a Quaker boarding school and subsequently obtained a Bachelor's degree in political science from the University of Jordan in 1969 and a Master's degree from WMU in 1997.

Leaving their lands in the West Bank left the Palestinians devastated with bitterness, pain and agony at their loss, says Shadia, but she and her family survived. Eventually she married and came to the United States with her physician husband. Over the years she has visited her native land many times but access there has become increasingly difficult. She explains how tragic it was for her to be allowed by the Israeli occupation forces to visit her native country only as a tourist traveling with an American passport. She can only stay there

---

[88] These areas were occupied by Israel in 1967 in the aftermath of the Six Day War and are referred to as the Occupied Territories. They are the West Bank and Gaza, constituting 22% of historical Palestine. All peace initiatives and U.N. and Security Council resolutions deal with this portion, which more recently was diminished to half by the Israeli settlements and the Separation Wall.

[89] Over 700,000 Palestinians fled to the neighboring Jordan, Syria, Egypt, or the West Bank and Gaza. They are the core of the Palestinian refugee problem which is at the heart of peace negotiations in the region.

on a three-month visa. If she wants to stay longer, she·has to leave the country and reenter with a new visa.

The plight of the Palestinians used to be a unifying issue for the 25 Muslim countries in the Middle East. Gamal Abdul-Nasser, president of Egypt (1952–70) and an advocate for the revival of the National Arab Movement, tried to unite and secularize the Arab nations. Since Nasser, Arab leaders still try to gain legitimacy for their regime by invoking the Palestine issue. This political and cultural movement continued with Saddam Hussein who offered the families of suicide bombers $25,000 compensation for their sacrifices. Of course, the latter is what the media capitalize on, says Shadia who adds that "Saddam was a butcher and a dictator. He used the Palestinian issue to further his cause, and the U.S. media capitalized on that linkage to diminish the Palestinians' right to freedom."

Since 1991 with the first Gulf War, the Palestinian issue that once served as a political unifier has become divisive. Arab countries are now dissociating themselves from the Palestinians because of U.S. pressure on their leaders and Israeli reprisals against them. Lebanon suffered a devastating invasion in 1982 to get the P.L.O. out (Palestine Liberation Organization under the leadership of Yasser Arafat).

"All the Palestinians have now is the stone (to use as a weapon) and civil disobedience. Their only card is resistance against Israeli occupation of their people. Yet, we keep hoping for a peace settlement." Suicide bombers have become the other weapon, I say.

"It is important to remember that the suicide bombers are members of extremist factions in Palestine, both Islamic and secular," says Shadia. "They have given up on peace and are resistant to the Israeli occupation because they believe they have a legitimate right to life under international law. No one condones their actions, but they are claiming their right to freedom from Israeli occupation and colonization. However, in its effort to curb what it calls terrorism, Israel is actually committing 'state-sponsored terrorism' on daily basis which systematically imposes a collective punishment against all Palestinians by bulldozing orchards and farm lands and uprooting hundreds of thousands of olive trees, demolishing buildings and assassinating wanted militant Palestinian leaders. The army protects the Jewish settlers who live on stolen Palestinian land in the midst of the Palestinian centers. The settlers often go on a rampage by smashing car windows, stealing crops, burning businesses and committing acts of kidnapping and murder."

"Many people blame Arafat," says Shadia, but the truth is that Palestinian society remains very divided politically. At one extreme are those who want peace at any price, lowering the bar continuously, at the other are the Islamic fundamentalists and other rejectionists who would rather die than compromise their basic rights. To survive you have to be a juggler of these factions and keep a level of balance. Arafat, a master politician, was able to do it as head of the PLO by keeping all the factions in check. [90] Everything he did was done with the idea of keeping to the middle ground. He also managed to negotiate the Oslo Accord (September 1993), which provides for a peace treaty between Israel and the P.L.O. by ending the occupation of West Bank and Gaza and creating a two-state solution. But the Accord failed to do that."

Actually, the plight of the Palestinians goes beyond Arafat, explains Shadia. It began in 1897 when Zionists[91] leaders met

---

[90] Yasser Arafat died on November 11, 2004.

[91] Zionism, the national movement for the return of the Jewish people to their homeland and the resumption of Jewish sovereignty in the Land of Israel, advocated, from its inception, tangible as well as spiritual aims. Jews of all persuasions, left and right, religious and secular, joined to form the Zionist movement and worked together toward these goals. Disagreements led to rifts, but ultimately, the

in Basel, Switzerland, and concocted the idea of finding a homeland for the Jews. This began a convergence of religion and politics in the Middle East. The Zionists looked at four places where this nation could be: Argentina, Canada, central Africa, and Palestine (which at the time was part of the Ottoman Empire). The Zionists voted for Palestine and rallied Jews to come to "God's Promised Land."

"The Zionists could capitalize on Palestine and sell it much better and get support for the land where they lived 2,000 years before the Roman Empire's exile of the Jews," she says. To corroborate her story, Shadia refers me to Dr. Norman Finkelstein, a political science professor from DePaul University, who came to Kalamazoo in October 2003 to talk about the origins of the Israeli–Palestinian conflict. Finkelstein's parents were Jewish Holocaust survivors. Shadia even loans me her original copy of his videotaped visit so that I can study it. This is typical Shadia: she will do whatever she can, take whatever time, and use whatever means she has to educate others on Palestine.

Actually, Shadia's passion for politics began when she was in the second grade and "became aware of King Abdullah (of Jordan) and his alleged complicity." She heard her father and brothers talking politics all the time and as she learned their stories, she "imitated" them and practiced their positions on her friends. "My family taught me information and the attitude

---

common goal of a Jewish state in its ancient homeland was attained. The term Zionism was coined in 1890 by Nathan Birnbaum (1864– 1937). In 1890, Birnbaum also coined the terms Zionist and in 1892, Political Zionism. In 1893, he published a brochure entitled Die Nationale Wiedergeburt des Juedischen Volkes in seinem Lande als Mittel zur Loesung der Judenfrage ("The National Rebirth of the Jewish People in its Homeland as a Means of Solving the Jewish Question"). Source: Jewish Virtual Library, www.jewishvirtuallibrary. org.

of nationalism," says Shadia, which characterizes her passion and identity. "It puts in focus the reason I am here."

Because they were a wealthy family, Shadia's parents began helping people who lost their livelihood and their homes in 1948 after the state of Israel gained sovereignty. Her mother sent poor people money in envelopes, a discrete way of providing the unfortunate with something to live on while preserving their dignity. Many others shared their own food with those devastated by the new regime. "Islam teaches that charity is supposed to be done in secret," says Shadia. "You don't do it to boast or impress others. That is not from the heart." Today, Shadia's mother, who is 80 and housebound, continues her various charitable works like providing shelter to those whose homes have been demolished, collecting blankets and food for distribution and organizing breakfast fundraisers to help the needy. And there are plenty of needy people in Palestine.

The Israeli occupation of Palestine has presented Palestinians with an extraordinary situation. There is no government, police, army, civil service or social service, nothing to take care of people's needs, she says. Some people live in houses with big holes in their walls caused by Israeli tanks or shells, which they can't repair because they have no materials. If they do manage to fix a structure, the Israelis often damage it again. Women bake bread to share with their neighbors and people from all over the world donate computers, sewing machines and the like, she says. Some charity groups bring Palestinian girls from their villages and educate them so they can return home and establish businesses in their community. They send them with a sewing machine or a computer to sustain themselves and their families.

Several European nations have also helped the Palestinians. The European Union maintains the municipalities in several towns with monetary and tangible aid. U.S.

official aid to Palestinians is minimal, but American and other international and local non-governmental organizations (NGOs) are a major source of aid there. Aid to the refugees is exclusively dependent on the United Nations Relief Works Agency (UNRWA), however, funding for this major service has been cut and is threatened to be completely stopped, which would have disastrous effects on the Palestinian refugees all over the Middle East. The other major source of funding for Palestinians under occupation is the money sent by family members who reside outside their country. They are called expatriates or expats for short. They are usually immediate family members, but in many cases they extend themselves further to help aunts and nephews and cousins.

Currently, World Bank statistics estimate that 75 percent of the Palestinians live on less than $2 a day, says Shadia spewing out the facts on Palestine like an encyclopedia. So if it were not for the private charity of families there or in the United States, many of the people would perish. Shadia and her husband contribute to Palestinian charities that support hospitals in her hometown. They also provide scholarships and sponsorships to students.

Shadia's two girlhood friends, who came from elite families and went to college together, are also involved in such activist efforts. Liana, a filmmaker, records the Israeli army's brutality and destruction and then shares her films with sympathizers all over the world for education and fundraising purposes. Anan started a charity group in Detroit that provides news and information about the Palestinian situation.

"If it weren't for charitable work, people would starve over there," says Shadia. "But I am not exceptional, I am doing the minimum. Sometimes I feel a little short from what others do. I should do more."

In Shadia's hometown resides the 5,000-year-old biblical tribe of Samaritan Jews. This Palestinian-Jewish tribe lives there peacefully even though they've never mixed their two cultures or integrated with the local Muslim Arabs. Their community is part of the social network of Nablus in Arab Palestine. They go to the same schools, work in public and city jobs and maintain close friendly relations with the Nablus families, including Shadia's. The community proudly boasts its possession of an original calfskin copy of the Bible.

Last summer Shadia and her husband wanted to visit their home, which they built on the hilltop adjacent to the Samarite village. (Her husband's ancestral home, 600 years old, was destroyed by Israeli F-16 bomber in April 2002.) So they went to see the Samarite village chief, whom they knew personally, to obtain special permission to travel through the many checkpoints the Israelis had set up on the mountain. At these checkpoints, Shadia's car, like everyone else's, was searched. When she arrived at her home, she found the Israeli army camped out on the driveway. Of course, it became impossible for the couple to stay at their home; it remains empty.

"We are privileged because we are Americans," says Shadia "and I knew the chief of the village who got us through the checkpoints. We didn't have to spend nearly as much time waiting." Such is not the life for most Palestinians and more hardship has recently visited them when Israel built a 28-foot high concrete wall extending 425 miles.

The wall, complete with razor-wire fences, trenches and watchtowers on the gerrymandered borders between Israel and Palestine,[92] presents Palestinians with ever more obstacles of

---

[92] On July 9, 2004, the Hague-based International Court of Justice (the World Court) declared the Separation Wall illegal and said it should be dismantled. Of course, this ruling is non-binding and Israel, with the U.S. backing it, does not accept it. Israelis claim the wall protects them from terrorists and Palestinians claim the Israelis are engaged in a land grab from territory the Jewish state captured. Source: www.gush-shalom.org/thewall/index.html

time and space as they attempt to get to jobs, markets and the homes of family and friends. Sometimes the wait at the checkpoints takes days and women give birth to their babies. The wall has essentially trapped 210,000 Palestinians living in 67 towns or villages in Gaza and the West Bank. In some places the wall literally surrounds a village, like a prison. There are 13 villages with 11,700 people who live like this. The wall has also reduced Palestinian territory by approximately 50 percent *within* the Green Line. Some of this territory includes rich farmland and centuries-old olive trees as well as the much coveted water aquifers.

As I listen to Shadia, my impression of the Palestinian cause seems so hopeless, and I ask her how and why she continues with it.

"My role is simple," she says. "I don't think I can do more, but I have the sense of satisfaction that I'm doing something even if it is sometimes frustrating."

The USA PATRIOT Act has also had an effect on Palestine, says Shadia, by intimidating many American Muslims from sending money to charities in Palestine because they are suspected of supporting terrorists. Shadia especially dreads the passage of PATRIOT Act II. "My agony and our dilemma now is that I could become a target because of my origin. Anyone could be stripped of her citizenship," she says.

In December 2003 local ACLU and BORDC leaders lobbied the City of Portage to treat the USA PATRIOT Act with the same non-cooperation stance with the federal government as Kalamazoo did in October. Shadia says that many people testified for this proposition, including a U.S. Marine who had served in Iraq. In speaking against the USA PATRIOT Act he said he "didn't put [his] life on the line" for this kind of treatment to American citizens. The Portage City

Commission tabled further action until February 10, 2004, and then voted 6 to 1 not to vote on the issue claiming that the USA PATRIOT Act was a federal issue, not a local one.

"I wanted to speak at that [December] commission meeting," says Shadia, "but I didn't. I have been in the United States for 33 years. I feel I've earned my place and paid my dues. I have gifted this country with four sons: one is a heart surgeon, one is studying to become a neurosurgeon, and the other two are businessmen in this community." "I feel I've earned the right to be comfortable, but I didn't have the heart to speak because my statement is more rhetorical and therefore weaker. And I didn't want to undermine the strength of those who spoke against the PATRIOT Act from their personal experience."

Unfortunately, the provisions of the PATRIOT Act have also led Shadia to suspect that *she* is under surveillance. For example, she has had a lot of problems with her telephone since 9/11 and wonders if she and her husband are being bugged. "I'm uncomfortable, but I'm not afraid," says Shadia. "We're careful about giving donations to our charities. We only give through official channels that are cleared by the State Department. We mainly help a hospital and an orphanage in Nablus. During these last two years the comfort level I enjoyed as a U.S. citizen has been taken away from me. I'm very sad about that, but will that stop me from my activities? NO! I could sit pretty, go to movies, wear diamond rings— and I have many. But what would be the value of my life, then?"

The post-9/11 environment has also changed Shadia's social life in Kalamazoo. For years Shadia has regularly played bridge with her women friends but the women only talk about safe subjects like families, food, fashion and social activities. Never politics. She has essentially gone along with this narrow field of conversation until this year.[93] What's more, her friends know she is involved politically, but they never ask her about her activities, they never talk about the Iraq War and they never bring up anything that might be controversial.

"It's like having a chessboard for each friend," says Shadia about this more strained and unnatural environment that exists for her. "I move my chess piece [by calling or visiting a friend] and then wait for her move." Frankly, Shadia is not sure whether her friends still accept her or not. So Shadia has become a passionate social activist, especially as the injustices against Muslims have increased since 9/11. She also channels much of her energy into KNOW and the Women in Black.

She had read about the Women in Black and knew about them from her visits to the Middle East, she says, but it wasn't until she first saw a demonstration on September 13, 2002, at a downtown Detroit art festival that she decided to start a group in Kalamazoo. The first Women in Black demonstration then took place in Bronson Park on March 23, 2003, after the Sunday peace vigil. Shadia invited 12 Christian and Muslim women to dress in black clothes and a black veil and hold a 20x30-inch placard she had made that read, "Women in Black: Mourning all victims of war and violence."

"The feeling I get from standing with the Women in Black is like I'm doing a long, sincere prayer. It is a cleansing experience," says Shadia. "It gives me completeness and a sense of belonging as well as the personal satisfaction of advocating for peace." As a result, she has become especially close to this core group of women who consistently show up for the hour-long silent vigils.

"We enjoy standing together," she says. "I look forward to being with them. They are like family," a phrase that Shadia uses to illustrate the intensity of feeling she has for others.

---

[93] A year later after this interview, Shadia told me she no longer associates with these friends.

Shadia has also made many new friends among the members of KNOW. Being with them gives her an "emotional supplement."

"KNOW has elevated me intellectually and spiritually and it has fulfilled a whole vacuum in my life," says Shadia. That KNOW people have listened to and extended their concern over peace and justice issues in Palestine has moved her greatly and she feels a sense of unity with them to her cause—and to peace in the world in general. For example, KNOW held a demonstration in Bronson Park to protest the 400-mile-long wall the Israelis built in Gaza and the West Bank. Several of the men made an 8x28-foot replica to illustrate the size of the wall. They then tore it down as a symbolic gesture of hope and peace among the Israelis and Palestinians. "They are a most sincere group," says Shadia. "Palestine is not their immediate cause, like it is for me, but they put forth tremendous effort."

Shadia's social activism has thrust her into a passionate new world that demands much time and psychic energy. For example, she organized a dinner fundraiser event at her home and raised $11,000 for the Palestinian Rowing Federation, which teaches Palestinian kids how to swim and trains coaches and swimmers for the Olympics.

"My husband worries about me personally," says Shadia. "He sees that the situation in Palestine is straining on me and making me tense. He tells me I have to slow down. He knows how agitated I am. My kids worry about me, too. They want me to read more fiction," she laughs.

Shadia has found that as devoted as she is to her work, she sometimes needs to withdraw from it all. Being alone and quiet renews her spiritually and reminds her of the peaceful and happy boarding school days she had with the Quakers, for example. It was with them that she learned to see the humanity in *all* people through the works of Gibran, Jesus,

Mohammed and Gandhi who all taught about peace, love and
dignity for all people.

"Being a Muslim moves me to make a statement of peace
toward Israelis," she says. "It allows me to make choices of
freedom out of my frustration over the Palestinian political
situation rather than to feed the violence." For that she finds a
venue in the Kalamazoo Interfaith Coalition for Peace and
Justice, which has hosted lively debates among the two sides in
quest for a permanent peace between the two peoples.

And what about the future for Palestine?

"I don't know," says Shadia. "I can only hope that the
American administration will see an objective, even-handed
policy and bring peace and security to the Middle East, but I
know this: no matter what gets done there in that region of
the world, it's all about Palestine."

Shadia contends that the focus on Iraq, Syria and Iran are
all cover-ups to the *real* problem, which is the Israeli and
Palestinian conflict. Instead, she believes that something will
be done when the United States, as the world's only
superpower, decides to do something about this situation.

"When Europe plays its hand, it tries to form partnerships.
When the U.S. plays its hand, it turns the tables and
monopolizes the process again." The so-called "Road Map"
was a solution started by the Europeans, the U.N., Russia and
the U.S. The U.S. assumed control over it and then allowed
Sharon to quash it.

I ask Shadia about Arafat's refusal to accept the peace plan
that President Clinton had frantically worked for during the
Camp David talks shortly before he left office. Arafat was
offered 95 percent of what he wanted. Why didn't he take
that?

"If he had signed the agreement, he would have accepted a
state with non-contiguous blocks of Palestinian population
separated by Jewish settlements and numerous Israeli army

check points. That mini-state would have no sovereignty over its borders; land, air or sea, its water resources or any aspect of sovereignty. The issue of the right of return for the millions of refugees and the issue of Jerusalem were unacceptable to the majority of the Palestinian people. If Israel wants peace, it has to withdraw from Palestinian lands, dismantle its settlements, compensate the refugees, and lose Israel's water rights and borders. Israel's strategy, however, has been to disrupt, cancel and sabotage the peace process—and the U.S. has been complicit. The United States is the only power capable of effecting change and tipping the balance."

For now, Shadia carries on a nearly single-handed campaign of education and consciousness-raising about Palestine and her people's predicaments. She hopes that by spreading the word about its plight, American citizens will call on legislators to change U.S. foreign policy in the Middle East. This hope comes from her belief and experience that there's nothing like the warmth of your own home and the decency of living comfortably with your family. However, she fears the worst for the people in her native land.

"I'm scared for my family in Palestine and I see my problems as nothing compared to theirs. I count my blessings but Muslims are fatalistic. So you can only do your best."

VII.

AFTERMATH

OF THE

WAR

JANUARY–JUNE 2004

Monday, May 3, 2004

POTUS VISITS KALAMAZOO

It isn't often that the President of the United States comes to your town. It is an exciting and historical event. George W. Bush came to Kalamazoo today, his fourth visit here in four years, twice as president. Only this time it is far more contentious and ugly. It starts with the distribution of admission tickets.

From Tuesday, April 27 until May 4, the *Kalamazoo Gazette* ran front-page stories about the president's visit planned at Wings Stadium, a 4,500-capacity arena. On Thursday, April 29 the paper announced that people could obtain the 3,500 available tickets beginning the next day from either the Chamber of Commerce in downtown Kalamazoo or a local law office in Portage. Many tickets were also reserved for dignitaries and special guests. So on Saturday, May 1, the paper reported that all the tickets were gone. Some people who had been promised tickets discovered they are "screwed" out of them. Many people had camped out at distribution sites as early as 6 a.m. while others stood out in the rain for two hours.

The peace people prepared for the Bush appearance, too, with two demonstration sites. Over 100 people show up at the Episcopalian Cathedral site near the Oakland Drive exit and I-94 where the Silhouette display (*see* page 375) is erected. It is big enough for the president to see from the freeway. At Wings Stadium on Sprinkle Road and I-94 I intend to talk to Bush supporters about the war. I haven't spoken to any of them for over a year and this event provides a good opportunity to interview people and compare their responses to last year's interviews (*see* Appendix I). However, I can't follow through with my plan because I need either a press pass or a rally ticket to enter the parking lot outside the arena, and I have neither. So I decide to spend my time with the Wings Stadium demonstration which is gathering at the UAW union hall nearby.

This once-vibrant UAW hall is pretty quiet today, except for the demonstrators and the clanging rusted hooks fastened to the deteriorating ropes hanging on the flagpole in front of the building. In 1998 nearly 1,100 UAW workers lost their jobs at the GM stamping plant nearby and that pretty much gutted the union presence around Kalamazoo.

In the late 1970s, when the GM plant was rated one of the most efficient in the country, I remember arranging a public relations photo of a manager right outside the plant building. He was the subject of a story I was doing for the Nazareth College alumni news. Security men watched me closely to make sure I focused only on the man standing against a dark corrugated cement wall of the building and nothing else. Such security measures seemed so silly to me; I couldn't see anything inside the building, no machinery or even the workers. All that is now left of the plant is a big, empty parking lot with fading yellow parking lines and weeds growing out of the cracks of the pavement. Economic development officers in Kalamazoo are having a difficult time selling the plant to another manufacturing company because of GM's deed restrictions on the property. So the plant just sits there, empty.

☮

While the people gather in front of the UAW building, authorities admonish them not to walk on the grass of the adjacent business because they will be trespassing on private property. The people who come to rally are in rather high spirits and they make a joke of the rule, seeing it a pointless demand but not worth the trouble of argument. When it is time for the demonstration to begin, Wade Adams, the leader from KNOW, calls the group to order as people collect their signs and prepare for the half-mile hike to the demonstration site. Strange things begin to happen—and they continue until the event and the demonstration are over.

Wade notices the Kalamazoo police videotaping the crowd so he walks over to ask them what they are doing. They say they always film protest groups. Then a young policeman lays down several rules, which have security ramifications, as can be expected for a presidential visit. People crowd around Wade and the policeman to listen, but the policeman hesitates in his explanations and seems unsure of the rules. He seems a little too green to me. He does manage to give one clear order: "You must stay on public property along Covington and Sprinkle Roads and you may not go toward Wings Stadium where the cars are going into the Bush event."

Since the Secret Service agents have just finished checking people into the rally at the Covington entrance, not far from the UAW meeting site, they are now free to oversee the demonstrators. The two agents in business suits walk with us as we start down Covington Road and toward to the "free speech zone" on Sprinkle Road and then meet us again near the designated site on the corner of Sprinkle and the side road leading into the stadium.

The walk to the site on the uneven, grassy terrain actually is exciting as the tension for the president's appearance mounts. Peace Momma is here. About 200 people are here. The Women in Black are here and they bring a new prop, a U.S. flag-draped "casket" they built as a response to the Pentagon's ban of media coverage of dead soldiers' returning caskets. This "casket" recently appeared at the Sunday peace vigils.

We settle into our designated site in front of a gas station and within shouting distance to people going into the rally. After 10 to 15 minutes, the demonstrators and the Bush supporters (in their cars driving to the parking lot inside the arena) exchange harsh words. Suddenly, the Secret Service decides to move our group across the street.

I must admit that I am miffed because this move seems to be a ploy to separate the demonstrators even further from the arena in order to keep them as far away from Bush's bus as possible. The news has already reported that people in presidential counter-rallies are regularly "penned in." On the other hand, I soon realize the authorities probably want to reduce the tension in the crowd, not heighten it. They are there to protect *all* the people and to keep things peaceful but not to antagonize them. I keep trying to tell myself this.

One young woman takes particular offense to the directive to move and starts to argue with the authorities. I gently take her arm to persuade her to be quiet, do what the authorities say and to act peacefully. There is no use arguing with the police.

"Take your hands off of me," she says to me indignantly. "I consider your action as violent as theirs." She startles me with her response. Suddenly, I become her enemy.

"We don't want to make trouble," I retort, recalling the way the peace people demonstrate at the Sunday vigils, without rancor no matter what anyone says to them. She then blathers some nasty, disdainful remarks and sneers at me as she walks away. "That is not peaceful demonstration," I say under my breath, wanting to spout my piece without having to confront this hothead any further.

"This crowd is not the same crowd as the Sunday vigil," I tell Wade who passes by a bit later, looking rather harried.

"Yeah, I know. I'm trying to avoid the Secret Service from finding me so that they don't make any other demands on us." Wade clearly has his hands full and none of the other KNOW regulars—the men, that is—is there to help him. The group proceeds to cross the street as the police stop traffic to get everyone to the other side rather than wait for the traffic light. A grumbling undertone ensues, but everybody moves peacefully.

Wade later told me that the gas station owners complained about our being on their front lawn. Also, he said that some demonstrators did not want to move and were contemplating egging on the police to arrest them. That prospect had not been discussed prior to the event and Wade said he was unprepared to deal with it. Fortunately, he persuaded these people to move without further incident.

"I was concerned about most of our people getting into more difficulty than they had signed on for," says Wade.

Although this demonstration is organized by KNOW, several people I have never seen before are here and it seems to change the flavor of the demonstration from one of vigil to one of protest—a very contentious protest at that. Some of these unfamiliar people make a very extraordinary presence in terms of clothes, hair, tattoos and demeanor. At times I wish I weren't there because the ambiance is hostile and unpleasant, but this is only the beginning of what will become a long afternoon.

After the demonstrators move across the street I meet a friendly woman and we talk about the crowd, the cold and the significance of the day's event. She has an accent so when I finally ask her about her nationality she tells me she is a Muslim from the Middle East. We eventually talk about what that means to her and how her life as a woman matters in her own country.

Suddenly, two Secret Service agents approach us. These men are the same two I met when I tried to enter the stadium parking lot. I give them a friendly hello and they respond in kind, but they are not there to socialize. They ask my new acquaintance if she has passed a dollar bill that says "Kill George Bush" on it.

"No, I never passed such a bill," says the woman with a combination of astonishment, worry and a beseeching look on her face. "I never saw such a bill."

The two men look through the woman as if to test her truthfulness as I stare at them suspiciously and with disgust. Wade Adams suddenly appears. The two men begin to bluster. Then they blurt out a kind of laugh and move on. My eyes follow the two agents as they walk along the line of demonstrators. I don't see them talk to anyone else about the mysterious dollar bill.

"Can you believe that?" I shriek at Wade. "I can't believe that!"

Wade shakes his head and the woman just freezes in place for a while.

"Are you alright?" I ask her. "Are you OK?"

She musters up her composure. "I don't know what happened?" she says, "or why they came to me."

The evidence seems too obvious, as the spot where we had our conversation is right in front of a Sheriff's Department patrol car. The deputy inside may have heard our conversation and felt it was his duty to have this Muslim, Middle Eastern woman checked out. Then again, he may have just wanted to hassle her. Once again, I see that as paranoia set in, trust dissipates.

I peer into the patrol car to see who is in it and who may have been responsible for this inquiry, but the tinted glass blocks my view. Nice. Bullies acting in secret, I think to myself. They stay out of reach and then laugh to themselves at the havoc they cause on others. I am incensed. I want to get away from that spot and suggest to my new friend that we move along. She resists. I am frustrated and then torn about whether to stay with her or not; not that I can protect her. I decide that if anything happens, I'll call Wade for help. I stay another 10 minutes until finally I can't stand it any more.

"I'm going to stand with the Women in Black," I say to the woman, hoping that she will follow me.

"OK," she replies. She doesn't move.

I feel so uncomfortable leaving her, but I can no longer sustain the rancor of standing in front of the patrol car. I need some relief so I stand behind the Women in Black and their "casket." Actually, what I really want to do is escape this whole crowd. It tastes like poison.

Standing behind the Women in Black with their flag-draped casket gives me a little relief because I know them and trust them. I tell Jean Gump about the incident that has just taken place and she shakes her head gesturing her lack of surprise. Jean is good-natured about it, though. "Don't worry about it. No harm done," she says in her usual clipped and optimistic way.

A few minutes later, the woman reappears at my side. I am glad—and relieved. Suddenly there is yet another change in mood as the police begin to line up in front of us. The president's bus must be getting closer.

"This is a no-free speech zone," says an invisible man over a blow horn. "You must stay on the curb or you will be arrested." He repeats his warning a couple times to make sure everyone understands. Then the street becomes a high security zone. Officers with billy clubs in hand line up in front of us about an arms' length apart from each other and a few feet from the curb. Some of them are so young they barely show their beards but they stand there stone-faced and solemn.

Some of the protesters recognize a few policemen and try to be friendly to them.   The cops look uncomfortable at this exchange and try to avoid eye contact and conversation.

Then there are the Sheriff's deputies on horseback, the tallest horses I've ever seen. They stand in front of the street's entry way to the arena.   I recall a scene from the movie, "Gandhi" where the people are suddenly attacked by a pack of galloping British cavalrymen.   Their steeds would have trampled the people had not one of the Indians told the group to lie down. He knew that horses didn't run over people lying down on the ground. The tactic saved them as the horses stopped just before the crowd. While I know the deputies won't let their horses rush us in the same way, their presence provides a stunning example of how the police use intimidation to make sure that the demonstrators don't try anything. They assume we are an unruly and dangerous crowd. It sickens me. All of a sudden, we don't belong, we are not wanted, and we have been declared a potential enemy to the president—and this is in our own community!

I walk to the furthest end of the line to watch for the presidential convoy. On the other side of the street I notice a small group of Bush supporters gathered and freely holding their signs. No police line or horses stand in front of them. The words of the president after 9/11 come to mind, "You're either with us or against us." With this difference in treatment I begin to see the gravity of Bush's statement and how the country has divided against itself.

The tension mounts as we await the president's bus. Suddenly, traffic on Sprinkle Road stops completely. Seconds before the procession arrives, a young woman demonstrator has squatted on the ground at the furthest end the line where I am and begins to chant a loud, wailing, eerie moan.   The presidential procession approaches. Squad cars come first. As they exit the freeway and drive onto Sprinkle Road, they execute a circle formation on the full width of Sprinkle rounding it two or three times as their cherry-tops flash, their sirens blare and their tires squeal. The woman's wailing grows louder and the scene more surreal. The cars break their circle formation and head toward the arena as the mounted Sheriff's deputies lead their horses to turn away from the demonstration and toward the stadium. A group of motorcycles then roars in from the freeway. The men wear heavy white helmets with tinted visors and tough black jackets. The lead bus follows with several others behind it. Press and staff buses, no doubt. I can't see the president in the first bus, although the evening news shows him standing in the front window of the bus waving at the crowds in his characteristically affable way.

This whole drama lasts less than a minute and then the police break their line and declare the area a "free speech zone" again. The tension breaks as I try to catch my breath.

"What a travesty," cries out a tall, well-built middle-aged man in his deep voice nearby me. "What an absolute travesty! Our tax dollars at work. The people we elect to serve us in this county have turned against us."

I begin to feel sick again over the next 45 minutes or so. I can't stand the crowd I'm in. I can't stand the event or the treatment we receive. I can't stand the cold dampness of this day where I've been standing outdoors for five hours. I've had enough and want to get out of there as fast as I can! But I am stuck here without a car—and with my own curiosity over what might happen upon Bush's departure.

I call my husband, Kurt, on my cell phone and tell him about my afternoon. He just listens and is not surprised. This conversation is one of the few comforts of the day. I know I will be home soon and I am looking forward to it.

"Let's go out to dinner," I say. "Chinese?" Comfort food. Comfort activity. Something to look forward to while I endure this. He knows my sentiments.

"OK, we can do that," he says.

A few people in the crowd have radios and listen to Bush and the other activities on stage. They will let us know when the rally concludes, although that soon becomes evident from our vantage point when the police line up in front of us again and their commander gives the warning that the street is now a "no-free speech zone." The Sheriff's deputies return to the entrance way on their mounted horses and wait. Finally, the lead bus comes and peels out onto Sprinkle Road and onto the I-94 entrance ramp. As the president's bus speeds by I have been so overwhelmed by his presence and the pent-up negative emotions of the day that I shake my fist in the air at him and even though I can't see him behind the bus's tinted glass, I shout: "Get out of my town, you bastard. Get the hell out!" Bush is gone. And it is finally over. Well, not quite. I gasp at myself. I am violent. I have become like those I accuse.

A couple days after the Bush rally, it comes out that people who are Democrats or known to be unsupportive of the president were unwelcome to enter the arena to see the president. Bush supporters standing in line for tickets are expected to report such individuals who are then denied tickets. A *Gazette* reporter subsequently tells me she witnessed such an incident in the ticket line a couple days before and I hear from a couple other people that it happened to them as well. Citizens reporting on other citizens. Is this where we are headed in this new age of terrorism?

This crowd-control tactic for the president becomes more public, however, when David Corn of *The Nation* reports in his May 5 website, "Capital Gains," that seven Kalamazoo College students from the College Democrats who acquire tickets for this event are spotted by their College Republican classmates at the arena and report them to the security guards. Security then orders the College Dems to leave the area or be arrested.

According to Corn's story the students checked the Chamber of Commerce's website that said, "The tickets are free and will be distributed on a first-come-first-serve basis." So they stood in line for two hours, submitted their photo ID and their addresses as procedure prescribed and received their tickets. Outside Wings Stadium the College Dems, like everyone else, passed through a series of checkpoints until security accosted them.

"They told us," one Dem recounts to Corn, "that we failed a background check, that we had been identified by volunteers as a potential threat and that if we didn't leave we would be arrested."

No one in Kalamazoo was ever told that the rally with the president of the United States is a "private event" for his supporters only. Certainly the *Gazette* didn't indicate this restriction when it told people how to obtain tickets for the event.

> "Several things anger us," one of the "K" Dems tells Corn. "It may have been a private event, but the tickets didn't say that and we were never told that. We felt misled. But we felt worse about the College Republicans. We were very disappointed that our peers singled us out for what they *thought* we might do. And we later heard they had been primed to find potential threats at the event. But we were not a threat. We're even friends with some of these College Republicans. This was a sad commentary about the bitter divide of American politics. Look how hard it was for us to hear a contrary view. We wanted to see the president and then talk about what he said

afterward. We felt like we were being blacklisted by our campus peers, and this is a campus that is supposed to be open to different political views.

David Corn called both the College Republicans and the regional spokesperson for the Bush campaign for comment but neither of them responded.

This story makes the *Kalamazoo Gazette* on May 10. Deb Buchholtz-Hiemstra, chairwoman of the Kalamazoo County Board and vice chair of the Kalamazoo County Republican Party, is quoted as saying that the rally was a campaign event and not a presidential visit. In an attempt to get as many Bush supporters together as possible, politicians typically try to rouse their base in order to campaign for him in the coming election. That's why he wanted to have his supporters there.

In stories pre-dating the event, people were told where to get tickets and the procedure for obtaining them. They were told security would be tight although not out of the ordinary for a high security visitor (even after September 11). They were told to avoid traffic jams around Wings Stadium. They were told how they would be checked on site. They were even told that the Secret Service would not pen in protesters in a separate and distant location. They were *not* told, however, that the president's visit was a private affair or a closed event—at least not until they arrived there or were in line for tickets, a disturbing development.

In its many announcements prior to the event, the *Gazette* never indicated that the president's visit wasn't a public event. People just assumed it was. But like so many strange things that happened that day, this event suddenly became a private event.

In his assessment of the day, Corn writes on his website:

But it's no surprise that the Bush campaign—
like other campaigns—stage-manages its
public events to the fullest extent possible and
tells non-supporters to keep out (or be locked
up). Bush did not engage in drive-by
campaigning in Kalamazoo to provide local
citizens the opportunity to see him in action.
He hit the town in search of a middle-of-
America backdrop, a screaming throng, and
upbeat footage on the local news shows.
After all, campaigns are about candidates, not
voters. So while [the students] did not get to
see Bush in person wax about the glories of
freedom they did at least receive a lesson in
modern politics.

June 5–19, 2004

THE SILHOUETTES

For a society infatuated with numbers, Americans aren't
getting many concrete ones these days about the war in Iraq.
The day-by-day reports of U.S. soldiers killed or wounded are
either lacking a cumulative total or skimmed down to combat
casualties only—leaving out the non-combat wounded and
dead. Iraqi deaths are not counted at all and the war in
Afghanistan is nearly forgotten—until the body bags are flown
home. That's why Mike Murphy built a large outdoor display
he calls "the Silhouettes." He wanted to help others
understand and reflect on the human cost of war.

"I was looking for a nonverbal way to communicate," says
Mike who has a penchant for images more than the written
word. He noticed that the signs people held at the Sunday

peace vigils were too numerous and too hard for drivers passing by to read. He wanted a message that would have more impact.

"I'm very conscious of delivering a message to the population that is seen and understood," says Mike. During the 1970s he was a stage lighting and set-up "roadie" for blues and pop music bands in Canada. He worked for stars like Leo Kottke and Taj Mahal.

Mike is also a Quaker, a spiritual path that teaches that prayer and love are revealed in action. He became a pacifist and social justice advocate when he discovered the Quakers in the mid-1980s and then joined them because he felt he needed to strengthen his own resolve for nonviolent activism through a faith community. However, the Quakers aren't simply against war, they teach that every person has a responsibility to educate and make others aware of society's injustices and urge them to become nonviolent.

"You could pray for peace all day long but you have to do something about it," says Mike.

Today Mike believes the United States is probably in the most dangerous period of its history. In his judgment, the decision to invade Iraq was not a consensus decision or the right thing to do to defeat terrorism; it was "a ruthless decision" by those in power to avail themselves of greater concentrations of power by telling lies and curtailing Americans' civil liberties. Bombing apartment buildings in Iraq, for example, was bound to hit civilians and legitimizing the torture of prisoners was a complete manipulation of language, "putting Orwell off by 20 years."

Mike wants to communicate his own thoughts and feelings about the war to ordinary people who don't think about it as much as he does, but at first he didn't know how. So like any Quaker would do: he sat silently and listened for the Spirit.

Because the Quakers have no pastor for their congregation, people learn to figure things out for themselves. However, they are not alone in this. Once a person gets an idea, he brings it to "meeting"[94] so it can be tested with the group and discerned through silence and consensus decision-making. The objective is to see where Spirit is leading.

"That's it. It's pretty simple," said Mike.

After six months of patient listening, Mike woke up one morning and with a picture of a display within his head. It originated from the images of people vaporized after the atom bomb explosion in Hiroshima in 1945. Their shadows were burned onto the sides of buildings, streets and sidewalks in the shape of whatever ordinary action they were performing at the moment of the attack.

In the Quaker way, Mike discussed his idea with others before he pursued it. He talked with his wife about the project and family members in Long Island about its construction. He spoke about its suitability to KNOW's mission to his fellow Quakers who then encouraged him to go to the next planning meeting to present it. In preparation for the meeting Mike made up quarter-inch plywood samples of a man and a woman in a motion pose. He used the outlines of the models from a Lands' End catalog to present his proposal.

The KNOW planners typically work thoughtfully and by consensus and once they adopt a plan for a project, people pitch in to make it happen. At the meeting several people suggest the types of figures to represent in the design: women and men, the young and elderly, the unborn, the healthy, the wounded, soldiers and a journalist. A few recommend possible sites for the sign as well as colors, size and, of course, ways to attract media attention. The caption of the sign, "Iraq, how many deaths?" plays off Bob Dylan's song line in "Blowing in

---

[94] A Quaker "meeting" is an hour-long worship service conducted in silence. People only talk when they are moved by the Spirit to speak.

the Wind," "How many deaths will it take 'til he knows, that too many people have died?" Mike thinks it aptly prompts more questions about the war like: How many American deaths? How many coalition and Iraqi deaths? How many more civilian deaths to come? How many deaths are we willing to endure?

Chris Orsolini, an artist, sketched out photos of the figures with chalk on big sheets of quarter-inch luan plywood. Steve Senesi, a local carpenter and artist, helped Mike cut out the 44 wooden Silhouettes while others attached them onto sticks and painted them white on one side. The group then constructed the 4 x 32-foot sign and painted it white with black letters. Over the next four to five weeks about 30 people attended workshops to complete the Silhouettes and within three months well over 100 people had done something on the project.

The Silhouettes' first official "gig" is March 20, in time for a candlelight vigil to commemorate the first anniversary of the start of the Iraq War. KNOW volunteers have finished ahead of schedule so they "unveil" the Silhouettes on Saturday, March 13, on the eight-lane highway in Portage (a suburb south of Kalamazoo), across from a major shopping mall. The display attracts a lot of attention that first day and the *Gazette* publishes a photo story on it. On May 3, the Silhouettes "greet" President Bush when he visits Kalamazoo. As the president's bus passes a hill overlooking the I-94 freeway and the Oakland Drive exit, he will be able to see 21 of the Silhouettes and the sign sitting on a 15 x 40-foot scaffold. The Silhouettes will also turn up at the Sunday peace vigils in front of the Federal Building as demonstrators substitute the individual figures for their regular placards. Everyone, including Mike, is in for a surprise when churches begin "adopting" the Silhouettes.

☮

Mike and KNOW members want the Silhouettes to provoke thought and response and that's exactly what they will get. As part of a pacifist congregation's observance of Holy Week and Easter (April 5–11, 2004) the Skyridge Church of the Brethren on the western side of town, decided to put the display on its front lawn. Shortly afterward, vandals tip over the Silhouettes. Within the hour, however, KNOW people are on the scene to put the display back together again. One or two strangers who happen to be on the road that day stop by to help. The Silhouettes remain on display without further incident.

In June the Sisters of St. Joseph (SSJ), who reside on the northeastern section of town, host the Silhouettes on their property within the confines of the huge stonewall that surrounds their campus. They hold a short prayer service to dedicate the sign and to renew their commitment to the peace and justice ministry.

"It is our hope that this sign will be a reminder to all who pass by of the sanctity of all life; of the human cost of war and violence tallied in pain, anguish, death and enduring physical and emotional injury; and the reality that we are all brothers and sisters sharing this earth," says Sister Christine Parks, vice president of the SSJs, in a welcoming prayer. The sisters pray for "all the victims of the war in Iraq, especially those whose deaths go unnoticed, and their loved ones" and to "cry out for an end to all the bloodshed."

Almost immediately after the service people in town begin calling the nuns to object to the Silhouettes. Someone even threatens arson. A couple of complaint notes are posted on the sign itself, including one that reads, "Freedom isn't free," but the sisters decide not to remove the notes. Then the notes mysteriously disappear. In another incident, someone crosses out Iraq on the sign and inscribes 9/11 so that the caption reads: "9/11, how many deaths?" Then someone else paints over that and puts "Iraq" back on the sign.

Two days after the Silhouettes are up a young man, a carpenter on his lunch hour, knocks on the front door of the motherhouse and shares his objections on the sign. Sister Irene Waldmann, a member of the SSJ *Pax Christi,* a peace and justice group that sponsored the Silhouettes, invites him in to sit and talk. When he finishes his piece, she apologizes that the sign has offended him. He suddenly calms down and listens to her explain the sisters' reasons for putting up the sign, namely, to encourage people to reflect on the loss of life in Iraq—for Americans, Iraqis and coalition forces.

"Thanks for hearing me out," he says to her. "I appreciate it and will tell the other guys."

Sister Irene is among several sisters who fielded over 250 calls about the Silhouettes. In the end, seven out of eight of those calls turn out to be positive. What disturbs her, however is the *quality* of the negative calls as they reflect the divisiveness of America. Here are some examples of people's objections:

* One grandmother claims her 10-year-old grandchild is concerned about "why the sisters would ever do this when we have troops in Iraq?"

* Another person who has to pass that corner every day says he is sickened by the sign because he has a son in the military stationed in Iraq.

* A veteran dislikes the sign's politicizing message and calls the nuns traitors because they support the Iraqi people.

* A hospital volunteer who works at the sisters' hospital, Borgess Medical Center, is so irate he vows not to render his services until the sign is taken down.

* One person points out that the Bible has war all over it; consequently, the war in Iraq is justified.

* Someone else believes that the sign represents anti-Bush, pro-abortion liberals.

* One caller tells the nuns that they are naïve and need to get out into the real world.

* A Catholic wonders what has happened to the "good, holy sisters" that they would do this, implying that the nuns are not acting in accordance with Church rule.[95]

A campaign worker for John Kerry is also among the callers. He thanks the sisters for making an "anti-war statement" and for showing voters that "it's wrong to follow Bush." But in a separate interview, Sister Christine retorts that if a Democrat were president and conducting this war, the sign would still be there. Death and destruction are the issue, not support for or against a presidential candidate or party.

"If every call were negative, I'd know we did the right thing in putting up the sign," says Sister Jan Kurtz, coordinator of the project and on leave from her missionary work in Peru. "We're not here to be people pleasers and we will not be controlled by public opinion. We'd lose our prophetic stance if we were controlled by whether something flies or not."

---

[95] The irony of the last caller isn't lost on Sister Irene who said that Pope John Paul II had strenuously pleaded with President Bush to "stop the killing of our brothers." The pope was among a multitude of mainline religious leaders who called upon Bush to avoid war in Iraq. According to Bishop Thomas Gumbleton of Detroit (May 9, 2003), Bush refused to confer with any clergy when he was making the decision to go to war, including those from the Methodist Church of which Bush is a member. Only Cardinal Pio Laghi, former papal nuncio and a friend of the president, is allowed access to the president.

"When the negative calls came they gave me the opportunity to dialogue with people," says Sister Irene who realizes that the sisters have created a unique opportunity in their reconciliation ministry to hear what people think about the Silhouettes and then to call them to reflect on the loss of life, but that sometimes proves difficult.

"You gals may be able to reflect on it, but what about the rest of us?" replies one caller to this explanation. What the sisters discover is that they have tapped into people's fears through the Silhouettes.

"People are reacting to a whole climate of real, manufactured and capitalized-on fear of terror," says Sister Christine, "despite evidence to the contrary. They are linking Iraq and 9/11. Anyone opposed to that idea is opposed to protecting us in the War on Terror."

"Many people have loved ones fighting in Iraq or they have bought into the whole story that we are there [fighting terrorism]," says Sister Jan. "Psychologically, they can't afford to question that belief because it would destroy all they have come to believe in and are committed to. It's easier to hang on to and defend what they've been told than to change their minds."

"They would feel disloyal to a family member in the military over there," adds Sister Irene. So when the negative calls came, especially during this time of war, upset and division, the sisters answered with calm reserve and love.

"Love is a positive strategy of being one with the members of the Universal Family where we see ourselves as brothers and sisters—with no boundary lines between countries," says Sister Irene. "It is also a way of countering all the fear and negativity that have gripped the American people. This is the message of peaceful nonviolence as espoused by Cesar Chavez, Martin Luther King, Jr., Gandhi and Rosa Parks: approach problems in a faith-filled and fearless way without vengeance for anything or anyone."

"The charism of the Sisters of St. Joseph is one of inclusive love and unity," says Sister Theresa MacIntyre, vice president of the SSJs. "Our prayer extends to those we meet, those we serve, and those we care for."

Two weeks later, when it is time to take down the Silhouettes, the sisters again celebrate in prayer—but not without incident. The service is held behind the Silhouettes where the crisscrossed scaffolding and unpainted wooden backs of the figures show. Looking at the display from this angle gives it a rough, unfinished appearance as if to symbolize what it takes to achieve peace.

The sisters use the same props they did at the prayer service two weeks before. A small table serves as an altar and on it sits a simple, red lantern as well as a banner inscribed Paz (peace in Spanish) that pictures a lion and lamb resting together. Behind the altar is a bulletin board with 17,970 written on it, the number of deaths among the Americans, Iraqis and coalition troops since the beginning of the war.

"That number has been increased by 200 since the Silhouettes went up," says Sister Jan in her introductory remarks.

"The more we understand how to do peace, the better a world we'll be," says Sister Irene. "Our prayer for peace over the years and last month, and certainly over these past two weeks, is about a hope that peace continues."

"Tear it down," shouts a man in a passing truck.

Undaunted, the sisters continue the service and offer a reading from Isaiah 2:2–5, which reflects the prophecy for peace, and Matthew 6:38–48, where Jesus calls his followers to avoid retaliating against other's faults and transgressions. In a short reflection, Sister Jan asks the question of whether it is naïve to think that God wants us to create a world of peace?

"We are dreamers, for without dreams we wouldn't be here," she says. "The sign, which was Mike's dream, became real by sharing the idea and its creation with others and then with us."

A woman stopped at the traffic light on the road in front of the Silhouettes begins screaming out of her gray truck, "Why don't you guys try to support Bush and our troops?" When the light changes, she drives on honking her horn and shouting: "Four more years! Four more years!"

Sister Jan continues. "Solidarity is essential in the process of making our dream come true. We have lived it out in a special way these last two weeks at Nazareth, thanks to all of you and many others who cannot be here physically, but are with us in spirit. Thanks to a lot of collaboration, people are reflecting and, in some cases, reacting. The question is before them as well as ourselves."

"But we MUST NOT lose hope," she says. "We CANNOT give up seeking lasting peace and justice for ALL. Let us give birth to our dream by weaving all the earth with heartstrings of love. Let us teach forgiveness and link hands in a circle of peace. Let us overcome our fears, share the sign, keep it moving and keep asking the questions. Let us listen and respond in love. Finally, let us renew the meaning of hope for ourselves, but especially, for our children and for generations to come."

Those gathered pray together a prayer for peace. They then pray for the dead and wounded and make special mention of Paul Johnson, a contractor who was beheaded in Saudi Arabia earlier that week.

After the closing song, "Let There Be Peace on Earth," Sister Jan cries out once more, "We are not naïve! We are not naïve!"

June 25–28, 2004
"FAHRENHEIT 911"

Marti Faketty and Dru Carter, members of Kalamazoo's CodePink, pass out flyers[96] (in shocking pink colors, of course) to movie patrons of "Fahrenheit 911" at its opening on Friday, June 25. As they distribute the flyers, they engage people saying, "If you're angry about what you just saw, here's a flyer to help you do something about it." As she grabs a flyer one woman responds, "I've been angry for four years." Marti has other tales to tell.

One couple tries to get tickets but the show has already sold out. Marti gives them two tickets and they throw their arms around her and cry. Their son has just signed up with Army recruiters because he felt he was doing his duty. Now he is terrified he'll end up in a body bag.

One woman is so distraught over the film that she vows to take her son to Canada to save him from military service in Iraq. "There no way he's going over there," she says.

A man and a woman, probably about ages 18 and 20, leave the theatre sobbing. They say they have several friends in Iraq and it is difficult to watch the soldier scenes in the film. The young man vows he is going to tell his friends about the film and discourage them from signing up for military service.

Marti says that distributing the flyers is unlike anything she has experienced during her time in the KNOW peace movement. People eagerly take them and some ask for

---

[96] The CodePink women discover the difference between "public property" and "private property." Bronson Park, the sidewalk at the Civic and the grass along highways near shopping malls—all are considered "public property," a shrinking commodity in our cities. Lack of public space contributes to curtailing the freedom of public assembly.

duplicates to give to their friends. "It was amazing to watch. I felt privileged to see the outpouring of determination from these people. I can't wait to go back and hand out more flyers."

Distributing flyers, however, becomes problematic when theatre managers tell the CodePink women they cannot do it on this property, which includes the parking lot that surrounds the theatre. There have been no complaints from patrons, rather it is a management decision. After a couple days the women stop the flyer distribution.

Some people are so upset with the Bush administration, especially after seeing the film, "Fahrenheit 911," that they are more determined than ever to defeat the president in the November 2 presidential election.

"There is a new energy that is a transforming influence on America," says the emcee of the "Moveon.org Meet-up with Michael Moore" that draws 110 people to Kalamazoo Valley Community College (KVCC) on Monday, June 28. "This proves to you that democracy still exists."

For 35 minutes beginning at 8:15 p.m. EDT, over 30,000 people gather in hundreds of house parties[97] and auditoriums all over the United States to participate in the meet-up and to discuss the strategies aimed at retiring George W. Bush from the presidency.

Michael Moore's introduction as a "true progressive hero" and the "top of Karl Rove's enemies list" excites the agitated crowd who desperately want to know what they can do to "take back the country." This is such a contrast to the 2000 election where most Americans believed there was no difference between Bush and Gore. Those were the days when

---

[97] At least three other house parties took place in Kalamazoo with 15 to 30 people assembled for the Meet-up.

Americans largely took our democracy for granted. Now that it has become apparent to at least half of the country that our democracy is threatened with a growing plutocracy, people at the grassroots are anxious to join the political fray to do something to stop it.

Participants in the Meet-up don't treat Moore as a star but rather as a critic of Bush. The documentary has unleashed a pent-up firestorm of anger, dread and discontent over the administration. Even movie theatres in the "red" states have sell-out crowds as the film becomes the largest weekend grossing initial release since "Rocky," according to a June 28 report in the *Gazette*.

Moore, sounding quite astounded but delighted at the success of the film cites several examples of people's reactions.[98]

* A man in Republican Long Island claims he became a "different man" as a result of seeing the movie which gave him pause to think about what was really going on in this administration and that there was "too much, too much to discount it." He bought three more tickets to give to friends.

* A young woman in Florida left the theatre in tears and said she could no longer be loyal to George W. Bush.

---

[98] Here's another example of a reaction in Kalamazoo. My hairdresser reports that his client, who has always been a Republican, sneaked out of her house to see "Fahrenheit 911" fearful that her Republican neighbors would find out. Instead, she sees *them* at the theatre and they all love the film. The woman has never voted for Democrats, but plans to do so in November to get Bush out. Her neighbors put Kerry bumper stickers on their cars. They are grandparents who don't want their kids killed in a needless war.

* At the end of the film in San Francisco a man in the audience threw a shoe at the screen during the last scene that featured Bush.

* In Connecticut a man stood up on his seat and exclaimed, "Let's go have a meeting!"

* Independents, Republicans and people who had not made up their minds about who to vote for in the November election decided to vote against Bush as a result of seeing the film.

Moore recalls that pundits predicted only Bush haters would attend the film but such stories disprove that theory. Fifteen months ago after his Oscar Award acceptance speech on "Bowling for Columbine," Moore staged an outburst of his anti-war stance. He says he felt alone back then, but has since noticed a shift in the country over the past few months. "I knew that the truth would eventually come out on Bush," says Moore. "And that once the people who had supported him in this war found out that they were betrayed, they would respond with a vengeance."

Although Moore says he didn't intend it, people are picking up on the fact that the mainstream media did not demand any evidence from Bush to justify war. For example, people who view the film typically come out of it saying, "Why haven't I seen this on the nightly news?" It is as though the American public had been mercilessly shielded from the truth about what is going on in their country—and to American soldiers in Iraq.

"The media are all mad at me and I expect them to keep after me," says Moore. "But the movie is solid [on the facts]."

Moore and Moveon.org want to keep the momentum going and they offer participants in the Meet-up several ideas about what they can do to make a difference in this year's presidential election. Here are their suggestions:

* Vote on November 2 and take the day off so you can volunteer to get out the vote.

* Go to a swing state for a weekend and volunteer to help in the presidential campaign.

* Identify five non-voters and adopt them. Make it fun, have a party, take them to the polls.

There are two choirs singing in this country, says Moore, the left and the left out. Then there are 50 percent of the American people who do not vote because they feel alienated and not represented by the parties or the government. Many of these people have been deeply affected by the movie. Moore also predicts that a lot of young people will vote for the first time because of this movie. "Many people have given up and watched on the sidelines. We've got to get them to participate in our democracy. If I've made a small contribution to that through this film, I'm hopeful for good things to come out of this election," says Moore.

Moore does have another agenda besides defeating Bush. He wants to see a Kerry administration switch to an international force in Iraq and bring American troops home. He wants universal healthcare to be offered as a right and he wants the country to acknowledge that we are running out of oil. He compares the search for alternative fuels as broad a move as President Kennedy's challenge for America to go to the moon.

"This election is Kerry's to lose," says Moore who fears that the Democrat may move to the right to get votes. "Energize the base. Give them a reason to vote." Moore says that 62 percent of the electorate is a combination of women, Blacks and Hispanics. Only 13 percent of African Americans even bother to go to the polls. "That means that two-thirds of the country is not white male. That's the strong base out there and Kerry needs to concentrate on that."

☮

After the Meet-up, about 30 percent of the KVCC audience volunteers for MoveOn.org's National Voter Registration Day scheduled for Sunday, July 11. People also sign up for a seat on the bus bound for the massive march set a day before the Republican National Convention in New York on August 29.

A couple of local candidates show up that night looking for campaign volunteers. Scott Elliott, candidate for the 6th U.S. congressional district, and Jim Houston, candidate for the 61st state representative seat, are running in impossibly-Republican strongholds, but the candidates remain upbeat and hopeful that a defeat of Bush would filter down the ballot to help them.

Sunday, June 27, 2004
PEACE VIGIL

The energy of today's vigil reverberates up and down the street, most likely an outcome of the "Fahrenheit 911" film released on Friday. Several peace activists have already seen it. Apparently, drivers have, too, as their horns honk more vigorously and more frequently than ever before. Only a few passing cars hurl negative comments but even these are reduced to one-word shouts like "Bush!" The tide seems to have turned against Bush in Kalamazoo.

"Michael Moore has got them scared to death," says John Mann who adds that the Carlyle Group[99] is planning to buy out

---

[99] The Carlyle Group is a private investment bank that focuses on the defense industry, telecom, property and financial services. Included in this group are former politicians like: George Bush (Sr.), James Baker III, Former Secretary of Defense and Deputy Director of the CIA Frank C. Carlucci, former Senator Alan Simpson (R-Wyoming),

the Loewe Theatres. "This will give the Right control over yet another media outlet so they can suppress and manipulate the truth. When I found out about the Carlyle Group, I was staggered."

John points out that over 40 corporate media outlets existed during the Clinton era. Now there are six. "It's a putsch. They have a stranglehold on power in this country." However, John also refers to today's *L.A. Times* editorial that declares the administration's experiment of pre-emptive war and invasion a failure. "This shows how quickly things are unraveling for the administration and how terrified they are of losing the election."

Many people think that the peace movement is a hippie movement of liberals in beards, beads and sandals, but the Iraq War has touched people, many people, from all walks of life and it is difficult to tell who the "typical" peace supporters are. For example, today a beautiful, blonde woman rolled up along the curb in her shiny, black Jaguar to stop to talk to some peace activists and to hand them a pile of flyers that contain information on the costs of war. She wants to do her part to spread a message. It turns out that she is a realtor (she attached her card to the flyers) who is supportive of the peace effort and passing out information to people one at a time. She has even been able to persuade Republicans to abandon

Richard G. Darman (White House Budget Advisor Bush / Clinton administrations), former British Prime Minister John Major. Source: www.informationclearinghouse.info/article3995.htm

According to its website www.carlyle.com, "The Carlyle Group is a private global investment firm that originates, structures and acts as lead equity investor in management-led buyouts, strategic minority equity investments, equity private placements, consolidations and buildups, and growth capital financings."

their support of Bush once they read the materials she distributes.

Some new and bright yellow signs appear today with the following captions:

They knew and did nothing

Prevent war, elect John Kerry

No link between Iraq & 9/11

No WMDs

☮

Sixty people show up for today's vigil and there seems to be a new spirit present, says Tom Small in his concluding remarks. Although his crowd count reached 60 people, Tom's multiplier effect includes the energy of those who wish they were there. That would mean 600 people came out for the vigil. The vigorous horn honks, and the numerous demonstrations taking place all over the nation would make the crowd well over 1,000.

Ron Kramer characterizes the June 30 "handover" as a fiction, a sham and not a true measure of sovereignty. "There was no reason for this particular date," he says. "It was timed to the election. True sovereignty means that the government has control over the military. We still have 138,000 Americans there on 14 bases. True sovereignty means that the government has control over its economic resources. There are foreign corporations that own these. We have $18.4 billion dedicated for reconstruction and only $3 billion has been doled out. True sovereignty has an administrative apparatus and the United States has the largest embassy with an expected staff of 2,000 to 3,000 Americans. This is a sham. It is a structure of domination by the United States. We must speak out and resist it. 'Fahrenheit 911' is a powerful film and it has gotten a lot of people angry at the Bush administration. The left is determined to get these criminals out of office in November."

Six women gather to demonstrate with the Women in Black today. They are planning for their first annual potluck for Wednesday, June 30, and continue at Shadia's house.

KNOW is arranging for a bus to take people to New York for the August 29th protest march against the administration, one day before the Republican National Convention begins.[100]

The Be-in-the-KNOW Film Series will continue every other week in July and August. Starting in September it will run for eight consecutive weeks until the election.[101] In order to help draw area college students, the first film in the fall will be on the draft.

---

[100] Forty-four people go on the bus trip, which begins on Saturday, August 28, at 7 p.m. with a send-off rally by supporters and well-wishers. They return on Monday, August 30, at 7:30 a.m. after two overnights on the bus. *USA Today* reporter Charisse Jones joins the group during the march and posts a story and photograph. (www.usatoday.com/news/politicselections/nation/2004-08-29-michigan-protestors_x.htm#). A preview story appeared on Friday, August 27 (www.usatoday.com/news/politicselections/nation/president/2004-08-26-protests-park_x.htm). The *Detroit News* also mentions the group as part of its larger report on the march (www.detnews.com/2004/politics/0408/30/a01-257921.htm).

[101] The "Be-in-the-KNOW" film team increased its showings to three times a week as the November election nears. (Source: www.beintheknowfilms.org)

ON THE WAY TO HANDOVER

Bush's approval ratings are melting down to 42 percent, about the same place he was before the September 11 attacks. Public opinion on the war also has turned against him with 53 percent of those polled believing the war in Iraq was a mistake, while 43 percent think the war is justified (*Los Angeles Times*, June 27, 2004). In November 2003 the numbers were reversed. In another indicator, 44 percent of the American people approve of Bush's handling of the war compared to 51 percent in March (AP, June 17, 2004). Finally, the Pew Research Center finds the country more divided than ever with 45 percent of Americans saying the U.S. plays a more important and more powerful role as a world leader than it did 10 years ago, while 67 percent say the U.S. is less respected (*New York Times*, Aug. 19, 2004).

One of the more startling events to impact the nation is the premiere showing of Michael Moore's documentary film, "Fahrenheit 911," which opens on June 25 in hundreds of theatres across the country. For its first weekend the film grosses over $26 million, the largest box office take in history. The film connects the dots of the past three years showing Bush's collusion with Saudi oil chiefs, the weakness of his leadership in handling September 11, and his general lackadaisical attitude toward foreign affairs even as he calls Americans to wage war with Iraq. Quite damning stuff that help solidify those against the president, further angering those in favor of him and maybe bringing a few undecided voters to doubt him.

Shortly before midnight on June 27, the U.S. Army announces a call-up of 5,674 members of the Individual Ready Reserve to support troop strength in Iraq later this year. At the time the United States has 140,000 troops in Iraq joined by nearly 25,000 international forces. There are 20,000 U.S.

troops stationed in Afghanistan. The Army's move represents the latest evidence of the strain placed on the U.S. military in Iraq and Afghanistan (Reuters News).

Americans grow increasingly fearful over a reinstatement of the military draft. The Ready Reserve call-up provides more evidence of this prospect despite administration and congressional officials' repeated claims that there will be no draft. Citizens continue to write letters against the draft's reinstatement. (Some of my own college students become alarmed at the prospect while others began to prepare themselves mentally for the possibility.)

"There is no need for it at all," says Secretary of Defense Donald Rumsfeld (AP, July 5, 2004) in referring to the draft.

"We cannot bring back a draft now and make some young men and women go into uniform and not bring in a whole lot of others to do different tasks," says Sen. John Warner, R-Va., on NBC's "Meet the Press." He argues that the cost of benefits would be prohibitive (AP, July 5, 2004).

At this point with five months to go before the election, the peace activists are sure that President Bush will be defeated. And even though many of them are disappointed about Kerry's instant win in the primaries they will support him, work for him, vote for him—and lobby for an end of the war starting with Inauguration Day.

Tuesday, June 28, 2004

The long-awaited day of passing sovereignty back to the Iraqis has finally come—two days before the official June 30 handover. Iraqi Prime Minister Iyad Allawi is installed in a private ceremony held in secret and ahead of schedule for security reasons.

U.S. military forces would remain, however, for an unstated period of time and with an unstated amount of power. During this occupation, 14 military bases are built as well as the largest American embassy. Insurgencies continue— and will escalate. It is unclear when we can expect our troops to return home. Over the next month, two soldiers a day are killed.

Thursday, June 30, 2004

The U.S. military has found Saddam Hussein but not the weapons of mass destruction. The idea that Saddam is tied to the September 11 attacks was unsubstantiated. Osama bin Laden, whom the Bush administration immediately blames for planning the September 11 terrorist attacks, remains at large somewhere in Afghanistan.

The total number of lives lost in Iraq is between 17,014 and 20,442, which includes 979 deaths among coalition troops,[102] including 858 Americans, 4,895 to 6,370 Iraqi military deaths and 11,143 to 13,096 Iraqi civilians.[103] Americans wounded in action amounts to 5,572 and at least double that number in non-combat situations (i.e., sickness, injury, stress).[104] If this war becomes anything like the first

---

[102] Figures obtained from the following websites:

        www.lunaville.org/warcasualties/Summary.aspx,
        www.Iraqbodycount.com
        www.costofwar.com
        www.infoshout.com.

Coalition forces other than the United States and Great Britain are July 30 figures.

[103] www.iraqbodycount.net. In October 2004, the mainstream media will report 100,000 Iraqi deaths.

[104] Sources: Bill Moyers "Now" (June 18, 2004) and "Democracy Now" (*Friday, April 2nd, 2004*) interview with U.P.I. reporter, Mark Benjamin, one of the few reporters investigating the numbers on the

Gulf War, it will take a decade before we see a bigger death toll caused by soldiers' and civilians' contact with depleted uranium, a substance that coats the tips of American missiles and causes a deteriorating death to those exposed to it and genetic damage to future generations.[105]

Iraq's U.N. Ambassador Mohammed Al-Douri leaves the country in March 2003 shortly before the U.S. invasion while other U.N. staff leave the following September. The leaders of the scant number of coalition forces President Bush collects are beginning to doubt the progress in Iraq after a year of war. They contemplate abandoning their commitment when hostilities mount, insurgencies increase and political pressure at

---

wounded. The Pentagon does not report the number of non-hostile wounded.

"The Pentagon is not doing a good job at explaining to the American people what that number means," said Benjamin. "To give you an example, I, of course, once got – once I got that 18,004 number asked the Pentagon, well, how many casualties does that mean? How many casualties. Casualties as we said, is anybody who is injured or ill or sick or wounded, because of the war. The Pentagon told me that at the Pentagon, they do not keep a centralized database of the number of casualties. They can say what they say the number of wounded are, but not the number of casualties. That makes it very difficult for a reporter, who – you know, we're trained to try to get the story right – wading through a bunch of statistics on the evacuations gives us a good idea of what's going on in the war, but not a precise idea. And I think a lot of reporters are frankly put off by the fact that the Pentagon is not doing a good job of communicating what the human costs of this war is."

[105] Of the 697,000 U.S. troops who took part in the first Gulf war, 30 percent of American GIs may have been affected and over 200,000 Iraqis have died from contact with depleted uranium. Source: Depleted Uranium Education Project, www.iacenter.org/depleted/du.htm

home negatively nudges them for supporting the war. The Spanish prime minister, for example, loses an election while Tony Blair, prime minister of England, is severely chastised by Parliament and populace alike. Iraqi exile Ahmed Chalabi, the Bush Administration's main intelligence source on Iraq, is found to be unreliable. When the U.S. bombs his headquarters in May 2004, Chalabi decides to divulge U.S. military and intelligence secrets to Iran.[106]

Many Americans, including several Republican leaders, question the administration's war planning in terms of troop strength and exit strategy. By spring 2004 Bush's polls dip to the low 40s and put him in the "danger zone" for re-election. Much of this downward spiral is attributed to revelations that Bush lied, or at least prevaricated, about his reasons for committing troops to Iraq and that he planned to get rid of Saddam prior to his 2001 inauguration. In March 2004 several books appear on the newsstands criticizing the administration. In April 2004 a scandal breaks over Americans' treatment of prisoners at the Abu Ghraib prison in Baghdad. Vice President Dick Cheney, a member of the "neoconservatives" who helped mastermind America's new foreign policy for global domination, is also accused of war profiteering through his former company, Halliburton.

The conflicts between Israel and Palestine continue despite overtures of peace. Everyone in the world seems to understand that peace in the Middle East is dependent on settling differences over territory on the West Bank and Gaza, everyone but the Americans, that is. Threats on Yasser Arafat's life are reported from time to time in early 2004 as Ariel Sharon, prime minister of Israel, claims that he will and then later that he won't have Arafat killed.[107] The Israelis build

---

[106] www.disinfopedia.org/wiki.phtml?title=Ahmed_Chalabi

[107] Arafat died on November 11, 2004.

a $1.4 billion wall[108] on the West Bank, designed to separate its territories from the Palestinians and to defend itself against Palestinian terrorists and suicide bombers. Although the wall has reduced the number of these incidents, it has increased the difficulties Palestinians must endure in their daily lives including long lines at checkpoints, personal harassment and random sweeps through their villages.

Bush has raised the $200 million he targeted for his re-election campaign, which begin this month,[109] but the $80 million he has already spent finds him trailing John Kerry in the polls. Kerry, who emerges as the "most electable" Democratic presidential contender in the Iowa Caucus and the New Hampshire primary, has already raised over $100 million. He receives great support from various non-profit groups (a.k.a. 527s) to help bump up his advertising assault on the president. Many people who donate to the 527s are "Anybody but Bush" supporters. Nevertheless, the Democrats' attempt to unseat Bush will end in bitter disappointment in November as the president wins by three million popular votes (51 percent to 49 percent) and 286 electoral votes to Kerry's 252. The election reveals to Democrats just how out of step they are with Middle America and its values of family, morality and religion.

The U.S. deficit is over $400 billion and the national debt is $7.1 trillion—and counting.[110] The Iraq War has already cost over $114 billion—and counting.[111]

---

[108] When completed, the Wall will be 280–400 miles long at a cost of $1.4 billion. By September 2003, the construction affects over 65 Palestinian communities with populations over 210,000. Source: www.endtheoccupation.org/article.php?list=type&type=68

[109] www.opensecrets.com

[110] www.brillig.com/debt_clock/

☮

They are still out there. Every Sunday at noon and every Tuesday at 4:30, the Kalamazoo peace activists are still out there at the Federal Building to stand for peace—and to hope and pray that the soldiers will return home soon.

---

[111] www.costofwar.com

400

APPENDICES

APPENDIX A

KNOW—
Kalamazoo Nonviolent Opponents of War

WHO WE ARE:
KNOW is a coalition of people and groups committed to nonviolent solutions to human problems, especially to the threats posed by international confrontation and by religious, ethnic, and class conflicts. Formed in summer 2002, KNOW arose in the wake of threats from the United States to begin pre-emptive military action against Iraq. KNOW conveners gathered together individuals and existing peace groups to develop plans for action in support of peace and justice locally, nationally, and internationally.

WHAT WE BELIEVE:
* This country is at a moment in its history when citizens cannot afford to be indifferent or passive.
* By challenging our government's policies, we, together with millions of people across the country, can help change those policies for the better.
* Our nation must find peaceful alternatives to violence and oppression to which the poor, the innocent, and the environment are subjected.
* Only through peace and social and economic justice can a nation achieve true security and preserve democracy.
* By untiring and passionate commitment to non-violent resolution of every kind of conflict, we can help create a better world.

WHAT WE SUPPORT (at the international level):
* Peaceful resolution of conflicts within and between nations.
* Global nuclear disarmament.
* An end to all nuclear testing.
* U.S. ratification of an International Criminal Court, a treaty abolishing use of land mines, and a biological weapons convention.
* U.S. leadership of efforts to halt and reverse global warming and to provide a decent life for everyone on the planet.
* Establishment of a United States Department of Peace. (For the text of HR 2459, to create a Dept. of Peace, go to www.house.gov/kucinich.)

WHAT YOU CAN DO:
* Stand for Peace each Sunday at noon and each Tuesday at 4:30-5:30 p.m. at the Federal building at Park and Michigan in Kalamazoo.
* Write and call your Congressional representative and senators.
* Write letters to the editors of local and national publications.
* Share this with your friends and colleagues.

KNOW meets the second and fourth Thursdays of each month from 4:30 - 6:00 p.m. at the Wesley Foundation on the Western Michigan University campus. For more information and suggestions, please visit our website at: http://www.kzoo4peace.org/ or call: 269-387-5284

APPENDIX B

LEADERS OF FAITH COMMUNITIES WHO OPPOSED THE WAR WITH IRAQ

Statements by religious leaders unite in a belief that war is not the answer to the problem of Iraq and the hope that political leaders will be guided by "the vision of a world in which nations do not attempt to resolve international problems by making war on other nations" ("Disarm Iraq Without War," a statement by Christian religious leaders in the U.S. and the U.K.).

In a "Statement of Conscience on the Iraq War," 125 Christian, Jewish, and Muslim leaders called on all people whose lives are "rooted in the sacred stories" to "act as responsible peace advocates." They condemned "actions resulting in the death and suffering of thousands of innocent people and fueling further terrorist acts" as "an offense to the ethical foundation upon which our country is founded."

Signers of these and other anti-war statements include the following:

Rev. Andrew Young, former UN Ambassador

Frank R. Jamison, President
Buddhist Assn. of Southwest Michigan

Dr. Nazir Khaja, Islamic Information Service

Rabbi Michael Lerner, Editor
Tikkun Magazine

Mary Ellen McNish ,General Secretary
American Friends Service Committee

Peter Price, Bishop of Bath and Wells
(and 21 other Anglican Bishops, including Archbishop
of Canterbury)

A. Roy Medley, General Secretary
American Baptist Churches USA

Dr. William J. Shaw, President
National Baptist Convention, USA

Bishop Wilton D. Gregory, President
United States Conference of Catholic Bishops

Judy Mills Reimer, General Secretary
Church of the Brethren

The Most Rev. Frank T. Griswold, Presiding Bishop
& Primate, The Episcopal Church, USA

The Rev. Mark S. Hanson, Presiding Bishop
Evangelical Lutheran Church in America

Jose Ortiz, Executive Director
Mennonite Central Committee USA

Archbishop Mor Cyril Aphrem Karim
Archdiocese of the Syrian Orthodox Church of Antioch
for Eastern USA

Jim Forest, Secretary
Orthodox Peace Fellowship

Rev. Fahed Abu-Akel, Moderator
214th General Assembly, Presbyterian Church (USA)

Wesley Granberg-Michaelson, General Secretary
Reformed Church in America

Rev. William Sinkford, President
Unitarian-Universalist Association

Rev. John H. Thomas, President
United Church of Christ

Riad Jarjour, General Secretary
Middle East Council of Churches

Rev. Robert Edgar, Secretary General
National Council of Churches

Canon Patrick Mauney, Chairman, Board of Directors
　　Church World Service

Corinne Whitlatch, Director
Churches for Middle East Peace

Marilyn Borst, Executive Director
Evangelicals for Middle East Understanding

Ronald G. Sider, President
Evangelicals for Social Action

Sr. Constance Phelps, SCL,Vice President
Leadership Conference of Women Religious

David Robinson, National Coordinator
Pax Christi USA

The National Council of Churches Executive Board,
representing 36 Protestant, Orthodox, and Anglican
denominations, with 50 million adherents, unanimously
approved a letter to President Bush concluding, "Mr.

President, we respectfully implore you to heed the strong beliefs of the broader faith community, which calls you to move, even now, away from war and toward peace with compassion."

An Interfaith Service of Prayer and Meditation in Time of War

Sponsored by the
Kalamazoo Interfaith Coalition
for Peace and Justice
First Presbyterian Church of Kalamazoo, Michigan
Friday, March 21, 2003, at 6:00 p.m.

All silently gather

Prelude   Judith Whaley
                                Kalamazoo Recorder Players

Words of Welcome   Rev. Dr. David VanArsdale
                                Pastor, First Presbyterian
                                Church

Reading of the
Statement for Peace   Lee Ann Johnson and Paul
                                Clements
                                Co-moderators, Kalamazoo
                                Interfaith Coalition for Peace
                                and Justice

As people of conscience and abiding faith, united by a concern for human dignity and justice, we call our nation and our world to peace.

The situation between the United States and Iraq has drawn us together and it demands that we speak out. The people of Iraq have suffered under tyranny and sanctions. War only adds to their suffering. They deserve a nonviolent solution.

The United States has the power, resources, and democratic tradition to build lasting bond of peace. As people of faith, we see the harm done to anyone as harm to everyone and we have a responsibility to speak out.

We support the people of Iraq and not its leaders.
We support diplomacy and not aggression.
We support inspections and not unilateralism.
We support democracy and not domination.
We support the U.N.'s efforts to promote the rule of law.
We oppose war as patriots seeking liberty and justice for all.

Now is the time for each of us to let this message be heard by our elected representatives and other decision-makers. As the role of the United States becomes that of the aggressor, we not only diminish ourselves as a people, but also neglect the pressing needs of the nation and the world. The strength of our faith and the courage of our convictions unite us in the belief that we can steer our grand nation from the darkness of war to the light of peace.

Readings and Prayers from Various Faith Traditions

Frank Jamison	*Buddhist*
Deacon Arthur Marsaw	*Pokagon Band of Pottawatomie Tribe, Hartford Catholic Church*
Azhwarsamy Jeganathan	*Chair, Outreach Committee Indo-American Cultural Center and Temple*
Balwinder Singh	*Sikh Temple Priest*
Gurman Gill	*Sikh Temple Member and Translator*

Hymn*
> *If the War Goes On*   John L. Bell
>   Sara Dorrien, *Soloist*

Reflections on Peace   Raelyn Joyce
                              Kalamazoo Friends Meeting

Litany for the   Frank Gross
Beginning of War   *St. Joseph Catholic Church*

Rock of Ages, God of our mothers and fathers; you who are
    and you will always be, we come in hope and sadness to
    pray for peace in this time of war. Hear what we ask
    you.

That every nation, every state, every person, every woman
    and man, every child, every soldier, every Muslim,
    every Jew, every Christian, all those of other religions
    and those without religion may cling to peace as best
    each one can . . .
        Let us hope. Let us pray.
That none of us ever forget the dignity and worth of all the
    peoples involved in this war . . .
        Let us hope. Let us pray.
That one day the terrible weapons of war will be beaten into
    ploughshares and cook stoves, and statues, and the roofs
    of houses and all other means whereby we live and
    move and have our being . . .
        Let us hope. Let us pray.
That we never forget that anger is dangerous and that the
    desire for revenge and the desire to main and kill other
    people is evil . . .
        Let us hope. Let us pray.

*Stand if able
**See* Appendix C-2, p. 415

That we remember to hold fast to the great rock on which
peace is built: the knowledge that all people everywhere
are sisters and brothers . . .
> **Let us hope. Let us pray.**

That this war which has just begun will end soon and that all
of those involved in the fighting will come home safe to
those near and dear to them.
> **Let us hope. Let us pray.**

Dear God, dear mother and father, dear master of the
universe, come to help us as we seek the peace to which
you have called us. Bring us closer throughout the
world. Help us know that all peoples are chosen, not
just ours alone. We pray this in the names of Jesus and
Mohammed and Moses and all your prophets who have
spoken for you throughout history.
> **Amen. Amen. Amen. Amen. That we
> remember to hold fast to the great rock on which
> peace is built: that of knowing that all people
> everywhere are brothers and sisters . . .**

Silent Meditation

The Peace

*Exchange signs of peace and reconciliation with the people
in and around your pew. Introduce yourself and spend some
moments in conversation sharing your deepest sadness and
your greatest hope at this time of war.*

Musical Interlude Janlee Richter
First Presbyterian Church Pianist

**Sharing the Candle
  of Peace** Judith Whaley
Kalamazoo Recorder Players

The worship leaders will share the flame of peace with those
sitting closest to the aisle. Please pass the light to your

neighbors in the pew. **You are urged to take this candle
with you to burn in a prominent place in your home until
peace has become a reality.**

| **Charge** | Rev. Kevin E. Holley |
| | *Assoc. Pastor, First Presbyterian* |

*Let us now go forth into the world in peace, being of good courage,
holding fast to that which is good, rendering to no one evil for evil,
strengthening the fainthearted, supporting the weak, helping the afflicted,
honoring all creation, loving an serving our Creator, and rejoicing in the
power of the One and Holy God.*

Blessing	Dr. Mushtaq Luqmani
	Board of Trustees
	Kalamazoo Islamic Center
	Elder Karl Wallace
	Church of God Pentecostal, Inc.
	Rabbi Steve Forstein
	Temple B'Nai Israel

Extinguish your candles at the conclusion of the blessing.

Recess in silence, following the peace drum into the world.

Worship Leaders

Paul Clements	Christian (Presbyterian)
Steve Forstein	Jewish
Gurman Gill	Sikh
Frank Gross	Christian (Roman Catholic)
Kevin Holley	Christian (Presbyterian)
Frank Jamison	Buddhist
Azhwarsamy Jeganathan	Hindu
Lee Ann Johnson	Christian
Raelyn Joyce	Christian (Society of Friends)

Muhthu Luqmani	Muslim
Art Marsaw	Native American
	Christian (Roman Catholic)
Robin Pollens	Jewish
Balwinder Singh	Sikh
David VanArsdale	Christian (Presbyterian)
Karl Wallace	Christian (Pentecostal)

Music Leaders

Sara Dorrien	Vocalist
Janlee Richter	Pianist
Judith Whaley	Recorder

Ushers

Eloise Crocker	John Petro
Juanita Holley	Sara Wick

Worship Planning Team

Frank Gross	Kevin Holley
Sara Wick	

Convened in January 2003, the **Kalamazoo Interfaith Coalition for Peace and Justice** *welcomes people of all faith and spiritual traditions who wish to engage in local, national, and international issues involving peace and justice. Meetings are the 1ˢᵗ and 3ʳᵈ Sundays of each month at 5:00 p.m. at different faith community locations . . . For additional information contact Paul Clements at 552-5570. Lee Ann Johnson at 342-9422, or check our web site at www.kalamazooicpi.org.*

The Kalamazoo Interfaith Coalition for Peace and Justice wishes to thank the First Presbyterian Church of Kalamazoo for making their worship space available for this service of prayer and meditation in time of war.

REFLECTIONS ON PEACE
by Raelyn Joyce

*Given at the Interfaith Service of Prayer and
Meditation in Time of War
First Presbyterian Church of Kalamazoo, Michigan
March 21, 2003*

I'm grateful and humbled to have been asked to say a few words of reflection as we face the beginning of a full-scale war on Iraq. At this time, words seem inadequate to express the jumble of emotions within me: sorrow, dismay, pain, outrage, sometimes gloom and despair, and then the question, what more can I do? What's the next step for me, for us?

Some might say that the grassroots peace movement in this country and around the world has tried to stop a war and has failed. On the surface, we might feel that our efforts in the last seven months in Kalamazoo: the rallies twice a week in front of the federal building, the speeches given before the city commission, the letters and phone calls to the White House and to Congress, the letters to the editor, the thousands of yards signs we've spread throughout the city and surrounding areas, the trips to rallies in Washington D.C. and New York, to Lansing and Grand Rapids, the interfaith gatherings, the weekly meetings of KNOW—all these and more have been for naught.

Yet, it doesn't take much thinking to realize what we, individually and collectively, have done for the cause of peace.

I'm a novice peace activist. From the beginning, which was not very long ago, my peace activism has grown from my Quaker beliefs. (For me, a pivotal moment was an interfaith meeting for worship held last September 11 at the Friends Meetinghouse, to reflect on the events of September 11, 2001. It was attended by people who have since been vitally involved in the local peace movement. The peace activists present that evening have become inspiring role models for me. I think you know who you are!) My activism is rooted in the historic Peace Testimony developed by Quakers in the 1600s, which expresses the belief that war and preparation for war are contrary to the spirit of Christ. And I have come to believe that peacemaking is a process that has to be lived daily, not a goal to be reached. For, as Thich Naht Hanh says, "Peace is every step."

Looking back over the seven months that we've worked together, I have so much to be grateful for. This isn't a new realization—I believe I've felt it all along. Our work together has astonished me, cheered me, and strengthened me in more ways than I can mention.

Jean Gump, a local veteran peace activist, who has spent time in federal prison for her acts of civil disobedience, a person whom I admired from afar after reading about her in Studs Terkel's books, told me that she had two main reasons for protesting and attending peace vigils: One is to feel the connection and the sense of community that develops when she's with people of like minds. The other is to lower her blood pressure.

I've had the pleasure of standing next to Jean in front of the Federal Building, of seeing her smile in encouragement and nod her head to the beat of my drumming. Attending peace rallies Sunday after Sunday I have come to realize the truth in Jean's words.

I've told a few friends that I've become addicted to peace rallies that attending them has become my drug of choice. When I arrive at the rallies and see the crowds of people and the friendly faces, I feel a surge of energy and joy. I do feel connected with all of you, even though I don't know most of you by name. I'm elated and inspired by your mere presence.

But I've had my moments of doubts and despair. I remember once a while back hearing someone say, "I'd come to the rallies if I knew they made a difference." I remember feeling discouraged and wishing there was something positive I could say. A friend helped me through that discouragement by saying, "Attending peace rallies is a form of prayer." And in a real sense, that has been true for me.

It's easy to be discouraged listening to the news and reading the newspapers, but driving around town I've been uplifted by the "Another Family for Peace" yard signs in front of homes. I remember when our yard sign was the only one in our Westside neighborhood, but in a few days 7 seven more signs sprung out of my neighbors' snowy front yards, and the next street,

Pinehurst, has even more. Across West Main, Dartmouth, I believe, wins the prize for having 6 yards signs in a row in front of homes. I smile as I drive by. Even though I don't know them, I feel a kinship with the people in those homes, a sense that we're all part of the Peaceable Kingdom. Yesterday I spotted a new yard sign on South Westnedge, nestled in a bank covered with ivy. A pretty sight! I would battle the traffic on Westnedge just to see it again!

I've taken courage and hope from the words of others. Our KNOW web site has had a statement about the "peaceable imagination" that resides in all people, like a light that can never be extinguished. The statement, now removed from the web site to make room for announcements, has nourished me for some time.

I'm heartened by the words of Robert Muller, the former Assistant Secretary General of the U.N., who recently in San Francisco called the present time "a miraculous time in history" because for the first time we're engaged in a huge global conversation about the legitimacy of war. Yesterday an American friend living in India forwarded an email that contained Muller's speech sent to her by an Indian who presumably had heard Muller give the speech in San Francisco. Think of how far Muller's speech has traveled, and how many times around the world, and how many people in different countries have read it!

And recently, the *Kalamazoo Gazette* carried an article about the German consul from Chicago, Alexander Petri, who just last week in Kalamazoo declared that because of its experience with wars, Europe has

"outlawed war as a means of achieving political ends."
Accurate or not, what marvelous words!

Two months ago, when I was racked with doubts, my
daughter Rebecca reminded me about the words of
historian Howard Zinn, who wrote about how
movements begin.   Howard Zinn says,

> The essential ingredients of struggles for
> justice are human beings, who, if only for a
> moment, if only while beset with fears, step
> out of line and do *something,* however
> small. And even the smallest and most
> unheroic of acts adds to the store of kindling
> that may be ignited by some surprising
> circumstance into tumultuous change.

Zinn goes on to explain, "Note how often in this
century we have been *surprised.* By the sudden
emergence of a people's movement, the sudden
overthrow of a tyranny, the sudden coming to life of a
flame we thought extinguished. . . . We are surprised
because we don't see that beneath the surface of the
present there is always the human material for change:
the suppressed indignation, the common sense, the need
for community, the love of children, the patience to
wait for the right moment to act in concert with others.
These are the elements that spring to the surface when a
movement appears in history."

I pray and believe that such a movement has begun. We
are vital parts of that movement. I pray that each of us
will continue to add to the "store of kindling" that will
ignite and lead to tumultuous change.

I pray for wisdom as we face the uncertain and troubling future. I would like to end with a poem by Thich Naht Hanh, which I hope we can continue to ponder on as we leave this gathering. It speaks of the need to see life whole, to see opposites co-existing in each of us, and it speaks of the importance of humility and compassion.

Do not say that I'll depart tomorrow
because even today I still arrive.

look deeply: I arrive in every second
to be a bud on a spring branch,
to be a tiny bird, with wings still fragile,
    learning to sing in my new nest,
to be a caterpillar in the heart of a flower,
to be a jewel hiding itself in a stone.

I still arrive, in order to laugh and to cry,
    in order to fear and to hope,
the rhythm of my heart is the birth and
    death of all that are alive.

I am the mayfly metamorphosing in the
    surface of the river,
and I am the bird which, when spring comes,
    arrives in time to eat the mayfly.

I am the frog swimming happily in the
    clear water of a pond,
and I am also the grass-snake who,
    approaching in silence,
    feeds itself on the frog.

I am the child in Uganda, all skin and bones,
    my legs as thin as bamboo sticks,
and I am the arms merchant, selling deadly
    weapons to Uganda.

I am the 12-year-old girl, refugee
    on a small boat,
who throws herself into the ocean after
    being raped by a sea-pirate,
and I am the pirate, my heart not yet capable
    of seeing and loving.

I am a member of the politburo, with
    plenty of power in my hand,
and I am the man who has to pay his
    "debt of blood" to my people,
dying slowly in a forced labor camp.

My joy is like spring, so warm it makes
    flowers bloom in all walks of life.
My pain is like a river of tears, so full it
    fills up four oceans.

Please call me by my true names,
so I can hear all my cries and my laughs
    at once,
so I can see that my joy and pain are one.

Please call me by my true names,
    so I can wake up,
and so the door of my heart can be left open,
    the door of compassion.

WAR IN IRAQ AND THE PROJECT FOR THE NEW AMERICAN CENTURY

THE PROJECT FOR THE NEW AMERICAN CENTURY (PNAC), A PLAN FOR GLOBAL DOMINANCE, IS NOT CONSISTENT WITH AMERICAN VALUES

- The Project for the New American Century, or PNAC, is a Washington-based think tank created in 1997. Above all else, PNAC desires and demands one thing: The establishment of a global American empire to bend the will of all nations.

- The fundamental essence of PNAC's ideology can be found in a White Paper produced in September of 2000 entitled "Rebuilding America's Defenses: Strategy, Forces and Resources for a New Century." In it, PNAC outlines what is required of America to create the global empire they envision.

- Most ominously, this PNAC document described four "Core Missions" for the American military. The two central requirements are for American forces to "fight and decisively win multiple, simultaneous major theater wars," and to "perform the 'constabulary' duties associated with shaping the security environment in critical regions."

- Two events brought PNAC into the mainstream of American government: the disputed election of George W. Bush, and the attacks of September 11th. When Bush assumed the Presidency, the men who created and nurtured the imperial dreams of PNAC became the men who run the Pentagon, the Defense Department and the White House. When the Towers came down, these men saw, at long last, their chance to turn their White Papers into substantive policy.

- Vice President Dick Cheney is a founding member of PNAC, along with Defense Secretary Donald Rumsfeld and Defense Policy Board chairman Richard Perle. Deputy Defense Secretary Paul Wolfowitz is the ideological father of the group. Bruce Jackson, a PNAC director, served as a Pentagon official for Ronald Reagan before leaving government service to take a leading position with the weapons manufacturer Lockheed Martin.

- PNAC is staffed by men who previously served with groups like Friends of the Democratic Center in Central America, which supported America's bloody gamesmanship in Nicaragua and El Salvador, and with groups like The Committee for the Present Danger, which spent years advocating that a nuclear war with the Soviet Union was "winnable."

- PNAC has recently given birth to a new group, The Committee for the Liberation of Iraq, which met with National Security Advisor Condoleezza Rice in order to formulate a plan to "educate" the American populace about the need for war in Iraq. CLI has funneled millions of taxpayer dollars to support the Iraqi National Congress and the Iraqi heir presumptive, Ahmed Chalabi.

- The PNAC Statement of Principles is signed by Cheney, Wolfowitz and Rumsfeld, as well as by Eliot Abrams, Jeb Bush, Bush's special envoy to Afghanistan Zalmay Khalilzad, and many others. William Kristol, famed conservative writer for the *Weekly Standard*, is also a co-founder of the group. The *Weekly Standard* is owned by Ruppert Murdoch, who also owns international media giant Fox News.

- The desire for these freshly empowered PNAC men to extend American hegemony by force of arms across the globe has been there since day one of the Bush administration, and is in no small part a central reason for the Florida electoral battle in 2000.
- On September 11th, the fellows from PNAC saw a door of opportunity open wide before them, and stormed right through it.
- The day after 9/11, before it was known who was behind the attacks, Rumsfeld insisted at a Cabinet meeting that Saddam's Iraq should be "a principal target of the first round of terriorism." Members of PNAC had called for regime change in Iraq in 1998 in a letter sent to President Clinton, long before 9/11. Ten of the eighteen who signed the letter are now in the Bush administration (they include Rumsfeld, Wolfowitz, Armitage, Bolton, Khalilzad).
- Bush released on September 20th 2001 the "National Security Strategy of the United States of America." It is an ideological match to PNAC's "Rebuilding America's Defenses" report issued a year earlier.
- PNAC had demanded an increase in defense spending to at least 3.8% of GDP. Bush's proposed budget for next year asks for $379 billion in defense spending, almost exactly 3.8% of GDP.
- In August of 2002, Defense Policy Board chairman and PNAC member Richard Perle heard a policy briefing from a think tank associated with the Rand Corporation. According to the *Washington Post* and *The Nation*, the final slide of this presentation described "Iraq as the tactical pivot, Saudi Arabia as the strategic pivot, and Egypt as the prize" in a war that would purportedly be about ridding the world of Saddam Hussein's weapons.
- Iraq is but the beginning, a pretense for a wider conflict. Donald Kagan, a central member of PNAC, sees America

establishing permanent military bases in Iraq after the war. This is purportedly a measure to defend the peace in the Middle East, and to make sure the oil flows. The nations in that region, however, will see this for what it is: a jump-off point for American forces to invade any nation in that region they choose to. The American people, anxiously awaiting some sort of exit plan after America defeats Iraq, will see too late that no exit is planned.

- All of the horses are traveling together at speed here. The defense contractors who sup on American tax revenue will be handsomely paid for arming this new American empire. The corporations that own the news media will sell this eternal war at a profit, as viewership goes through the stratosphere when there is combat to be shown. Those within the administration who believe that the defense of Israel is contingent upon laying waste to every possible aggressor in the region will have their dreams fulfilled. The PNAC men who wish for a global *Pax Americana* at gunpoint will see their plans unfold. Through it all, the bankrollers from the WTO and the IMF will be able to dictate financial terms to the entire planet. This last aspect of the plan is pivotal, and is best described in the newly revised version of Greg Palast's masterpiece, "The Best Democracy Money Can Buy."

- There will be adverse side effects. The siege mentality average Americans are suffering as they smother behind yards of plastic sheeting and duct tape will increase by orders of magnitude as our aggressions bring forth new terrorist attacks against the homeland. These attacks will require the implementation of the newly drafted PATRIOT Act II, an augmentation of the previous Act that has profoundly sharper teeth. The sun will set on the Constitution and Bill of Rights.

- The American economy will be ravaged by the need for increased defense spending, and by the aforementioned "constabulary" duties in Iraq, Afghanistan and elsewhere. Former allies will turn on us. Germany, France and the other nations resisting this Iraq war are fully aware of this game plan. They are not acting out of cowardice or because they love Saddam Hussein, but because they mean to resist this rising American empire, lest they face economic and military serfdom at the hands of George W. Bush. Richard Perle has already stated that France is no longer an American ally.

- As the eagle spreads its wings, our rhetoric and their resistance will become more agitated and dangerous. Many people, of course, will die. They will die from war and from want, from famine and disease. At home, the social fabric will be torn in ways that make the Reagan nightmares of crack addiction, homelessness and AIDS seem tame by comparison.

- This is the price to be paid for empire, and the men of PNAC who now control the fate and future of America are more than willing to pay it. For them, the benefits far outweigh the liabilities.

- The plan was running smoothly until those two icebergs collided. Millions and millions of ordinary people are making it very difficult for Bush's international allies to keep to the script. PNAC may have designs for the control of the "International Commons" of the Internet, but for now it is the staging ground for a movement that would see empire take a back seat to a wise peace, human rights, equal protection under the law, and the preponderance of a justice that will, if properly applied, do away forever with the anger and hatred that gives birth to terrorism in the first place. Tommaso Palladini of Milan perhaps said it best as he marched with his countrymen in Rome. "You fight terrorism," he said, "by creating more justice in the world."

- The People versus the Powerful is the oldest story in human history. At no point in history have the Powerful wielded so much control. At no point in history has the active and informed involvement of the People, all of them, been more absolutely required. The tide can be stopped, and the men who desire empire by the sword can be thwarted. It has already begun, but it must not cease. These are men of will, and they do not intend to fail.

- Excerpts from an article by William Rivers Pitt, "The Project for the New American Century." Pitt is a *New York Times* bestselling author of two books—*War On Iraq* (with Scott Ritter) available now from Context Books, and *The Greatest Sedition is Silence*, available in May 2003 from Pluto Press. Excerpts also from an article by Gary Dorrien, "The War Against Iraq and the Permanent War."

- Search www.google.com (The Project for the New American Century") for more.

LETTER FROM PNAC TO PRESIDENT CLINTON

January 26th, 1998

The Honorable William J. Clinton
President of the United States
Washington, DC

Dear Mr. President:

We are writing you because we are convinced that current American policy toward Iraq is not succeeding, and that we may soon face a threat in the Middle East more serious than any we have known since the end of the Cold War. In your upcoming State of the Union Address, you have an opportunity to chart a clear and determined course for meeting this threat. We urge you to seize that opportunity, and to enunciate a new strategy that would secure the interests of the U.S. and our friends and allies around the world. That strategy should aim, above all, at the removal of Saddam Hussein's regime from power. We stand ready to offer our full support in this difficult but necessary endeavor.

The policy of "containment" of Saddam Hussein has been steadily eroding over the past several months. As recent events have demonstrated, we can no longer depend on our partners in the Gulf War coalition to continue to uphold the sanctions or to punish Saddam when he blocks or evades UN inspections. Our ability to ensure that Saddam Hussein is not producing weapons of mass destruction, therefore, has substantially diminished. Even if full inspections were eventually to resume, which now seems highly unlikely, experience has shown that it is difficult if not impossible to monitor Iraq's chemical and biological weapons production. The lengthy period during which the inspectors will have been unable to enter many Iraqi facilities has made it even less likely that they will be able to uncover all of Saddam's secrets. As a result, in the not-too-distant future we will be unable to determine with any reasonable level of confidence whether Iraq does or does not possess such weapons.

Such uncertainty will, by itself, have a seriously destabilizing effect on the entire Middle East. It hardly needs to be added that if Saddam does acquire the capability to deliver weapons of mass destruction, as he is almost certain to do if we continue along the present course, the safety of American troops in the region, of our friends and allies like Israel and the moderate Arab states, and a significant portion of the world's supply of oil will all be put at hazard. As you have rightly declared, Mr. President, the security of the world in the first part of the 21st century will be determined largely by how we handle this threat.

Given the magnitude of the threat, the current policy, which depends for its success upon the steadfastness of our coalition partners and upon the cooperation of Saddam Hussein, is dangerously inadequate. The only acceptable strategy is one that eliminates the possibility that Iraq will be able to use or threaten to use weapons of mass destruction. In the near term, this means a willingness to undertake military action as diplomacy is clearly failing. In the long term, it means removing Saddam Hussein and his regime from power. That now needs to become the aim of American foreign policy.

We urge you to articulate this aim, and to turn your Administration's attention to implementing a strategy for removing Saddam's regime from power. This will require a full complement of diplomatic, political and military efforts. Although we are fully aware of the dangers and difficulties in implementing this policy, we believe the dangers of failing to do so are far greater. We believe the U.S. has the authority under existing UN resolutions to take the necessary steps, including military steps, to protect our vital interests in the Gulf. In any case, American policy cannot continue to be crippled by a misguided insistence on unanimity in the UN Security Council.

We urge you to act decisively. If you act now to end the threat of weapons of mass destruction against the U.S. or its allies, you will be acting in the most fundamental national security interests of the country. If we accept a course of weakness and drift, we put our interests and our future at risk.

Sincerely,

Elliott Abrams	*William Kristol*
Richard L. Armitage	*Richard Perle*
William J. Bennett	*Peter W. Rodman*
Jeffrey Bergner	*Donald Rumsfeld*
John Bolton	*William Schneider, Jr.*
Paula Dobriansky	*Vin Weber*
Francis Fukuyama	*Paul Wolfowitz*
Robert Kagan	*R. James Woolsey*
Zalmay Khalilzad	*Robert B. Zoellick*

APPENDIX E

The following article is a mini-version of Gary Dorrien's book Imperial Designs: Neoconservatism and the New Pax Americana *(Routledge, 2004). He presented this talk in April 2003 at a local church where over 200 people attended. Dorrien was the Kalamazoo College Parfet Distinguished Professor and Chair of Religious Studies. He presented a similar talk to an audience of 600 on Sunday, February 23, 2003, after Catholics, Protestants, Jews, Muslims, Hindus, Baha'i's, and Buddhists marched from the Federal Building and the Kalamazoo Islamic Center to converge at Stetson Chapel at Kalamazoo College. The march was held in protest of possible war with Iraq.*

Currently, Dorrien, an Episcopalian priest, is the Reinhold Niebuhr Professor of Social Ethics at Union Theological Seminary and Professor of Religious Studies at Columbia University. A second paperback edition of Imperial Designs *will be published by Routledge in spring 2006.*

IMPERIAL DESIGNS: RESISTING THE PERMANENT WAR
by Gary Dorrien

For three weeks we watched our country kill people and destroy things in Iraq; for one afternoon we shared in the celebration of Saddam's figurative and literal downfall in that country, which marked the end of a vicious dictatorship; and for many years to come we shall deal with the occupation and reconstruction of Iraq that are now upon us.

We are told that it was necessary to overthrow the Baathist regime in Iraq to defeat the kind of terrorism that "changed everything" for Americans on 9/11. But Iraq had no connection to 9/11; we cannot diminish terrorism against the United States by incinerating Arab countries and causing most of the world to despise the United States; and if the architects of this war get their way, it will lead to further wars.

The Bush administration is loaded with officials who advocate an ideology of world dominion that its founders call "unipolarism." These officials have no intention of stopping with Iraq; some of them have demanded a war against Iraq since the mid-1990s; and they fervently believe that the U.S. must use its immense military and economic power to create an American-dominated world order. To understand how the ideology of *Pax Americana* became the foreign policy of the United States, we need to recall some Cold War history.

In 1947 the intellectual godfather of American neoconservatism, former Trotskyist James Burnham, argued in his book *The Struggle for the World* that World War III had already begun and that the United States could not win this war—the Cold War against Communism—if it did not adopt an aggressive ideology of its own. America's foreign policy establishment was dominated by liberal internationalists and realists who shunned ideological warfare, Burnham argued. What was needed was an assertive American ideology that proclaimed the superiority of the American system, the need to fight against Communism everywhere in the world, and the need to establish American military bases in every region of the world. In the 1950s a new kind of American conservatism, one that emphasized geopolitics, military expansion, and anti-communist ideology, based itself on these claims.

In the 1970s and 1980s, the neoconservatives built a powerful intellectual movement and won numerous top-level positions in the Reagan administration. Repeatedly they insisted that the Soviet Union was superior to the United States in nuclear capability, military strength, political efficiency, and ideological effectiveness. Often they warned that democracies have great disadvantages in competing with totalitarian regimes for world power. Some of them blasted Reagan for negotiating with the Soviets, and as a group, they were the last believers that Communism works. Thus the neoconservatives were not well prepared in the early 1990s for the disintegration of the Soviet Union. I wrote my book *The Neoconservative Mind: Politics, Culture, and the War of Ideology* during this period, when some of my subjects were suffering from severe intellectual shock. In conducting my interviews for the book, I found it almost embarrassing to ask them, "What happened to the towering, world-conquering colossus described in your writings?"

But most of the neoconservatives quickly recovered, and that is my point. While the Soviet Union unraveled and then disintegrated, some neoconservatives opted for realism or liberal internationalism, but most of them opted for a new ideology of American domination. They argued that the "unipolarist moment" had arrived. More than ever, the United States needed to use its immense military and economic power to America's maximal advantage. A major neoconservative leader, Norman Podhoretz, told me that younger neoconservatives like Paul Wolfowitz and Charles Krauthammer needed to lead the way; they had the youth and ambition to launch a new crusade and defend it from its critics. Krauthammer coined the term "unipolarism" to describe the movement's ideology, and though the term didn't catch on, the idea was seized upon by nationalistic unilateralists, democratic globalists, foreign policy hawks who needed a rationale for increased military spending, and old-style imperialists.

Not all the neoconservatives went along with this transition. A few of them defected from the cause, notably Edward Luttwak and Michael Lind; and some rediscovered their realism, such as Irving Kristol and Jeane Kirkpatrick. Kristol characteristically opined that "no civilized person in his right mind wants to govern Iraq." But the key players made the transition to unipolarism: Kenneth Adelman, Elliot Abrams, John R. Bolton, William F. Buckley, Jr., Stephen Cambone, Dick Cheney, Angelo Codevilla, Eliot Cohen, Devon Cross, Eric Edelman, Douglas Feith, Frank Gaffney, Donald Kagan, Robert Kagan, Lawrence F. Kaplan, Robert Kaplan, Charles Krauthammer, William Kristol, Michael Ledeen, I. Lewis Libby, Joshua Muravchik, Michael Novak, Richard Perle, Daniel Pipes, Norman Podhoretz, Donald Rumsfeld, Ben Wattenberg, James Woolsey. In his article "Universal Dominion: Toward a Unipolar World," Krauthammer spelled out the unipolarist idea: "America's purpose should be to steer the world away from its coming multipolar future toward a qualitatively new outcome—a unipolar world" shaped by American power.

Wattenberg urged nervous politicians not to be shy about asserting American superiority: "We are the first universal nation. 'First' as in the first one, 'first' as in 'number one.' And 'universal' within our borders and globally." Because the United States is uniquely universal, he reasoned, it has a unique right to impose its will on other countries on behalf of an American-style world order. With a lighter touch, Wattenberg declared, "A unipolar world is a good thing, if America is the uni." Muravchik put it plaintively: "For our nation, this is the opportunity of a lifetime. Our failure to exert every possible effort to secure [a new world order] would be unforgivable. If we succeed, we will have forged a *Pax Americana* unlike any previous peace, one of harmony, not of conquest. Then the twenty-first century will be the American century by virtue of the triumph of the humane idea born in the American experiment."

All of this was in the early 1990s, while the first Bush administration argued internally about unipolarism. In 1990, faced with demands for a sharp decrease in American military spending, Secretary of Defense Dick Cheney commissioned Paul Wolfowitz, Lewis Libby, and Eric Edelman to devise a new strategic plan for the United States. Wolfowitz outlined a global empire strategy that called for unilateral military action, new military bases in areas of strategic and economic interest, and the preemptive use of force. But the first Bush administration was dominated by moderately conservative realists who spurned Wolfowitz's aggressive vision of global Americanism, and the Wolfowitz strategy sparked an embarrassing controversy for the Bush administration after it was leaked to the *New York Times*. The more traditional conservatism of Colin Powell and Brent Scowcroft won the day, though Powell made important contributions to unipolarist ideology.

After Bill Clinton won the presidency in 1992, the unipolarists refined their strategic vision and regrouped organizationally. Under the leadership of Cheney, Wolfowitz, Donald Rumsfeld, William Kristol, and Donald Kagan, the unipolarists launched a think tank in 1997--the Project for a New American Century (PNAC)--and subsequently forged an alliance with George W. Bush. In 1998, the PNAC unipolarists wrote a letter to President Clinton that called for a preemptive war against Iraq. Two months before the presidential election of 2000, the PNAC unipolarists issued a position paper that spelled out the particulars of a global empire strategy: repudiate the ABM treaty, build a global missile defense system, develop a strategic dominance of space, increase defense spending by $20 billion per year to 3.8 percent of gross domestic product, establish permanent new forces in Southern Europe, Southeast Asia and the Middle East, and reinvent the U.S. military to meet expanded obligations throughout the world. When Bush won the presidency, the unipolarists came with him: Cheney, Rumsfeld, Wolfowitz, Kenneth Adelman, John R. Bolton, Stephen Cambone, Eliot Cohen, Devon Cross, Douglas Feith, I. Lewis Libby, Richard Perle, Daniel Pipes, and James Woolsey.

This time they had the upper hand. The Bush administration rejected the Kyoto Protocol, withdrew from the ABM Treaty, abrogated the Land Mine Treaty and the Comprehensive Test Ban Treaty, and denounced the International Criminal Court. On some issues the Wolfowitz/Rumsfeld/Perle group didn't get its way--they wanted military confrontation in the Middle East--but after the fiendish attacks of 9/11, they took control of Bush's foreign policy. Three days after 9/11, Wolfowitz declared at a press conference that the U.S. government was committed to "ending states who sponsor terrorism." That remark earned a public rebuke from Colin Powell, who countered that America's goal was to "end terrorism," not launch wars on sovereign states. But the differences between these objectives soon blurred in the administration's foreign policy.

Wolfowitz had argued for years that the U.S. should overthrow Iraq; immediately after 9/11, he went to work on President Bush, repeatedly pressing for an invasion. He pressed so hard and persistently that Bush reportedly became irritated with him. The president worried that there was no connection between 9/11 and Iraq; Wolfowitz replied that even if that turned out to be true, overthrowing Saddam was the key to changing the political culture of the Middle East. Other unipolarists in the administration agreed with Wolfowitz, who cast the war on terrorism as a world-wide crusade. On September 20th, President Bush declared that any nation that sponsors, aids, or harbors terrorists is an enemy of the United States. One year later he declared the right of the United States to wage pre-emptive wars. The following month,

Wolfowitz asserted: "This fight is a broad fight. It's a global fight...that must be pursued everywhere."

Many of the unipolarist leaders are now in the Bush administration, and the rest are more free to say what they think. Persistently, their talk is way beyond Iraq. Donald Kagan says that the way to stifle Arab criticism is to show that the U.S. will not hesitate to use overwhelming force against Arab governments. Angelo Codevilla says that the United States must overthrow the governments of Syria and the Palestinian Authority as soon as possible. Frank Gaffney says that the U.S. must overthrow Iran and the Palestinian Authority and that Bush needs to sweep away most of the longtime professionals in the State Department. Norman Podhoretz says that "we ought to 'kill' the regimes" in Syria and Palestine, that the U.S. must overthrow Iran and Lebanon as soon as possible, and that Egypt and Saudi Arabia belong on the list of enemy targets. Michael Ledeen says, "once the tyrants in Iran, Iraq, Syria, and Saudi Arabia have been brought down, we will remain engaged." William F. Buckley, Jr. says that the U.S. is in a world war against all nations that shelter terrorists and that Iraq is merely a "manageable" opening target. Robert Kaplan remarks: "The real question is not whether the American military can topple Saddam's regime but whether the American public has the stomach for imperial involvement."

It has long been assumed in these circles that Iraq, Iran and North Korea constitute an "axis of evil," as President Bush called these nations last year, and much of the in-house debating among unipolarists concerns the ranking of Syria, Egypt, Yemen, the Palestinian Authority, and Saudi Arabia on this list.

The unipolarist ideology constitutes a fourth basic perspective in foreign policy doctrine. Liberal internationalists seek to secure world peace and stability by securing collective agreements from nation states to comply with international law; realists seek to ensure a balance of power among competing regimes; principled anti-interventionists renounce the use of military force for all reasons besides self-defense; unipolarists maintain that the U.S. has a moral and ideological obligation to establish a new Pax Americana. They argue that if this is imperialism, it is not the classic imperialism that ruled by direct conquest and the subjugation of populations, because America advocates democracy and freedom.

Krauthammer has recently capsulized the argument: "The new unilateralism argues explicitly and unashamedly for maintaining unipolarity, for sustaining America's unrivaled dominance for the foreseeable future...The future of the unipolar era hinges on whether America is governed by those who wish to retain, augment and use unipolarity to advance not just American but global ends, or whether America is governed by those who wish to give it up--either by allowing unipolarity to decay as they retreat to Fortress America, or by passing on the burden by gradually transferring power to multilateral institutions as heirs to American hegemony. The challenge to unipolarity is not from the outside but from the inside. The choice is ours. To impiously quote Benjamin Franklin: History has given you an empire, if you will keep it."

Today the Bush administration is desperate to install a pro-American government in Iraq as soon as possible, one built around former Iraqi exiles, because it needs the political cover and is alarmed that anti-American Shiite clerics could end up running the country. The Bush administration is almost equally desperate to find the hundreds of tons of chemical weapons it claimed that Saddam possessed. Even if it finds some chemical and biological weapons, however, the Bush administration will be forced by the circumstances of occupation and postwar turmoil to increasingly invoke its ultimate reason for invading and occupying Iraq--that the transformation of the Middle East required it. Saddam is a sadistic thug and totalitarian wannabe who gassed the Kurds in 1988, when he was an ally of the United States. His regime was despicably abusive toward its people, but the same arguments that rationalized the invasion of Iraq will apply to Syria, where the same party is in power; and Saudi Arabia, which has an atrocious human rights record; and North Korea, which has a huge army and the bomb. Saddam may have retained some mustard gas or anthrax, but the same thing is true of other governments that detest the United States, and before long we shall be hearing a great deal about them.

The war was a species of social engineering. Even White House officials have begun to acknowledge this fact, but they couldn't say it before we went to war, and thus they stumbled in explaining why we had to invade Iraq. They began by claiming that Saddam was building a nuclear bomb. That didn't pan out, so they switched to the claim that he was connected to terrorism. That didn't pan out either, so they switched to the possession of weapons of mass destruction. They found no evidence of that either, so finally Americans were called to war because Saddam failed to cooperate with inspectors.

Today the United States spends as much on defense as the next fifteen nations combined. When military spending by U.S. allies is excluded, the United States is spending nearly *twice* as much on "defense" as the rest of the world combined. American troops are stationed in 75 countries; each branch of the armed services has its own air force; and in the next year we may learn if the U.S. can occupy Iraq and fight another war at the same time. After 9/11, most Americans are quite happy to spend more on warfare than the next fifteen nations combined. They trust in the assurance of our leaders that if we overwhelm our enemies and kill enough of them, we will be safe.

The realism that we need has to do something about that illusion. True realism distinguishes between international police action to curb terrorism and wars of aggression against governments and their civilian populations. Realism tells us that there will always be bad leaders that have to be coped with and contained. A war fought for the reasons that we are being given leads inevitably and necessarily to more wars, exactly as its advocates insist. Recently James Woolsey declared at U.C.L.A. that the war against Iraq marks the beginning of World War IV—following Eliot Cohen, he counts the Cold War as World War III—and that America must now fight against Syria, Iran, and Lebanon. Woolsey is a close friend of Wolfowitz's and is playing a major administrative role in the occupation of Iraq.

This war will deliver an immense relief to many Iraqis who suffered under Saddam, but it will also create a chaotic nightmare in Iraq for the United States to manage; it will make America the lightning rod for all the frustration and rage in that part of the world; and it will create enormous problems for America's relationship to the rest of the world. Two weeks ago Pentagon staffers told reporters that the U. S. plans to maintain permanent military bases in Iraq; even Rumsfeld panicked at that one, hurriedly claiming that it isn't so. Later he was asked if the U.S. will tolerate a Shiite government in Iraq. Sixty percent of the country is Shiite, but Rumsfeld emphatically replied that the Bush administration will not stand for a government shaped or directed by Shiite clerics.

I have long assumed that Saddam retained some chemical weapons, and I never doubted that he was evil enough to use them again, though former UNSCOMB inspector Scott Ritter insists that 95% of his capacity to use them was destroyed in the 1990's, and we have not found any weapons of mass destruction. In his State of the Union address, President Bush claimed that Saddam retained 500 tons of chemical weapons, 25,000 liters of anthrax and 38,000 liters of botulinum toxin. If Saddam possessed even a fraction of these weapons, it is very strange that he did not use them. But Saddam was not chosen as America's first target of preemptive war because he threatened the United States. He was chosen because he was too weak to have to be dealt with diplomatically, and because his regime was the key to the unipolarist vision of a Middle East transformed by American power.

From a Christian standpoint it is supposed to be nearly impossible to morally justify the murderous violence of war. The world worships power, but Jesus lived and taught the way of agape—the power of self-sacrificial divine love. To the early church the cross symbolized the fellow-suffering way of Christ, which contradicted the way of violence and domination. Subsequently most of the churches taught that war can be morally justified as a last resort in defense of the innocent if proportional means are available and a right intention prevails. But now we are waging wars that don't pretend to take these criteria seriously. The doctrine of preemptive war is a flat-out abandonment of the mainstream Christian moral tradition.

For decades Americans felt safe from the problems and dangers of other countries, often while being oblivious to the suffering that we caused in the world. On 9/11 we lost the former illusion, but our leaders are invoking that experience to reinforce our hubris and obliviousness. This war has been and will be tremendously popular; President Bush will get a huge political windfall from it; and many Americans will feel safer. President Mubarak of Egypt offers a different perspective: Before the war there was one Osama bin Laden, Mubarak observes; now there will be a hundred.

The administration's decision to single out Iraq began with Wolfowitz, who convinced Bush that it didn't matter if Saddam had any real connection to international terrorism; his evil regime deserved to be overthrown in any case. But the Bush administration believes the same thing about Iran, North Korea, and Syria. I believe that Iran is next, but regardless of who is next, the same arguments will be used. Pope John Paul II calls it "the logic of war"; unipolarists call it "draining the swamp."

Because this is a permanent war, it is not too late for Americans to say, no, you are draining my country of its good name and its claim to the good will of other nations. I don't want my country, the country that I love, fighting wars of terror and destruction in the Middle East. I don't want my country to be dragged into wars that don't come remotely close to being a last resort. Not in my name do you create thousands of terrorists and wage a permanent war in the name of making America safe.

CORRESPONDENCE BETWEEN SARA WICK AND REPRESENTATIVE FRED UPTON

[Letters retyped to fit book format.]

March 28, 2003

The Honorable Fred Upton
Sixth District, Michigan
House of Representatives
157 South Kalamazoo Mall, Suite 180
Kalamazoo, MI 49007

Dear Congressman Upton:

On March 1 at your town meeting in Parchment, I presented
your staff with three copies of a speech given by Dr. Gary
Dorrien a few days earlier at an Interfaith Service of Peace at
Kalamazoo College. Dr. Dorrien's speech included references
to some of his research for the past 10 years on
neoconservatism and global domination. He brought attention
to the Project for the New American Century (PNAC), a
frightening plan that calls for the United Stares to assume the
role of God and impose its will on the rest of our planet. It's
devoid of any moral leadership for our country. I trust you
and your staff have read this document and at least one of the
other reports mentioned, "The National Security Strategy of
the United States" (a report on the White House web site).

As my Congressman, I am asking that you:

- Publicly denounce the PNAC and rebuke the efforts of the creators who currently serve in any branch of our government;
- Carefully scrutinize all appropriation bills and vote against any that use our tax dollars to initiate any part of this plan which would include spending for this current pre-emptive war;
- Meet with the Kalamazoo Non-Violent Opponents to War (KNOW) and Dr. Gary Dorrien to discuss needed changes in U.S. foreign policy;
- Sign on as a co-sponsor and passionately support Representative Dennis Kucinich's legislation to establish a United States Department of Peace;
- Vote "no" on the PATRIOT ACT II; and
- Read and reflect on the attached text of Mark Twain's <u>War Prayer</u> that was written around 1900 but not published until after his death (at his request) because he thought it would be too controversial. It was reissued in 2002 in a beautifully illustrated paperback. As our country engages in this immoral, illegal war and supports our troops with prayer, people of all faiths must remember what we are really praying for. The best way to support our troops is to bring them home immediately so all the killing can be stopped.

May you be blessed with peace and hope during this sad time,

Sara L. Wick

Congress of the United States
House of Representatives

April 17, 2003

Sara Wick

Dear Sara,

I do appreciate your taking the time to contact me regarding the war with Iraq. Like you, I to have put much thought and reflection into this issue over the last few months.

Starting last summer, the Administration shared information through classified briefings to Republican and Democratic Members of Congress. I participated in many of these briefings. I left those meetings with the firm belief that the Iraqi regime indeed was an extremely hostile one—not only to its own people but to U.S. interests both here and abroad. I left convinced that they were building weapons of mass destruction and were pursuing a nuclear weapons program as well.

On October 10th, the House passed a resolution authorizing military force by a bipartisan vote of more than 3-1. The Senate, even with the support of Sen. Hillary Clinton and Sen. John Kerry, passed the same resolution by better than 3-1. I supported President Bush in obtaining UN Resolution 1441, which explicitly stated that Iraq has "a final opportunity to comply with its disarmament obligations." This was the 16th UN Resolution on Iraq since the war ended in 1991. Failure to comply with this resolution would yield "serious consequences."

With Iraq, we've tried diplomatic means for 12 years without success. A few more months would have seen Iraq succeed in developing nuclear weapons which would have created a very ugly dynamic in the Middle East.

The war is largely over now and I am heartened by the welcome we have received from many Iraqi citizens who have been oppressed by Saddam Hussein and his brutal regime. But there is much work to do to help this country recover from both the Hussein regime and the war to liberate them. I am committed to supporting this effort. I am also very proud of our military and how hard they worked to avoid mass civilian casualties. These fine men and women make many sacrifices in the service of our country and have done an outstanding job.

Thank you again for contacting me. With the start of the new year, busy times lie ahead for all of us. As a Senior Member of the Energy and Commerce Committee and Chair of the Telecommunications and Internet Subcommittee, I am constantly working to ensure that each and every one of my constituents is equipped with the tools necessary to achieve the American Dream.

My priorities, first and foremost, are to enhance and strengthen our national security and to get our economy moving again. I'm pleased to announce that the Pentagon, recognizing the need, has approved my request for a Michigan-based rapid response anti-terrorism civil support team. This team is located in nearby Augusta, Michigan, ensuring the safety of all of us. In order to receive a quicker response in the future, feel free to write or call either of my two Michigan offices or email my office in Washington (tellupton@mail.house.gov). My offices are located in downtown Kalamazoo and the Twin Cities.

Sara Wick
Page 2, *continued*

God Bless America!

Very truly yours

Fred Upton
Member of Congress

FSU:

The Patriot Act II has not been introduced. I do not subscribe to the PNAC Theory.

SURVEY RESULTS:
APRIL 12–26, 2003

During the most critical period in our nation's history, Americans stop talking to one another. As we enter the war—and as the war drags on—we become more divided and more hostile toward each other. Kalamazoo is no different. Neither the peace activists nor the Bush supporters interact in a public forum nor do they take the opportunity to know or understand what each other thinks. Only at the street rallies do people encounter each other and that is through the impersonal horn honks of approval, drive-by shoutings or obscene gestures.

Over the past couple decades Americans have adopted the habit of associating only with people who hold views similar to their own.[1] On TV talk shows, pundits and politicians from opposite sides don't discuss issues any more; they shout their positions until they subdue their opponents. Hosts on Conservative Talk Radio lead out invectives against "liberals" and hosts on Liberal Talk Radio fight back, albeit with less a following or exposure. Congressional leaders' rivalries become more intense, more vicious—and more obvious with the impeachment proceedings against President Bill Clinton in 1999. Some of this is payback for Democratic shenanigans such as "borking" Republican presidential confirmations[2] at

---

[1] My thanks to Professor Gary Dorrien for this insight.

[2] Failure to confirm Robert Bork for the U.S. Supreme Court touched a raw nerve among Republicans because of Democrats' mistreatment of him during hearings based on their fear that this conservative judge would reverse Roe v. Wade. Actually, Bork had previously "borked" Special Prosecutor Archibald Cox when he was

the time the Democrats were the majority party in Congress. Republicans' payback comes in 1995 when they become the majority party. Veteran legislators reminisce about the "good old days" when senators and representatives from different parties disagreed but at least talked together, socialized and hammered out compromises. But those days are over.

At the grassroots level this divisiveness in America expresses itself not in policy but in such things as media preferences, tastes in entertainment, clothes, food choices and cars. These externalities typically represent class status but they grow into more distinctive symbols of Americans' identification with the country's divisions along "cultural" lines, as Thomas Frank points out in his book, *What's the Matter with Kansas*. As a result, today more than ever, people avoid political debate because of its potential volatility—and with the result that citizens are more ignorant of each other's positions now more than ever before. These divisions among Americans have even evolved into hate speech, as exemplified on the Internet Yahoo News message boards, and growing hate crimes, as reported in the newspapers. There the battle between the Clintonites and the Bushies continues unabated as they embrace a tribe-like behavior that resembles high school football rivalries or worse, the gang wars of the Jets and the Sharks depicted in Leonard Bernstein's 1957 hit, "West Side Story." Even the map of America has morphed into a conflict between the "red" states and "blue" states, recalling the bitterly contested divide between Republicans and Democrats in the 2000 election. These national divisions make me all the more curious to find out how the Bush and the peace contingencies in Kalamazoo perceive the war in Iraq.

Although I talk with people throughout the 18 months of this project, for three weeks I conduct a survey with people

investigating the Watergate scandal and the Nixon White House. Cox was subsequently fired from his job—for doing his job.

from both sides who attend rallies in front of the Federal Building by asking them the following questions:

> Why are you here demonstrating?
>
> Are the demonstrations partisan?
>
> What do you think of the other side? How do you characterize them?
>
> Are you familiar with the Project for the New American Century?
>
> Are you familiar with the Bush Doctrine?
>
> Where do you get your news on Iraq?
>
> What incidents have occurred at home or work as a result of your stand on the war?
>
> Victory is near, what is your assessment of the next steps.
>
> How long do you plan to demonstrate?
>
> Do you see U.S. going into Syria?[3]

I interview 12 Bush supporters (all identified with pseudonyms) and eight peace activists (in their own names unless otherwise indicated). Respondents are very cooperative in expressing their opinions and willing to share their thoughts. While the results are not conclusive, they provide some notion of what motivated local activists on both sides to demonstrate in April 2003, the first month of the war.

One of the most surprising results of this inquiry is that the Bush supporters and the peace activists agree on many things:

---

[3] This question is provoked when the administration begins talking about Iraqi insurgents escaping into Syria. Syria is one of the rogue states fingered for invasion in the PNAC document.

* They need a public outlet to express their concerns and opinions.

* They judge this war by the degree of trust they have in the president.

* They judge this war by their perceptions and biases of the Vietnam War.

* They fear terrorism, but Bush supporters want to stop it directly and peace activists fear the war will instigate more terrorism.

* They support the troops.

* They hold negative impressions of each other, namely, that the other side is uninformed, unrealistic and naïve.

* They believe the war would be over quickly and the United States would win.

* They question the meaning of patriotism.

* They tend to group themselves along partisan lines.

* They mistrust and are dissatisfied with the media.

The survey unearths the differences between these two groups as they reflect on what they think is happening with the war and how citizens should respond. Below is a more detailed account of the survey results.

Media

The Bush supporters obtain their information from a variety of media sources including MSNBC, NPR, WKMI radio, the Internet, CNN, *Detroit Free Press*, *Kalamazoo Gazette*, Fox News. However, they are dissatisfied with the media because they deem it too liberal and, therefore, more interested in the "anti-war protesters" than in support for the president. They think their side should receive more news coverage. What I think they mean is that they need evidence of *grassroots* support for the president—and there isn't much, except for their rallies and supporters' car bumper stickers or "Support the Troops and the President" yard signs. They also resent TV news coverage that focuses on wounded Iraqi children and not enough on the war's progress.

> *"I brought grandkids [to the rallies] who were so enthused. My wife couldn't believe how much support we have. You don't see that on TV, just the anti-war demonstrators."*
>
> **— George Tower**

The peace activists' news sources are more varied and include mainstream media outlets like the *Kalamazoo Gazette*, *New York Times* and PBS, but they also tune into the alternative media made possible by the Internet (True Majority, Moveon.org, CommonDreams.org, other independent and international media) and a cable TV show entitled "Democracy Now." None of them cite Fox News as their news source. The peace activists are also very dissatisfied with the media because they think it favors the administration. They complain that most of the media is owned and controlled by conservative media moguls like Rupert Murdoch and the "Big 10" pro-Bush corporations[4] who benefit from the Federal Communication Commission's (FCC) relaxation of monopoly regulations in the media. Secretary of State Colin Powell's son, Michael, the chairman of the FCC, promoted this change in 2002.

The peace activists feel the media has also minimized reports on the national and international activities of millions

---

[4] The Big 10 consists of AOL/Time-Warner, AT&T, General Electric, News Corporation, Bertelsmann, Walt Disney Company, Viacom, Vivendi Universal, Sony, Liberty Media Corporation.

of people around the world who demonstrate against President Bush's drive toward war. The *Gazette* covers most of KNOW's local events, especially between the late fall 2002 and up to May 1, 2003. After that, coverage is sparse. The readership has apparently tired of the war and especially of the peace demonstrations and the local media has responded in kind.

Patriotism, Partisanship and Protest

Both the Bush supporters and the peace activists believe they are in touch with the truth about the war and that this truth provides them with a lens to understand and evaluate the president and his performance. They also hold deeply-felt assumptions about how citizens should act in a time of war.

The Bush supporters like President Bush's leadership and don't hesitate to identify with the Republican Party. They are unwavering in their support for the president and the troops *because* the country is at war. This, they believe, is the way Americans are supposed to act in a national emergency. However, much of their attitude comes not only from their admission of partisanship but from statements that reveal nationalistic and ethnocentric attitudes.

> *Yes, definitely, this side is Republican. You see a lot of Bush supporters. The peace rallies are actually anti-Bush, not anti-war.* — ***Ann Perkins***

> *I back Bush 150 percent. I'm a diehard Republican . . . This war is not a partisan issue. It's time to unite. When we're at war, we stand behind our country. Love it or leave it.* — ***Patsy Donovan***

Patsy, a self-proclaimed Republican, makes red/white/blue ribbons to pass out to demonstrators. She says she did this after 9/11. "It was something I could do to support our country." Ann sees the war as a critical time for all citizens to rally round the president:

> *Because I totally support President Bush and the troops. I wasn't convinced at first but trusted the authorities. Then when it started, we had no choice but to support it.*

Martha Duncan, feels the same way as Ann and Patsy, only she bases her conclusions about this war on her experience in Europe during World War II when the Americans liberated the Netherlands from the Nazis. She was six years old at the time. She equates the Americans in Iraq as liberators, as they were in her native land 59 years before.

> *I've been here demonstrating since March 6, just before the war. I lived in Netherlands during World War II and saw the other side. I know what happens when people take over your country. The Iraqis feel oppression. Americans liberated the Dutch.*

Martha's husband, also in the Netherlands during World War II, wears a Bush cap and carries big American flag. As he speaks, he points to the veterans in the crowd:

> *They enabled us to stand here. I've seen what a despot and a tyrant can do. The black shirts gunned down people. When the Americans came to liberate us we knew we were free. These guys are doing it again. We don't want to allow a bully to go on forever. Even though FDR lied a bit to get the war going, I'm glad he did. There are 8,306 graves in Netherlands. Many are of young kids 17–19 years old. They died so we could do this [demonstrate in public]. If we had appeasement with Hitler, we'd be goose stepping instead of standing here with the stars and stripes. Jews, Gypsies, and the handicapped were all gone.*
>
> **— Craig Duncan**

The Bush supporters generally believe the peace activists are anti-Bush and sore losers over the 2000 presidential election; they are using the war to protest against the president.

> *Some [peace] people weren't demonstrating anti-war with Clinton when Haiti, Somalia, Bosnia came up. War is an excuse to be anti-Bush. They are using the troops by saying 'Bring the troops home.' I feel real strong about it. I'm obviously pro-Bush.* — **Ann Perkins**

George Tower expresses a more cynical opinion of the peace activists, thus implying partisanship without naming it and questioning their motives for demonstrating as well. He justifies his position by calling freedom of speech an American value that troops are protecting in Iraq—and in all our wars. This is a common theme Bush supporters add to their comments.

> *Those against us don't know what's going on: we're trying to free a whole nation. Some people demonstrate because that's the thing to do to get in the news—right or wrong. They have a right to demonstrate but forget if it weren't for the vets, they couldn't protest on camera.* — **George Tower**

The peace activists say they are unsupportive of President Bush and his decision to go to war, not out of partisanship but because they don't want war to be a response to 9/11. They believe they attract people from all political persuasions.

> *People from all parties attend the vigils. There's concern across the spectrum. Peace activists are present here. A number of Vets for Peace have been here since we began last summer. Some people know Iraqis. Some families are divided over this war by political party loyalties or religious perspectives.* —**Tobi Hanna-Davies**

> *Some of us are active in political parties. It's opposition to*
> *the powers that be—both parties are sold on the myth of*
> *domination and have to show we are more powerful and in*
> *control.* — ***Rev. John Fisher***

I know many of the peace activists to be Democrats or Green Party members but few identify themselves with either party. Many of them will favor Howard Dean or Dennis Kucinich in the 2004 presidential election, the only two Democratic presidential candidates who denounce war with Iraq. When John Kerry (who voted to give the president the power to go into Iraq in October 2002) wins the primaries, the peace activists unite with him in a common cause: to defeat George W. Bush in 2004.

The Bush supporters define patriotism as supporting the president in a time of war, regardless of what a person thinks about the war or who the president is. They remain stalwart in their support of the troops, I believe, mostly because they don't want them to be treated with hostility and disrespect as the Vietnam veterans were. This memory of Vietnam plays an important role in shaping both sides' perceptions of the war in Iraq. Many peace activists protested the war 30 years ago—or they are protesting this war because they didn't protest the Vietnam War. Many Bush supporters have never participated in public rallies before. Both sides have veterans in their demonstrations. Most of the pro-Bush veterans served during Vietnam or afterward while many of the peace activists are vets from Vietnam, World War II and Korea.

Among the Bush supporters are veterans who identify with the current soldiers in the field. George Tower, a Marine 1954–56, waves a big red Marine flag at the rallies. He has a niece in the army who is stationed in Kuwait and who, he figures, will probably go to Iraq. Tony Freedman, a Marine from 1976–88, who served most of his time as a reservist, has a special empathy for the reserve troops pulled into service for this war. He also says he feels a part of the "Marine brotherhood," something that he cherishes deeply. Ken Webber, a veteran, 1967–71, remembers the poor treatment he and other veterans received when they returned from Vietnam. He wants to make sure that isn't repeated with this war. Vietnam affects non-veteran demonstrators, too, like Martha who says:

> *I support the troops and the president. It's important so it's not like the last time (referring to Vietnam) when troops were not supported and then booed when they returned.*

The painful lingering pain of some veterans I meet is hard to take but the real heartbreakers are parents or family members of troops. They show up at the pro-Bush rallies because they feel there really isn't any place else for them to go—and they feel a need to attend a public demonstration to express themselves. They regard the peace activists as anti-war, anti-Bush and therefore non-supportive of the troops who happen to be *their* sons and daughters who are risking their lives for the country. Such perceptions also give Bush supporters reason to call the peace activists "traitors." Among these military families their major concern is the safety of their children and they show up at the rallies to relieve their worries a little bit and to be around people who avidly support the troops.

> *My nephew is in the Marines. He's at Cherry Point, NC. Joined just before 9/11. My sister works and she can't come here, so I'm here. I would prefer that we ended this war now instead of waiting five years when my son is over there. He wants to serve as a Navy Seal, the toughest one of all and he wants to do it.* — **Shirley Johnson**

Other people express their lack of concern about partisanship on the war issue; they are there to support the troops, too.

> *Hard to tell [if it is a partisan issue] but probably. There are hardcore people on both sides. I support Bush but that's not why I'm here. I support the troops.*
> — **Craig Duncan**

> *I have no idea if people support the war or are against it. I'm just here to support the troops.* —**Shirley Johnson**

> *There are few people here we know. The Republicans started the demonstrations, probably because they were in support of Bush.* — **Martha Duncan**

> *Strong leaning one way for each group—a guess, I don't know.* —**Tony Freedman**

Although they are concerned about the deaths of American troops, Bush supporters consistently avoid this topic but concede that it is an unfortunate consequence of war. Instead, they express more worry about the threat of terrorism and see the campaign in Iraq not only as a step toward stamping it out, but as a necessary means of protecting the American way of life. They support the troops because they regard them as heroes taking on this important and difficult charge.

While the peace activists support the troops, they do it by arguing that American soldiers should come home rather than to fight an "unjust, immoral, unnecessary" war in Iraq. They are also upset over the administration's emphasis on defense spending and war profiteering as the administration cuts domestic social programs for Americans, including benefits for veterans. (The Bush supporters never discuss these issues; the war is the single-minded focus of their demonstrations.) The more religious members of the group speak of their faith as a motivation *not* to conduct this war and a few cite the Beatitudes and Jesus's calls for peace and justice as their inspiration toward this position. While they are concerned about the deaths of hundreds of coalition troops, the peace activists also worry about the deaths of thousands of Iraqis, especially the civilians, which the Bush supporters do not speak about at all and the media never report—except in October 2004 when the word is out that 100,000 Iraqis have died in the war. There seems to be no public reaction to this fact, however.

Need for Public Expression

Through my observations of the Bush rallies and the peace vigils, I gain a new appreciation for the Constitution's provision for public assembly, a First Amendment right. Public assembly[5] allows individuals the opportunity to express

---

[5] "The right to peacefully gather and parade or demonstrate to make one's views known or to support or oppose a public policy is based upon the twin guarantees of the freedom of speech and the right to peaceably assembly.

"On October 14, 1774, the Declaration and Resolves of the First Continental Congress declared, among a list of other demands, `[t]hat the inhabitants of the English colonies in North-America, by the immutable laws of nature, the principles of the English constitution, and the several charters or compacts, have the following RIGHTS: *Resolved, N.C.D.8.* That they have a right peaceably to assemble, consider their grievances, and petition the king; and that all prosecutions, prohibitory proclamations, and commitments for the same, are illegal.'

their thoughts and ideas to a mass audience without suppressing it. Public assembly goes beyond speeches, letters to the editor and, of course, private conversations with family and friends. It signals that an issue needs to be aired in public. If large numbers of people join a public assembly, the media notices that and is moved to examine the issue. So public

---

"Later, the declarations of rights of the newly formed states of Pennsylvania (1776), North Carolina (1776), Massachusetts (1790), and New Hampshire (1784) included guarantees for peaceable assembly and petition.

"That Pennsylvania should be the first state to recognize the right to peaceably assemble is no accident. The founder of the colony William Penn was arrested in 1670 on Gracechurch Street, London, for delivering a sermon to an orderly assembly of Quakers in the street in front of his assembly hall. The hall had been locked by London officials and Penn had been forbidden to preach in any building. He was charged with unlawful, tumultuous assembly that disturbed the king's peace. The judge in the case tried to force the jury to return a verdict of guilty for William Penn and his supposed co-conspirator William Mead. This was a bitter memory for those who believed in religious freedom and the right for people to assemble peacefully.
"In *De Jonge v. Oregon*, 299 U.S. 353 (1937), the U.S. Supreme Court unanimously ruled that the right to peaceably assemble for lawful discussion, however unpopular the sponsorship, cannot be made a crime. The decision applied the First Amendment right of peaceful assembly to the states through the due process clause of the Fourteenth Amendment.

"The right of peaceable assembly protects the right to picket which has been used in labor disputes and civil rights and anti-war demonstrations. In general, picketing is protected when it is for a lawful purpose, conducted in an orderly manner, and publicizes a grievance of some kind. Generally, parades or demonstrations can be controlled by local time, place, manner regulations as long as they are applied in a nondiscriminatory fashion and do not block such protected expression" (source: First Amendment Cyber-Tribune, http://fact.trib.com/1st.assemble.html).

assembly can be a political tactic designed to attract attention that something is awry with the system. In this sense, it is the citizens' check on government policy.

As the war in Iraq approaches, the tension agitates the Kalamazoo peace activists—and millions across the United States and the world—enough to get them out on the streets to express their concerns. Based on my research, they demonstrate for three major reasons:

* they want to express their opinion of the war

* they act on memories from past wars

* they need to be among others who share their opinion on the issue.

Many activists who protested the Vietnam War in the 1960s and early 70s and the arms race in the 1980s, are philosophical about their reasons for demonstrating this war.

> *I feel so strongly our nation is making a big mistake. I want the U.S. to be a force for good in the world. No war on our own soil—many people don't realize how evil war is in itself. My Mom and Dad were WWII vets. Mom in the British Navy came to the U.S. at 19; in England during the Nazi attacks she joined the Navy to defend her country. Dad was in the U.S. Navy in the Pacific on the first ship in the harbor of Japan.*

> **— Tobi Hanna-Davies**

Rev. John Fisher offers a Scriptural explanation of his reasons for demonstrating, which end up taking a toll on his congregation:

> *It is a religious thing for me. It's an illusion that violence brings peace. Jesus taught us to resist evil and that nonviolence is the best way. He overcame evil with peace. When the bombing started I tore my vestments as an act of*

> *humility and grief for the suffering the U.S. is causing. I*
> *include myself in this act because I'm an American. It*
> *represents a failure of the Church to teach a viable*
> *alternative to war. We haven't done our part. When the*
> *war started my congregation split on two sides.*

Eileen Pearson goes to Washington and Lansing with four other women to march against the war. She attends KNOW meetings and candlelight vigils and wants to be around a group of people she can identify with because it affirms her self-respect, even though it is not a popular thing to do. Here she compares her experience with the peace activists in Kalamazoo to those in Chicago, which gives her hope that the anti-war position will be heeded because so many people take to the streets:

> *On March 21 I went to Chicago to pick up my sons. One*
> *son is in college and went to a march. It started at 5 pm.*
> *When people were coming out of work. Thousands joined*
> *the march and the police were disoriented. They shut down*
> *Lakeshore Drive for two hours. People were stopped in*
> *traffic but they gave huge support. Many left their cars and*
> *joined the march.*

The peace activists are so passionate and so committed to the anti-war agenda that they vow to continue their vigils indefinitely. They still demonstrate twice a week in front of the Federal Building and they continue to hold activities and events against the war. The Bush supporters are just as passionate about their commitment to their cause of supporting the troops and the president. Shirley Johnson has two daughters, 8 and 11, who come with her to a Bush rally even though they are sick. They stay in the car across the street while their mother demonstrates on the street for a couple hours that morning. She says that her kids insisted on coming to the rally so she compromises with them on this

arrangement. Shirley holds a poster she made with photos of
Marines and summaries of the war dead. Ann Perkins has a
son-in-law in the National Guard. He has not been called up
yet, but he has been in Kuwait preparing bases since
December. Her niece and nephew are in the Coast Guard in
California.

While Shirley and Ann focus on the safety of their family
members, one man believes his son is fighting this war for a
just cause:

> *I support my son and his efforts. He's a Marine reservist
> (3½ years) and he's in Iraq. I believe we need to step
> forward on this situation (terrorism) and stop it at its
> source before it gets totally out of hand. We created the
> monster, Saddam, we should put him to rest.*
> — **Bill Katz**

Convincing himself that his son is in a just war doesn't
make it any easier for Bill to endure his concern:

> *I spoke to my son on the phone on Feb. 22 and saw him in
> January. His last letter was March 18, two days before
> war. He's in water purification projects and he's pretty
> busy. I got a letter from one of his buddies yesterday in the
> same unit. They got split up working on other projects.
> I'm behind the war from the get go. My son was the first
> one called from our employer. Then several others followed.
> Everybody at the plant supports him. (He was the kick-off
> point.) Every Wednesday people come up and ask about
> my son. The first couple weeks were hard after he left. It's
> harder on his mother than me. I keep assuring my wife
> that the Marines are an elite corps and well-trained.*

The Bush supporters express a commitment to continue
their rallies, but organizers indicate the rallies will no longer

meet at the end of April when they believe the president will
call a halt to the war.

> *I'll be here till it's over. It will be over when the president
> declares the fighting is done. He's the one that said 'let's
> roll.'* — **Patsy Donovan**

> *There was a woman here a few weeks ago who gave a
> reporter a big list of reasons why she was here. It takes a
> lot to get a woman out of bed on Saturday when she works
> during the week, has three kids and gets up every morning
> at 6 a.m. It's a real commitment . . . . I would be here
> all summer long but this is the last week we will be holding
> a rally. I hope we get Saddam out of there before my kids
> have to go and fight him.* — **Shirley Johnson**

Amy Crain feels the rallies are important but she expresses
her displeasure about the numbers of people who don't attend:

> *Being here with a 200,000 population in this county, it's
> disappointing that we are so few in numbers. I don't mind
> giving up a Saturday. We all lead busy lives and have
> other priorities, but without this action we wouldn't be able
> to enjoy those busy lives and other priorities.*

Judging from cars passing the demonstrations,
Kalamazoo's response to the pro-Bush rallies is generally
positive and, unlike the peace activists who experience varying
amounts of negativity during their vigils and in comments from
the LETTERS TO THE EDITOR *in the Gazette.* (It is possible that
being out on the street for only seven weeks is not time
enough to receive much critique. I am unaware of any national
media coverage of pro-Bush demonstrations. All the coverage
is on the peace activists. Likewise, in Kalamazoo there are
only two stories on the Bush supporters.)

Trust in the President

The Bush supporters see the president as an honest, strong, and forthright leader who has responded adeptly and appropriately to 9/11 by mounting on a "war on terrorism." The Bush supporters have an implicit trust in him and his ability to protect the country from terrorists because he shows courage, personal morality and admits to a close faith relationship with God.

> *Bush is not looking to be re-elected, he just wants to keep us safe. I'm sorry for all the stuff he's been through, but he's doing a damn fine job.* — **Madge Baker**

> *I support him 100%. When he tells you something, you can take it to the bank. When he says something, he means it. He's not wishy-washy. He's an honorable man with high morals and I admire a man like that. You don't have to disinfect the Oval Office. Clinton was the biggest disgrace in my life. The presidency is an office you respect whether it's occupied by Democrats or Republicans. The last 8 years I had no faith in that man Clinton at all. Those sex scandals.* — **George Tower**

Bush implies (and Vice President Cheney directly insists even during the 2004 presidential campaign) that there is a link between Saddam and Al Qaeda and that Saddam has weapons of mass destruction.[6] These are good reasons to go to war: to

---

[6] Several news reports have declared that Iraq has no WMD (CIA Report by David Kay to Senate and House Select Intelligence Committees, Oct. 2, 2003; *USA Today*, March 2, 2004; BBC News, Dec. 17, 2003; CBS News, September 25 BBC News, September 24, 2003).
On July 28, 2004, David Kay, the CIA-appointed position of chief U.S. weapons hunter who steps down in January 2004, says that the

liberate Iraq from the brutal dictator who kills his own people and to bring democracy and freedom to that country.

> *I believe Bush when he says that Osama bin Laden has ties to Saddam Hussein. Then, when we see what Saddam has done to his own people, how can we not go into Iraq? If we had done it 12 years ago, maybe we would not be in Iraq today.* **—Patsy Donovan**

---

administration should give up the "delusional hope" that Iraq has WMD so they can move on with reforms suggested by the 9/11 Commission Report that recommends overhauling U.S. intelligence, including creating a national director to oversee the 15 spy agencies. (Reuters)

In July 2004, the 9/11 Commission declares that there are no ties between Saddam and Al Qaeda even though a July 22, 2004, project memorandum by Daniel McKivergan, PNAC Deputy Director, says that the 9/11 Commission report *does* confirm the ties between Iraq and Al Qaeda. "With the release of the September 11 Commission report, some media outlets may ignore or mischaracterize the fact that the report offers more confirmation of Iraq—Al Qaeda ties. It is especially noteworthy, however, that the previous staff report's finding of no 'collaborative relationship' between Iraq and Al Qaeda has been significantly modified. While the commission found no evidence of a 'collaborative operational relationship' for 'carrying out attacks against the United States,' they did find that the connection between Iraq and Al Qaeda to be more extensive than many critics of the administration have been willing to admit. And, as the CIA's Counterterrorism Center previously remarked, 'Any indication of a relationship between these two hostile elements could carry great dangers to the United States'"
Source: www.newamericancentury.org/iraqmiddleeast.htm

A January 12, 2005, the *New York Times* reports that the search for illegal weapons (WMD) is over and that the United States has not found any.

I don't doubt he had them or had them and would have used them. After seeing the way he treated his people (prisons and torture), it's a matter of human rights and we're justified going in there. People demonstrated there, makes me want to throw up. Why didn't we come over the last 12 years? — **Ann Perkins**

Iraq developed WMD and can pass them on to terrorists. That's where Iraq is involved. It had the money and resources to sell or give weapons to terrorists. Atomic or chemical weapons pose a very serious threat, not just for us but for the whole world. — **Ken Webber**

They're there, we just haven't found them yet. Inspectors were there before and saw the weapons and knew they were there. Saddam showed them. Either they're well-hidden or in Syria or some place. We'll find others. — **Bill Katz**

However, with that trust in the president comes an unnerving sense of the fear of terrorism threatening America and the American way of life.

Saddam lied about not having weapons of mass destruction. The middle of the U.S. could be the next target. — **Patsy Donovan**

I wish they would find Saddam.[7] — **Shirley Johnson**

Support for this war becomes a means of stomping out terrorism. Iraq can serve as an example to other would-be

---

[7] Saddam is found in a six to eight foot-deep spider hole in Ad Dawr on December 14, 2003. As of July 2004 he resides in a 10 x 13-foot military prison cell. He is restricted from television or radio but has access to books donated to him by the Red Cross (Associated Press, July 26, 2004).

terrorists that the United States will not tolerate terrorism in the world. This position implies that the U.S. is indeed the world's policeman, a position that has been unresolved since the end of the Cold War and before 9/11. Now people regard this new role as our responsibility.[8]

> *Hopefully, others have seen what we can do and they'll work with us to eliminate terrorist threat of any group out to destroy freedom....9/11 was the start of the whole war. We were attacked by a foreign organization.[9] That was an*

---

[8] Critics on the left, however, see the U.S. role in Iraq as that of the world's bully because it ignores international law. The 1989 coup in Panama, ordered by President George H.W. Bush, and the 1998 bombing raids on Iraq, ordered by President Clinton, show bipartisan agreement that such action is justified. CounterPunch writer Robert Jensen notes that, "All this talk about being the world's policeman helps obscure a simple reality: U.S. policy-makers routinely ignore international law and act as rogues."
Source: www.counterpunch.org/jensen1118.html, Nov. 18, 2002

[9] In a three-part series entitled "The Power of Nightmares" broadcast in England by the BBC2 starting on Wednesday, Oct 20, 2004, the narrator states that Al Qaeda is not an organization at all and it does not have sleeper cells all over the world. The 9/11 hijackers were a small group of extremists who pulled off the attacks on the World Trade Center and the Pentagon. Osama bin Laden then used the term, "Al Qaeda," as a rallying cry to recruit more terrorists.
Sources: The BBC (news.bbc.co.uk/1/hi/programmes/3755686.stm) and *The Guardian* www.guardian.co.uk/terrorism/story/0,12780,1327904,00.html)

Thom Hartmann made the American public aware of this broadcast on a Dec. 7, 2003, in an essay for alternative press website Common Dreams www.commondreams.org/views04/1207-26.htm.
Hartmann is a Project Censored Award-winning, best-selling author and host of a nationally syndicated daily progressive talk show, "The Thom Hartmann Radio Program." His website is www.thomhartmann.com.

*act of war. Iraq is a continuation of that. You can argue
that we weren't attacked by a country.* — **Ken Webber**

Some Bush supporters believe that war will bring peace to
the Middle East, even though others doubt that peace in that
region is possible.

> *This is the beginning of peace for the Middle East region.
> Conflict has been going on for thousands of years. It's tied
> to Israel and Palestine.* — **Amy Crain**

> *We also want peace, but we have to fight for it. We tried
> peace and then came 9/11.* —**Patsy Donovan**

A couple of people support this war for religious reasons.
"God is not for war," says Patsy Donovan. "Evil is in the
world and we must stand up against it." She also refers to
Matthew 24:1–8 as proof that God is against war. Here is the
reference from the Bible:

> Jesus left the temple and was going away,
> when his disciples came to point out to him
> the buildings of the temple. But he answered
> them, "You see all these, do you not? Truly, I
> say to you, there will not be left here one
> stone upon another, that will not be thrown
> down."
>
> As he sat on the Mount of Olives, the
> disciples came to him privately, saying. Tell
> us, when will this be, and what will be the sign
> of your coming and of the close of the age?
> And Jesus answered them, "Take heed that no
> one leads you astray. For many will come in
> my name, saying, 'I am the Christ,' and they
> will lead many astray. And you will hear of

> wars and rumors of war; see that you are not
> alarmed; for this must take place, but the end
> is not yet. For nation will rise against nation,
> and kingdom against kingdom, and there will
> be famines and earthquakes in various places:
> all this is but the beginning of the sufferings.

Another woman sees the war as a signal of on Armageddon
and the End Times.

> *We've been headed that way . . . .Don't worry, it's going to*
> *happen sooner or later.* — **Madge Baker**

The Bush Doctrine

The Bush supporters focus on the purpose of the war
while the peace activists are obsessed over its consequences,
especially after they learn about the Project for New American
Century (PNAC) and its influence on the Bush administration.
Most of the Bush supporters have no idea what PNAC is. (It
is also called the Bush Doctrine although the name never
catches on.) Almost no one I interview has ever heard of
PNAC by name but, curiously, they have opinions about it.
(This response, perhaps, reflects an aspect of American culture
that we like to express our opinions on an issue even when we
know nothing about it; this is our conception of freedom and
free speech. In articulating an opinion, people seem to adopt
the opinions of those of people they admire.[10] (For this survey
people may have manufactured an opinion to project their
positive perceptions and hopes about the president and his
policies. They want him to succeed, especially after the
Clinton disaster; he must be right about what he is doing; he

---

[10] Thanks to Bill Mahr for this insight during his interview with Terry
Gross's PBS show, "Fresh Air" on August 8, 2004.

has responded to our fears about our vulnerability to the terrorists; he is a man of God and we trust him.

Craig Duncan ventures a guess that the Bush Doctrine is "about doing things together and coalition building." Ken Webber, 54, who is recognized by his fellow rally mates as a man who "reads everything," is unfamiliar with PNAC and says he has only vaguely heard of the Bush Doctrine, but he can't describe it or comment on it. Only Tony Freedman has some idea of what PNAC is, and he expresses his reservations about it: "I'm not real comfortable with pre-emptive strike, but once the first shot is fired, I support the troops."

At the time of these interviews the administration begins talking about Syria as a potential haven for terrorists escaping Iraq. I ask Bush supporters if they think we should go after Syria.

> *Depends on what Syria and neighboring countries decide to do. Hopefully, they'll see differently after seeing what our Marines have done. The next objective would be North Korea. We need to set down some ground rules and have both sides talk. We've worked it out in Russia, why not do it with North Korea? We don't need World War III.*
> **— Bill Katz**

Raymond Salizar shares his concerns about the United States getting along in the world and he expects the U.S. diplomatic corps to allay further war, but he trusts the president's judgment for any further action in the Middle East:

> *I was pleased we tried to use diplomacy [with Iraq in 2003]. I watched George Bush, Sr., leave us short . . . . I don't think we should expand this any further than Iraq and Afghanistan right now. I don't think we should give the Arab countries a reason for hating us. But if we do go in, I support our troops.* **— Raymond Salizar**

Other pro-Bush respondents either want to avoid further war or they don't want to think about that possibility.

> *Hope not. Before Iraq I was more worried about North Korea. That could be a bad situation. They DO have weapons that can reach us. That's why I want Saddam out before he does have weapons that can reach us.*
>
> **— Shirley Johnson**

> *If war started it would be in Korea.[11] If we have to, we'll go burn the barn to get the rats out of the chicken house, too. My concern is to get the Iraqi yahoos out.*
>
> **— Martha Duncan**

> *No. North Korea, China, Japan – it's up to them. It impacts them. It's up to them to sort it out, maybe with our help.*
>
> **— Amy Crain**

> *Don't know—don't think so, hope not.*
>
> **—Tony Freedman**

---

[11] North Korea is one of the three countries Bush names as the "axis of evil" in his 2002 State of the Union speech. Secretary of State Colin Powell is later quoted then as saying, "It does not mean that we are ready to invade anyone or that we are not willing to engage in dialogue. Quite the contrary," (BBC February 6, 2002). On May 6, 2002, the BBC reports that Cuba, Libya and Syria have been added to the list of "rogue states" that sponsor terror or pursue WMD programs. In a speech entitled "Beyond the Axis of Evil," U.S. Under Secretary of State, John Bolton says that America will take action "to prevent the next wave of terror," referring to the September 11 attacks in Washington and New York that killed 3,000 people. "States that sponsor terror and pursue WMD must stop. States that renounce terror and abandon WMD can become part of our effort, but those that do not can expect to become our targets," he said.

Haven't been watching the news. — **Martha Duncan**

Can't say for sure. It depends on their behavior.
—Bill Katz

From these comments it appears that the Bush supporters assume that the United States is acting defensively rather than offensively. Their belief has several cultural precedents to assume that business in our relationships is going on as usual. For example, the U.S. Constitution states that the Congress shall provide for the common defense and have the power:

> To declare War, grant Letters of Marque and Reprisal, and make Rules concerning Captures on Land and Water;

> To raise and support Armies, but no Appropriation of Money to that Use shall be for a longer Term than two Years; (Article 1, Section 8, Clauses 10 and 11)[12]

Upon leaving office George Washington cautions the young nation to stay out of Europe's affairs to avoid its constant war and strife, which results in our tendency to be isolationist. This attitude is only enhanced by our geography that separates us physically from the world by two oceans. One interesting outcome of these three precedents is that Americans have come to assume a position of innocence in the world scene. We are only drawn into wars to help others, as in World War I and II and we wouldn't think of starting wars or

---

[12] Bush obtains congressional approval for a resolution (H.J. Res. 114) authorizing the use of military force against Iraq on October 11, 2002. He maintains, however, that Article I does not restrict a preemptive war.
Source: shs.westport.k12.ct.us/socst/Iraq_files/ JointRes.htm

causing them. This posture has been largely successful and believable—even when it isn't true.

According to Chalmers Johnson in his book, *Sorrows of Empire* (Metropolitan Books, 2004), the United States has been pursuing a militarism quest for economic empire since the early 19th century. September 11 catches us by surprise, especially as the world's only super-power. Through our innocence we believe we have been attacked without provocation. President Bush's response, which resonates with most Americans, is to "hunt down" the terrorists, a typical militaristic response. He later tells us that we must go after Saddam Hussein because he harbors terrorists in Iraq and is connected to 9/11 mastermind, Osama bin Laden.

The Bush supporters believe the president and support him unremittingly even in the face of contradictory facts. It is perhaps an explanation for why they demonize the peace activists as anti-American, negative, effeminate (*i.e.,* refusing to want to "hunt down" the terrorists) traitors. The peace activists, on the other hand, want to examine U.S. relationships with the Middle East, particularly our dependence on oil. This approach is deemed completely off-base and counter-productive.

When the end of the Cold War leaves the United States as the only remaining superpower, PNAC proposes to the Clinton administration a new policy of aggression against "rogue states" and organizations[13] that pose a terrorist threat to the United States. Clinton rejects it. Prior to his inauguration in 2001, the Bush administration adopts PNAC's strategy to establish a "new American century" of world dominance. It includes the option of unilateral, pre-emptive strike, which we

---

[13] The Neoconservatives list 40 countries that pose threats to the United States and President Bush added 20 more (source: Professor Gary Dorrien speech at Kalamazoo College, May 13, 2004).

eventually employ against Iraq. Dealing with terrorists in the "war on terror" is different from dealing with nation-states, he says, so the Geneva Convention provisions are irrelevant. Bush supporters buy these arguments even though Iraq has nothing to do with 9/11. Later the administration will justify torture at Guantanamo Bay Detention Facility and Abu Ghraib.[14]

The peace activists are convinced that the Bush administration is looking for another war because PNAC's plan of *Pax Americana* requires "perpetual war." (It is a "we make the peace with war" argument.) Consequently, whenever the administration discusses another threat in the region, like Syria, the peace activists see it as a signal for another invasion.

> *I believe this administration is looking for another war.*
> *Read the words of Cheney, Rumsfeld, Wolfowitz*
> *(PNAC). They call for war against Iraq long before*
> *9/11. It's a myth that there was an Al Qaeda and Iraqi*
> *connection . . . . The vigil will continue. KNOW decided*
> *that as long as the Bush administration follows the*
> *Neocons and PNAC that means American empire.*
> *KNOW is addressing a variety of aspects about the war;*
> *PNAC is one of them.*

> **— Tobi Hanna-Davies**

Bush's approach to foreign policy has made the peace activists very fearful of him. They want a better America and a more just America but they point out the contradictory way America deals with the world, like outlawing WMDs for everyone but ourselves.

---

[14] Judge Alberto Gonzales, White House counsel and the nominee for the Attorney General spot in 2005, advises the president that the Geneva Conventions are irrelevant in a war on terrorism and that torture against presumed terrorists is OK and appropriate.

WMD—we're the only country to use them on Hiroshima and Nagasaki. Then we justified them. It was a perceived problem of hypocrisy. Now others have WMD.
—Barbara Frisbie

Yes, I'm concerned. Before the war inspectors said they didn't believe so many had been destroyed. We weren't kicked out in 1998 by Saddam. Inspectors pulled out because the U.S. would bomb Iraq (Operation Desert Fox). Iraq wouldn't let them come back.
—Tobi Hanna-Davies

He probably had WMD but he's not the only one. It wasn't a great threat to us but was the justification for the war. If we don't use this, we'll find some other justification. What worries me is PATRIOT Act I and II. How quickly people are willing to give up their rights. It changes the tenor of the nation. **— Rev. John Fisher**

The peace activists are terrified and morally outraged by PNAC's aggressive ideas because PNAC resists finding peaceful solutions to world conflicts. It detracts from an overall goal of bringing democracy to corrupt or dictatorial governments.

Yes, it's immoral. Second century Roman historian talked about the invasion of Britain, "You created a wasteland and call it peace." I fear that's what we're about. It's good to end oppression but we've gone about it the wrong way. Winning peace is more difficult than winning battles. We need active resistance, not passive resistance.

— Rev. John Fisher

PNAC is terrifying. It's a ruse that we're bringing democracy [to Iraq]. We're destroying it at home and abroad. For example, in Turkey, we are trying to find representative government in a very difficult position

geographically and culturally; they have suffered many
different things. There is great jeopardy now if we push
them. Turkey has militant Islamic forces which endanger
women. **—Barbara Frisbie**

Tobi Hanna-Davies also associates the Bush Doctrine with
the lies that brought us to the Iraq War because, she believes, it
was planned.

> *One reason after another was given by the Bush*
> *administration to attack Iraq. Every time reasons were*
> *countered by fact, another reason was given. The*
> *administration was determined to go to war, no matter*
> *what. For years the U.S. supported Saddam and supplied*
> *him with weapons. During the Iran–Iraq War, the U.S.*
> *was friends with Saddam, even though he committed*
> *atrocities against his own people. The U.S. had a great*
> *deal to do with creating the terror in Iraq, including*
> *supplying ABCs.*

Amy Crain, a Bush supporter, isn't familiar with PNAC
but she handles my questions about PNAC by applying middle
class American values to foreign policy.

> *Don't know what our diplomatic relations are with them,*
> *Iraq. I hope we don't offer asylum to Saddam. We want*
> *to finish what we started.*

Ken Webber has a similar sentiment and bemoans the fact
that Bush's father didn't finish the job on Saddam.[15]   His

---

[15] In his memoir, *A World Transformed*, George H.W. Bush explains
why he didn't push into Iraq in 1991. "Trying to eliminate Saddam
. . . would have incurred incalculable human and political costs.
Apprehending him was probably impossible . . . We would have been
forced to occupy Baghdad and, in effect, rule Iraq . . . there was no
viable 'exit strategy' we could see, violating another of our principles.
Furthermore, we had been self-consciously trying to set a pattern for

comments also reflect George W. Bush's own impatience with Saddam.

> *I'm not for war, but I'm in favor of doing something about Saddam after 20 years of his dictatorship and what he's done to his own people. When it comes to WMD, we must eliminate those threats. That we could negotiate with him was ridiculous. We spent 12 years and we didn't get anywhere with him.* — **Ken Webber**

Impressions of the Peace Activists

The Bush supporters' positions on partisanship focus on the nature of patriotism during war and whether or not it is right to criticize the president. It also appears that many of their impressions about the peace activists come mostly from what they see on television rather than what is happening in Kalamazoo. For example, Craig Duncan speaks about a congressman who says he hopes we'll lose the war. "That's downright treasonous to want troops to die. It's wrong." Then he continues with his opinion of the peace activists in general:

> *I'm just a supporter of our troops and our country and freedom. Not sure what they call themselves....They believe they're peacemakers. There comes appeasement with Saddam. Only 600 Iraqi civilians died.[16] That's*

---

handling aggression in the post-Cold War world. Going in and occupying Iraq, thus unilaterally exceeding the United Nations' mandate, would have destroyed the precedent of international response to aggression that we hoped to establish. Had we gone the invasion route, the United States could conceivably still be an occupying power in a bitterly hostile land."

[16] According to www.iraqbodycount.net/, between 5,094–6,237 Iraqis had been killed by the end of April 2003.

incredible it's only that many. Saddam has killed
hundreds of his own— and those in neighboring countries.

Patsy Donovan cites instances where peace activists are lying in the streets, hooking themselves together: "That required extra police to take care of them. How much did New York lose? $900,000 to get them out of the road." Then she recalls the right of free speech, an American value that the Bush supporters address continuously: "The soldiers are there fighting for our freedom of speech so that we have a right to stand out here."

Craig Duncan says he talked to a peace guy "who doesn't agree with us, but he can disagree because those guys [American soldiers] are paying the price. Freedom doesn't come free." Bill Katz prefers to call the peace activists "anti-war protesters."

They need to think about what they're doing. If it wasn't
for my son and people like him, they couldn't demonstrate.
He stood up and fought for their rights.

As veteran, Tony Freedman vows to protect the Kalamazoo peace activist's right to speak against the war. He points toward the small group of counter-demonstrators across the street who consistently show up at the Saturday rallies across the street from the pro-Bush rally:

I don't agree with them, but if anybody tries to stop them,
I'll be right there. I watched a peace guy across the street
during our demos and made up my mind to protect him if
anything happens.

Martha Duncan, who also speaks of her experience of Kalamazoo peace activists, is nevertheless unimpressed by them:

> *Peace supporters. Not much dealing with them. One day some were here when we were. They were not very patriotic at all. Not dressed neat. All in black. Never been here when they demonstrate on Sundays and Tuesdays. Everyone is entitled to their opinion.*

Patsy Donovan relates the story of a local incident at the St. Patrick's Day parade where a few peace activists interfered with the Bush supporters' demonstration, "They were rude. We got in a group to decide what to do and then walked away. The peace activists then took over the corner."

Ken Webber takes a different track by recognizing the new age of terrorism that has come upon us. He retains a disdain for the peace activists, whom he regards as "liberals,"[17] and expresses himself in a language similar to Bush's, another common pattern in many of the Bush supporters comments:

> *The peace activists are misguided and have a difficult time facing facts. They live in a different world than I do [like they're back in the 60s]. And it's a different world than 30 years ago. In the 60s we had clear-cut enemies and organized states. Now we have no borders. There are people who hate Americans or the Western style of life. We have to ban together. The terrorists' objective is to destroy freedom and our way of life. We have to stop terrorism by reducing the threat from countries that support terrorists.*

---

[17] Thomas Frank in *What's the Matter with Kansas* addresses this as the "cultural war" in America where ordinary people are run by those who are despicable, self-important and divisive among the classes. "Our culture and our schools and our government, backlashers insist, are controlled by an overeducated ruling class that is contemptuous of the beliefs and practice show-offs. They are effete, to use a favorite backlash term. They are arrogant. They are snobs. They are liberals." (pages 114-115)

This comment and those of former Marine, Roger Woodson, and a few others at the pro-Bush rallies illustrate a theme that replays the conflicts of the 1960s. Bush supporters I've met continually refer to the peace activists as hippies or the children of hippies. (In an ironic twist, Woodson, although he carries a Marine Corps flag, wears a long beard and old clothes.)

"They look like the kids of the 60's people," said Patsy Donovan. Unlike so many others, however, she is at least seems willing to encounter them—with some qualifications: "If they go home and take a bath, we'll talk."

The peace activists are unfamiliar with the Bush supporters as Tobi Hanna-Davies's statements indicate, but they reflect a certain compassion toward families of soldiers:

> *Haven't seen a lot of them. We're getting a lot of people honking at the peace vigil. It's understandable if your loved one or friend is in the Gulf and that you want to believe that the U.S. policy that is putting them in harm's way is for a good cause. It's totally understandable.*

Rev. John Fisher has some idea who the Bush supporters are and he can identify with them in many ways.

> *I talked to a man that carried a sign saying, "Wage war for peace." We shared our views and I shook his hand and thanked him. "I'm on the other side" but we're all for peace. It's not us and them. Some people like labels. I have a nephew [in Iraq].*

> *My stepsister lives in Kuwait. She said Saddam is awful and none of us is supportive. But there is better resistance to him than violence to remove him. Her youngest son is a Marine in Iraq. His mother has me here and a grandson there and is appreciative of both.*

We have to change the way we live. That's what has kept me here. Waging peace has brought invigorating diversity here. For example, the inter-faith service for peace at Stetson Chapel (February 23, 2003) was filled with the most diverse group (multicultural, generational, ethnic, age) of people all making historic positions of peace. What gives me hope is that this cross-section that draws people together to work on common ground. War divides people.

Prognosis for Peace

By mid-April 2003 Americans are antsy for the war's end, probably because they expected a repeat of the 100-hour engagement of the Gulf War in 1991. I ask Bush supporters how long they think the rallies will continue.

> *No idea. Don't want troops to come home like the Vietnam vets did."* — **Craig Duncan**

> *Don't know until the general mood when things are under control, then we slack off. Numbers are fewer every week here.* — **George Tower**

> *Until soldiers come home. At least the next couple weeks and Memorial Day parade."* — **Martha Duncan**

> *I'll be in the Memorial Day parade—hope to be there."* —**Tony Freedman**

The peace activists remain skeptical about a presumed victory in Iraq or an end to the war. Mostly, they fear the consequences:

> *Victory? More like domination. My concern is that peace isn't fizzling out. I've been here [demonstrating] since October. Seems like the issue is gone, as the real tragedy of*

*war becomes evident, more people are committed to the peace
movement in other ways besides wearing buttons.*

— **Barbara Frisbie**

*Be aware of how Bush will operate in Iraq—on his own or
with the UN. We need to keep protesting so he doesn't set
up a Western dictatorship, that is, the Iraqi people trade
one dictator for another.*   **—Sarah Boyce**

When they talk about the war's end, neither the Bush supporters nor the peace activists believe it will be very soon. They both account for the need to subdue the insurgents and America's responsibility to rebuild the country after bombing it, in the same way we rebuilt Europe with the Marshall Plan after World War II. The president has alluded to this same idea as well, but in their portrayal of this "long, hard slog,"[18] the Bush supporters insist that America is helping Iraq.

*It's a long way off. The Iraq army will continue on-going
battle with suicides and snipers.*   — **Craig Duncan**

*It's over when the last man comes home. We have to take
care of everything there and it will take months to get new
government established. Then we'll get out.*

— **George Tower**

*We have to help people get back on their feet. Common
people are oppressed so much. They probably don't know
what it's like to be free.*   — **Martha Duncan**

A couple peace activists continue to assess the war from a moral standpoint:

---

[18] October 22, 2003, Secretary of Defense Donald Rumsfeld's assessment of the war.

> *I'm heart-broken at the whole turn-out and can't figure out why the administration can't hear or see the mind of the people.* **—Sister Mary Bader**

> *I don't see it as a victory or peace-making effort. As long as countries believe they can make a decision without support from the rest of the world, I don't think we can live in peace.* **— Audrey Wierenga**

Two Marine veterans, Art, a Vietnam vet from the peace group and Tony, a Marine reservist from the Bush group, turn out to be the most prescient observers of the war:

> *The war isn't over. I expect we'll go to North Korea, they will re-establish the draft and we will be dangerous as the only Superpower. I don't foresee us having peace. I blame the media and us absorbing the information. This causes hate and aggression of the whole world.* **— Art Orzel**

> *There may be some problems if we don't find WMD. That was the justification for going in the war. We'll look foolish in eyes of rest of world. We'll look more belligerent than we needed to come across.* **— Tony Freedman**

APPENDIX H

The Kalamazoo City Commission
241 West South Street
Kalamazoo, MI 49007

Re: Community Resolution to Protect Civil Liberties

Dear Mayor and City Commissioners:

This letter is written in support of the Community
Resolution to Protect Civil Liberties as proposed by the Task
Force for the Defense of the Bill of Rights. I (we) support
the Community Resolution as a necessary tool to protect the
civil rights of the residents of Kalamazoo. The Community
Resolution is of particular importance to the population of
Kalamazoo for the following reasons:

The USA PATRIOT Act, by expanding the definition of
"terrorism," subjects political and religious organizations to
surveillance, wiretapping, harassment, and criminal action
for political or religious activity. By enacting the
Community Resolution, the City will decline to expend City
Resources for surveillance of individuals or groups based on
activities protected by the First Amendment without further
suspicion of criminal activity.

The USA PATRIOT Act expands the ability of law
enforcement to conduct secret searches of the residents of
Kalamazoo. The City will refrain from voluntary compliance
with federal requests for expenditure of City resources in the

secret search of any resident of the City whose property is the subject of the search.

The Attorney General plans to enlist local law enforcement agents to enforce federal immigration laws. The Kalamazoo Department of Public Safety will be directed not to voluntarily engage in the enforcement of federal immigration laws, and the Community Resolution affirms the City Commission's strong support for the rights of immigrants.

The USA PATRIOT Act permits the detention of a person without charge and denies the right to counsel under such circumstances. Under the Community Resolution, the City will decline to expend City resources, including use of city personnel, for the detention of individuals without charge and without access to an attorney.

The Community Resolution urges the members of the Michigan Congressional Delegation to actively seek the revocation of sections of the USA PATRIOT Act, or any other federal legislation, order or directive which limits or violates the fundamental rights and liberties of persons as found in the United States and Michigan constitutions, and to restore the checks and balances inherent in our constitutional tradition.

I would like to impress upon the City Commission the need to take a stand against the USA PATRIOT Act and other federal policies that curtail the civil rights of the residents of Kalamazoo. I urge the City Commission to enact the Community Resolution as soon as possible.

Sincerely,

BE SURE TO INCLUDE YOUR FULL NAME AND
ADDRESS

FOR MORE INFORMATION, GO TO THE WEB SITE
FOR THE BILL OF RIGHTS DEFENCE COMMITTEE:
www.bordc.org

APPENDIX I

Survey Results: May 2004

When the Bush campaign announces a visit to Kalamazoo on May 3, 2004, I realize I have an opportunity talk to Bush supporters who have pretty much disappeared from the public scene since last year. I plan to interview people as they wait outside the arena where the president will speak, but fail to get a press pass. Fortunately, prior to the event I happen to be walking downtown (I'm covering a story on Daniel Schorr, who is speaking at the Radisson) and see people waiting in line to obtain tickets for the event at the Chamber of Commerce. I interview them even though my questions are not planned out nor are they the same ones I will ask the peace activists at the Sunday vigil a few days later. Although this survey is not scientific, it does capture the voices and moods of ordinary people, the purpose of this book.

It is interesting to note that the Bush supporters I talk with are unlike those I spoke to last year at the rallies in front of the Federal Building in that they are not self-selected individuals attending a public assembly. In fact, they are very hesitant to talk with me, so I promise to record only their gender and age and to use pseudonyms in order to preserve their anonymity. I ask five people (three men and two women) the following questions:

* Why are you a Bush supporter?

* Where do you get your news?

* Did you support the war in Iraq in the beginning? Why?

* Do you believe Saddam was involved in 9/11?

* Do you believe there will be a reinstatement of the draft? Why or why not?

* WMD were not found. What do you think about that?

* Are you willing to go into other countries to fight terrorism?

I speak with six peace activists (two men and four women) to contrast the views of the Bush supporters with this set of questions:

* Why don't you support Bush?

* How would you characterize this war with Iraq?

* What should we do in Iraq?

* What do you think of Bush supporters?

* Why do you think the president still has supporters—almost 50% of the people polled?

* Do you think there will be a draft? Why or why not?

* Why do you still stand here on the street for peace?

* Where will you be on Monday, May 3 during the Bush visit?

Support for the President

The Bush respondents speak excitedly yet sternly about the president's leadership, morality and character.

*I like his firm hand and determination; he's had a lot of
stuff dropped in his lap; he handled 9/11 very well.*
— Cal Hoover

He's against gay marriage and abortion.
— Randy James

*He's a man of good character who speaks the truth. He
believes in what America stands for and hasn't forgotten
that there's a God.* **— Tom Mason**

Many of the respondents identify themselves as
Republicans. Edna Cole, 50, turns out to be the most
outspoken person on this point. Her story also reflects a
changing America that has gone unnoticed regarding people's
political moves from party to party. She doesn't reveal the
nature of her husband's disappointment with the Democrats
but she certainly illustrates the nature of party loyalty that the
Republicans have been able to garner during this election, a
special characteristic of the Bush administration in particular:

*We've been long-standing Republicans and supported
[George W. Bush] and his father. My husband worked
for Bush Senior. I had a son in Iraq. My daughter is at
OSU and what she sees there influenced her to become a
Republican. My husband was a Democrat in the 70s, a
staunch Kennedy supporter. He was in Vietnam and saw
the country tarred from that war. He worked for
Republicans and volunteered for the GOP.*
— Edna Cole

Respondents also see Bush as a capable leader able to
handle terrorists, which Cal Hoover best reflects, "Terrorism is
expanding to other countries. Bush says 'you're either with us
or against us.' It depends on the attitude of the rest of the
countries that support terrorism." This comment is key

because it not only illustrates how Bush has defined the new world after September 11, but it shows that some citizens have adopted it. During the Cold War, two major adversaries surface—the capitalists and the communists represented by the United States and the Soviet Union respectively. The rest of the countries in the world align themselves with either one or the other. After the fall of communism in 1989, however, we are unclear about our role in the world as the only remaining superpower, especially with several "rogue states" in our midst. It will be a decade before we flesh out what that means. The term, "terrorist" will also be used more widely. With Bush's comment, "You're either with us or against us," he sets up two types of nations—and individuals: those who sponsor or harbor terrorists and those that don't; those who go along with U.S. policy and those who don't.

When Bush pumps up the nation for war against Iraq, he claims that Saddam is connected to the chief perpetrator of the September 11 attacks, Osama bin Laden and Al Qaeda, and that Saddam also has weapons of mass destruction which pose a threat to the United States.[1] Saddam's ties are implied by the administration and later debunked by the 9/11 Commission and the WMDs are never found. Still pro-Bush respondents recognize that the world has changed and that the United States now has the responsibility of taming terrorism and preventing WMDs from spreading to other countries, including our own. Their comments also reveal that they have adopted a more bellicose attitude to threats in the region than the Bush supporters of one year ago.

---

[1] British Prime Minister Tony Blair, Bush's main supporter for the war on Iraq, also proclaims that Saddam has WMD; in fact, he said that Saddam could launch an attack on Great Britain in 45 minutes. This statement is later recognized as an exaggeration.

> *Terrorism is spreading in the Middle East, so we may*
> *possibly have to go in. I am supportive of that.*
> — **Randy James**

> *Only if we need to.* — **Edna Cole**

> *If they are attacking us—then I hope we do go into every*
> *[country]. Saddam was killing innocent people. He was*
> *nuts. We don't do that. Well, we kinda do, but not that*
> *way.* — **Tom Mason**

This last comment points to what America has become as a result of this new way of looking and acting in the world. The respondent appears not to have quite dealt with the contradictions of U.S. actions yet. In another interesting turn, Cal Hoover remains loyal to Bush but is frustrated with our progress in Iraq,

> *I supported the war but have become a little more skeptical.*
> *It's a can of worms opened up. There will never be peace in*
> *the Middle East, no matter what we do. We try to give*
> *them direction and purpose so they may have a good life,*
> *but their ethnic and religious beliefs pull it apart too much.*
> — **Cal Hoover**

Bush hints at a connection between Saddam and Osama bin Laden, but his lack of evidence produces a "faith-based politics" in foreign policy, which allows the administration— and later grassroots Bush supporters—to rationalize the war out of their beliefs or suspicions rather than from any concrete evidence. The comments below illustrate the shaky ground respondents know they hold, even as they back Bush's contentions about Saddam and WMD:

> *Saddam and the Muslim conflict and the whole Middle*
> *East was definitely in support of [the 9/11 attacks]. He*

may not have masterminded 9/11 but he funded it. I
believe he funded the whole Middle East.
— **Randy James**

I believe he was involved in some way. Saddam supported
terrorist training camps in Iraq. It's all part of the same
thing. — **Juanita Gonzalez**

He didn't give the order but in some way shape or form,
he's connected. He is at least guilty by association. He
hangs around with unruly people. — **Tom Mason**

Nevertheless, U.S. military forces' accomplishments seem to be invisible, a common complaint of Bush supporters who blame the "liberal media" for this omission. Randy James agrees: "I'm positive about what we've done: electricity, water, new construction. We are turning the country around. I totally agree with the reform of Iraq."

☮

As much as the Bush people like the president, the peace activists remain appalled and fearful of him. They regard him to be untrustworthy and the members of his administration to be ruthless and lawless. They blame Bush for intensifying the terrorist threat by starting a war against Iraq and believe his policies misguided; their derision toward him intensifies:

He promoted a policy of pre-emptive, unprovoked war on a
sovereign nation. In the process, he is not helping the war
on terror. Clearly, the level of terrorism has increased.
Iraq has become a magnet to terrorists. When he says
Iraqis are thugs and terrorists, what would we do if soldiers
came here? People would fight with all their might and yet
people don't appreciate this. —**Wade Adams**

> *He's a liar. All neocons lie, cheat and steal. Lie after lie after lie. He only wants money.*
> — **Stephanie Dobbs** (a pseudonym)

Most of all they fear his assault on Americans' civil liberties.

> *It's endless. I feel like he's been extremely detrimental to our basic freedoms (speech, choice, the environment, the world community and our presence in it). He lies all the time. He's different from all politicians lying. It undermines the basic foundation of our country. He is the first president who has made more amendments to the Constitution. He gets on TV and says one thing and does another (his first State of the Union, he sounded like a Democrat.)* — **Sharon Tattum** (a pseudonym)

The peace activists characterize the war with Iraq as a "disaster," a "fiasco" and "unnecessary, immoral and illegal."

> *It's like all wars which are for nothing but money and control of oil reserves.* — **Stephanie Dobbs**

> *He went against American public opinion and world opinion. He shouldn't have done that. Even McNamara (the former Secretary of Defense who presided over the Vietnam War) says: if you're the only country going to war, you better rethink it.* — **Sharon Tattum**

While the Bush supporters see terrorism spreading, the peace activists worry about the decline of the United States' reputation in the eyes of the world and repudiate the idea that we have turned into global bullies:

> *We have made so many enemies in the Muslim world. Bush had thousands of Iraqis held in prison for months in*

*3x4 foot cells in the dark—like Saddam. How do we
teach people democracy doing that? These are people picked
up on raids in their homes*
> **— Wade Adams**

*Unnecessary, divisive, horrible. It is a no-win situation for
either side. I feel for the Iraqi people and our soldiers and
their families because this is all greed-inspired. We're
alienating our allies and not winning any friends.*
> **— Sara Wick**

Of course, always looming in the background of any Bush-opposition contingent is the 2000 election and the Kalamazoo peace activists are no different.

*Bush is only in it for the money (oil). He misled the
American people by saying he wanted to free Iraq of a
dictator who had WMD. We are led by a president who
swindled the election. He went to war to export democracy
when in fact, his ulterior motive was to imperialize the
Middle East and take the oil, which is abundant.*
> **— Art Orzel**

Sara Wick is utterly discouraged with Bush's ideas about religion, war and the spending of taxpayers' money:

*I don't believe what he believes. He has a narrow-minded
view of religion and what's good for this country. War is
unilateral. That's not my style. He's not compassionate
and he doesn't bring people together but rather invites
division, lack of dialogue, and billions of dollars of military
spending when so many other needs exist like senior citizens
services, health, education, jobs. I'm not sure what world
he lives in but it's not my world or the world of my children.*

While the peace activists express their vehement dislike for Bush, Sharon Tattum articulates one of the major reasons why. Her comments also reveal a new focus among this group—Bush's fundamentalist religious beliefs.[2]

> *Everyone is afraid of him. If you do the slightest critical thing, they'll get you. There's not much I like about him. He's a simplistic thinker, a fundamentalist Christian. I don't like fundamentalism under any guise. It will be the end of the U.S. and any civilization. His policies will affect women adversely.*

So, why do almost 50 percent of the American population polled at the time still support Bush? The peace activists think the president has four things going for him: his Christian background, his appeal to strength and discipline, the influence of Fox News and Americans' ethnocentrism as a nation:

> *A certain segment of his supporters vote for him irrespective of what he does. These are mostly one-issue people, like Right to Life. To me he seems contrary to the old Republican values of individual freedom without the government dictating what's best.*
>
> **— Wade Adams**

> *A lot of these people tend to fall in line and follow the leader. (They raise their hand before they talk, don't color out of the lines, and follow instructions.) They are mind-numbed and do what they're told and listen to Fox News.*
>
> **— Stephanie Dobbs**

---

[2] Religion will become a major force leading to Bush's victory in the 2004 campaign and leave the Democrats dumbfounded as the separation religion and politics becomes more blurred.

*He has the power of the news media. The American people
are very nationalistic and patriotic by nature. We think
we're a democracy but we're fueled by capitalism and we are
a nation focused on imperialistic commerce and money. We
are like pre-World War II Japan.*   **— Art Orzel**

*A lot of people are not very well informed. Most of their
news is from evening TV, if they get any news at all, and it
does not give a complete picture. Many people are not into
getting out of their comfort zone.*
                                        — Kay Chase

*They are comfortable and not understanding the
consequences of Bush's actions. There is no discernment of
U.S. history of world involvement. We need to get outside
ourselves and understand what other people have gone
through. We're in great denial.*   **— Sara Wick**

The influence of the media over people's perceptions of
Bush cannot be overstated, according to the peace activists.
Some of this is guided by what the administration tells the
media and some of it the media plays up through
misinformation, an appeal to fear, a narrow view of the
consequences of U.S. actions in Iraq—and good show
business. Sara Wick summarizes the dynamic here by
emphasizing what she thinks is the broader relationship of how
America must fit into the global community. After all,
according to "Outfoxed," the documentary film that features
former Fox News reporters, such material sells.

*They (the pro-Bush people) are probably very honest,
forthright people who have not done much thinking about
9/11. Bush is inflaming them with fear. They need to
know what the world situation means and why other
nations disrespect us. People want a comfortable American
lifestyle and they don't think of the consequences. I don't*

> *know how we can keep up with the demand for oil and the amount we consume. Other countries are starting to demand more. I'm not real optimistic. We have a huge deficit, enormous military spending, disparity between the rich and poor. Where we are evolving, I'm not sure how it will all work out. We may need to define a different level of comfort.*

So, what should we do in Iraq? Unfortunately, I only asked the peace activists this question and they overwhelmingly believe that the United Nations should get involved, more diplomacy should be extended, more contracts should be shared and the United States should get out of Iraq. Stephanie Dobbs adds, "We shouldn't have been there in the first place. Iraq and Saddam did nothing to us and they had nothing to do with 9/11 or Al Qaeda."

Draft Reinstatement

One of the implications of the war in Iraq and the war on terror is the availability of necessary troop strength to conduct these operations. The possibility of reinstating the draft surfaces more widely and more openly during the spring of 2004 among those most affected by it—the young.[3] In November 2003 the Skyridge Church of the Brethren holds a training session anticipating the need to inform young people vulnerable to the draft about the option of Conscientious Objector status.

---

[3] I do not see the concern in the local press but I hear many college students on my campus discuss the prospect of a reinstatement of the draft. It even comes up in class one day, the first time in four years that my students have talked openly about 9/11, the war with Afghanistan or the war with Iraq. We spend 25 minutes on this subject as a result.

In this survey, both the pro-Bush people and the peace activists doubt America will have a draft, although the peace activists, who consistently tend to fear the political, social and economic consequences of the Iraq War, believe reinstatement is more probable.   Only one Bush supporter, Randy James, who had just volunteered for the National Guard and would begin service in July after high school graduation, is gung-ho about the draft and military service in general:

> *If there is [a draft], I support it. We should be mandating that everyone give two years of mandatory service. The government supports the troops very well. You get three square meals a day, bonuses and good pay. They take care of you.*

Randy's comment is especially interesting.   To leave home to be taken care of by the government seems to be a contradiction to Republican ideology of reducing government and promoting self-sufficiency.   To begin a massive national service program for all young people would, of course, require financing.   This idea of national service, particularly in the military, also reflects the population's growing acceptance of militarism.

The consequences of a military course of action is not lost on peace activists like Art Orzel, a Vietnam combat Marine, who believes a draft is imminent because, "We're spread too thin, especially if we stay in Iraq."   Wade Adams, another Vietnam vet who obtained Conscientious Objector status after he was drafted, sees the possibility for reinstating the draft dependent on what happens in Afghanistan and Iraq, "If they think they can attack Syria, for example, we're in deep trouble."

Vietnam War vets seem more sensitive to the draft issue than the rest of the respondents, but people on both sides still agree that "the political ramifications are too great" and that "the country's not ready for a draft."   Sara Wick, takes a different view and regards the current composition of our military forces unfair when lower class people serve and middle class kids do not. The film, "Fahrenheit 911" illustrates her point in the scene where Marine recruiters aggressively and deliberately target potential candidates at the lower class shopping malls. Sara, like Wade Adams, also fears that the abundance of personnel a draft would bring into service will give the administration license to "police the world" even further.

Meanwhile, Bush supporter, Juanita Gonzalez, prefers a volunteer military force over conscription, "My son volunteered. Besides, there will be enough people to volunteer without having to drag them in." In fact, commanding the military is one of Bush's greatest appeals to her, "I believe what's going on in Iraq. We need a good defense and he's a good person for it."

Public Demonstrations

It has been 20 months since I first began covering the peace vigils. Some of the people have been demonstrating for at least a year. I ask them why they still do it and, clearly, it is because they find purpose as individuals and as a member of a larger cause:

> *As an American citizen I'm morally responsible for the death of Iraqi citizens. My sense of consciousness tells me to do it. My heart also grieves for American soldiers and veterans.* — **Art Orzel**

> *It's become a habit. A lot of other people feel it's important enough to come. We get a lot of positive response (honking cars) and we keep the issues in the public eye. We make sure people think.* — **Kay Chase**

*To inform the public that we believe what the U.S. is doing
is wrong. I am patriotic in doing this. I am also a
Vietnam War veteran.* — **Wade Adams**

*To get my word out, get the message out. There's not much
more left to do. This is nonviolent direct action.*
— **Stephanie Dobbs**

*This is my right. We haven't evolved much since the last
Iraq War. I have to be reminded to go in a non-violent
and peaceful direction.* — **Sara Wick**

Four of these five peace activists plan to demonstrate
against the president when he comes to Kalamazoo on May 3.

Heroes of a Different Stripe

ABOUT THE AUTHOR

The Sisters of St. Joseph first brought Olga Bonfiglio from her hometown of Melvindale in downriver Detroit to Kalamazoo in 1976. As a nun she worked for nine years in public relations for their college and hospital, and became involved as a professional and volunteer with numerous institutions, community boards and organizations in town. She received a W.K. Kellogg National Leadership Fellowship in 1984 and studied intercultural communication on four continents. After obtaining her doctorate in international education at Michigan State University, she taught at University of Michigan-Dearborn, and then turned her energies to the Kalamazoo community.

Olga has been a professor at Western Michigan University and Kalamazoo Valley Community College. In the late 1990s she produced and hosted "Public Voice," a community-access television talk show that featured local and a few national personalities discussing political, economic development and social justice topics. In 1999–2000 Olga served as chair for the Kalamazoo County Democrats and ran for county treasurer.

Her freelance writing career, specializing in religion and social justice issues for the local newspaper, began in 2002. Olga has also published articles in *Christian Science Monitor*, *America*, *National Catholic Reporter*, *Presbyterians Today* and *Christian Camps & Conferences*. *Heroes of A Different Stripe* is her first book.

Currently a professor at Kalamazoo College, she lives with her husband, Kurt Cobb, and Tucker the Cat in one of downtown Kalamazoo's historic neighborhoods.

www.olgabonfiglio.com

INDEX

SUBJECT INDEX

Note: Compound locators that consist of a page number and a small case italic *n* followed by an ending number, e.g., 98*n*23, refer to footnotes on that page. This example indicates footnote 23 on page 98.

Not in Our Name (organization),
200
Nuclear Freeze petition drive, xxi,
300–301
Nuclear weapons, 336, 445
bombing with, 184, 186–189,
190–191, 196
build-up of, 109, 314
club of nations with, 4, 138
depleted uranium from,
241n61, 397, 397n105
international law and, 238, 240,
316
Ron Kramer's work on, xxi,
300–301
North Korea and, 18, 185, 309
protests against, 180, 184–186,
197, 235–238, 243, 308 (*see
also* Plowshares (organization))
See also Weapons of Mass
Destruction (WMD)
Nuns. *See* Catholics, women
religious as; Dominican
nuns as demonstrators;
Sisters of St. Joseph (SSJ)

O
"O Finlandia" (Sibelius), 198
"Ode to Joy" (Beethoven), 203n55
Ogston, Maria Wong, 61–62, 92–93
Ogston, Walter, 91, 208–209
Ohio National Guard, Kent State
protest and, 311–312,
312n72
"On a Clear Day, You Can *See*
Forever" (Lane & Lerner),
52
Orsolini, Chris, 378
Orzel, Art, 96
on Iraq War, 484, 495
on the military, 193–195, 499
peace vigils and, 102, 500, 501
"Outfoxed" (film), 327n80, 497
Oxford Pledge, 290, 290n67

P
Pacem in Terris (Pope John XXIII),
245n63, 293
Pacifists, 244, 309, 376
Pagan, Kristy, 30
Palestine, Zionism and, 350–351,
350–351n91
Palestine Liberation Organization
(P.L.O.), 349–350, 350n90
Palestinian-Israeli conflict, 141, 201
Fr. Chacour on, 251–254, 260
living conditions during, 196,
353–355, 399
Michigan Peace Team and,
324n76
politics of, 347–353, 358–360,
398
Parks, Sr. Christine, 379, 380, 382
Parks, Rosa, as peacemaker, 382
Patriot Act. *See* USA PATRIOT
Act
Patriotism
9/11 and, 18, 213
Bush supporters and, 73, 115,
214, 453–454, 456
flags and, xxviii, 120–121, 222,
454
God and, 203–204
peace activists and, 74, 93, 197,
326
Pax Americana, xxivn2, 53, 317,
425–426, 431–442
Pax Christi (organization), 380
Payden-Travers, Chris, 300
Payden-Travers, Jack, 300
Peace, 14
definitions of, 76, 214, back
cover
major conferences on, 288, 290,
307
quotes about, by
Pres. Eisenhower, 346
Mother Teresa, 68
George Orwell, 99
religious motivation for, 214,
245n63

To order more copies of

HEROES OF A DIFFERENT STRIPE
HOW ONE TOWN RESPONDED TO THE WAR IN IRAQ

Each copy is $26.95 with 40% discount for 10 or more copies:

copies _____ x _____ = $_____

Shipping and Handling:
USA Media Mail $3.00 for first book,
$1.00 for each additional book $_____

Tax: Michigan residents, add 6% sales tax $_____

Total $_____

Checks payable to: **Global Visions**

Mail order form and payment to:
Global Visions
310 Elm Street
Kalamazoo, MI 49007

Send book/s to (please print)

Name _____

Street _____

City _____

State/Province _____ Postal Code_____

Please allow three weeks for delivery